Real-L Writing Activities

for
Grades 4–9

Cherlyn Sunflower

THE CENTER FOR APPLIED
RESEARCH IN EDUCATION
Paramus, New Jersey 07652

Library of Congress Cataloging-in-Publication Data

Sunflower, Cherlyn
    Real-life writing activities for grades 4–9 / Cherlyn Sunflower.
        p.   cm.
    Includes bibliographical references.
    ISBN 0-13-044979-2
        1. English language—Composition and excercises—
    Study and teaching (Elementary)   2. English language—
    Composition and excercises—Study and teaching (Secondary)
    3. Language arts (Elementary) 4. Language arts (Secondary)
    5. Letter writing. I. Title.

    LB1576.S892 2002
    372.6—dc21   02-040468
                                                                        CIP

Printed in the United States of America

10   9   8   7   6   5   4   3   2   1

ISBN 0-13-044979-2

Also published as *Real-Life Writing Activities for Young Authors* (ISBN: 0-87628-448-7).

ATTENTION: CORPORATIONS AND SCHOOLS

The Center for Applied Research in Education books are available at quantity discounts with bulk purchase for educational, business, or sales promotional use. For information, please write to: Prentice Hall Special Sales, 240 Frisch Court, Paramus, NJ 07652. Please supply: title of book, ISBN, quantity, how the book will be used, date needed.

**THE CENTER FOR APPLIED RESEARCH
IN EDUCATION**
Paramus, NJ 07652

www.phdirect.com/education

In honor of

Benjamin Franklin, inventor,

and

our young authors, who—reacting to real-life experiences with electricity and excitement—invent new ways to communicate

Dedication

This book is dedicated to my mom and dad, Alberta and Robert Henrickson, who have supported my curiosity and creative thinking.

Acknowledgments

I want to express my thanks to Win Huppuch, my editor, who saw the value in my approach to teaching writing; Gene Shepherd, who has guided my search for teaching excellence; Joyce and Weil for their study of teaching models and how teachers acquire new professional knowledge; Donald Graves, who studied the writing process of adult writers; Gail Tompkins, for sharing her knowledge of Language Arts with me; and my elementary and middle school students, who taught me how children learn language.

I'm grateful to Marie Lucero who carefully edited and gave creative suggestions on this manuscript; the hundreds of classroom teachers who helped refine the real-life writing activities; Jim Coomber, Chair of the English Department at Concordia College and Director of Concordia's Regional Reading and Writing Conference; the Fargo–West Fargo–Moorhead Teacher Center; and Cheryl Price at the Connecting Point for their support.

I am also grateful to the following clip art companies that supplied illustrations: Imprint Graphs, Dynamic Graphs, Art Master, AAACE's Clip Art, A.A. Archbold Clip Art, Cobb Shinn Art-Pak Illustrations, Dover Clip Art Series, Northern Light Clip Art Series, The Advertising Illustration Clip Book, Agricultural Communications in Education Clip Art Book 5, and others.

ABOUT THE AUTHOR

Cherlyn Sunflower (B.A., M.Ed., University of Texas; Ph.D., University of Oklahoma) has been actively involved in elementary education as an educator for over 25 years. Her experience includes 12 years as a classroom teacher and resource room teacher in the Austin, Texas Public Schools, and 18 years as a teacher educator at Minnesota State University in Moorhead.

Dr. Sunflower has given many presentations on the subject of language arts at the national, regional, and state levels. She has also authored several other practical teaching/learning resources, including *Really Writing!*; *75 Creative Ways to Publish Students' Writings*; *URICA—Using Reading in Creative Activities*; and *LATTS—Learning Aids and Teaching Tools*. The first focuses on the writing process and writing for real audiences and purposes. The second shares ways to call attention to and give value to children's oral and written compositions. The third is designed to help children become more effective readers. The fourth provides teachers and students ideas for tools to assist learning.

Cherlyn is an Associate Professor of Education at Minnesota State University, Moorhead.

ABOUT THIS RESOURCE

Students must become effective speakers and writers to succeed in today's extremely complex world. To achieve proficiency, young authors need to learn the process effective writers use and to view writing as an exciting and rewarding form of communication.

When they approach process writing instruction, many teachers ask:

- How can I motivate my students to write?

- What can I do to help young authors generate and organize ideas?

- How do I teach the thinking steps used by effective writers?

- What kinds of writing do young authors need to be effective at home, school, and work?

- How do I help young authors discover new genre?

- What can I do to interest young authors in self-evaluating and improving their first drafts?

- How do I teach conventions of the English language effectively?

- What are some meaningful purposes and real audiences for young authors?

Real-Life Writing Activities for Grades 4–9 answers these questions and more. This book provides 40 real-life writing activities that capture young authors' attention and improve their writing. The activities are designed for students in grades 4 through 9 who are just learning the composing process, as well as for advanced writers who are ready to experiment with a variety of writing and speaking genres.

The lessons and activities in this resource follow the fundamental steps of the writing process. As you look at each lesson, you will see the following steps: Outcomes, Motivators, Group Brainstorming, Group Composing, Individual Brainstorming and Composing, Responding to Students' Writing/ Revising, and Publishing. Each step is explained in detail in the section titled "Tips for Using Real-Life Writing Activities."

Each of the *Real-Life Writing Activities* includes a general outcome and specific outcomes that are based on national, state, and local standards. Standards-based instruction takes place in context at two points: during Group Brainstorming and during Group Composing. This instruction in specific standards occurs *before* young authors write a rough draft. If writers do not achieve a desired outcome, reteaching takes place during the Responding to Students' Writing/Revising step.

Real-Life Writing Activities for Grades 4–9 teaches the different types of speaking and writing genres students need to succeed in the real world. As you already know, teaching young writers the writing process is not enough; they must also experience daily the oral and written genres in use in real-life if they are to become effective *life-long* speakers and writers.

Yet, how do you and your students know what the essential elements of particular genre are?

- As part of a science unit on endangered species, your young writers want to write and circulate *petitions*. How does a petition usually begin? What should it include to help potential signers make up their minds?

- In another class, your young writers feel they owe their principal an oral *apology*. What does a thoughtful and caring apology contain? How are those ideas effectively organized?

- Two teachers want to tie language arts with a social studies unit on citizenship by involving your young writers in writing *legislative bills* and sending the bills to their U.S. Senators and Representatives. What must an effective bill contain?

- In another classroom students want to write *eulogies* for Samson, the school mascot, who has just died. What goes into a thoughtful and memorable eulogy?

In the Group Brainstorming step of each lesson the essential elements of each genre are taught through the use of key questions that stimulate young writers' thinking.

Real-Life Writing Activities for Grades 4–9 includes instruction in all basic language modes:

descriptive
persuasive
directional
narrative
poems

These basic language modes correspond to the writing skills required to meet state and national graduation standards.

Real-Life Writing Activities for Grades 4–9 offers an interactive questioning approach that stimulates students' higher-level thinking in each language mode. This interactive instructional approach involves young writers in an apprenticeship in thinking. This apprenticeship prepares students for the more independent writing that takes place in Writer's Workshops or when writing independently.

This valuable resource:

- meets the growing concern about when and how the conventions of the English language—such as grammar, capitalization, and punctuation—should be taught. This instruction takes place in context both *before* young authors compose a rough draft as well as during and afterwards.

- is designed to keep you, the teacher, out of the editorial role by providing "responding techniques" that help young authors learn to self-evaluate and revise their own compositions. In addition, the real audiences and authentic purposes for writing built into each lesson give young authors a meaningful reason to improve their compositions.

- provides a valuable resource for setting up real communication experiences that teach young authors not only *HOW* to write, but also *WHEN* to write.

- assists you in providing for the wide range of writing abilities that exist in most classrooms. Each lesson has an overall outcome that every student can meet. You can meet students' varied needs with only slight adjustments in each lesson. Suggestions for such adjustments are given throughout each lesson. Thus, young authors of all abilities can participate and succeed through your instruction.

- includes reproducible pages designed to support your teaching. These reproducibles, because of the big spiral-bound format, are easy to photocopy. Web sites to aid instruction and stimulate your students' exploration of the Internet (as a valuable writing resource) have also been included.

The *Real-Life Writing Activities* in this resource are appropriate for adult learners, adolescents, and children who are in the process of acquiring a second language. When working with these students, curtail the writing process to Motivator, Group Brainstorming, Group Composing, and Publishing. The group composition can be published and read and reread as a language experience chart.

Real-Life Writing Activities for Grades 4–9 will help you reinforce your language arts curriculum, meet state and national standards, and serve as a resource for interdisciplinary units in science, health, math, social studies, and literature.

Cherlyn Sunflower

CONTENTS

∽ *Genre* ∽
A French word often used as a synonym for a type of communication.

SECTION 1
DESCRIPTIVE COMPOSITIONS FOR YOUNG AUTHORS *1*

SECTION 2
DIRECTIONAL COMPOSITIONS FOR YOUNG AUTHORS *131*

SECTION 3
PERSUASIVE COMPOSITIONS FOR YOUNG AUTHORS *225*

SECTION 4
NARRATIVE COMPOSITIONS FOR YOUNG AUTHORS   *385*

SECTION 5
POEMS AND SONGS FOR YOUNG AUTHORS *417*

TIPS FOR USING REAL-LIFE WRITING ACTIVITIES

Each real-life writing activity follows these process writing steps:

- **Outcomes**

- **Motivators**

- **Group Brainstorming**

- **Group Composing**

- **Individual Brainstorming & Composing**

- **Responding to Students' Writings/Revising**

- **Publishing**

Use these steps to teach students a writing process (motivation, brainstorming, composing, revising, and publishing) that will serve them throughout their lives. You may follow the real-life writing steps in each lesson as described or add, omit, and/or change parts to fit your students' knowledge, skills, or interests and/or your curriculum needs.

Now let's consider each of these instructional steps.

Outcomes

An overall outcome is provided at the beginning of each lesson that every student can master at some level. An example of an overall outcome is:

- **Each student will write a compliment for a friend.**

More specific "idea" and "mechanic" outcomes that young authors are expected to meet by the end of the lesson are taught during Group Brainstorming and Group Composing. Here are two examples of specific "idea" outcomes:

- **Include three positive describing words in the compliment.**

- **Use at least four details—such as size, shape, color, and weight— to describe the object.**

Here are two examples of specific "convention" or "mechanic" outcomes:

- **Insert commas between ideas in a series.**

- **Put the exact words of a speaker in quotation marks.**

When young authors do not achieve a desired outcome, reteaching takes place during the step titled "Responding to Students' Writings/Revising."

After selecting the outcomes you want your class to accomplish, consider individual differences among your students. It may be necessary to lower or raise some requirements. For example, if your outcome is "Each student will write a three-paragraph science report including hypothesis, materials, procedures, and results," you could reduce this standard for a *beginning writer*. The young author could achieve the outcome by writing a one-paragraph report built from three pattern sentences:

I thought _____ **would happen.** (hypothesis)
I did _____ **using** _____. (procedures and materials)
I found out that _____. (conclusions)

Likewise, some young authors may need a greater challenge than the group as a whole. Therefore, the *advanced writer* might be expected to add a fourth paragraph that tells how the results of the science experiment could be applied in the real world.

Whether requirements are raised or lowered, realistic expectations reduce stress and boredom. Realistic expectations are the key to young authors' long-term growth and success.

Assess Learning After young authors complete the writing process, you can easily assess your students' learning because the general and specific outcomes of each lesson have been identified. There is no need to compare one student's work with another's; instead, each student's composition can be checked to determine whether the general and specific objectives have been met.

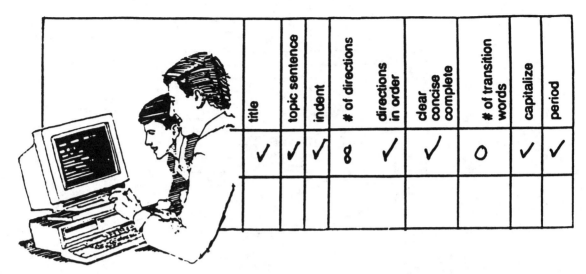

	title	topic sentence	indent	# of directions	directions in order	clear concise complete	# of transition words	capitalize	period
	✓	✓	✓	8	✓	✓	0	✓	✓

One way to keep track of a student's long-term writing growth is to use 5 × 8-inch index cards, a three-ring notebook, or a computer. Assign one card, page, or document to each student. You may want to organize your files alphabetically. Then, once a week or once a month, add to each student's card/page a brief dated note regarding outcomes mastered. You can evaluate students' work during the Revising step while conferencing with a student or before young authors share their compositions with their intended audience.

Modifications   For your convenience in *Real-Life Writing Activities*, modifications for beginning and advanced writers have been integrated into each step of the writing process. The modifications embedded in the activities are of three types:

> **Modification of Outcomes (expectations)**
> **Modification of the Writing Process**
> **Classroom Management Suggestions**

Modifications for increasing or decreasing difficulty are brought to your attention in three ways:

- the terms *beginning writers* and *advanced writers*

- the word *optional* which, if included, signals added difficulty

- *notes* to the teacher

These modifications give you tools to meet the needs of beginning writers and challenge advanced writers.

Motivators

Since today's students must learn to think creatively and critically, teachers have the added responsibility of stimulating young authors' minds before inviting them to think.

The motivators in *Real-Life Writing Activities* are designed to mentally prepare young authors to think and communicate. Each *real-life writing activity* provides several possible motivators at the beginning of the lesson.

Have young authors look at photos of themselves when they were younger before writing memories.

Show young authors political flyers before they write campaign speeches.

Share a story about a bike accident you had before young authors write safety tips.

Some motivators require only a few minutes; others may take a whole class session. You may pick one or two motivators that appeal to you, use all the motivators that are provided, or create your own. In a few lessons one or more motivators are essential. These motivators will be obvious as you glance through the lesson you are considering.

Creating Your Own Motivators   The motivators provided in _Real-Life Writing Activities for Young Authors_ aren't the only motivators you can use. They are only ideas to get you started. The key to creating effective motivators is selecting or designing ones that are appropriate for your students' interest and grade level. Basic ideas for motivators (which you can tailor to meet your needs) include having young authors:

Observe a person, animal, thing, or place.
Read a newspaper article, magazine, or piece of literature.
Remember or recall an experience.
Survey a person or a particular group of people.
View a movie or videotape.
Discuss a particular topic.
Interview a person.
Role-play, use a puppet, or do an oral reading.
Use visual imagery.
Experiment and document results.
Draw pictures, paint, or doodle.
Listen to stories, music, sounds.
Draw upon a current event or a chance event, such as a new student or a tornado warning, to capture students' natural excitement.

The most powerful and natural motivator is, of course, to have a **real audience** and a **genuine purpose** for communicating. These motivators are addressed in the Publishing step.

Classroom Management Suggestions During the Motivator, Group Brainstorming, and Group Composing steps, it is helpful to have young authors bring their chairs into a semicircle or double semicircle around the chalkboard or overhead screen. Even though moving chairs takes time and makes noise, the "pay off" in management makes it worthwhile. This physical arrangement signals it is time to think as a group and creates a more intimate atmosphere that personally involves young authors. Later, when young authors return to their desks to individually brainstorm and compose, the change to a new physical setting again energizes students.

Another advantage of pulling together young authors for the Motivator, Group Brainstorming, and Group Composing steps is that when one or more students are disruptive, they can be removed from the group and directed to return to their desks until they choose to listen quietly, keep their hands to themselves, or share appropriately. Students with a history of behavior problems may need to be excluded from the group several times before they realize they are missing out on the fun. Don't worry about temporarily excluding these young authors from the prewriting activity; they will still hear and learn even though they are at their desks. Bring the student back into the group as soon as he/she signals readiness to act appropriately.

Group Brainstorming

In each *real-life writing activity* you will find key questions and other information needed to lead brainstorming for the genre being taught. During Group Brainstorming, young authors actively participate in the process of idea generation.

Brainstorming Brainstorming is the process of generating a large number of ideas in a short amount of time. The rules for brainstorming are:

- Start ideas flowing; the more ideas the better.

- Accept every idea as possibly valuable. Save evaluation for later. Often crazy or "off-the-wall" ideas lead to something useful.

- Involve every young author in active participation.

There are two major methods for capturing young authors' ideas: listing of ideas and visual displays.

1. **Listing** Listing is a linear way to capture and organize thinking. Listing, which includes brainstorming multiple lists, is a very powerful technique for guiding and coaching young writers in *new* genre. Here is one example:

Rocks						
Size	Texture	Hardness	Color	Number of Materials	Weight	Other

2. Visual Displays   Effective visual displays for capturing thinking include webbing, mapping, clustering, and outlining. Visual displays are useful techniques for writing *independently* in a *familiar* genre. Here is an example:

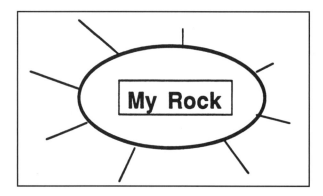

Genre   The most difficult part of teaching young writers is figuring out the idea categories writers must brainstorm for a particular genre. While effective writers have developed "mental pictures" of what is needed in a particular type of composition, frequently the rest of us must do considerable thinking and/or research to "come up" with the needed brainstorming categories:

- **If a writer were going to compose a letter to the editor about environmental waste, he/she might brainstorm (1) opinions about waste and (2) reasons to recycle, reuse, and reduce waste.**

- **If a writer were going to compose travel directions for someone, he/she might brainstorm (1) starting points, (2) directions, (3) distances, and (4) landmarks along the way.**

The brainstorming categories for different genre are provided for you and your students in the *real-life writing activities*. These categories shouldn't be taught to young writers; rather, your young authors will internalize the genre they use frequently and invent their own brainstorming categories.

Idea Generation   To encourage students to generate ideas, you need to use five basic techniques: (1) thought-provoking questions, (2) longer wait-time for students to think, (3) high levels of participation, (4) responses to students' ideas that support and encourage higher-level thinking, and (5) praise.

1. Thought-Provoking Questions   In addition to the brainstorming categories built into each *real-life writing activity*, you will find examples of key questions that promote higher-level thinking in the chosen genre. These questions are written in bold type for your convenience. How key questions are worded makes a tremendous difference in how young authors' respond.

Compare the following pairs of questions. Which column of questions, in your opinion, encourages more thinking?

Can you tell me who got you interested in your hobby?	**Who helped you get interested in your hobby?**
Do you have a reason why gum should not be chewed at school?	**Why do you think students should be allowed to chew gum in school?**
Should you put a question mark at the end of an asking sentence?	**What punctuation is needed at the end of your sentence?**

As you become comfortable wording key questions for each genre category, you will see the difference in the quality of your students' thinking and writing.

2. Longer Wait-time   After asking young authors key questions, it is important to be aware of the amount of time you allow before expecting a response. As you begin asking thought-provoking questions, you may feel uncomfortable pausing for longer amounts of time, such as 30 seconds, a full minute, or 3 minutes. It usually takes time to get comfortable waiting, but the rewards are immense. The amount of wait-time needed after higher-level thinking questions depends on the type of thinking required of young authors, the experiential background students have on the topic, and the needs of each individual student.

- **When recall questions are asked, students should be expected to show their knowledge by quick, correct responses.**

- **When thought-provoking questions are asked, it is essential to allow more time for thinking before expecting a response.**

Young authors who are accustomed to responding with "correct" answers may also need time to adjust, since being wrong is something students have been taught to avoid. It is more risky generating and sharing one's own thinking than it is to share a predetermined answer. At first students won't know how to succeed. Consider telling your students before you lead Group Brainstorming why you will be waiting longer for responses. Explain that they should be thinking during the silence and that when an idea comes to mind, he/she should quietly raise a hand.

3. **High Level of Participation**   During the Group Brainstorming step it is important to actively involve all young authors in contributing ideas. Pull quiet students in by directly calling on them. Young authors who cannot or won't contribute creative ideas can be involved when it comes time to "choose" an idea. Choosing someone else's idea from the brainstormed lists is safer than sharing an idea of one's own. For example, you might ask, "Out of all our ideas for clues in our mystery, which clue(s) do you want us to use?" Result—another student is actively and successfully participating.

4. **Responding**   Also during Group Brainstorming young authors need to be reassured that their growing abilities to think creatively and critically are on the right track. Here are three simple, yet effective ways to respond:

- **When a young author shares an idea, model respect by looking at the student, listening intently, writing students' ideas on the board or overhead, and encouraging other students to look at the idea sharer when he/she is speaking.**

- **Accept all ideas (99%) no matter how strange; otherwise the young author, especially one who has had a history of failure, may not risk sharing in the future. (The main exceptions are obscene language and racial/sexual/gender slurs.)**

- **Reinforce the idea sharer by writing the young author's actual words on the board or overhead under the brainstorming category, and making a positive oral response.**

5. Praise When encouraging creative and/or critical thinking, high levels of praise are needed *until* young authors acquire an inner sense of what is needed to succeed. It is important to note that praise differs in effectiveness. When asking questions that have a "correct" answer, general praise works, since all the young author needs to know is whether the answer was correct. When promoting creative and critical thinking, more specific feedback is needed.

Compare the following pairs of praise:

Wow! That sounds great.	**Wow! Each of your reasons for chewing gum in school is very convincing.**
Great Idea!	**Your title "Ten Reasons for Putting Off Doing Homework" will certainly catch readers' attention.**
Terrific!	**You indented all five of your paragraphs. This will really help your readers know when you plan to shift to a new idea. Terrific job!**

The "quick" general responses (found in the left column) are useful in keeping ideas flowing. The specific positive comments (found in the right column) are valuable anytime, but are essential when (1) a student, who does not usually participate, risks sharing or (2) an idea is especially unique/valuable. Here's an actual example.

In one seventh-grade classroom, while brainstorming students' wishes for a new year, most students were wishing for *things*, such as a new computer, CDs, and soccer equipment. Then one student offered a wish for "no more rainfall in Iowa" (where there had been extensive flooding). This creative response deserves special recognition because it was not a material object and because it was something for others, instead of for oneself.

Classroom Management Suggestions While many writing experts suggest all ideas that young authors risk sharing during brainstorming be accepted, in practice there are two types of answers that require special responses.

- **If a student shares something offensive, it is best to ignore the comment, then give specific praise to the next few students who are on the "right track." If the student continues in an inappropriate manner, a warning followed by removal from the group is usually effective.**

- **If a young author *thinks* he/she is on the "right track" but isn't, it is best to intervene. For example, the following incident occurred during a fifth-grade language arts lesson on composing math word problems. When the teacher asked young authors to brainstorm "where a problem might take place," one student suggested putting a soccer ball in the problem. The class was brainstorming places, not objects.**

Two respectful ways the teacher could redirect this student who is "off track" include:

1. **Ask where the soccer ball would be used. If the young author responded "playground," write "playground" under the brainstorming category "Place" and praise the young author for his/her contribution. Then return to brainstorming "where a math problem could take place."**

2. **Acknowledge the young author's idea (soccer ball) is an object that could be in a word problem, and list soccer ball under the brainstorming category "Object" before returning to brainstorming "Places."**

Group Composing

Group Composing is an instructional strategy for selecting the best ideas from those brainstormed, organizing them, placing the ideas on paper, and applying conventions. Group Composing makes the individual composing less threatening, improves young authors' attitudes toward writing, and positively affects the quality of the final product by helping young authors visualize and understand expectations.

Teaching Idea Organization   During Group Composing, you model how writers select and organize their ideas and guide young authors through a collaborative effort to compose a particular writing genre (such as an editorial, a recipe, or a complaint letter) before releasing young authors to write alone. The "interactive guidance" provided in Group Composing is an active apprenticeship that has a tremendous positive effect on young writers.

Teaching Conventions   Group Composing is also the time young authors are involved in applying the conventions/mechanics of the English language (capitalization, punctuation, spelling, correct grammar, and usage). As you use *Real-Life Writing Activities*, you will notice that "Thinking About Mechanics" boxes are included within each lesson so you can involve your young authors in making decisions about how to apply conventions *in context*. Use this information to ask young authors where and how to apply conventions.

> **Thinking about Mechanics:** Which of our landmarks in our directions are names for particular places? How do we show our readers this? (Capitalize the first letter of each proper noun.)

Modeling Error Recovery   Another useful technique is error recovery. This technique models for young authors how to handle mistakes in a nonthreatening way. Writers of all ages need to see that everyone makes mistakes or improves a composition during and after making a rough draft.

During Group Composing, model error recovery by calling attention to any accidental or intentional errors you made. State out loud, even be a little dramatic, that you really do not want to start over. Then cross out words and sentences you want to eliminate, draw arrows to reorder ideas, add words, circle words that may be misspelled, or leave blanks for future ideas. Explain to young authors that during creation of the rough draft the most important thing is getting ideas down on paper; correctness and a clean copy will come later. Once young authors realize errors aren't permanent, they will concentrate on the ideas they want to communicate.

Individual Brainstorming & Composing

At this point young writers have the opportunity to put their own thoughts into written form. There are two parts to this step: Individual Brainstorming and Individual Composing. Earlier, during the Group Brainstorming step, idea generation was modeled for young writers. Now is the time for them to brainstorm alone and capture their own unique ideas about the topic. During the earlier Group Composing step, organization of ideas into a draft and application of conventions/mechanics of the English language were modeled. Now young writers have the opportunity to organize their own ideas into a draft.

After young authors participate in Group Composing, keep the beginning writers with you and send the more confident advanced writers to their seats to brainstorm and compose their own rough drafts. Review with the beginning writers the task before them (a Comprehension Check). Once all the young authors have begun their rough drafts, move through the room, encouraging and coaching young authors as they get their ideas down on paper.

Comprehension Checks   Comprehension checks are extremely valuable modifications for students because they offer a chance to rehearse again before writing alone (during the Individual Brainstorming and Individual Composing steps). Comprehension Checks cut down on raised hands and questions such as "What do I need to do now?"

After Group Composing send advanced writers back to their seats to begin brainstorming and composing on their own. Keep the beginning writers and students who need supervision with you. Display the Group Brainstorming and Group Composing charts generated by your class. Then ask general questions to see how much these young authors understand regarding what they are to do when they return to their seats to write:

- **What do you need to brainstorm?**

- **How can ideas be organized?**

- **Where do the conventions of the English language need to be applied?**

If young authors need more assistance, ask specific questions. For example:

- **After you decide** (which school parties to have next year), **what do you need to brainstorm next?**

- **Which words in your title will need to be capitalized?**

There is a wonderful opportunity to reinforce their knowledge when young authors know the answers. If young authors don't recall what to do, you now have their attention and an opportunity to reteach. Most young authors will outgrow the need for Comprehension Checks when writing activities are geared to their level and as they gain self-confidence through repeated success experiences.

Responding to Students' Writings/Revising

The goal of responding to young authors' writing is to teach young authors to self-evaluate their ideas and conventions (mechanics), rather than to produce "error-free" or "everything perfect" compositions. It is extremely important to teach young authors to assume responsibility for rethinking or "reseeing" their compositions, instead of depending on teachers and parents to edit for them. Both responding to students' compositions and teaching them to revise are effective methods to help young writers achieve these goals.

Responding

Responding to young writers' compositions can take place during the creation of the rough draft or during revising. Responding at both points is valuable. Informal responding or conferencing occurs while writers are drafting their compositions. Circulate around the room holding brief one- to three-minute conferences with young authors who need particular attention. Formal conferencing, when desired, occurs after young authors' rough drafts are completed. The *real-life writing activities* give you tools to replace the traditional correcting and suggestion-giving approaches.

Responding techniques include specific positive comments, question and listen, and read aloud. These ways of responding are designed to teach self-reflection while maintaining student ownership. The following tools will guide your students to think creatively and critically during informal or formal conferencing.

1. **Specific Positive Comment Technique** This technique involves applauding or complimenting specific aspects of a composition that are effective. This type of response differs from the more typical general praise because it focuses on the composition or the intended audience, not how wonderful the student is.

Feedback that Makes the Student Feel Good	Specific Positive Comments that Help the Student Learn and Feel Good
Outstanding!	"My Skateboard" is a terrific title because it tells everyone the subject of your article.
You're incredible.	"Cutting down on pollution" is a terrific reason for convincing the public to recycle newspaper.
On target!	Outstanding! You used your spell checker to find the correct spelling of brontosaurus! Now the other students will know exactly which dinosaur you are describing.
Way to go! You're catching on!	In your direction "Turn left at the library," you have provided a useful landmark that all the students will know.

In addition to receiving positive reinforcement, young authors with low self-confidence need to be taught to see their own strengths and to reinforce themselves through positive self-evaluation.

2. **Question and Listen Technique** This technique involves asking probing or open-ended questions that encourage the young writer to think creatively and critically. These "who," "what," "where," "which," "why," and "how" questions focus on a particular aspect of the composition, yet keep the young author in the role of decision-maker.

NOTE: Questioning should not be limited to guiding young authors to resee only weak areas; questioning should also be used to guide young writers to view their strengths.

Poor Questions	Better Questions
Is there a way the dragon could escape?	How could the dragon escape from the castle?
Do you know when to stir in the chocolate chips?	When should the cook stir in the chocolate chips?
Do you need to start a new paragraph here?	Where do you change ideas? How can you signal your readers that you are starting a new idea?

3. Read-aloud Technique   This technique involves reading part or all of a composition out loud to see how it sounds so the young writer can determine whether he/she has communicated what he/she wishes to say. Two variations are effective with young authors:

- **Someone such as the teacher, a parent, or a peer reads the composition out loud to the young writer.**

- **The young writer reads his/her own composition out loud to the teacher, a parent, a peer, or someone else such as a janitor/ school aide/neighbor.**

A third version, that of an author orally or silently reading the compositions to him-/herself, is less effective until writers gain experience in revising critically and have an internal sense of writing for a particular audience.

Revising

Young authors must learn to self-evaluate two aspects of their compositions if they are to revise effectively:

- **Revising Ideas:**   adding ideas, making ideas more accurate and clear, removing ideas, or reordering ideas

- **Editing/Proofreading:**   locating and correcting errors of punctuation, capitalization, indenting, usage, grammar, spelling, and handwriting

The following revising techniques are designed to teach self-reflection while maintaining student ownership.

1. Checklist   One useful technique to assist young authors in self-reflection is the revising checklist. A checklist promotes independence while guiding young authors' revising. Checklists can be completed by the young author, a peer, and occasionally the teacher. Checklists are provided in many of the real-life writing activities.

Town Brochure Assistant

_____ 1. Does my town sound like an interesting place to move to or visit?
_____ 2. Does the Town Brochure contain lots of useful information (details)?
_____ 3. Is my information accurate?
_____ 4. What is the best part of my brochure?
_____ 5. Which words have I used that are worn out? What specific vibrant words could I choose to replace each worn-out word?

After using checklists for a period of time, advanced writers can be taught to create their own checklists as a review before independent writing.

In order for young authors to effectively use a checklist, they must be taught (1) how to look in their composition for each item on the checklist and (2) to make the revision before marking an item off the checklist. Without instruction in using a checklist, many young authors will read the checklist and mark off *every* item as accomplished. While it may appear these young authors are "lazy," in fact most have an immature conception of the task of revising. Modeling correct checklist use results in more effective utilization by students.

One way to maintain effective checklist use is to randomly or systematically meet with each student and evaluate each item on the checklist with the young author. Some teachers date and save revising checklists along with a copy of selected student compositions in a growth-oriented portfolio. Other teachers assign points to each item on the checklist and use this information for grading.

You'll find that the general and specific outcomes in each *Real-Life Writing Activities* revising checklist correlate well with local, state, and national standards.

2. Peer Feedback   Peer feedback provides an opportunity for young authors to get reactions from readers about how well they have communicated.

Over time as your students are the recipients of positive comments, questioning, and read-aloud "responding" techniques described earlier, they will gradually acquire skills in asking questions, sharing specific positive comments, reading aloud parts of compositions, and making suggestions that help their peers.

Real-Life Writing Activities includes suggestions for assigning young authors to peer partners and small cooperative revising groups. When arranging pairs, consider how to balance the groups. Generally you'll want to pair strong writers with weaker writers and young authors who have trouble controlling themselves with task-oriented partners. Before using small cooperative groups of three to five students, be sure that students are task-oriented, possess cooperative group skills, and know how to select a strong student leader.

3. Read-aloud Technique   This technique, addressed in the responding section, can be used again to reevaluate the composition. Reading aloud involves the young writer reading his/her own composition out loud to the teacher, a parent, a peer, an aide, etc., to see how it sounds and to determine whether or not the writer has communicated what he/she wishes to say.

A Few Tips about Revising

1. **"Red Pencil" Approach**   Beginning writers rarely benefit from having their compositions corrected, nor should they be pressured to revise. Writing, like speaking, develops with growth. If students were criticized for their speaking as much as they are for their writing, most would have never learned to talk.

2. **Real Audiences and Purposes**   One important part of a teacher's role is to create authentic reasons for students to speak and write. When young authors want to communicate, revising becomes a meaningful task. When writing to a senator to convince him/her to vote for/against solar energy, for example, getting the message across takes priority in young authors' minds. However, when the only purpose for writing is to learn to be a good writer and the only audience is the teacher as a grader, many young authors fail to see a reason to improve their compositions.

3. **Meaning Takes First Priority**   The meaning or ideas in the composition should be given first priority. This is particularly important when working with beginning writers, since they learn best when faced with only one or two improvements per lesson. ***Note:*** If convention/mechanic outcomes are important, then consider lowering the difficulty level of the idea objectives so that young authors can focus successfully on applying the conventions of the English language.

4. **Amount**   The amount of revising should depend on the degree of refinement that is needed for a particular audience and for achieving a particular purpose.

5. **Quantity vs. Quality of Writing**   Until young authors become comfortable writing, channel their creative talents into many short, easy writing situations. Frequent (daily) writing is more effective in producing long-term growth than one or two finely tuned writings a week.

Publishing

Since writing is a form of communicating, authentic communication situations with audience and purpose are necessary for writing to be meaningful. Young authors need a chance to present their finished composition to various audiences. Such opportunities are the primary motivation for students to write and speak.

Audiences   Audiences include family members, other supportive and trusted adults in students' lives, classmates, unknown readers, and, of course, self. Having multiple audiences also benefits you, since teachers do not have time to read and respond to every composition.

Purposes   Reasons for communicating in written form include: to convey information, to request something, to extend memory, to organize ideas, to clarify feelings, and to entertain.

Teachers often ask these questions about publishing:

1. **Should poor or weak writing be published?** Give every student the opportunity to publish. Take time to educate students, parents, fellow teachers, and administrators that differences are normal. Help these people understand that writing is a developmental process and that errors are signs of growth.

2. **Should young authors recopy their rough drafts?** Do not require a "clean" final copy until young authors have become skillful writers. Beginning writers of all ages are rarely motivated to recopy their revised drafts. Most view recopying as a meaningless task and generalize from it that writing as a whole is useless.

   Consider saving the requirement of a clean, corrected final copy with excellent handwriting for very special writing occasions. Once students learn keyboarding and word-processing skills, a clean final draft often becomes more rewarding.

3. **How can young authors' work be published?** One or more publishing methods are suggested in each *real-life writing activity*. For additional publishing ideas, consider this valuable reference: *75 Creative Ways to Publish Students' Writings*, Cherlyn Sunflower (New York: Scholastic Inc., 1993).

We'd Love to Hear from You!
Tell us what you think!

We hope you enjoyed teaching with *Real-Life Writing Activities* or our book *Really Writing*.

If you have a success story, run into a problem, find an error, want to make a suggestion, or need assistance designing the brainstorming for a genre not covered in these books, please let us know. If you are interested in a workshop, contact us for information.

Mail to: Dr. Cherlyn Sunflower
c/o Prentice Hall Direct
240 Frisch Court
Paramus, NJ 07652

or e-mail us at www.PHedu.com

Be sure to include your street or e-mail address and phone number with area code if you desire a response.

SECTION 1

Descriptive Compositions for Young Authors

Writers use a descriptive pattern when they want to describe a person, place, thing, event, or ideas. A descriptive composition helps the reader clearly visualize what is being described.

- **Simple Descriptions** A simple descriptive composition consists of two or more detail sentences.

- **Complex Descriptions** A complex description consists of a topic sentence and three or more detail sentences. The type of details given depends on what is being described. Complex descriptions often end with a summary sentence.

Details in a sensory composition consist of visual, auditory, olfactory, tactile, and gustatory information. Details in a factual composition often include who, what, when, where, how, and why. Details in a compare and contrast paragraph tell how two people, things, places, or events are alike and different.

Both simple and complex descriptions make use of adjectives (telling how many and what kind), similes (comparing one thing to another), and adverbs (telling how, when, where, and to what extent).

Reports

Reports are an even more complex form of descriptive composition. A report pattern is useful when writers want to share a quantity of knowledge. There are two types: the "all about" report and the research report.

- **Simple Report** The "all about" report is based on knowledge that students have already acquired. The students must recall their knowledge on a particular subject, organize that knowledge, and put it into a written form that someone else can understand.

1

• **Complex Report** In a research report, students ideally decide what they want to learn and then search for information on the subject before they organize their knowledge and put it into written form. This search often includes interviews, observations, experiments, and/or library research. It may include note-taking and the citing of knowledge sources.

Some Forms of Descriptive Writing

"All about" Books	Friendly Letters	Report Cards/
Announcements	Job Application	Progress Reports
Book Summaries	Letters	Research Reports
Business Brochures	Legal Contracts	Riddles
Character Sketches	Magazine Articles	TV Program
"Dear Santa" Letters	Math Story Problem	Summaries
Definitions	News Bulletins	Thumbnail Sketches
Fact Books	News Stories	Time Capsules
Fan Letters	Observational Notes	Visitor's Guides
Feature Articles	Pen Pal Letters	Wanted Posters
Field Trip Reports	Predictions	Weather Forecasts

LESSON 1

People/Fact Hunt

OUTCOME Each student will construct a game and use it to learn new things about his/her classmates or to review/introduce academic content.

MOTIVATORS

1. Discuss meeting people and how hard it can be to get to know other people. Point out that one way of meeting people is through traditional introductions. Choose one or two students to role-play introductions with you.

   Introduce yourself.
   "Hi/Hello" or "Let me introduce myself."
   "My name is _____."
   Then share something interesting about yourself.

   Introduce another person.
   "I would like you to meet _____." or "I would like to introduce you to _____."
   Then share something interesting about the person you are introducing or something that the two people have in common. This information is to encourage the people to open up and start talking.

   Now pair each student with another student. Ask them to formally introduce themselves to each other. Afterwards inquire how comfortable students felt.

2. Explain that there are other ways to get acquainted. Suggest that one way to get acquainted with someone is to ask questions. Pull one of your more quiet students to the front of the room. Then ask him/her four or five yes/no questions. Nod at each response, but DO NOT inquire further. Finally, ask your class how effective this method would be to get to know a new friend. (It acquires very little information.)

   Were you born in a large city?
   Do you wear contacts?
   Are you the oldest child in your family?
   Can you calculate percentages?
   Have you ever built a water tornado?

3. Play "Twenty Questions—Who Am I?" with your class.

You are IT first. Choose a person your students know (principal, president of the country, popular musician, etc.) and have students try to guess the person. Students should ask questions that can only be answered by Yes or No. Since students must correctly guess within twenty questions, select another student to count the number of questions asked.

The student who guesses the person correctly gets to be IT and choose the next "secret person." If twenty questions are asked without guessing the correct answer, IT chooses the next student to be questioned.

GROUP BRAINSTORMING

Let's create a People Hunt, an interesting activity during which students get to know each other.

NOTE: If you want young writers to create yes/no questions about facts in an academic subject, choose brainstorming categories to facilitate this. *For example:* If you are studying pollution, you could choose brainstorming categories such as air pollution, water pollution, and other types of pollution. Then students would brainstorm questions about each of these areas. In this case, brainstorm who, what, when, where, how, why, what kind of, how many type questions.

Activities	Family	Interests & Other Stuff
likes to bowl	has an older brother	likes pizza
plays guitar	owns a cat	favorite color is green
	lived in Oklahoma City	has never walked on the moon

Key Questions

Since creating these yes/no questions is more difficult than it looks, a list of verbs that work well with yes/no questions is included on the next page.

NOTE: A good interview question is specific, so that many, but not everyone can answer.

Activities

Praise students' responses and record them on the board or use an overhead projector under the heading "Activities."

1. **What yes/no questions could you ask other students about hobbies?**

2. **What yes/no questions might you ask new friends about sports?**

3. **What yes/no questions could you ask peers about special talents?**

4. **What yes/no questions might you ask classmates about schoolwork?**

Family and Friends

Praise students' responses and record them on the board or use an overhead projector under the heading "Family and Friends."

1. **What yes/no questions could you ask other students about family?**

2. **What yes/no questions might you ask new friends about pets?**

3. **What yes/no questions could you ask peers about where they were born?**

4. **What yes/no questions might you ask classmates about where he/she lives or lived?**

Interests and Other "Stuff"

Praise students' responses and record them on the board or use an overhead projector under the heading "Interests."

1. **What yes/no questions could you ask new friends about favorite foods?**

2. **What yes/no questions might you ask peers about a favorite color?**

3. **What yes/no questions could you ask classmates about their appearance (hair, eyes, clothes)?**

4. **What is something you have never done?** Wait for a response. **What question could you ask about this activity?**

NOTE: Encourage some obscure questions so that not everyone can answer every question.

likes
likes to
can do
has been to
can play
is/has
owns
should
would
is
are
were
has
will
shall
may
am
was/were
have/had
can
could
might

GROUP COMPOSING

Ahead of time make an overhead of the blank grid found at the end of this lesson on reproducible 1–1.

People Hunt Get acquainted. Find someone who can answer "yes" truthfully to one of your questions. Talk to him/her. Then get the person to sign his/her name and phone number or e-mail address.			

Now let's create a People Hunt together. Display the blank People Hunt.

NOTE: The grid is called a People Hunt even when hunting for people who have the answers to academic facts.

You will use the People Hunt later to help you get acquainted with new friends or know old friends better. Eventually when we play the game, a friend who can honestly answer "yes" to one of your questions will write his/her name and phone number or e-mail address in the box on the grid.

1. **First, let's select our four best questions from each of the brainstormed categories. "Best" could mean neat ideas, characteristics of people we want to meet, or some other criteria. That will give us twelve questions—our twelve best ideas.** The People Hunt will be more challenging if students choose yes/no questions that narrow the possibilities a classmate can answer "yes," but more fun if they also add questions that will include everyone. **What is one question we want to include on our People Hunt?** Circle questions as they are chosen.

2. **Next, we want to arrange our questions so that questions about the same idea don't end up together. What is a good question for our top left box?** Accept ideas.

3. **Let's write our question in the box. If there is room, we'll draw a picture below it so the person who signs this box has room to write his/her name and phone number/e-mail address below it.** Demonstrate how to write the question in the box and still leave open space.

4. **What question shall we insert into the People Hunt next?** Circle that question. **Where might we insert this question?** Write the question on the People Hunt grid.

> **Thinking about Mechanics:** What should I do to the first letter in a sentence? (capitalize) What punctuation should I place after each question to let others know that they need to make a response? (question mark)

5. **Select a student to draw a corresponding picture in the upper part of the box with colored markers.**

6. **Continue inserting questions until your students understand how to create their own People Hunt.**

INDIVIDUAL BRAINSTORMING & COMPOSING

Tell students that they now get to draft questions for their own get-acquainted or fact hunt game. Direct students to turn a sheet of notebook paper so the holes are at the top.

Get-Acquainted Game

To brainstorm for a get-acquainted game, have students fold the paper into thirds and crease the folds. Write "Activities" at the top of the first column, "Family & Friends" at the top of the middle column, and "Interests & Other Stuff" in the third column of the notebook paper. Have students brainstorm these questions.

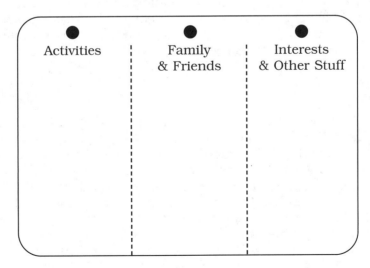

Academic Facts Game

To brainstorm for the academic facts game, have students fold the paper into fourths and crease the folds. Write "Who," "What," "When," "Where," "How," "Why," "What Kind of," "How Many" brainstorming categories at the top of each column. Have students brainstorm these questions.

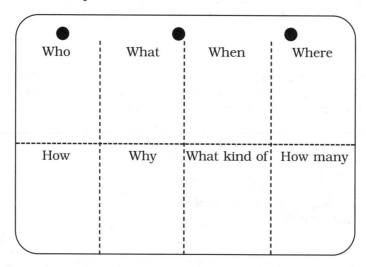

As students brainstorm questions, walk around the classroom noting productive starts. Make positive comments about interesting questions relating to activities, family and friends, and interests. Also compliment illustrations that go with each question. Later, these illustrations can be reduced to fit the space.

NOTE: When students are finished drafting questions, they can locate clip art to illustrate each question.

RESPONDING TO STUDENTS' WRITINGS/REVISING

As students finish the rough drafts of their get-acquainted questions, ask them to find a revising partner. Have each read his/her question aloud to the other person to (1) see which questions will help get to know other students and (2) decide if most of the questions are too easy or too hard. A mixture is best. Make one or two suggestions regarding how to improve the questions. Allow time for revisions.

PUBLISHING

Ahead of time make copies of the People Hunt reproducible (1–1). If you are short on time, students can fold their own grids. A sheet of 8-1/2 × 11-inch paper can easily be folded to make 20 usable boxes. Instruct students to fold the sheet of paper in half four times. (Crease each fold.) The folds delineate the boxes. To produce 18 slightly larger boxes, fold the sheet of paper in half, then in thirds, and then in thirds again.

Give each student a grid so that he/she can add questions and perhaps illustrations. If you have a large group, make two copies of the grid for each student. Caution students that their handwriting must be legible, or have students word-process their questions and tape them to the grid. Once questions and illustrations are added, they can be glued or stapled to a file folder before the People Hunt begins.

Allow students to save their originals to copy and use at People Hunt parties.

Interview Grid

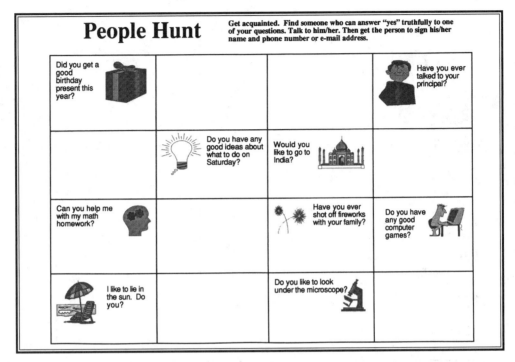

Now you (*audience*) **are going to use your People Hunt to get acquainted with each other** (*purpose*) **or to review academic material** (*purpose*). **Here are the rules.**

Directions

1. **Go up to a person. Say, Hi/Hello, I'm _____.** (Insert your first name.)

2. **Then the other person must do the same thing. If he/she doesn't respond, ask "Who are you?" and wait for a reply.**

3. **Ask a question from your People Hunt sheet until you find one to which the person can truthfully answer "yes." Then ask the new friend to write his/her name and phone number or e-mail address inside the box just below the question.**

If the People Hunt is constructed about academic facts, then the person must accurately answer the question before signing his/her name. For example, "How can a person save water while showering?" (Turn down the volume of water coming in and/or take a shorter shower.)

NOTE: This process provides for lots of oral conversation and takes time to complete.

Alternate Directions

If you want a faster publishing method, instead of doing an oral interview, the student can hand the get-acquainted sheet to the other student to find a question and sign.

NOTE: This alternative is useful when students are searching for the answers to academic facts. It is less effective as a get-acquainted activity and can turn into a "rush to see who can get the most signatures" or who can get their card filled first. While this is entertaining, it often loses the value of getting to know other people and the experience of interviewing another student.

People Hunt

Get acquainted. Find someone who can answer "yes" truthfully to one of your questions. Talk to him/her. Then get the person to sign his/her name and phone number or e-mail address.

LESSON 2

Autograph/Memory Book

OUTCOME Each student will create, circulate, and read entries in his/her personal memory book and respond in other people's books to remember this year together.

MOTIVATORS

1. Share examples of some autograph books, signed memory books, or high school yearbooks of your own or from friends/family members. Read eight to ten titles that sound interesting.

> Favorite Subject
> Worst Moment
> Outstanding Athletic Play
> Best Teacher
> Funniest Moment
> Cutest Guy/Gal
> Hardest Class

Read some entries that are not too personal. Here are a few examples of what students in my class wrote.

> Ryan, I really enjoyed being your partner in science lab. It was exciting when you blew up the volcano and it spit sparks all over Mrs. Loffery's room.

> Carrie, I knew we would be best friends when you walked into English in Guess jeans. I'm glad you were a great speller. I liked writing reports with you.

2. Ask students what they remember about last year in school. Who were their friends last year/the year before? What special events took place this school year? Explain that the purpose of an autograph book is to help you remember your friends and events of the year.

3. Tell students that instead of filling prenamed pages created by an adult, we're going to create the pages on which our friends and classmates will respond.

GROUP BRAINSTORMING

Let's brainstorm some different topics we might want for pages in our autograph/ memory book. (Put information on chart paper so it can be saved and used later in the lesson.)

Key Questions

We're going to write questions to place at the top of each memory/autograph page for peers and friends to answer. Explain that since closed questions request yes/no answers, they don't work in autograph/memory books. Explain that we need open-ended questions that begin with question words like *which, where, when, how, why, who,* and *what.* Write the questions students offer on chart paper, the board, or an overhead.

> ### Entertainment
>
> What was your favorite movie this year? Why?

Entertainment

1. **What question can we compose about TV shows or movies this year?** Add each idea in abbreviated form to the board or chart.

   EXAMPLES: What movie meant the most to you? Why? / What TV show did you
   watch every week? Why?

2. **What question can we compose about celebrities?**

   EXAMPLE: Who did you think deserved an Academy Award? Why?

3. **What question can we compose about songs or other music?**

   EXAMPLE: What song do you hum or whistle to yourself? Why?

Fashion Trends

What outfit did you wish you had never worn this year?

Fashion Trends

1. **What questions can we compose about (style of) clothes?** Add each idea in abbreviated form to the board or chart.

   EXAMPLE: What kinds of jeans were fashionable this year?

2. **What questions can we compose about hair styles/cuts?**

   EXAMPLE: How did you wear your hair this year? Why?

3. **What questions can we compose about shoes?**

   EXAMPLE: Who in our class has the coolest shoes?

4. **What questions can we compose about places where you "hung out"?**

   EXAMPLE: Where was your favorite hangout at school? after school?

5. **What questions can we compose about places to shop?**

   EXAMPLE: Where was the most popular place to shop? Why?

6. **What questions can we compose about new foods on the market?**

   EXAMPLE: What new food did you try this year? Did you like it? Why or why not?

Political Events

What was the most important political event that took place this year? Why did you select this event?

Political Events (Advanced Writers only)

1. **Which politicians were in the news this year?** Praise good ideas. **What questions can we compose about these politicians?** Pause for at least 30 seconds to give students time to think. Add each idea in abbreviated form to the board or chart.

   EXAMPLE: Which public office (job) would you like to have? Why?

2. **What important events occurred this year?** Praise good ideas. **What questions can we compose about important events in the news?** Pause for at least 30 seconds to give students time to think.

   EXAMPLE: What unfortunate news happened this year regarding our environment?

3. **What issues were debated this year?** Praise good ideas. **What questions can we compose about issues being debated?** Pause for at least 30 seconds to give students time to think.

   EXAMPLE: About what "hot" issue do you feel strongly? Why?

4. **What did our society achieve this year?** Praise good ideas. **What questions can we compose about achievements we made?** Pause for at least 30 seconds to give students time to think.

   EXAMPLE: What did you do this year to make our neighborhood a safer/cleaner/happier place?

School

What was your most memorable school day this year? Why?

School

1. **What questions can we compose about subjects or classes?** Add each idea in abbreviated form to the board or chart.

   EXAMPLE: Which class/teacher taught you the most?

2. **What questions can we compose about people at school such as the principal, teachers, custodians, secretaries, bus drivers?**

   EXAMPLE: Who will you never forget? Why?

3. **What questions can we compose about special activities or events at school?**

   EXAMPLE: What sporting event was the most exciting this year? Why?

4. **What questions can we compose about school achievements?**

   EXAMPLES: What did you do this year that made you especially proud? / What difficult thing did you accomplish this year?

5. **What questions can we compose about problems we experienced?**

   EXAMPLE: What was the most difficult thing you had to deal with related to your parents?

Yourself

Why am I so terrific?

Yourself

1. **What questions can we ask about our pet peeves?** Add each idea in abbreviated form to the board or chart.

   EXAMPLE: What bugs you the most about detention? Why?

2. **What questions can we ask about embarrassing situations?**

   EXAMPLE: What was your most embarrassing moment? Why?

3. **What questions can we ask about bummers or regrets?**

   EXAMPLE: What do you wish you could do over, and do better?

4. **What questions can we ask about wishes or the future?**

   EXAMPLE: What teacher do you hope to get next year? Why?

Explain that questions should not contain people's names. Names can be placed in the responses in private memory books, but not in public view.

GROUP COMPOSING

Ahead of time tape several different colors of butcher paper on the wall to represent different pages in the Autograph Book.

Now let's create several pages for our group autograph book.

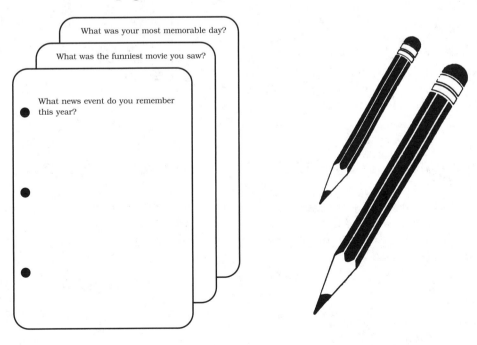

1. **Since we brainstormed questions about entertainment, fashion, trends, political events, school, and ourselves, let's choose two questions from each area for our group autograph book.**

2. **Out of all our ideas, which two shall we choose from entertainment?** Circle these ideas. **from fashion trends?** Circle these ideas. **from political events?** Circle these ideas. **from school?** Circle these ideas. **about yourself?** Circle these ideas.

3. **Which of these questions would we want to put first, second, etc., in our autograph or memory book?** As you number the selected questions, choose students with legible handwriting to write that question at the top of one of the butcher paper sheets you taped on the wall earlier.

INDIVIDUAL BRAINSTORMING & COMPOSING

Suggest young writers find a private spot in the room to draft questions for their Autograph/ Memory Books. You may want to institute these two rules:

1. Any spot, even under a desk or lying on the floor, is fine as long as you don't talk or bother a classmate.

2. If you can't handle the freedom, then you may compose questions at your desk.

Before they begin, encourage students to write one question on a line and then skip the next line so ideas will be easier to read.

Note: As students brainstorm and compose the titles for the pages in their Autograph/Memory Books, consider creating the titles for *your* autograph book. If you choose this option, alert your students to give you privacy. Explain that you'll assist them during the revising step.

● What was your most memorable day?

What bugs you about guys/gals?

What news event do you remember this year?

● What world event shook you the most this year?

What was the funniest movie you saw?

What will you always remember about this year?

●

RESPONDING TO STUDENTS' WRITINGS/REVISING

As students finish the rough drafts of the questions for their autograph/memory books, ask them to find a revising partner. Direct each student to read his/her questions aloud to the other person and decide if the questions will help you remember the writer and the events of the year.

Encourage revising partners to:

- Make two to three specific comments on what they like about the titles for each page of their autograph/memory books.

- Give one to two suggestions for how to improve a question for the Autograph/Memory Book.

Next, write these questions on the board or overhead to guide autograph book creators as the peer evaluates each question.

Does the question begin with an open question such as who, what, when, where, why, how, which one? Have you avoided "yes"/"no" questions?	Yes	No
Will the question help the person respond with something memorable?	Yes	No
Can friends/peers respond to this question without embarrassment?	Yes	No
Does each sentence begin with a capital letter?	Yes	No
Does each question have a question mark at the end?	Yes	No
Have you included a variety of questions?	Yes	No
Do peers get a sense of who you are by the kinds of questions you have written for your autograph book?	Yes	No

After this is completed, the author should make at least one or two revisions to improve his/her questions.

Finally, before writing their questions in the Autograph/Memory Book, revising partners should trade compositions and look for capitalization, punctuation, and spelling errors that might hinder peers from responding to the questions in the Autograph/Memory Book in a memorial way.

PUBLISHING

After students assemble their autograph/memory books, explain that they'll pass their books around and get messages from classmates (*audience*) so they will be able to remember the year they had together (*purpose*).

Autograph Book

Assemble Memory Book

1. Get one sheet of notebook paper for each of your questions.

2. Write a question on the first line at the top of each piece of notebook paper.

3. Place your "Thoughts from Your Teacher" page on the table or your desk. This will be your last page. (optional) Place the "Nominations for _____" page on top of this.

4. Lay your notebook pages in order on top of this final sheet.

5. (optional) Position a resealable bag over these sheets to store photos and mementos of classmates. The bottom of the bag should be at the top, the opening at the bottom.

6. Ahead of time choose and reproduce a cover appropriate for the age of your students. (See reproducibles 2–2 and 2–3.) Decorate your cover with colored markers or pencils, then place it on top of the stack of papers. Staple the pages two or three times across the top.

NOTE: Students may want to staple the Autograph Book on the left side. Discourage this. It is easier to write in the book if it is stapled at the top.

Thoughts from Your Teacher

Nominations for _____

Write the first name of the person in our class
who best fits this description.

Great Listener   _____

Creative Thinker   _____

Responsible Partner _____

Terrific Joke Teller   _____

Friendly   _____

Shares Generously   _____

Cooperative Team Member _____

Awesome Ideas   _____

Most Helpful   _____

Dependable   _____

_____   _____

Trade Memory Books

1. Once you have traded Memory Books, find a question to which you want to respond.

   • Begin the response with the word "To" followed by the name of the person for whom the message is aimed.

   • Answer the question posed by the Memory Book owner.

   • Respect the reader's feelings. Avoid hurtful remarks.

   • End with the word "From" followed by your name.

2. Respond to one to two questions. Leave room for other people to write.

3. Pass the autograph/memory books around so everyone has an opportunity to sign. (optional) Return the memory book to its owner so he/she can pass it to another student or read what was written.

For the next week/two weeks give students ten minutes at the end of school/each class period to exchange memory books. Or complete this writing activity on a day when you are having a class party, so students have an opportunity to exchange memories in a casual, nonstructured time frame.

Revising Assistant

for Autograph Books

This checklist will assist you in evaluating your Autograph/Memory Book questions.

Revising Partner

1. Have you included a variety of questions?

2. Will the question help the person respond with something interesting or memorable?

3. Do peers get a sense of who you are by the kind of questions you have written for your autograph book?

4. Can friends/peers respond to each question without embarrassment?

5. Does the question begin with a *who, what, when, where, why, or how* word? Have you deleted all "yes"/"no" questions?

6. Does each question begin with a capital letter? Does each question end in a question mark?

Overall Comments (Which questions do you like the best? Why?)

Memory Book

Name:
Date:
Classroom Teacher:

Memory Book

Name:
Date:
Classroom Teacher:

Nominations for _____

**Write the first name of the person in our class
who best fits this description.**

Great Listener _____

Creative Thinker _____

Responsible Partner _____

Terrific Joke Teller _____

Friendly _____

Shares Generously _____

Cooperative Team Member _____

Awesome Ideas _____

Most Helpful _____

Dependable _____

_____ _____

Thoughts from Your Teacher

LESSON 3

Captions

OUTCOME   Each student will write humorous captions for three pictures.

MOTIVATORS

1. One option is to coordinate this lesson with a learning activity in which you take pictures of what occurs. Tell students that they are going to write captions for the photos taken during the activity so that parents and other students in their school (*audience*) can see what we have been doing/learning (*purpose*).

2. Ask students to sit on the floor in a circle. Play "Face Charades" with your students. Ask students to closely watch as you make a facial expression. Then ask students to guess how you were feeling. Inquire which clues helped them guess your feeling. Repeat six to eight times with a different student making the facial expression each time.

    Divide the class into two groups to play "Face Charades." One student takes a turn making a facial expression. Have him/her whisper the feeling word to you before starting. Students on the opposite team guess the emotion. Alternate teams.

    Pull everyone together and discuss how facial and body expressions help us predict what a person is thinking.

3. Share several pictures with humorous captions that you have found in a magazine or newspaper or ones you created from imagination. Ask students for other ideas for what the subject in the pictures (such as a person, animal, or object) could be saying or thinking.

4. Tell students they are going to write captions for the pictures to entertain (*purpose*) each other. *Ranger Rick*, published by the National Wildlife Federation, regularly has humorous captions of wild animals. This magazine can often be found at the public library or an elementary school library.

   Collect used or recycled magazines and distribute one magazine per student or pair of students. Explain that each person should select three pictures. Point out that pictures selected must show expressions, feelings, and/or actions that are open to various interpretations. Use a paper cutter or scissors to trim each picture that is selected. Mount the pictures on separate pieces of colored construction paper with a staple, tape, or glue so that captions can be added later.

   More advanced students can be asked to glue a figure cut from one picture to an unlikely background of another picture.

5. An alternative is to find a full-page picture of a human or animal face in a magazine and cut out around the face. Then cut the face in half vertically or horizontally.

   Glue one half of the face to a sheet of construction paper. Have students use a pencil or pen to complete the face.

GROUP BRAINSTORMING

Ahead of time choose a large picture from a magazine so that students at the back of the class can see the picture easily. **Let's brainstorm a caption for this picture.**

"Recycle? Sure we recycle. My owner recycles empty dog food cans and I recycle all the leftover bones. I crush them with my powerful jaws," Nelson smiled smartly.

Name	Feeling	Reason	Said	How
Austin	sad	salesman poked finger at him	cried	quickly
Jeb	silly	kids teased him	moaned	furiously
Sassy	playful		chirped	playfully
Barbie	angry		growled	carefully
Yolanda			whispered	confidentially

Key Questions

1. **What could be the name of the person, animal, or object in the picture? Who is speaking? Who or what is thinking?** Pause for at least 30 seconds to give students time to think. Write their ideas under the "Name" column.

2. **How is the subject feeling? What emotion could he/she/it/they be having? What word captures the feelings in the picture?** Pause to give students time to think. Write students' ideas under the "Feeling" column.

3. **Out of all the feelings we considered for this picture, which might lead to a humorous caption?** Choose a withdrawn or uninvolved student to select a feeling. Circle the feeling.

4. Ask students to look back at the list of feelings generated in step 2. **What situation could cause the subject to feel this way? Why do you think the _____ is in this mood? Why might the subject be feeling _____?** Pause to give students time to think. Write students' ideas under the "Reason" column.

5. **Out of all the reasons we generated for the subject to feel this way, which reason could lead to a humorous caption?** Choose a withdrawn or uninvolved student to select a reason. Circle the reason.

6. Ask students to look back at the list of feelings generated in step 2. **What is a word like "said" that we could use to attribute the quote? What is a more precise word for "said" that we could use to fit the situation? For example, what "said" word could work for an angry person? for a person feeling silly?** Pause to give students time to think. Praise good ideas. List students' ideas under the "Said" column.

> **Thinking about Mechanics:** For example, in the quote "The oldest pig exclaimed, 'Wee, wee, wee all the way home,'" the phrase "the oldest pig exclaimed" shows who was doing all the whining. The whining was attributed to the oldest pig.

Other Words for "Said"

whispered	declared	replied
shouted	muttered	objected
chirped	cried	explained
exclaimed	insisted	hollered
whined	screamed	growled
denied	responded	answered
shrieked	called	echoed
complained	gasped	protested
mumbled	howled	announced
yelled	argued	vowed
barked	sighed	concluded
reported	roared	asked

7. Ask students to look back at the list of feelings generated in step 2. **How is the subject speaking? If the subject is reflecting, how is he/she/it/they thinking?** Pause to give students time to think. List these adverbs that tell how under the "How" column.

GROUP COMPOSING

Ahead of time cut large speech bubbles (see reproducible 3–1) from butcher paper so drafts of the group caption can be written on them. **Now, we are going to draft a humorous caption together to get acquainted with the procedure.**

   1. Considering the subject's feelings and reasons, what do you think the person, animal, or object is saying? What is the subject saying about the situation he/she/it/they are in? Pause to give students time to think. Write one student idea per speech bubble. Write one possible quote at the top of a bubble, another possible quote at the bottom, and finally half of the quote at the top and the rest at the bottom of a speech bubble so that the three basic ways to write a quote can be demonstrated.

   NOTE: The rest of each caption will be completed in steps 2–7.

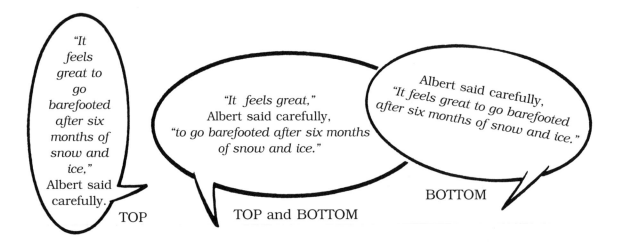

2. **What punctuation would be appropriate at the end of this quote? Is the subject asking a question?** (question mark) **shouting or yelling?** (exclamation point) **whispering or talking normally?** (period) Add the correct punctuation.

3. **What final punctuation do we need to place around the exact words of someone?** (quotation marks at the beginning and the end of the exact words of the person quoted) Place the quotation marks around the quote.

4. **Which name should we choose for the speaker or thinker?** Choose a quiet or uninvolved student to select a name. Add the name to the caption.

> **Thinking about Mechanics:** What should we do to the name of the speaker or thinker? (capitalize the first letter of a proper name)

5. **Which of our words for "said" would add to the humor?** Add that word to the caption.

6. **Out of all the words that describe how the quote was said, which word** (adverb) **would make it humorous?** Add that word to the caption.

7. **What could we change so the quote will make readers laugh? How can we change it to make it sound funnier/more humorous?** Pause to give students time to think. Revise the caption as students make suggestions.

8. Repeat for the other "quotes" generated in step 1.

INDIVIDUAL BRAINSTORMING AND COMPOSING

Tell students that now they get to draft their own ideas for captions for pictures they have chosen. As students brainstorm ideas, walk around the room. Make positive comments and ask questions to expand and clarify the feelings in each student's picture, why the person/animal/object is feeling this way, what the subject might say, and how it is stated. Particularly comment positively on what makes a student's caption humorous.

Advanced Writers   Suggest students locate and cut out cartoons that they like from the daily or Sunday newspaper. Have these young writers compose one or two captions for each picture in the cartoon sequence. For now have young authors write each quotation on a strip of paper.

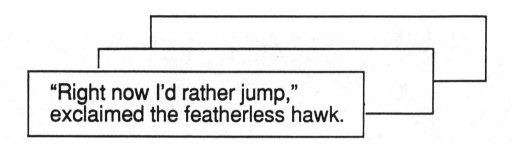

**"Right now I'd rather jump,"
exclaimed the featherless hawk.**

Later, these captions can be published in a special cartoon sequence. See alternate publishing method titled Cartoon Sequence in the *Publishing* section of this lesson.

RESPONDING TO STUDENTS' WRITINGS/REVISING

As students complete their three captions, ask them to find a partner and read each caption aloud. Ask partners to point out which of the three captions is the most humorous and explain why it is humorous. Then the partner can make suggestions for the other two captions.

Examples of three separate captions:

Spike whispered prickly, "I stand here all day long and no one even notices."

"All right, no more Jello for dessert," said Terrance swiftly as he dived for the rabbit.

"It feels great to go barefooted after six months of snow and ice," said Albert carefully.

Finally, direct students to proofread for a capital letter at the beginning of each sentence in the caption, quotation marks before and after the speaker's words, an adverb telling how the statement is said, and a period, question mark, or exclamation point at the end of each sentence in the quote. Write the following information on the board or overhead to guide your students' revising.

Caption

Ideas

_____ 1. Is the situation (picture and caption) funny?

_____ 2. Is the person/animal/thing quoted named? Is this funny or thought provoking?

_____ 3. Does it include how the quote is stated? Is this funny or descriptive?

_____ 4. What is the best part of your caption?

Conventions

_____ 1. Are quotation marks placed at the beginning and end of the quote?

_____ 2. Does the sentence begin with a capital letter?

_____ 3. Has end punctuation been used?
  • a period at the end of a statement
  • a question mark at the end of a question
  • an exclamation point at the end of a statement expressing strong emotion

_____ 4. Has a comma been used to separate part of a quote from the rest of a sentence and the attribution?

PUBLISHING

After students finish revising their captions, explain that they'll publish them on signs in the hallway so that the other students in school (*audience*) can read and enjoy them (*purpose*).

Hangings/Garlands

Materials

copy paper, scissors, glue, hole punch, yarn

Directions

1. Draw a speech bubble large enough for your caption or duplicate one from those found at the end of this lesson.

   NOTE: Speech bubbles can be turned around or flipped over so they point toward the speaker.

2. Write your caption neatly inside the bubble.

3. Cut out this bubble and glue it to your picture.

4. Punch holes at the top of your picture on the left and right sides.

5. String yarn through the holes and tie a knot; or string several hangings together for a garland. Hang the hanging or garland where it/they can be seen and read.

Cartoon Sequence

Materials

construction paper, comics, scissors, glue

Directions

1. Cut a sheet of construction paper in half the long way. Save one half for a different cartoon sequence.

2. Fold the bottom edge of the construction paper up about one and a half inches. Crease the fold and reopen. Eventually the captions will be written on both sides of this fold.

3. Fold the construction paper in four or five sections depending on the number of cartoon sections. Crease and then reopen.

4. Glue one part of the cartoon (pictures without dialogue) in each section.

   NOTE: Stay above the imaginary dotted line.

5. Cut a notch along the bottom edge between each comic section to make the folded edge of dialogue easier to turn.

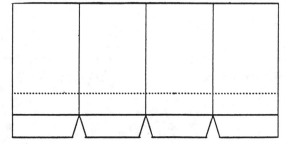

6. Write the dialogue/captions for one speaker on the open flap. Refold the bottom edge and write the dialogue for the other speaker on the closed flap. Repeat for each section of the comic.

Speech Bubbles

Speech Bubbles

Lesson 4

Consumer Survey

OUTCOME Each student will compose written questions and gather people's opinions about particular brands of a product.

MOTIVATORS

1. This lesson is great for days when students need to release some energy. Bring in two brands of one product (soda, gum, candy, or chips), some small cups, and a water pitcher. For this lesson we'll presume your class will evaluate chips.

   Select a student to distribute a napkin and a small sample of an unidentified brand to each student in your class. Direct students to label this product "Brand X." Pass out a sample of the second brand. Instruct students to label it "Brand Y." While students are labeling their products, have another student pass out small cups and another student fill the cups half full of water.

   Explain that students will be doing consumer testing of the two brands to see which is better. Direct students to slowly drink, chew, or consume Brand "X," savoring the taste. Then sip a little water to clean away all smells or tastes. Direct students to slowly drink, chew, or consume Brand "Y," savoring the taste. Ask students to decide which brand they liked better. Tell students they are going to create a class Consumer's Guide.

2. Explain that Consumer's Guides contain buying wisdom about major consumer products and different brands of these products. In order to advise or guide people accurately on the pros and cons of different brands/models, data is collected through reader surveys, panel tests, laboratory tests, and expert judgments. Sometimes data on some products includes repair histories and the suggested retail prices.

   Once this information is analyzed, one or more brand(s)/model(s) of a product is judged excellent quality (or superior to the other brands that were evaluated). If brand(s)/model(s) of a product are judged high quality and low price, it receives a "Terrific Buy" rating.

GROUP BRAINSTORMING

In order to collect data for our Consumer Guide we must first create a consumer survey. In order to do this we need to consider what characteristics or features influenced us to like and dislike these two brands. We will use these characteristics/features later when we create our consumer surveys.

NOTE: This step is for generating criteria, not for comparing the two products. Comparisons will come later.

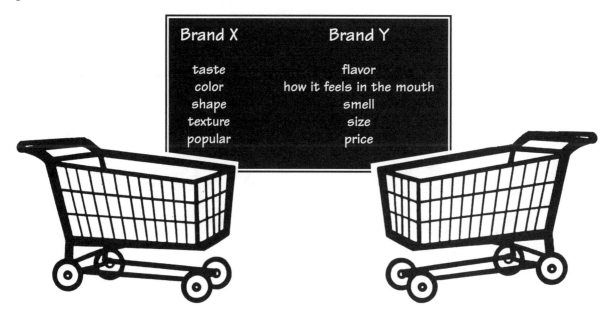

Brand X	Brand Y
taste	flavor
color	how it feels in the mouth
shape	smell
texture	size
popular	price

Key Questions

1. Take a quick poll. **Silently raise your hand (with two fingers crossed) if you liked Brand X better.** Quickly count hands. **Silently raise your hand (with two fingers open in a "y" or "v" shape) if you liked Brand Y better.** Quickly count hands. **Silently raise your hand (turned flat) if you couldn't decide.** Count hands.

2. Direct this question to students who voted for Brand X. **Why did you think Brand X was the better brand? Why would you buy it or tell other people to purchase it?** Write students' ideas on the board or overhead under the words "Brand X."

3. Direct this question to students who voted for Brand Y. **Why didn't you like Brand X? Why wouldn't you buy Brand X? Why were you uncertain?** Write students' ideas under the words "Brand X" along with the things that were liked.

4. Direct this question to students who voted for Brand Y. **Why was Brand Y the better brand? Why would you buy it or tell other people to purchase it?** Write students' ideas under the words "Brand Y."

5. Direct this question to students who voted for Brand X. **Why didn't you like Brand Y? Why wouldn't you buy Brand Y? Why were you uncertain?** Write students' ideas under "Brand Y" along with the things that were liked.

6. Show the students the brands they tasted.

INDIVIDUAL BRAINSTORMING

We need to consider products and the brands of those products about which you'd like to gather information. A blank grid for the overhead can be found at the end of this lesson. **After that we'll brainstorm some characteristics or features you may want your consumers to evaluate when deciding which brand to purchase.**

NOTE: Brands will be brainstormed last, since the point of this task is to model generating characteristics.

1. **For which types of food products would you like to evaluate the quality?** If a student offers a brand name, accept it; then ask what type of food it is. Write the type of the product on the board, not a brand name.

2. **About what other products would you want to survey people?** Record ideas on the board.

3. Ask an uninvolved student to choose a product. Star that product and move across the grid horizontally. Explain that later students will choose at least two brands so they can compare them. Skip this brainstorming category for now.

Product	Brands	Characteristics/Features			
soda		flavor	smoothness	no aftertaste	price
gum		chewy	flavor	smell	amount
cereal		freshness	taste	crunch	healthy
chips		taste	salty	eye-appeal	freshness
pizza					
movies		action	actors	music	scenery
jeans		last	look sharp	popular style	
shoes		sturdy	in style		
parks		scenery	things to do	cleanliness	crowded
motorcycles		handles	accelerates	smooth ride	speed
software					

4. **What characteristics or features are important to this product? What makes it special? What makes people want to buy or not buy it?** Move across the grid horizontally and record student ideas under the heading "Characteristics/Features."

5. Choose an uninvolved student to select a product.

6. What brands of this product could be tested? Write two brand ideas under the heading "Brands" across from that product.

7. Repeat questions 3 and 4 for about eight products so students will be prepared to generate this information for their own surveys. To save time brainstorm brands for just two or three types of products.

8. You will use this information (a product, two brands, and at least five characteristics or features of this product) when you each create and conduct your own survey.

9. Now each of you needs to select a product. After that, what should you do next? (Brainstorm at least five characteristics or features.) **What do you need to do next?** (Choose two brands.)

10. Give students time to complete steps 8 and 9.

GROUP COMPOSING

Ahead of time make overheads of the Consumer Survey and the two blank survey forms. Show students the forms and explain that we'll use them to organize their own ideas. **Now we'll create a group survey based on the characteristics or features we generated from Brands "X" and "Y." Later, you'll create your own survey to evaluate the product and the brands you selected.**

Consumer Survey

Sponsored by _____

We need your assistance in evaluating ___ brands of _____.

Please read each question about these brands of _____, then decide whether you liked or disliked that characteristic. Circle one number on the rating scale and explain your reasons why in the space provided.

Distributed by _____

Consumer Survey Cover

1. Who is sponsoring our survey? (us) Insert your group's name on the cover sheet.

2a. Next, we need to request people's assistance. Point to this sentence: **"We need your assistance in evaluating _____ brands of _____."**

2b. How many brands did we evaluate? What type of product did we evaluate? Insert this information on the survey cover.

   Tell Advanced Writers that when they compose their own surveys on different products, they can vary this survey introduction and the directions to meet their own needs.

3. Now we'll complete the directions on the survey cover. Read: **"Please read each question about these brands of ___, then decide whether you liked or disliked that characteristic. Circle one number on the rating scale and explain your reasons why in the space provided."**

4. Finally, when you create your own consumer survey cover, you will fill in your name at the bottom after "Distributed by."

```
┌─────────────────────────────────────────────────┐
│                 Survey Form                     │
│                                                 │
│  Brand: _____                        │
│                                                 │
│  1. How would you rate _____?           │
│                        1_____2_____3          │
│                     _____          _____      │
│  WHY? _____ │
│  2. How would you rate _____?           │
│                        1_____2_____3          │
│                     _____          _____      │
│  WHY? _____ │
│  3. How would you rate _____?           │
│                        1_____2_____3          │
│                     _____          _____      │
│  WHY? _____ │
│  4. How would you rate _____?           │
│                        1_____2_____3          │
│                     _____          _____      │
│  WHY? _____ │
│  5. How would you rate _____?           │
│                        1_____2_____3          │
│                     _____          _____      │
│  WHY? _____ │
│  6. How would you rate _____?           │
│                        1_____2_____3          │
│                     _____          _____      │
│  WHY? _____ │
│                                 Consumer # ____ │
└─────────────────────────────────────────────────┘
```

Survey Forms

1. Leave the survey cover and move to the two survey forms. **Earlier we tested Brands "X" and "Y." What are the names of the two brands we evaluated earlier? We'll write one brand on each survey form.** Insert one brand on the line after the word "Brand: _____."

2. **Which characteristic/feature should we place on our survey first? Let's insert this term in the first question, "How would you rate _____?" Insert the term.**

3. (optional) **Under the characteristic/feature, we need a rating scale so survey takers can indicate how much the brand was liked or disliked. We can use the terms disliked and liked, with disliked getting a rating of 1, and liked getting a rating of 3.** Explain that the rating system will make it easier for the people surveyed to respond.

1_____2_____3
Disliked   Liked

4. (optional) **What other positive and negative terms could we use?**

Negative Terms			Positive Terms
1	2		3
Yucky			Yummy
Poor			Excellent
Awful			Tasty

5. State that consumers need a place to add comments. Point out that after each rating scale there is the word "Why."

6. Which characteristic/feature (taste or flavor, smell, crunch, texture, salt, and size) should we place on our survey next? Let's insert this term in the next question, "How would you rate _____?" Insert the term.

7. Repeat for the other brand on the second survey form. Tell students to keep the characteristics/features in the same order to make tallying data easier.

INDIVIDUAL COMPOSING

Now that you have experienced creating a survey, you get to compose your own survey for the product you selected earlier. Later you will make multiple copies of your survey and collect your own data.

Comprehension Check

Cover Page

   1. What goes at the top of your consumer survey cover sheet under the title? ("Sponsored by _____")

   2. Next, what is needed to inform the person who will be completing the survey what to do? (directions)

   3. What goes in the first blank of the directions? (the number of brands) **What goes in the second blank?** (the product)

   4. What goes in the blank after "Distributed by"? (student's full name)

Survey Form

   1. What goes into each question on the survey form? (a different feature or characteristic)

   2. (optional) **What do you need under the characteristic or feature?** (a rating scale so survey takers can indicate how much the brand was liked or disliked)

   3. (optional/Advanced Writers) **What do you need to do if you don't like the terms liked/disliked? What other positive and negative terms could you use?**

   4. After you complete your first survey form, what do you do next? (Repeat the same steps for the other brand on another survey form.)

GROUP REVISING

Ahead of time make multiple copies of the group survey.

Tell students since the wording and appearance of a survey is very important, we'll look at our group's survey and see where it can be improved. **"What would make it clearer? Easier to understand? Easier to complete?"**

Together inspect the title, sponsor, number of brands, type of product, names of two brands, and positive and negative terms for accuracy and clarity.

INDIVIDUAL REVISING

This step is for students who are creating their own survey.

Let's use what we learned when we revised our group survey to revise your survey. Allow students time to revise.

PUBLISHING

Students will need one cover page and two survey forms. Make multiple copies of each student's packet. Reproducibles can be found at the end of this lesson. Direct students to add their information before making packets for each student. Each student will need one to three packets depending on how many people you decide to have them survey.

Explain that students will use their surveys to see what consumers like and dislike. Tell students that in the next lesson they'll use the information they collected to create a Consumer's Guide, full of many different products. The Consumer's Guide will help consumers (*audience*) take charge of their lives and purchase the best products (*purpose*).

1. Role-play how to hand a consumer survey and a pencil to a consumer and request this person to complete the survey in a courteous and professional manner.

   NOTE: Direct students to go to another person if the consumer hasn't tried both/all brands being surveyed.

2. Direct students to collect a designated number of surveys (two or three is a reasonable number).

3. Give a due date for students to complete the data collection. Check on students' data collection halfway through and assist students who need help.

Product	Brands	Characteristics/Features			

Consumer Survey

Sponsored by _____

We need your assistance in evaluating ____ brands of _____.

Please read each question about these brands of _____, then decide whether you liked or disliked that characteristic. Circle one number on the rating scale and explain your reasons why in the space provided.

Distributed by _____

Survey Form

Brand: _____

1. How would you rate _____?

1_____2_____3

_____   _____

WHY? _____

2. How would you rate _____?

1_____2_____3

_____   _____

WHY? _____

3. How would you rate _____?

1_____2_____3

_____   _____

WHY? _____

4. How would you rate _____?

1_____2_____3

_____   _____

WHY? _____

5. How would you rate _____?

1_____2_____3

_____   _____

WHY? _____

6. How would you rate _____?

1_____2_____3

_____   _____

WHY? _____

Consumer # _____

LESSON 5

Consumer's/Buyer's Guide

OUTCOME   Each student will write a product review based on information collected during the Consumer Survey, Lesson 4.

MOTIVATORS

1. Show students copies of various consumer reports. See your school librarian or public library for copies. Encourage students to scan articles that interest them. Ask what kind of products they found in the consumer reports. List these on the board.

   If you have access to limited copies, place students in pairs or make an overhead of one article. Select a topic that appeals to your students. Read the article together and discuss what it contains. Ask students what features or characteristics of this product were evaluated.

Explain to your students that they are going to write their own consumer reports for other students and parents to use based on the information they collected.

2. Ask students who have finished doing all their surveys to raise their hands. Find out what problems they had getting people to complete the surveys. Make suggestions. Allow more time if needed.

3. Pass out copies of the survey created by your class in the Consumer Survey lesson.

   a. Have each student complete a survey on the food product he/she tested in your class during the Consumer Survey lesson.

   b. Collect the completed surveys.

Survey Form

Brand: _____

1. How would you rate _____?
   1_____2_____3
   _____   _____
   WHY? _____

2. How would you rate _____?
   1_____2_____3
   _____   _____
   WHY? _____

3. How would you rate _____?
   1_____2_____3
   _____   _____
   WHY? _____

4. How would you rate _____?
   1_____2_____3
   _____   _____
   WHY? _____

5. How would you rate _____?
   1_____2_____3
   _____   _____
   WHY? _____

   Consumer # _____

c. Make an overhead of a tally sheet for your own use and paper copies of the tally sheet for each student. A blank tally sheet can be found at the end of this lesson.

d. Demonstrate on the overhead how to compile the Brand X and Brand Y data on the tally sheet by writing the rating (1, 2, or 3) for each consumer in the column under each feature/characteristic. To determine which characteristics or features of each brand rated higher, total the ratings for each feature, then divide by the number of consumers in the survey. Ask students what conclusions they draw from the data. Discuss their findings.

Tally Sheet

	Feature 1	Feature 2	Feature 3	Feature 4	Feature 5	Feature 6	Feature 7
Brand _____							
Consumer 1	1	3	1	1	3	3	1
Consumer 2	1	2	1	1	1	2	1
Consumer 3	2	1	1	1	1	1	1
Total	**4**	**6**	**3**	**3**	**5**	**6**	**3**
Brand _____							
Consumer 1	2	2	2	3	2	2	2
Consumer 2	3	1	1	1	1	3	3
Consumer 3	1	1	2	1	2	1	1
Total	**6**	**4**	**5**	**5**	**5**	**6**	**6**

e. Distribute another blank tally sheet to each student. Give students time to compile their data from their own consumer surveys. After students finish tallying data on each characteristic or feature for each brand on their surveys, allow time to share their findings in pairs or groups of three. Put these second tally sheets away or collect them to use when students compose their own consumer reports.

GROUP BRAINSTORMING

Direct students to pull out their first tally sheets constructed during motivation step 3.
Let's consider what we learned about the two brands we tested in the Consumer Survey lesson.

Brand X	Reasons	Recommendation
	taste	preferred by more people surveyed
	crunch	
	texture	
	bought for years	
Brand Y	Reasons	Recommendation
	flavor	favorite of many people
	cost	
	would like more cheese smell	

Key Questions

1. **According to our survey data, which brand did we like better? What was the name of Brand "X"? What was the name of Brand "Y"?** Write the names of brands under "Brand X" or "Brand Y" on the board or overhead.

2. **What reasons were given for liking Brand "X" better than the other brand(s)?** Briefly jot down reasons on the board or overhead under the heading "Reasons."

3a. **What conclusion can we make about Brand "X" from the survey data? What conclusions can we draw from the comments written on the surveys?** Briefly jot down conclusions under the heading "Recommendation" on the board or overhead.

3b. **What recommendation can we make to potential consumers about Brand "X"? What are our suggestions to readers of this consumer report?** Write this information under the heading "Recommendation."

4. Repeat steps 2 and 3 for Brand "Y."

GROUP COMPOSING

Let's compose an entry in our consumer's or buyer's guide for the brands we tested as a class.

Chips

We surveyed our class (32 consumers) to determine which chips we thought were better. The brands evaluated were Lays Sour Cream and Dorito Nacho Cheese. Each chip was evaluated on six criteria: taste or flavor, smell, crunch, texture, salt, and size.

Lays Sour Cream   We liked the taste, crunch, and texture, but disliked the amount of salt and the small size. The comments of the people surveyed indicated people had purchased this product for at least 6 years.

Dorito Nacho Cheese   We liked flavor and cost, but disliked crunch and lack of smell. Some people commented that they wanted more cheese smell.

Shopping Tips

Shop for freshness.

In summary, we preferred Lays Sour Cream Chip over Dorito Nacho Cheese based on taste, crunch, and texture, but Dorito Nacho Cheese is a favorite of many. Since results were so close, we recommend you purchase and enjoy both products.

1. **Let's begin our consumer's or buyer's guide with the type of product on which we gathered information. What kind of food did we evaluate? We'll make this our title.** Write this at the top for the title.

   > **Thinking about Mechanics:** Where should the title be written? (at the top, in the center)

   > **Thinking about Mechanics:** What do we need to remember when writing a title? (capitalize the first word and all words except articles such as *a*, *an*, or *the*)

2. **Next, we need an opening sentence to tell readers what we did, how we collected information, and from whom we collected it. What could we say?** Pause to allow students time to think. Praise ideas that have two or three ideas in them. Have a student choose one. Add this to the review.

   > **Thinking about Mechanics:** How do we show we are beginning our first paragraph? (indent)

3. **Now we need to name the brands we evaluated. How can we say this?** Pause to give students time to think. Add the first good idea to the review.

> **Thinking about Mechanics:** How can we show that we are going to leave our introduction and begin discussing one of the brands that we tested? (begin a new paragraph and indent)

4. **Next, readers will want to know the characteristics or features we used for evaluation. How can we share this information?** Pause to give students time to think. Add the first good idea to the review.

> **Thinking about Mechanics:** What punctuation do we use after a sentence to indicate that a list will follow? (colon—The words in front of a colon must be a complete sentence.)

5. **Now we are ready to use the characteristics or features to describe each brand. Which brand shall we describe first?**

6. **Let's write the name of our first brand.**

> **Thinking about Mechanics:** How can we show readers that we are starting a new idea? (indent)

7. **Based on our survey data, what do we know about this brand regarding the first characteristic or feature?** Compose a sentence describing performance on this characteristic or feature. Repeat for the other features of this product.

> **Advanced Writers:** How shall we start this sentence?
> **Beginning Writers:** Let's start the sentence, "Consumers liked . . ."

8. **Based on consumers' comments, what do we know about this brand?** Add this information to the paragraph.

9. Repeat steps 6, 7, and 8 for the other brand.

> **Thinking about Mechanics:** How can we show we are changing to a new product? (indent)

10. **How can we summarize the information we learned about these two brands of
    _____? What is our recommendation?** Add this information to the consumer
    report.

    EXAMPLES: The new software, Go Westward, is better than _____, but it has
              some drawbacks.

              Oat Snack is the best cereal for a number of reasons.

              A Razorback Bike makes other bikes seem _____.

              We found that some consumers preferred _____, while others _____.

11. (optional) **Let's make a boxed-off section in our report for shopping tips. What
    tips could we give readers about how to shop for our product?** Add this infor-
    mation to the consumer report.

    EXAMPLES: Shop for freshness.

              To get the freshest chip, check the date code on the top of the bag.

INDIVIDUAL COMPOSING

Tell students it is time to use the survey information they collected and compiled on
their tally sheets to compose their own consumer reports. Display the group composing
chart so students can refer to it as needed.

   Advanced Writers   Send your Advanced Writers to their seats to begin.

NOTE: Advanced Writers may have collected data on more than two brands. Be alert to
this as they compose their consumer reports. These writers will need to compose an
additional paragraph and make other modifications to their review.

   Beginning Writers   Do a comprehension check to assess whether Beginning Writers clearly understand the task before them. Reteach where necessary. Allow Advanced
Writers who wish to attend to participate.

Comprehension Check:

1. **What information should your title contain?** (type of product)

2. **What needs to be included in your opening sentence?** (what you did)

3. **What do you need to report next?** (the brands evaluated)

4. **Now what do readers need to know?** (the features or characteristics to be
   evaluated)

5. **What do we need to decide next?** (which brand to describe first)

6. **For this brand, what information do we need to describe first?** (rating for each
   feature)

7. **What needs to be described next for this brand?** (comments)

8. **If you want to add some special information on shopping tips, where can you
   do it?**

9. **How will you wrap up your consumer report?** (recommendation, conclusions,
   and/or suggestions)

As students get situated, walk around complimenting students who have good starts on their consumer guide reports. Make positive comments to students who are referring to their survey data and comments as they write. Praise effective topic sentences, accurate details, powerful summary statements or recommendations, and useful shopping tips. *For example:* (Read paragraph to student.) **Your opening paragraph is very clear about who did the survey and which criteria were evaluated.**

RESPONDING TO STUDENTS' WRITINGS/REVISING

As students complete drafts of their consumer reviews, ask them to find a revising partner with whom they haven't worked. Direct each revising partner to read his/her partner's review out loud to the writer to see if it is easy to understand the information, makes sense, and the recommendation is clear. Trade back. Ask each reviewer to make at least two revisions to improve his/her review.

Circulate around the room assisting students who need help with the opening paragraph, the description of one or both brands, and/or the conclusion/recommendation.

- **Introduction/opening paragraph:** If a student has written a strong opening paragraph, make a positive comment such as "Your introduction will be really clear to readers because you have told the type of product and the brands that were evaluated and explained what you did in your investigation."

  If a young writer is having trouble, ask a question such as "What were the five characteristics/features that you investigated?"

- **Description of one or both brands:** If a student has written a strong descriptive paragraph, make a positive comment such as "Your paragraph on resealable bags describes precisely and clearly which characteristics the people surveyed liked and disliked. Also you have woven in the comments people made in a way that helps elucidate the information from the ratings."

  If a young writer is having trouble, ask a question such as "Which characteristics were rated the highest? the lowest? How can you describe this information in your consumer report?"

• **Conclusion/recommendation:**   If a student has written a strong concluding paragraph, make a positive comment such as "You have really summarized the survey data accurately. Your recommendation is in line with your data."

If a young writer is having trouble, ask a question such as "Based on the critical feedback you received on your survey(s), what suggestions could you make to the readers of your consumer survey report?"

Before publishing, have revising partners trade reviews and look for capitalization, punctuation, spelling, and grammar errors that might hinder a reader from acquiring useful information that could help them make good purchases.

PUBLISHING

Explain that students will publish their consumer guide to help other students, parents, and neighbors (*audience*) decide which brands to purchase (*purpose*). Compile all the reports, place them in alphabetical order, and add a cover and an index.

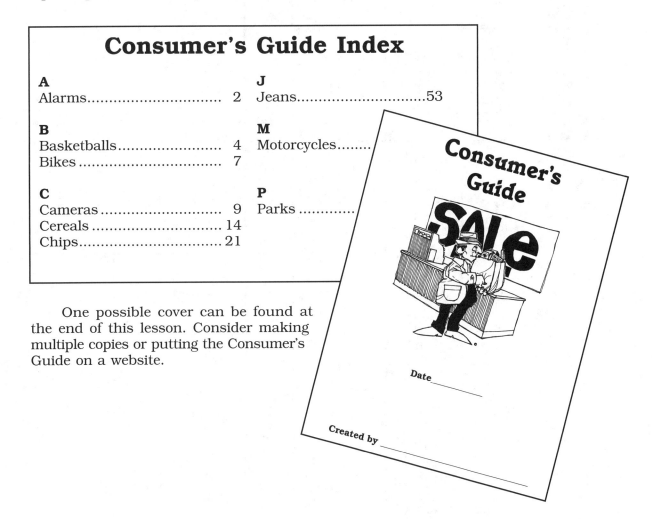

Consumer's Guide Index

A
Alarms............................ 2

B
Basketballs...................... 4
Bikes 7

C
Cameras 9
Cereals 14
Chips............................. 21

J
Jeans..............................53

M
Motorcycles........

P
Parks ....

One possible cover can be found at the end of this lesson. Consider making multiple copies or putting the Consumer's Guide on a website.

Tally Sheet

Brand _____	Feature 1	Feature 2	Feature 3	Feature 4	Feature 5	Feature 6	Feature 7
Consumer 1							
Consumer 2							
Consumer 3							
Total							
Brand _____							
Consumer 1							
Consumer 2							
Consumer 3							
Total							

Consumer's Guide

Date_____

Created by _____

LESSON 6

Letter of Introduction

OUTCOME At the end of the school year each student will write a letter of introduction to his/her teacher(s) for the coming year.

or

OUTCOME At the beginning of the year each student will write a letter of introduction to you or a new principal, teacher, or staff member who will
have contact with the entire class.

MOTIVATORS

1. Talk about the coming school year.

2. Share a letter a student sent to you before entering your class or use this one.
   Explain how the information was/is useful to you and how it got the year off to a
   good start.

May 3, 20XX

Dear Future Teacher,

I'm anxious about taking eighth-grade chemistry so I thought we might get off to a good start by telling you a little about myself. First, I'll tell you about my school work. Next, I'll tell you about my interests, friends, and family. Last of all I'll tell you about how you could help me succeed next year in school.

I'll start by sharing several things about school. My favorite subjects are math and computers. The most difficult thing I did this year was to set up my own website. Next year I hope to do all my school projects on computers.

Outside of school I have several interests. I run five miles each morning. After school I walk my neighbors' dogs. I have eight dogs I walk six days a week to earn money for clothes and lunch money. In the summer I mow lawns.

You could help me by not assigning too much reading. I try hard, but I'm not a good reader. If you assign reports, I'll need you to help me. I have trouble putting my ideas on paper. I have good ideas, but poor spelling and handwriting.

I'm looking forward to your class.

Sincerely,
Amy

3. Invite one of next year's teachers to visit with your class and talk about the coming year.

GROUP BRAINSTORMING

We are going to compose a letter to the teacher(s) you will have next year. Since most teachers want to know about your academic work, let's brainstorm that first.

School	Interests	Assistance
favorite subject—gym	after school play basketball	leave glasses at home, can't see
finally learned long division	work at laundry—empty trash	like working in small groups
love writing sports accounts	Mom bugs me try harder in science	need extra help with math
	hang out with next door neighbor	

Key Questions

School

Write students' ideas on the board or overhead under the "School" column.

1. **What is the most important thing you learned this year?**

2. **What is your favorite subject? Why? What do you like to learn?**

3. What was the most difficult part of this last year?

4. What are you good at?

5. What do you hope to do or change this coming year?

6. How do you get along with other students?

7. What else would you like to share about your school work?

Interests, Friends, Family

Write students' ideas under the "Interest" column.

1. What are your out-of-school interests?

2. What are your after-school activities?

3. What do you do to earn money?

4. Who do you hang out with? Who are your best friends?

5. What are your friends like?

6. What do you like to do with your friends?

7. What do you want me to know about your family?

8. Who helps you with your schoolwork?

9. If you need to talk to someone, to whom do you talk?

10. What does your family want you to accomplish/achieve?

Assistance

Write students' ideas under the "Assistance" column.

1. **How do you learn best?** (books, lectures, small-group work, projects, working alone, other)

2. **What might you need help with in my class? What may be difficult for you?**

3. **What can I do to assist you?**

4. **Do you wear glasses? take medication? Do you have a disability about which I should know?**

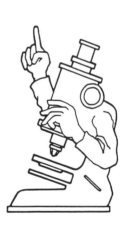

GROUP COMPOSING

Before you compose your letter of introduction, let's compose one together.

> May 20, 20XX
>
> Dear _____,
>
>   I'm looking forward to sixth grade and to being in your class. I'm going to share some things you might want to know about me. First, I will share school things, then my interests, and finally things you should know to help me learn . . .

1. **What is today's date?** Ask about mechanics, then add the date to the letter.

2. **How shall we say hello in a formal way?** Pause to give students time to think. Add a formal greeting.

Paragraph 1: Introduction

1. **What introductory sentence can we write to let the teacher know the purpose of this letter?** Pause for at least 30 seconds to allow students time to think. Choose one idea and add it to the letter.

   > **Thinking about Mechanics:** How can we show the reader that we are beginning a new idea? (indent)

2. **What topics will we address in our letter?** Praise accurate responses. **What will we say to let the teacher know the topics we'll discuss in this letter?** Praise skillful ways to say this. Add one topic sentence to the letter.

Paragraph 2: School

1. **What topic sentence can we write to let the teacher know this paragraph will be about our school life?** Praise successful topic sentences. Choose one and insert it in the letter.

   > **Thinking about Mechanics:** How can we show the reader that we are beginning a new idea? (indent)

2. **Out of all the ideas we brainstormed about school, which shall we choose to include in our letter?** Circle two to four ideas.

3. **In which order shall we put them in this paragraph?** Place numbers [1st, 2nd, 3rd] next to the circled ideas.

4. **How shall we state our first idea about school?** Add this information to the letter. Repeat for the other ideas.

Paragraph 3: Interests, Friends, and Family

1. **How should we begin our "interests" paragraph so that the teacher will know this paragraph is about our out-of-school interests?** Praise successful topic sentences. Choose one and insert it in the letter.

> **Thinking about Mechanics:** How can we indicate that we are beginning a new idea? (indent)

2. **Out of all the ideas we brainstormed about our interests and family, which shall we choose to include in our letter?** Circle two to four ideas.

3. **How shall we order our ideas?** Place numbers [1st, 2nd, 3rd] next to the circled ideas.

4. **How shall we share our first idea about our interests and family?** Add this information to the letter. Repeat for the other ideas.

Paragraph 4: Assistance

1. **How can we begin our paragraph on "assistance" so that the teacher will know what this paragraph is about?** Praise successful topic sentences. Choose one and insert it in the letter.

2. **Out of all the ideas we brainstormed about our special needs, which shall we choose to include in our letter?** Circle two to four ideas.

3. (optional) **How shall we order these ideas?** Place numbers [1st, 2nd, 3rd] next to the circled ideas.

4. **How shall we share our first idea?** Add this information to the letter. Repeat for other ideas.

Closing

1. **What is a respectful way to close this formal letter of introduction?** Choose one suggestion and add it to the letter. (Sincerely, Kind regards, Adios, etc.)

2. **How will the teacher know who this letter of introduction is from?** (signature) **Since some people judge others by looking at their signature, what impression might you/we want to give?** (Ask a volunteer to sign for the class.)

INDIVIDUAL BRAINSTORMING & COMPOSING

Tell students they now have the opportunity to compose their own letters to their next year's teacher(s). Before students begin brainstorming, ask them why this letter of introduction is such an important and special opportunity. Ask how this letter can help them.

Direct students to fold a sheet of notebook paper in thirds. Have students label one part "School," one part "Interests," and the last part "Assistance."

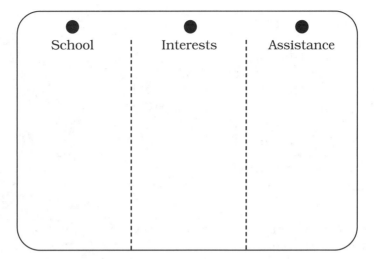

As students begin brainstorming ideas for their letters, walk around the room and converse with your young writers who need individual guidance or encouragement. Ask young writers questions to help them "come up" with important and sincere ideas to share.

RESPONDING TO STUDENTS' WRITINGS/REVISING

As your young writers complete their initial drafts of their letters of introduction, request they find a revising partner, someone new with whom they haven't worked. Have the revising partner read his/her letter of introduction out loud to the other person to see if it sounds sincere and if it provides lots of useful information.

Write the following on the board, a chart, or the overhead to guide the peer revising teams:

> • Make two or three specific comments about what is valuable in the letter. For example:
>
> > The information about how you work until 11:30 P.M. every night and on weekends at your dad's store tells why you have trouble getting homework done on time.
>
> • Ask questions to help the writer consider the impact of his/her ideas and handwriting on the teacher. For example:
>
> > How will telling the teacher about your interest in Sci-Fi help the teacher help you have a good year?
> >
> > What impression will your handwriting give your future teacher about you?

After this is completed, ask each letter writer to make one or two revisions to improve the effectiveness of his/her letter.

PUBLISHING

Collect students' letters. Tell students that you'll sort the letters and give them to the correct teachers before school starts next year. That way students' teachers (*audience*) will know a little about them so the students can have a great year (*purpose*). Encourage students to attach a personal or school photograph, or a drawing of themselves.

Here are two publishing methods to consider when creating personalized stationery for the letter of introduction:

1. Center a school photo on a sheet of blank paper and scan it with a computer.

2. Use the special "Introducing" paper that can be found at the end of this lesson. Once students' compositions have been written on this stationery, consider scanning all their letters and saving to a disk for future teachers' use.

Introducing

LESSON 7

Report Card/Parent Conference Letter to Parents

OUTCOME   Before a parent conference or report card distribution, each student will engage in reflection and then write an honest letter to his/her parent(s) about how he/she is doing in school.

MOTIVATORS

1. Ask your students what the role of report cards is. Inquire what information can be found on report cards (progress in each subject, comments on where improvements are needed, and the behavior of student). Then ask students to share their thoughts on why parents and teachers have conferences.

2. Share a report card that you received as a child or teenager and your parent(s)' responses(s). (A copy of my report card from third grade can be found at the end of this lesson. Feel free to revise it and use it with your students.) Ask students what their reactions are when getting a report card. Next, inquire how their parents usually react.

3. Ask students if they would like to take the teacher's place at a parent conference. Share the following letter written by an anonymous sixth-grade student from the viewpoint of his actual teacher.

Dear Mr. and Mrs. Collins,

   I am your son's teacher and I would like to say he is having a little bit of trouble in Math on multiplication like the 7's and 8's. With his multiplication I would like you to make him some flash cards for use at home.

   I think his behavior is awesome, except he talks in class. He got his name on the board a couple of times in Music. Also he is having a little trouble in class by turning around and talking to neighbors a couple of times every day.

   He is doing fine in Science, but he is having trouble in Social Studies.

   Signed,
   Jim for Mr. Elliot

Organize your students in teams of three: a teacher and two parents. In each team place a strong student in the role of teacher. Give each student who role-plays the teacher an information sheet that prompts the "teacher" with actions to take to make the performance realistic. Tell how the imaginary student is doing in each subject, the behavior of this student, and where he/she is having trouble. Also give an information sheet to each of the students who are role-playing the parents. The complete information sheets can be found at the end of this lesson.

Information Sheet:
Teacher

1. Greet the parent. Welcome him/her to your school. Show the parent(s) where to sit.

2. Again, thank the parent(s) for coming to the parent conference.

3. Tell the parent(s) the good news—what this student's best subjects are and his/her strengths:

   Reading, English, P.E., Art, Music, Health, Social Studies.

4. Tell subjects where the student is having difficulty—what this student's hardest subjects are and where improvement is needed:

   Handwriting, Math, Science; Shoves other students in the hall.

5. Explain how the parent(s) can help this student.

   Look at student's papers every night.
   Make sure student takes time to do homework after dinner.
   Talk about how to solve problems peacefully.

6. Encourage the parent(s) for their interest. Thank the parent(s) for coming to your conference. Say a final positive statement about the student.

Information Sheet:
Parent

1. Say hello to the teacher. Wait for the teacher to tell you where to sit.

2. State that you are interested in your child's progress.

3. Listen to what the teacher is saying. Ask questions about things you are curious.

4. Express pleasure at your child's progress and disappointment at weaknesses.

5. Thank the teacher for teaching your child. Say goodbye. Leave with any student papers.

To get students ready for the role-plays, read and talk through each information sheet. Then demonstrate how the parent conferences will take place. You can play the role of teacher. Select two students to play the parents. After the "conference" ask your class to critique which parts of the conference were effective. Next ask for suggestions regarding how to make the conference more realistic.

NOTE: The noise level of this activity may get a little loud so schedule the role-play when it won't disturb other classes or sign up for an activity room in your school.

GROUP BRAINSTORMING

We are going to brainstorm ideas for a letter explaining how you are doing in school. You'll want to be accurate since your parents will be getting a report card at the same time. If it helps, think about what I might say.

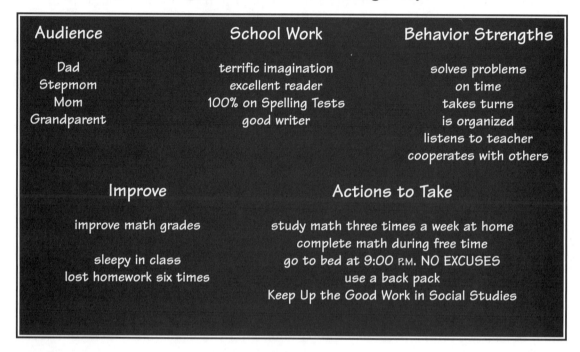

Audience	School Work	Behavior Strengths
Dad	terrific imagination	solves problems
Stepmom	excellent reader	on time
Mom	100% on Spelling Tests	takes turns
Grandparent	good writer	is organized
		listens to teacher
		cooperates with others

Improve	Actions to Take
improve math grades	study math three times a week at home
	complete math during free time
sleepy in class	go to bed at 9:00 P.M. NO EXCUSES
lost homework six times	use a back pack
	Keep Up the Good Work in Social Studies

Key Questions

1. **Who reads your report card? Who comes to your parent conference? Later you'll write your letter to one of these people.** Praise students. Write students' responses on the board under "Audience."

2. **What is your best subject? In what subject do you excel? Why? What will I/your teacher say about your academic strengths? What classes do you enjoy? What do you do well in school? What goals have you achieved?** Praise students. Write students' responses on the board under "School Work."

3. **What will I/your teacher tell your parents about how you get along with others? What good habits do you have? Regarding your behavior, what do you do well?** Praise students. Write students' responses under "Behavior."

4. **What will I/your teacher tell your parents about your most difficult subject? In what subjects do you need to improve? In what class do you need to put forth more effort?** Praise students. Write students' responses under "Improve."

5. **What will I/your teacher tell your parents about how to improve your behavior? Where/when do you need to be more cooperative?** Praise students. Write students' responses under "Improve."

6. **How can your parents help you?** Praise students. Write students' responses under "Actions to Take."

7. (optional) **What is your parent doing already that is helping you do well in school? For what good habits can your parents praise you?** Write student responses under "Actions to Take."

GROUP COMPOSING

Before you compose a letter to your parents about how you are doing in school, let's compose a letter together. Explain that it is important to tell the truth in the letters. Remind students their parent(s) will be getting a report card from school after meeting your teacher(s) at a parent conference, but they should hear their son's/daughter's viewpoint first.

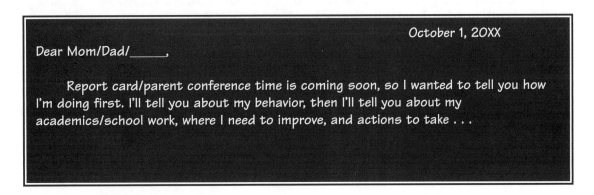

October 1, 20XX

Dear Mom/Dad/_____,

Report card/parent conference time is coming soon, so I wanted to tell you how I'm doing first. I'll tell you about my behavior, then I'll tell you about my academics/school work, where I need to improve, and actions to take . . .

1. **What is today's date?** Ask students about mechanics. (capital letter on the month and comma between day and month) Then place this date on the letter.

2. **How will we greet your parents?** Add this information to the letter.

Paragraph 1

1. Explain that the letters should be in a formal style. **Let's start with this topic sentence: "Report card/parent-teacher conference time is coming soon, so I wanted to tell you how I'm doing."** Write this information in this letter. Give Advanced Writers this example, then ask them for other ways to open the letter.

> **Thinking about Mechanics:** How do we indicate a new paragraph? (indent)

2. **We brainstormed academic strengths, behavior strengths, improvements needed, and actions to take. Which area do we want to share first? second? third? last?** Number the brainstorming categories on the board.

3. **We need to brief our reader on the contents of our letter. How could we put the contents of our letter in one sentence to orient our readers concerning what can be found in our letter?** Pause so students can think. Praise good topic sentences. Choose an uninvolved student to select one. Add this topic sentence to the letter.

   EXAMPLES: I'll tell you about _____, _____, and _____.
     You'll be curious about how I'm doing in my school work, behavior, and where I need to improve.

Thinking about Mechanics: What punctuation do we need to place between the three contents of our letter to show these are separate ideas? (commas in series)

Paragraph 2

1. **What would be a good topic sentence to let our readers know we are going to talk about academic strengths/school work first?**

   EXAMPLES: First, I'll share my academic strengths.
     You'll want to know where I'm doing well on my school work right away.
     I knew you'd want to hear about how I'm doing in my classes first.

Thinking about Mechanics: How do we indicate to readers that we've changed to a new subject? (new paragraph)

When do we start a new paragraph? (when a new idea/subject is started, i.e., from what we'll cover in our letter to now talking about academic strengths)

---

2. Direct students to look at the brainstorming chart. **Which of our academic strengths shall we share first?** Ask a low-achieving student to select an academic strength.

3. **What shall we say about it?** Choose a volunteer to word the statement.

4. Repeat until two or three strengths have been inserted into the letter.

Paragraph 3

1. **What would be a good topic sentence to let our readers know we are going to talk about our behavior strengths next?** Pause so students can think. Praise good topic sentences. Choose an uninvolved student to select one. Add this topic sentence to the letter.

2. **Which behavior strength shall we share first?** Ask a low-achieving student to select a behavior strength.

3. **What shall we say about it?** Choose a volunteer to word the statement.

4. Repeat until two or three strengths are inserted into the letter.

Paragraph 4

1. **What would be a good topic sentence to let our readers know we are going to talk about needed improvements and actions to take?** Pause so students can think. Praise good topic sentences. Choose an uninvolved student to select one. Add this topic sentence to the letter.

2. **Which area of improvement shall we share first?** Ask a low-achieving student to select an improvement.

3. **What shall we say about it? What actions need to be taken to remedy this problem?** Choose a volunteer to word the statement.

4. Repeat until two or three improvements are inserted into the letter.

5. **How can we close this letter respectfully?** (Your son/daughter, Yours truly, Adios, Love, etc.) Ask about mechanics, then add a closing to the letter.

6. **Now what final thing must the writer do?** (sign the letter) Encourage students to sign the group letter.

INDIVIDUAL BRAINSTORMING

Give students their portfolios or packets of work from one or more subjects.

Ask students to turn a sheet of notebook paper sideways and fold it in fourths. Write the following brainstorming categories on the paper: where they are doing well academically and in the area of behavior, where they need to improve, and what actions to take. As students reflect, ask them to jot down their ideas on the paper.

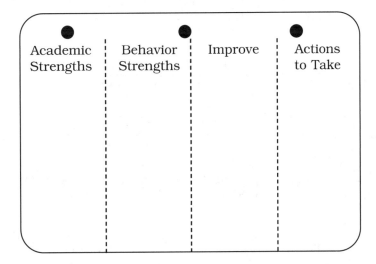

INDIVIDUAL COMPOSING

Once students have reflected and taken notes about how they are doing in school, they are ready to create a rough draft of their thoughts.

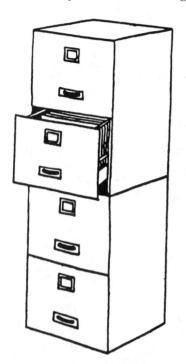

Walk around the classroom praising students who have begun their letters to their parents. Since this will be a tough task for many young writers, conference informally with those who need assistance to get started. Ask them to whom the letter will be addressed and what good things they'll share first. If a student says nothing, brainstorm together, then encourage the young author to add these additional ideas to his/her brainstormed list. Once the student has started, move on to another young author.

After a while return to the students who have difficult letters to write. Conference informally with these young writers. Praise the accurate strengths they have included in their letters. Ignore inflated positive perceptions of self. Consider these as the young author's point-of-view. His/her point-of-view will become more realistic via the report card/parent conference.

Focus your questions about the school work and behavior areas where the student needs to improve. Avoid the term "weak" or "poor work." If a student says nothing or denies the need to improve, brainstorm or look at the portfolio of work together. Sometimes a question such as "What subject is most challenging to you?" may fail. If so, reword it. For example, "If you do not need to improve in any areas, in what subject can you challenge yourself to do even better?" Have the young author add these ideas to his/her brainstormed list. Once the young author has started again, move on to another student.

RESPONDING TO STUDENTS' WRITINGS/REVISING

1. As students finish the rough drafts of their parent letter, ask the students to read their letters to themselves to see if they sound honest and accurate and whether they make sense.

2. Next, pass out the Revising Assistants. A condensed version is given on the next page. A complete version can be found at the end of this lesson.

Revising Assistant
for Letter to Parents

1. Date
____Have you included the date?
____Have you capitalized the month?
____Have you placed a comma after the day of the month?

2. Greeting
____Did you greet your parents respectfully?
____Did you use Mrs., Ms., Mr. and Mrs., or Mr. in front of their names?
____Did you place a comma after your parent(s)' names(s)?
____Did you capitalize the names?

3. Body of the Letter
____Did you indent the introductory paragraph?
____Did you begin your letter by telling why you wrote this letter?
____Did you describe what your letter contains?
____Does each sentence begin with a capital letter?

____Did you indent the academic (school work) strengths paragraph?
____Do you have a topic sentence for your academic strengths paragraph?
____Did you describe at least two academic strengths?
____Are examples given?

____Did you indent the behavior strengths paragraph?
____Do you have a topic sentence for your behavior strengths paragraph?
____Did you describe at least two behavior strengths?

____Did you indent the needed improvements and actions-to-take paragraph?
____Do you have a topic sentence for the needed improvements and actions-to-take paragraph?
____Did you describe at least two needed improvements and their corresponding actions to take?

____Have you been completely honest on each point in your letter? (If not, correct it.)
____What has been left out that needs to be included? (Add this information to your letter.)
____What else might your mom/dad/stepparent/grandmother want to know? (Add this information to your letter.)
____What praise or encouragement should be included for your parents?

4. Close
____Did you close your letter in a formal manner, such as *Sincerely* or *Yours truly*, and a comma?

5. Signature
____Did you sign the letter with your full name?

Use the Revising Assistant to evaluate these real letters written by some sixth graders.

Dear Mr. Clarence,

Your preteen is doing well in my class. She might need help in social studies. She is doing o.k. in spelling, but she has trouble with long and short vowels when reading. Her behavior is good, but she has to be told to turn around and get to work a couple times. You should help her at night.

Sincerely,

Madility for Ms. Trim

Dear Mom and Dad,

Mrs. Anderson will tell you that my best subject is math. Generally I behave well in school. I get along great with my classmates. She will tell you that if I pay more attention in class and study more I can improve my grades. Mrs. Anderson thinks you should help me study for tests. I think my teacher is going to tell you I'm kind of slipping in spelling, but otherwise I am doing fine in math, health, and all that stuff comes easy for me. I like working on a computer every week. I'm o.k. in music. I'm o.k. in gym. I think I'm flunking writing. Thanks for coming to my parent conference.

Hopefully good grades,
Casey

3. Ask students to use the complete Revising Assistant to self-evaluate and then make two or three improvements to their letters. Especially stress word choice. Let each student be responsible for his/her own viewpoints and for improving letters through self-evaluating. Encourage but don't require young authors to share their letters with you.

4. Before publishing, give students the option to trade compositions and look for capitalization, punctuation, spelling, grammar, and other errors that might hinder a parent from understanding and appreciating his/her son's/daughter's important information.

NOTE: Alert parents that the goal of revising should be self-evaluation and improvement, not perfection.

PUBLISHING

Tell students that when report cards are sent, their letters will be sent to their parents (*audience*) so the parents can hear the students' own viewpoint regarding academic strengths and weaknesses (*purpose*). Suggest that students discuss the content of the letters with their parents.

Pocket Folder

Place the letters in a double pocketed folder along with academic examples and share during parent conferences.

Card

Fold a sheet of construction paper and two sheets of typing paper in half. Place the typing paper inside the folded construction paper. Staple the typing paper in place. Cut around the edge of construction paper with decorative scissors. Glue the word NEWS on the cover.

   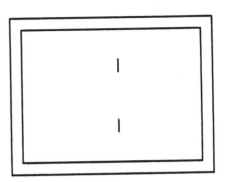

Sample Report Card

COLUMBIA PUBLIC SCHOOLS
COLUMBIA, MISSOURI
School Year 195_5_ and 195_6_

SCHOOL _Robert E. Lee_

PRINCIPAL _____

TEACHER _____

PART I.
The √ check indicates satisfactory growth. Improvement is desired if an item is not checked.

Quarters 1 2 3

READING
Understands what he reads
Reads aloud smoothly and naturally
Attacks new words independently
Reads during spare time

LANGUAGE
Tries to use correct language
Expresses self clearly orally
Expresses self clearly in writing

WRITING
Uses correct letter formations
Tries to improve writing

SPELLING
Masters new words
Spells correctly in written work

ARITHMETIC
Works accurately with numbers
Reasons out problems

ART
Uses art materials as directed
Shows creative imagination
Finishes work

MUSIC
Takes part eagerly
Tries to make correct responses
Tries to understand music

HEALTH AND SCIENCE
Understands materials studied
Practices good health habits
Appreciates simple science facts

SOCIAL STUDIES
Takes part in discussion
Cooperates in activities
Understands materials studied

Notebook work

PROGRESS REPORT OF
Cherlyn Sue

Grade _3_

Quarters	1	2	3	4
Absences	c	2	1½	1
Tardies	c	o	o	o

Part II.
ATTITUDES, HABITS, AND CHARACTER TRAITS

The √ check indicates the pupil's rating.

Respects rights of others
Obeys and respects authority
Takes correction in good spirit
Is able to work independently
Takes care of books and property
Tries to keep clean
Has good posture
Keeps objects out of mouth
Shows self-confidence
Works and plays well with others
Begins work on time
Does work accurately
Does work neatly
Works consistently
Follows directions
Uses extra time to advantage
Asks for help only when needed

© 2000 Cherlyn Sunflower

Information Sheet:
Teacher

1. Greet the parent. Welcome him/her to your school. Show the parent(s) where to sit.

2. Again, thank the parent(s) for coming to the parent conference.

3. Tell the parent(s) the good news—what this student's best subjects are and his/her strengths:

   Reading, English, P.E., Art, Music, Health, Social Studies.

4. Tell subjects where the student is having difficulty— what this student's hardest subjects are and where improvement is needed:

   Handwriting, Math, Science; Shoves other students in the hall.

5. Explain how the parent(s) can help this student.

   Look at student's papers every night.
   Make sure student takes time to do homework after dinner.
   Talk about how to solve problems peacefully.

6. Encourage the parent(s) for their interest. Thank the parent(s) for coming to your conference. Say a final positive statement about the student.

- -

Information Sheet:
Parent

1. Say hello to the teacher. Wait for the teacher to tell you where to sit.

2. State that you are interested in your child's progress.

3. Listen to what the teacher is saying. Ask questions about things you are curious.

4. Express pleasure at your child's progress and disappointment at weaknesses.

5. Thank the teacher for teaching your child. Say goodbye. Leave with any student papers.

Revising Assistant
for Letter to Parents

1. Date

____Have you included the date?

____Have you capitalized the month?

____Have you placed a comma after the day of the month?

2. Greeting

____Did you greet your parents respectfully?

____Did you use Mrs., Ms., Mr. and Mrs., or Mr. in front of their names?

____Did you place a comma after your parent(s)' names(s)?

____Did you capitalize the names?

3. Body of the Letter

____Did you indent the introductory paragraph?

____Did you begin your letter by telling why you wrote this letter?

____Did you describe what your letter contains?

____Does each sentence begin with a capital letter?

____Did you indent the academic (school work) strengths paragraph?

____Do you have a topic sentence for your academic strengths paragraph?

____Did you describe at least two academic strengths?

____Are examples given?

____Did you indent the behavior strengths paragraph?

____Do you have a topic sentence for your behavior strengths paragraph?

____Did you describe at least two behavior strengths?

____Did you indent the needed improvements and actions-to-take paragraph?

____Do you have a topic sentence for the needed improvements and actions-to-take paragraph?

____Did you describe at least two needed improvements and their corresponding actions to take?

____Have you been completely honest on each point in your letter? (If not, correct it.)

____What has been left out that needs to be included? (Add this information to your letter.)

____What else might your mom/dad/stepparent/grandmother want to know? (Add this information to your letter.)

____What praise or encouragement should be included for your parents?

4. Close

____Did you close your letter in a formal manner, such as *Sincerely* or *Yours truly*, and a comma?

5. Signature

____Did you sign the letter with your full name?

LESSON 8

Restaurant Review Checklist

OUTCOME Each student will create a checklist to collect information on area restaurants' strengths and weaknesses.

MOTIVATORS

1. Show students menus from area restaurants or wrappers from fast-food restaurants. Ask students what are their favorite eating establishments. Share what your favorite restaurants are and why you like them.

2. Direct students to close their eyes and visualize the following restaurants as you read these reviews.

Italian Meatball Castle

When I walked into the Italian Meatball Castle with my mom and dad, a hostess greeted us with a smile. I smelled delicious food, and that made me hungry. We had to wait twenty minutes to get seated, which was frustrating. I watched the goldfish in the lobby's fountain while we waited. When we finally sat down, I looked around at the restaurant. It was very fancy, with candles on all the tables, real cloth napkins, and soft music. There were a lot of choices on the menu, but I had plain old spaghetti. It was tasty. The waiter was cute and he gave us mint ice cream after dinner. It was very expensive, but we had a great time.

Fish Sticks Haven

When I entered the Fish Sticks restaurant, I felt like I was on a pirate ship. The room was decorated with fish nets, old oars and boats hanging from the ceiling, and even a gangplank. But that's where the fun ended. Even though our waiter was nice and almost looked like a real pirate, the food was awful. The fish sticks were greasy, and the French fries tasted like fish sticks! We had a good time, but the owners put too much thought into the atmosphere, and none into making the food taste good. The price was reasonable, but I won't go back to Fish Sticks.

3. Ask students to describe the positive and negative aspects of a restaurant where they've eaten recently.

4. Ask students to describe their "dream" restaurant. Where would it be located? What kinds of food would the restaurant serve? How would it be decorated? What kind of entertainment would it have? Who would be the waiters and waitresses? How would they be dressed?

GROUP BRAINSTORMING

We are going to design a checklist so we can collect data on strengths and weaknesses of area restaurants.

Restaurants	Characteristics	Criteria
Country Kitchen	Great waiter	
	Inexpensive	
Showbiz Pizza	Large amount of food	Food Quality
	Yummy salads	
Jimmy's Diner	Dirty bathrooms	
	Expensive	Cost
Hamburger City	Interesting lighting	
	Poor service	
Chung Wong	All-you-can-eat buffet	
	Decorated walls	Atmosphere
Franks to Go	No games to play	
	Awful spaghetti	
Radison Inn	Low cost	
	Pretty fish tanks	Entertainment
Nick's Deli	Intolerably loud music	
	Juicy steaks	Food Quality
Carol's Cafe	Shows movies	Entertainment

Key Questions

1a. Which restaurants do you like? Which fast-food places do you like? What other restaurants are in our area? Write students' ideas on the board, overhead, or chart paper under the heading "Restaurants."

1b. What is your least favorite eating establishment? Write students' ideas on the board under the heading "Restaurants."

2a. Have a quiet or uninvolved student select a restaurant. **Why do you like this restaurant? What is special or unique about it? What else is good about it?** Write students' ideas under the heading "Characteristics."

2b. What problems does this restaurant have? What do you dislike about it? Write students' ideas under the heading "Characteristics."

2c. What do other people need to know about this restaurant to decide whether to eat there? Write students' ideas under the heading "Characteristics."

3. Repeat steps 1 and 2 for three or four other restaurants.

4. **Since we are going to evaluate these restaurants and other eating establishments, we need to decide the criteria we will use for evaluation. Let's analyze our list of characteristics to aid us in setting up some common criteria.** Choose one or two similar characteristics from the brainstormed list and circle them with colored chalk (or marker).

Then ask questions like:

- **What do "juicy steaks," "awful spaghetti," and "yummy salads" tell us about restaurants?** (food quality or something similar) Write the term the students generate under "Criteria."

- **What criteria do "interesting lighting" and "pretty fish tanks" point to for evaluating restaurants?** (atmosphere or something similar) Write the term the students generate under "Criteria."

- **What do "shows movies" and "no games" show us about criteria for evaluating restaurants?** (entertainment or something similar) Write the term the students generate under "Criteria."

- **What criteria do "expensive" and "low cost" tell us about evaluating restaurants?** (cost or something similar) Write the term the students generate under "Criteria."

Continue grouping and questioning until all the brainstormed characteristics have been used to generate criteria.

NOTE: Other criteria that may surface include amount of food, size of servings, type of people who eat there, variety of food on the menu, food items for vegetarians or diabetics, number of free toppings, type of seating, how food is prepared (fried or broiled), length of wait before seating or serving, location of restaurant, parking, comparisons to other restaurants, free gifts, etc.

5. Tell students that we've left out one criterion that is very important. **What criterion can we add to our survey so we can determine if the restaurants are accessible to people with handicaps?** Add this term under "Criteria."

GROUP COMPOSING

Now that we have some common criteria for evaluating restaurants, let's create a checklist for all of us to use when we go out to eat.

Criteria	Poor	Good	Excellent	Comments
1. Food Quality	1	2	3	
2. Amount	1	2	3	
3. Decor	1	2	3	
4.	1	2	3	
5.	1	2	3	
6.	1	2	3	

1. **We'll leave space at the top of our checklist to write the name of the restaurant we decide to review.** Point to this spot.

2. **Now let's create a grid with five vertical columns and six horizontal rows.** Quickly draw this or have it drawn ahead of time. An overhead reproducible can be found at the end of this lesson.

3. **We'll write "Criteria" in the upper left box.** (first row, first column) Demonstrate this.

4. **Next, let's list the criteria we selected below it. Which criteria shall we list first? second?** Explain that often the most important criteria is placed first. Add this information on the checklist by a number. Tell students if they would like to add a final criterion of their own, they may.

5. (optional) **Next, we need to decide how we'll rate each restaurant on a particular criterion. We could use the terms:**

Awful ⟶	Good ⟶	Terrific
Icky	Pretty Good	The Best
Don't go	Go	Delightful Experience
Poor	Good	Excellent

   We need three terms that we can use for all six criteria. Choose one set and add it to the restaurant checklist.

6. **Let's place a rating term at the top of each column.** Choose a set of rating terms. Then write 1, 2, 3 in the boxes under these terms. Explain one number will be circled by the rater for each criterion.

7. **We'll put "Comments" at the top of the final column of the checklist.**

GROUP REVISING

Let's look at our group's checklist. How can we improve our checklist?

- **How is our spacing? Is there enough room for comments?**

- **Which words may be misspelled?**

- **Have we capitalized the first letter in each word of the restaurant?**

- **Where could our handwriting be more legible?**

Make improvements as students suggest them.

INDIVIDUAL COMPOSING

Tell students now they get to select and evaluate a restaurant. Ask students to volunteer to evaluate the restaurants generated earlier. To make sure the final restaurant review the class creates covers many restaurants, check off the names of the restaurants already chosen. Give first choice to students with limited income and/or transportation problems. Direct students to add the name of their restaurant at the top of the checklist.

Consider having students compose a brief note to their parents explaining the project.

NOTE: If you desire, students can be allowed to complete their checklists based on previous visits.

Advanced Writers   Since there is little composing to do, consider having Advanced Writers choose another business or service industry to observe and evaluate. Review the steps the class took to create the group checklist.

Comprehension Check

1. **First, you'll choose a different service such as type of store, lawn mowing service, bike repair, movies, babysitting, etc.—NOT a product.** See Consumer Survey, Lesson 4 for products.

2. **After we decided on restaurants, what did we do?** (brainstormed many restaurants)

3. **Once we generated a list of restaurants, what did we do?** (We thought about why we liked or disliked the restaurants. Then we listed good and bad characteristics.)

4. **How did we come up with criteria?** (We decided what the good and bad characteristics have in common.) **How many criteria must you have?** (at least five)

5. **What special criterion did we add?** (handicapped accessible) **We thought of physical barriers. You'll want to consider other barriers too, that might prevent people from being included.**

6. **What goes to the right of each criterion to make the checklist easy to complete?** (rating terms, such as bad, good, excellent) **How many?** (three to five)

Encourage Advanced Writers to create other terms for rating each different criterion. Suggest the young writers think of the best or worst term first. For example, if I thought the price was "too expensive," would that be my positive or negative term? (negative) Then I'd need to think of a positive term. What could be a positive descriptor for cost? (cheap, inexpensive, great value) Now we need a middle term to go between "too expensive" and "cheap." What term describes price, but is neutral? *For example:*

> If criterion is number of people: packed   pleasant   few
>
> If criterion is service: never saw the waiter   helpful   exceptional
>
> If criterion is music: intolerable   pleasant   uplifting
>
> If criterion is cost: overpriced   average   inexpensive
>
> If criterion is length of wait: 40 minutes   10 minutes   immediate

7. **Where do all these ideas go on the checklist?** Add this information to the checklist.

INDIVIDUAL REVISING

Ask Advanced Writers who are creating their own checklists to make at least one improvement on their checklist.

PUBLISHING

Explain to students that they'll (*audience—self*) use their checklist to collect and organize information (*purpose*) on the restaurant or other service they chose to review.

1. Duplicate multiple copies of the checklist with the group's criteria and rating terms, but without a restaurant's name.

   NOTE: You'll also need a class set of checklists to use in Lesson 28, Restaurant Review, motivator 1.

2. Distribute the checklists to students.

Criteria				Comments
1.	1	2	3	
2.	1	2	3	
3.	1	2	3	
4.	1	2	3	
5.	1	2	3	
6.	1	2	3	

3. Post the list of restaurants.

4. Ask students to volunteer to observe and collect information on one restaurant. Have students initial the selected restaurant so a variety of restaurants will be reviewed.

5. Set a date for completion.

6. See Lesson 28, Restaurant Review, to compose reviews from the data collected.

Criteria	1	2	3	Comments
1.	1	2	3	
2.	1	2	3	
3.	1	2	3	
4.	1	2	3	
5.	1	2	3	
6.	1	2	3	

LESSON 9

Horoscope

OUTCOME Each student will compose a forecast for his/her zodiac sign, forecasts for each of the twelve zodiac signs, or forecasts regarding one zodiac sign for a whole week or month.

MOTIVATORS

1. Ask students what a horoscope is. A horoscope is a written document thought to be based on astrological information, such as the position of the planets when the person was born. A horoscope is thought to forecast/predict a person's future, but is mainly written and read for entertainment.

2. Display a list of zodiac signs or a zodiac chart.

ZODIAC SIGNS	DATES
Aquarius	January 20–February 19
Pisces	February 20–March 20
Aries	March 21–April 20
Taurus	April 21–May 20
Gemini	May 21–June 20
Cancer	June 21–July 22
Leo	July 23–August 22
Virgo	August 23–September 22
Libra	September 23–October 22
Scorpio	October 23–November 22
Sagittarius	November 23–December 21
Capricorn	December 22–January 19

Share your zodiac sign. Ask students who don't know their signs to give his/her birth date. Point to his/her astrological sign on the chart. Bring in a horoscope from the daily newspaper or the World Wide Web.

VIRGO (Aug. 23–Sept. 22)
You will be lucky today. Go out of your way to please your mom and/or dad. Getting outdoors will lift your spirits and help you make a new friend.

LIBRA (Sept. 23–Oct. 22)
Your success at school will grow stronger today. Curb a tendency to make negative comments. Take time to talk to your sister/brother.

3. Give each student an index card with his or her name and an horoscope from the newspaper or personally written by you. Ask for volunteers to read their horoscope. Discuss that horoscopes usually are general enough to apply to almost anyone, yet may contain words of wisdom/valuable advice.

> **Brian**
>
> Today is a good day for making a new friend. Don't run across any busy streets. Be nice to your sister. If you work hard, you can earn lots of money.
>
> Jan. 20–Feb. 19

4. Ask students what they would do with their lives if they could really predict the future.

GROUP BRAINSTORMING

Most people are curious about the future. Today, we are going to write our own horoscopes and share them with each other.

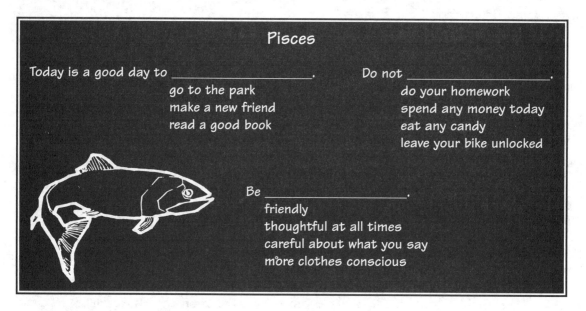

Pisces

Today is a good day to _____.
    go to the park
    make a new friend
    read a good book

Do not _____.
    do your homework
    spend any money today
    eat any candy
    leave your bike unlocked

Be _____.
    friendly
    thoughtful at all times
    careful about what you say
    more clothes conscious

Key Questions

1. **Which zodiac sign shall we use?** Write this at the top of the board or overhead.

2. **What might be a good thing to do today? What activity or task have you put off? What exciting thing would you want to happen? What could you do to lift your spirits?** Give specific, positive feedback after each response; for example, " 'Making a new friend' is an excellent idea for a horoscope. It is something to which anyone who reads this horoscope can relate."

3. **What are some things you shouldn't do today? Tomorrow will be a bad day to do what? What should you avoid?** Give specific positive feedback after each response; for example, "Any student who reads the advice about not doing their homework will be very pleased if they believe in horoscopes."

4. **What kind of person do most people want to be today? How would you like people to describe you? What positive characteristics might a reader have that would make him/her successful tomorrow?** Give specific positive feedback after each response; for example, "The suggestion about being thoughtful is a wise choice for a horoscope. It is something everyone needs to do more often."

GROUP COMPOSING

Let's write a horoscope together. Write "Your Daily Horoscope" on the board or overhead.

1. **Which zodiac sign did we choose?** Write this on the board or overhead. **What are the corresponding dates?** Add this information to your horoscope. As you write the horoscope entry, ask other students about indenting, capitalizing, and periods needed in the horoscope.

> **Thinking about Mechanics:** What abbreviations could we use if we wanted to shorten the date of our horoscope? (Jan., Feb., March, April, May, June, July, Aug., Sept., Oct., Nov., Dec.)

> **Thinking about Mechanics:** Where do the commas and spaces belong when writing dates? (Jan. 1, 20__ or December 27, 20__)

2. **Which ideas shall we select for our horoscope?** Point to the group brainstorming board. Ask three or four quiet students to select one idea from each list. Circle each idea as it is selected.

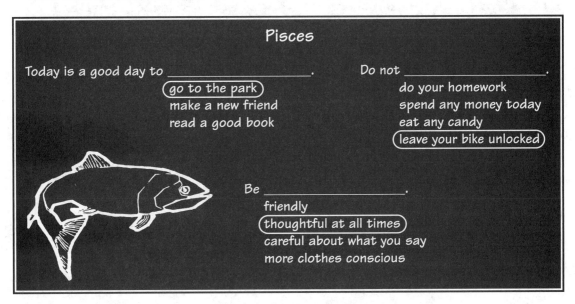

3. Which of the brainstormed ideas should we put first in the horoscope? Choose a new student to decide. Number the ideas that are selected.

4. To keep your students on task as you write on the board or overhead, ask your class to slowly read aloud each sentence so it can be written into a horoscope. To keep students' rate of reading slow enough for you to write, stop writing any time they get ahead of you.

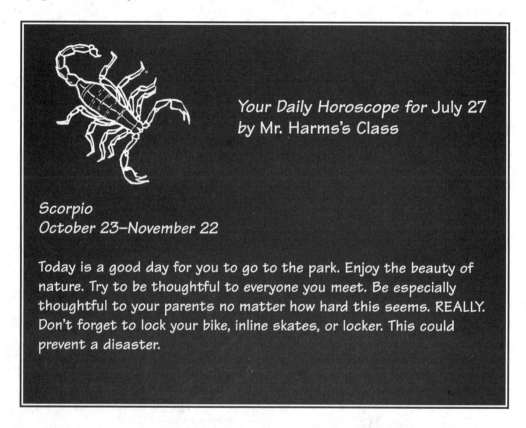

*Your Daily Horoscope for July 27
by Mr. Harms's Class*

*Scorpio
October 23–November 22*

Today is a good day for you to go to the park. Enjoy the beauty of nature. Try to be thoughtful to everyone you meet. Be especially thoughtful to your parents no matter how hard this seems. REALLY. Don't forget to lock your bike, inline skates, or locker. This could prevent a disaster.

5. Class, let's read the horoscope together to see if it makes sense and sounds convincing. Ask students what they think. Praise the group's horoscope.

INDIVIDUAL BRAINSTORMING AND COMPOSING

Explain that now students have the opportunity to compose their own horoscopes. Later they'll publish them so other students, teachers, and adults can locate and read their daily or monthly horoscope.

1. Ask students to write horoscopes for all twelve zodiac signs. An alternative is to divide your class into twelve groups. This can be done randomly or by birthdays. Each group should write horoscopes for a particular zodiac sign.

2. Provide copies of the List of Horoscope Patterns (found at the end of this lesson) to get your students started. Encourage students to use their own ideas for beginnings of horoscopes or use ideas from the list when needed.

List of Horoscope Patterns

Be prepared for _____.
Avoid _____.
Count on _____.
Reach out and _____.
Keep away from _____.
Today brings a chance to _____.
Schedule time to _____.
Your best friend needs _____.

It's time to _____.
You will be invited to _____.
You are pleased by _____.
Hold out for _____.
You will find _____.
Your problems will be resolved by _____.
Focus on _____.
Be careful when _____.
Remember to _____.
Enjoy _____.
Don't forget to _____.

Grin and bear _____.
Make plans to _____.
Catch up on _____.
You must be ready to _____.
Get a grip on _____.
Try not to _____.
Don't neglect _____.
Get involved in _____.
You're on a roll. Keep ____.
HOT TIP: Take care to _____.

3. As students begin brainstorming, walk around the classroom noting innovative beginnings and/or creative endings.

4. Ask questions to help students generate predominately positive endings and prevent forecasts that are totally gruesome.

RESPONDING TO STUDENTS' WRITINGS/REVISING

1. As students finish the rough drafts of their horoscopes, ask them to find a revising partner. Have each student read his/her horoscope aloud to see if the horoscope makes sense, sounds convincing, and is interesting.

2. Encourage students to make two to three specific comments on what they like and to offer suggestions for how to help make sure the horoscopes are positive and entertaining.

3. After step 1 is completed, require each writer make at least one or two revisions to improve the horoscope forecast or advice.

4. Finally, before publishing the horoscopes, have students trade compositions and look for three punctuation, capitalization, spelling, and other errors that might keep readers from *valuing* their advice.

PUBLISHING

After students finish revising their horoscopes, have each student type his/her "horoscope" on the word processor. Then bind and share with family and neighbors (*audience*) for entertainment and insight (*purpose*).

Book Cover

For an individual or class book, duplicate the horoscope book cover. (See cover at the end of the lesson.) Place the cover over the twelve horoscopes written by one person and staple.

Class Book

Duplicate horoscopes by different students and create multiple copies of the class book for each student to read.

Individual Horoscopes

For individual horoscopes make copies of the Zodiac sheets. (See sheets and cover at the end of the lesson.) Have students write their names above the zodiac symbol and date. Then write one horoscope on the paper below it. Post the horoscopes around the room for other students to read.

Web Page

Another way to publish the horoscopes is on a website that your class updates each day, week, or month.

ZODIAC SIGNS   DATES

ZODIAC SIGNS	DATES
Aquarius	*January 20–February 19*
Pisces	*February 20–March 20*
Aries	*March 21–April 20*
Taurus	*April 21–May 20*
Gemini	*May 21–June 20*
Cancer	*June 21–July 22*
Leo	*July 23–August 22*
Virgo	*August 23–September 22*
Libra	*September 23–October 22*
Scorpio	*October 23–November 22*
Sagittarius	*November 23–December 21*
Capricorn	*December 22–January 19*

ZODIAC SIGNS   DATES

ZODIAC SIGNS	DATES
Aquarius	*January 20–February 19*
Pisces	*February 20–March 20*
Aries	*March 21–April 20*
Taurus	*April 21–May 20*
Gemini	*May 21–June 20*
Cancer	*June 21–July 22*
Leo	*July 23–August 22*
Virgo	*August 23–September 22*
Libra	*September 23–October 22*
Scorpio	*October 23–November 22*
Sagittarius	*November 23–December 21*
Capricorn	*December 22–January 19*

List of Horoscope Patterns

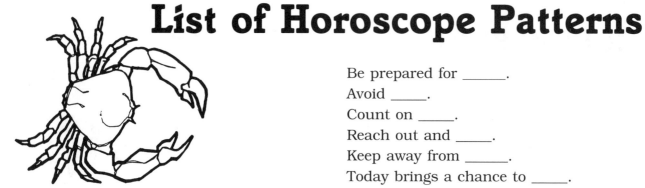

It's time to _____.
You will be invited to _____.
You are pleased by _____.
Hold out for _____.
You will find _____.
Your problems will be resolved by _____.
Focus on _____.
Be careful when _____.
Remember to _____.
Enjoy _____.
Don't forget to _____.
Remember to save for _____.
HOT TIP: Take time to _____.
True friends will _____.
Keep a level head when _____.
Keep on top of _____.
Hang out with friends who _____.
Guard against _____.
Others admire your _____.
Spend more time with ____ because ____.
You'll get caught ____.
Postpone _____.
Spend less on ____ and more on ____.
Be willing to _____.
Ask family members before _____.
The timing couldn't be better for _____.
Surround yourself with _____.
Stand up for _____.
In a flash you'll understand _____.
Share your feelings with _____.
Be on your best behavior during _____.
Be careful (around) (about) (with) _____.
You must not ____ or ____ will happen.
Get your priorities straight about _____.
Your plans for _____ may change abruptly.

Be prepared for _____.
Avoid _____.
Count on _____.
Reach out and _____.
Keep away from _____.
Today brings a chance to _____.
Schedule time to _____.
Your best friend needs _____.
Grin and bear _____.
Make plans to _____.
Catch up on _____.
You must be ready to _____.
Get a grip on _____.
Try not to _____.
Don't neglect _____.
Get involved in _____.
You're on a roll. Keep ____.
HOT TIP: Take care to _____.
Your friends complain you _____.
Talk to an adult or teacher about _____.
Make up with _____.
Listen carefully to _____.
Deep down you _____.
Don't despair _____.
Get together with _____.
Send an e-mail to _____.
HOT TIP: Contact _____.
When discouraged be open to _____.
You have the strength to _____.
Ask for _____.
Stick to _____.
Don't get sucked into _____.
Today is a good day to _____.
Suddenly ___ comes your way.
Think about ____ before you ____.
You'll meet (who) (where) & (do what).
Good luck comes to you because ___.
Choose to _____ instead of _____.
Success comes easily when you ____.
_____ is a problem you must overcome.
Ask _____ for help regarding ____.
Today you must not _____.

Taurus

Horoscope

Astrological Forecast
for _____

Capricorn

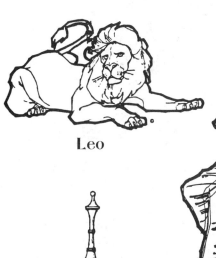

Leo

Virgo

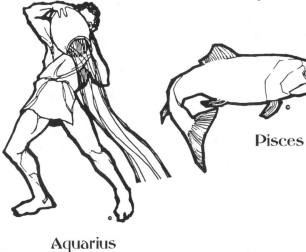

Aquarius

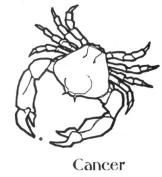

Pisces

Libra

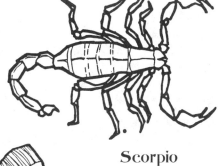

Scorpio

Gemini

Cancer

by _____

Aries

Sagittarius

Your Daily Horoscope

by _____

Aquarius
January 20–February 19

Your Daily Horoscope

by _____

Pisces
February 20–March 20

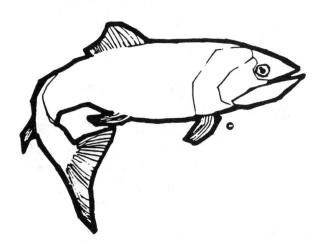

Your Daily Horoscope

by _____

Aries
March 21–April 20

Your Daily Horoscope

by _____

Taurus
April 21–May 20

Your Daily Horoscope

by _____

Gemini
May 21–June 20

Your Daily Horoscope

by _____

Cancer
June 21–July 22

Your Daily Horoscope

by _____

Leo
July 23–August 22

Your Daily Horoscope

by _____

Virgo
August 23–September 22

Your Daily Horoscope

by _____

Libra
September 23–October 22

Your Daily Horoscope

by _____

Scorpio
October 23–November 22

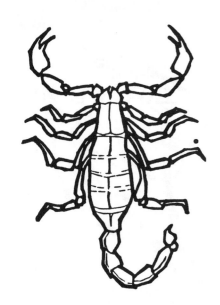

Your Daily Horoscope

by _____

Sagittarius
November 23–December 21

Your Daily Horoscope

by _____

Capricorn
December 22–January 19

LESSON 10

Sports Account/Article

OUTCOME   Each student will cover a recent sports event and write or tell about it so the action comes alive for the readers.

MOTIVATORS

1. Ask students about recent sports events they have seen or heard. Find out the details: time and place, players' names, action highlights, and who won the game. Encourage each student to draw a picture of an action highlight.

2. Share one or two current sports accounts from your local paper.

Gophers Do It Again

A fight broke out in Saturday afternoon's game between the Gophers and the Ice Sharks. Two players were kicked out of the game, but that didn't hinder the Gophers' win. The intensity of the hockey game was heightened by Gopher John Hasbrouck, who holds the most consecutive goals in the state. The Gophers are by far the best team in the state.

Lakers Sweep Ahead Winning by Six Points

The basketball game between the Lakers and the Cowboys was action packed. People filled the auditorium on Saturday night at the Moorhead Civic Center. Final score of the game was Lakers 86, Cowboys 80. Twenty-year-old rookie Dean Garret had 14 points and 16 rebounds for the Lakers. "He's been a key element of our success lately," said Coach Rogers. For the first time since 1989 the Lakers have carried a season of no losses. With only two games left, the Lakers are on the road to the state championship.

Taylor Breaks the Record

Friday night in Fergus, MN, Megan Taylor broke the Minnesota Girls Basketball Scoring Record. The record-breaking three-pointer was just part of Taylor's 41 points in Dilworth's exciting win against Lake of the Woods. If Dilworth goes to the state tournament, Taylor could break the All-Time record for girls' basketball.

As students view various sports accounts, ask them how the information is ordered. Lead students to notice that the most important information is usually reported early in the article and the least important information is presented last.

3. Tell students that they are going to write a sports article about one of their favorite sports to get classmates excited about that sport or team. Brainstorm types of team sports such as ice hockey, tennis, softball, floor hockey, dodge ball, basketball, gymnastics, swimming, track, debate, or chess. Ask your students which sporting events are currently taking place.

Since some students may not follow sporting events, tie this lesson to a sport played in P.E. or set up a sporting event during recess. Before playing the sport, brainstorm on a large sheet of paper which parts of the event a reporter would want to remember and report to readers: who, what, when, where, how. This will help students remember some of the important details.

GROUP BRAINSTORMING

Let's brainstorm some ideas for our group sports account.

Key Questions

1. **Who were the two teams that played in our game/the game we watched together? Which individuals competed against each other?** Add each idea to the board under the "Teams/Individuals" column. Praise names of teams and individuals who competed. **What type of sports event was it?** Write each student's idea on the board.

2. **Which of these sporting events should we select for our group report?** Select a quiet student or nonparticipator to choose the sporting event. Circle this idea and use it all through the lesson.

Teams/Individuals	Time	Place	Outcome/Final Score
Vikings	this afternoon	in Dallas	game went into overtime
MSU	on Saturday	on the track	scored the winning point
Ice Sharks		at the Gold Stadium	captured the lead
Angels		in the ice arena	won the gold metal
football			defeated in last __ seconds
hockey			

Action Highlights	Your Opinion	Background Information
8 tackles	exciting	one game left to end the season
4 touchdowns	gutsy	3rd year with an unbeaten record
homerun	terrific	Sally has more goals than anyone
9th basket		else in the State
took the lead		

3. **When did this/our spectacular sports event occur? What is another way to say this?** Write each student's idea on the board under the "Time" column. Repeat these questions until three or four ideas have been written on the board.

4. **Where was it held? What descriptive words can we use to make our readers visualize the location?** Write ideas under the "Place" column. Repeat these questions until three or four ideas have been written on the board.

5. **What was the outcome of the game? Who won the game? What was the final score?** Write students' ideas under the "Outcome/Final Score" column. Praise creative ways of stating this information.

6a. **What was an action highlight early in the game?** (run, shoot, kick, jump, etc.) Accept each idea orally, but hold off writing it on the board until you ask the next two questions. **Who performed this important play/feat? What action words could you use to describe the action highlight to make the event come alive for readers? Now, how can we combine these ideas?** Write improved information under the "Action Highlights" column.

6b. Here are some more introductory questions to use. **What was another highlight of this game? What was an important play/event early in the game?**

6c. **What exciting play did your team make that put them in the lead? What other thrilling or memorable things happened?** Write these ideas under the "Action Highlights" column. Praise statements that will help the reader visualize the game.

7. Repeat the above process several times.

8. **How did you feel during the game? How would you describe your feelings as you watched the game? How did the crowd react? How can you communicate the excitement that the crowd felt?** Write ideas under the "Your Opinion" column. Praise opinions that really give information to future readers.

9. **As the sports reporter or sportscaster, what was your opinion of the game?** Guide students to generate *opinions* such as "They played expertly during the second half of the game," not *information* such as Kate Rau, freshman at NDSU, scored 19 points and had 14 rebounds. **What did you think of the team?** Write students' ideas under the "Your Opinion" column. **the plays?** Write students' ideas under the "Your Opinion" column. Praise opinions that really give information to future readers.

10. (optional) **What interesting half-time events should be reported?** Praise information that future readers will find interesting.

11. **What background information might your readers want to have about the teams or individuals? about the coaches? about the pregame preparation? game statistics?** Write ideas under the "Background Information" column. Praise information that may be interesting to future readers.

GROUP COMPOSING

Let's write a sports account together.

1. Show students these headlines (or have students cut out some from your local newspaper) and question students about what a good headline is. Then ask whether headlines are written in past tense or present tense. (present tense)

    EXAMPLES:

    ### Headlines for Individual Sports

    Sally Donald Wins 5 to 7
    Russ Stone Does It Again
    Tennis Star Tia Burke Breaks her All-Time Record

    ### Headlines for Team Sports

    Cowboys Win 18 to 4
    Dragons Do It Again
    Wrestlers Break their All-Time Record
    Angels Beat Sioux in Overtime
    Dragons Score 3 Baskets during Final Minutes of Game

2. **What would be a good headline for our sports account? How could we get our readers' attention so they will want to read about this game? What was the outcome or final score of the game?** Before you write each suggested headline on the board, ask students to think about mechanics. Then write each suggested headline on the board (or chart paper) so all the students can see.

> **Thinking about Mechanics:** What should I do to the first letter in important words in the title? (capitalize) What important words must be capitalized? (team and school names, players and coaches, names of towns and states, etc.)

After students have suggested five or six headlines, ask a nonparticipating student who looks alert to choose the headline that he or she likes best. Circle the chosen headline.

Headlines

Gophers Win and Go to State

(Gophers Do It Again)

What a Season for the Gophers!

3a. Explain that we need a lead sentence to begin the sports account. The lead sentence for a sports account tells which individuals or teams played (who), what kind of game it was, and the outcome. Insert this information in a pattern sentence or lead students to generate several of their own lead sentences.

    EXAMPLES: Yesterday's exciting football game between __ and __ ended in a tie.
          The hockey game at ____ was tough, but in the end ___ lost to ___.
          On ___ the ____ won their ____ game of the season.

3b. Which two teams played? What kind of game was it? What was the outcome? Get four or five suggestions for a lead sentence before asking a quiet student to choose one lead sentence for the group to use.

4. If "when" or "where" information hasn't been reported in the lead sentence, then elicit this information next. **Now let's tell when and where the sporting event was held. How can we give our sports readers this information in a sentence?** Choose an uninvolved student to decide how to state this information. Before you write this information down, ask students to think about mechanics.

> **Thinking about Mechanics:** What should I do to the first letter in a sentence? (capitalize) How should I end this sentence? (with a period or exclamation point)

> ### Gophers Do It Again
>
> A fight broke out in the Metro Dome during Saturday's football game, but that didn't stop the Gophers from beating the Angels 27 to 9. The game was typical of the Gophers' winning season.
>
> The fans in the stadium cheered wildly as Jason Smyth scored three points in the last minutes of the game. This reporter is looking forward to watching the rest of the Gophers' winning season. The Gophers' 8 and 1 record makes for a team spirit that's catching!

5a. In what order did the action highlights and other events occur? Choose an uninvolved student to decide how to order the action highlights. As the student gives you the information, number the action highlights on the board.

5b. Which of these events/action highlights are the most important to share with readers? Choose a withdrawn student to decide the most important action highlights. As you add these ordered and prioritized action highlights to the sports account, have the class read this information slowly so you can add it to the group composition.

5c. As students select highlights, ask this before writing information into the Sports Account. **How can you help your readers see and hear the game?**

> **Thinking about Mechanics:** What descriptors can be added to the action highlights to make the sports account "come alive"?
>
> How can we describe/tell what kind of player, equipment, crowd, etc.? (adjectives describe people, things, and places; for example: The mammoth-sized track was full of state-of-the-art jumps.)
>
> How can we tell how a player ran/hit/threw/captured the ball? (adverbs describe how an action is done and often end in "ly"; for example: Cole grabbed the ball furiously and quickly ran toward the goal.

6. What else should we be sure to include? What was your opinion of this game? Ask a student who is quietly raising his or her hand to choose which opinion to add to the group sports account. Add this information to the group sports account.

7. Finally, which background information about the team, coaches, players, or game statistics do you want to share with your readers? Ask a quiet student for one piece of background information to add to the sports account. Add it to the group sports account.

"SET UP" HOMEWORK ASSIGNMENT

1. **What different kinds of sporting events could we report on? What individual or team sport would you like to choose? What sporting event could you watch? What individual or team sport is going on now?** Encourage students to jot down sporting events that they would like to attend as a sports reporter.

2. Point out that choosing a sport with which the student is familiar will make it easier to observe and compose the report. Ask students to choose a game or sporting event to attend.

3. Direct students to take notes during the game so the sports account will be more accurate. Suggest that they use a clipboard or spiral notebook and a pencil or pen for taking notes. Explain that reporters do this so that information will be accurate for readers. Distribute copies of the Note-taking Assistant, a reproducible found at the end of this lesson.

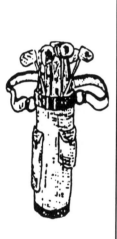
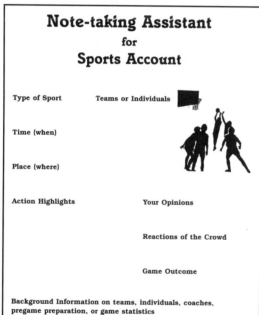

Note-taking Assistant
for
Sports Account

Type of Sport   Teams or Individuals

Time (when)

Place (where)

Action Highlights   Your Opinions

Reactions of the Crowd

Game Outcome

Background Information on teams, individuals, coaches,
pregame preparation, or game statistics

INDIVIDUAL COMPOSING

After attending (viewing) a sports event, ask students to use their notes to recall the sporting event *or* compose their own versions of the game played earlier in P.E. or at recess. Provide the Group Brainstorming chart for these students to help them recall the event. Do not share the Group Composing chart.

Walk around the classroom noting productive starts. If a young writer is having difficulty getting started, ask him/her to retell the sporting event to you or another student before composing. Make positive comments when students are using their notes and the inclusion of a title, lead sentence, team/players, action highlights, the writer's opinions, etc. Ask questions about the same elements when important ideas have been left out or to help students order their ideas about their own sporting event.

RESPONDING TO STUDENTS' WRITINGS/REVISING

As students finish the rough drafts of their sport accounts, ask them to find a revising partner. Have each read his/her sports account aloud to the other person to see how it sounds and if it makes sense. Write the following on the board:

> Encourage peer teams to:
>
> • Make two to three specific comments on what they like about the sports account such as the title, lead sentence, action highlights, opinions, or background information.
>
> • Ask questions to expand the action highlights or clarify the order of events.
>
> • Make one to two suggestions for improving the sports account, such as noting places where descriptive words could be added to show the excitement of the sporting event, and making it "come alive" for readers.

After this is completed, ask each sports writer to make at least one or two revisions to improve his/her sports article. Ask Advanced Writers to add three descriptive words ("what kind of _____" player, "what kind of _____" equipment, "what kind of _____" crowd is being described) or (tell "how" an action is done) to the sports account to make it "come alive."

Before publishing, revising partners should trade compositions and look for capitalization, punctuation, spelling, and other errors that might hinder a reader in acquiring useful information and enjoying the sports account.

NOTE: The goal of revising should be self-evaluation and improvement, not perfection.

PUBLISHING

After students finish revising their sports accounts, explain that they'll publish them in a Midweek newspaper (*format*) so that classmates (*audience*) can learn about and experience the excitement of the games they missed (*purpose*).

Midweek Newspaper

Materials

Midweek newspaper (a half-sized paper) *or* the Midweek News sheet at the end of this lesson, scissors, white glue or tape

Directions

1. Type or print a sports account in columns of appropriate width.

2. Cut off the front page of a half-sized newspaper or use the Midweek News sheet.

3. Place the revised sports article on the newspaper page and move it around until you find a place where it looks good. Usually this means that the masthead of the newspaper is not covered and a few other columns on the front page can still be read.

4. (optional) Draw a picture of a game highlight.

5. Glue the sports article and drawing in position.

6. Once it has dried, trade with other students so they can experience the game.

Midweek News

Volume ____ , Number ____   Date

Lakers Win by Six Points

The basketball game between the Lakers and the Cowboys was action packed. People filled the auditorium on Saturday night at the Moorhead Civic Center. Final score of the game was Lakers 86, Cowboys 80.

Twenty-year-old rookie Dean Garret had 14 points and 16 rebounds for the Lakers. "He's been a key element of our success lately," said Coach Rogers. For the first time since 1989 the Lakers have carried a season of no losses. With only two games left, the Lakers are on the road to the state championship.

Note-taking Assistant

for

Sports Account

Type of Sport   **Teams or Individuals**

Time (when)

Place (where)

Action Highlights   **Your Opinions**

Reactions of the Crowd

Game Outcome

Background Information on teams, individuals, coaches, pregame preparation, or game statistics

Midweek News

Volume _____ , Number _____   Date

LESSON 11

Advice-Column Problem Letter

OUTCOME Each student will write an anonymous letter to an "expert" describing a real personal problem and requesting advice.

MOTIVATORS

1. Ask why people write to a columnist for advice. What types of problems do these people have?

    Read these two problem letters to your class. Consider how to help these people.

    Ask students to name an advice column (such as Dear Abby, Dear Ann Landers, Dear Abigail, Miss Manners, Dear Shabana, and others).

2/24/20XX

Dear _____,

    I just bought a CD that my dad doesn't like. When I asked why, he said if he doesn't approve of the music, I can't play it on his new CD player. What makes me really angry is he's never even listened to this CD! I wish I could open up his mind a little to my kind of music. What should I do now?

          Sincerely,
          Burned Out

10/7/20XX

Dear _____,

    My best friend gave me a goofy hat for my birthday. She knows I collect interesting hats. My mom and dad just split up and my friend has been worried about me. Perhaps she was trying to be nice to me and make me laugh, BUT the hat is orange with two large eyes that light up as they spring out of the hat. What should I do now? I don't want her to get me another hat like this one.

          Sincerely,
          Embarrassed Hat Lover

Wonder aloud if all problem letters sent to magazines and newspapers are answered or published. (Advice columnists publish answers to questions that are interesting and will help the most people.) Encourage students to bring advice columns to class.

2. Pass out the poll of "common problems adolescents have" to your students. (A problem poll can be found at the end of this lesson.) Instruct students to check every problem that they or a friend has experienced. Give students 10–15 minutes to read and fill out the poll anonymously. Point out that at the bottom of the poll are several blanks. Encourage students to add personal and relationship problems that weren't on the list.

Poll of Common Problems

Please check any of the following problems that you or a friend has had in the last year. If you have time, add any personal and relationship problems that weren't on this poll on the blank lines at the bottom. *Do not write your name on this poll.*

___ 1. You share your _____, but your friend won't share his/her _____ with you.
___ 2. Another student cuts/butts in front of you and grins.
___ 3. You feel lonely, left out.
___ 4. Another student, brother, or sister teases and torments you.
___ 5. You worry about being good, strong, handsome, or attractive enough.
___ 6. You accidentally told a secret that you swore never to tell anyone else.
___ 7. Your mom/dad doesn't keep promises.
___ 8. Someone steals your best friend.
___ 9. No one will listen to your side of the story.
___ 10. Some kids want you to try smoking, alcohol, or drugs for fun.
___ 11. Two friends want you to do different things at the same time.
___ 12. Another student calls you names.
___ 13. You're shy, but you want to make more friends.
___ 14. You ruined something, but it was an accident. Now everyone is mad.
___ 15. Your mom/dad won't listen to you.

___ _____

___ _____

___ _____

Collect the polls, shuffle, and redistribute them, making sure students don't get their own poll back. This will help prevent embarrassment and teasing by peers as group results are reported. Also give each student a copy of the 2-page Problem Graphing Sheet. (The Problem Graphing Sheets can be found at the end of this lesson.)

To quickly tally data, ask students (item by item) to raise a hand if the item is marked on their poll. A student helper can count hands. Another student can place totals for each problem on the overhead or a blank Problem Poll.

EXAMPLE: _24_ 1. You share your _____, but your friend won't share his/her _____ with you.
          _9_ 2. Another student cuts/butts in front of you and grins.

While results are being tabulated, instruct students to record and graph the results on the Problem Graphing Sheet. Alert students that you'll expect them to reflect and give reasons for these results.

While you are compiling group data, ask two students (who can work independently) to make a master list of the problems students added in the blank spaces at the bottom of the poll.

Once data have been tabulated and graphed, investigate which problems are more frequent (common) and which are less frequent. (See the Problem Graphing Sheets.)

25	20	15	10	5	Problem
			▓▓	▓▓▓▓	1. You share your ___, but your friend won't share his/her ___ with you.
				▓▓▓	2. Another student cuts/butts in front of you and grins.
		▓▓	▓▓▓	▓▓▓	3. You feel lonely, left out.
▓▓▓	▓▓▓	▓▓▓	▓▓	▓▓	4. Another student, brother, or sister teases and torments you.
			▓▓	▓▓	5. You worry about being good, strong, handsome, or attractive enough.
				▓	6. You accidentally told a secret that you swore never to tell anyone else.

Point out that one way we are alike is that our problems are similar. This will help students see that it is normal to have personal and/or relationship problems—everyone has them. This will also help students be more willing to contribute genuine concerns to the advice columns and not make fun of others' problems.

Discuss with your class that some students may have very serious problems with far-reaching consequences. Stress that students need to respond to all problems in a sensitive, supportive, and caring manner.

GROUP BRAINSTORMING

Now you will get the opportunity to request advice from an expert to solve a personal or relationship problem.

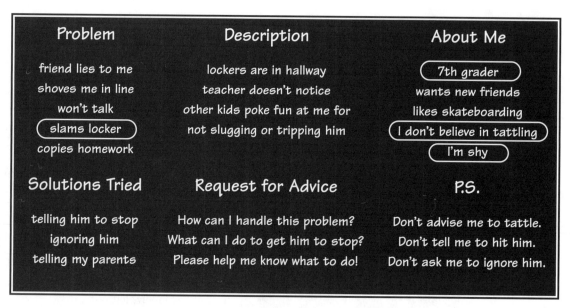

Key Questions

1. **What are some problems many students face? What problems do you have to deal with? What is a common problem your friends or other adolescents face? What problems do _____ graders have?** Pause for at least two minutes to give students plenty of time to think. Write each idea under the "Problem" column. Praise sincere problems. Ignore any silly comments designed to get attention.

2. **One of these problems needs to become the focus of our advice letter. Out of all the problems we listed, which one do many of us face?** Choose a quiet or uninvolved student to select a problem. Circle this idea and use it through the whole lesson. If other students object that their problem wasn't chosen, remind students that they get to write about their own personal or relationship problem later.

3. Point out to students that they'll need to respond as though this problem is their own. Suggest that they imagine themselves in this person's shoes and react honestly. Explain that when they write their own problem letters, they won't have to imagine. **How can we describe or explain this problem to someone else? What are the details?** If students need assistance in generating details, ask a few of the following questions:

   a. **When and where did the problem start?** For each question pause to give students time to think. Write students' ideas under the "Description" column. Praise freely.

   b. **How did it start? Who was involved? What happened?**

   c. **What is happening now/currently?**

d. **How do you feel about it? Why is it a problem?**

e. **What might happen if this problem is not resolved?**

4. **What solutions have already been tried? What were the results? What else have you already considered to make things better?** Write their ideas under the "Solutions Tried" column.

5. **What should we tell the advice giver about us? Who are you? What should the reader know about you before giving advice?** Write their ideas under the "About Me" column. Praise information useful to advice giver.

   NOTE: This column is second on the brainstorming chart, but brainstorm now because this will facilitate group and individual brainstorming.

6. **What can we say to request advice about the problem? How can we plea for help?** Write their ideas under the "Request for Advice" column. Praise thoughtful ways to request advice. **What should we say to request help in solving a problem? How can we request assistance for this problem?**

7. (optional) **Let's add a P.S.—a final thought. What did we forget to say? What advice do we absolutely not want to hear?** Write their ideas under the "P.S." column. Praise both serious and funny ideas.

GROUP COMPOSING

Let's organize our thoughts into a letter requesting advice.

March 6, 20XX

Dear Advice Giver,

I am a seventh grader with an embarrassing problem. A kid who uses the locker next to mine bothers me a lot. He slams my locker and shoves me. The lockers are in the hallway and all the other kids notice him bullying me—but the teachers don't seem to notice.

Don't tell me to ignore him because I've already tried that. The other kids make fun of me for not fighting back, but I'm shy and not very strong.

How can I get him to stop?

Sincerely,
Beat up and Bored with a Bully

P.S. Please don't tell me to tattle.

1. **What is today's date?** Write the date on the board.

> **Thinking about Mechanics:** What punctuation should I put between the day and the year? (a comma) Why? (so they won't run together and cause the reader to misunderstand)

2a. **What greeting (such as "Dear ____") shall we use?**

> **Thinking about Mechanics:** What should I have done to the letter "d" in "Dear _____" ? (capitalize)

2b. **To whom will you write for advice?** Before adding the advice giver's name, ask students to think about mechanics.

> **Thinking about Mechanics:** What do we need to do to the name of the person to whom we are writing? (capitalize each part of the name)

> **Thinking about Mechanics:** What punctuation should I put after the advice giver's name? (a comma)

3. Direct students' attention to the group brainstorming chart columns of "Problem" and "About Me." **What should we say to introduce ourselves and our problem? How can we introduce ourselves and briefly describe our problem in one sentence (the topic sentence)?** Listen to several responses. Choose one, but don't write it on the board until you ask students to think about mechanics.

> **Thinking about Mechanics:** What should I do to the first word in a paragraph to let the reader know this is the beginning of a new idea? (indent)

4. Direct students' attention to the "Description" column of the group brainstorming. **Which details will help the advice giver understand our problem so he/she can give us good advice? How can we describe the problem? What examples can we give?** Pause for at least 30 seconds to allow students time to reflect on the pieces of the problem. Praise insight. Add this information to the group problem letter on the board.

5. **Out of these important details, which ones are critical?** Circle these details. **Which details should we include first, second, third?** Number them 1, 2, 3, etc. Add the ordered details to the letter.

6. **What solutions have we already tried?** Star these ideas. **This knowledge will help the advice giver so he/she won't recommend things that we've already tried.**

7. **Of all the solutions that have been tried, which attempts should we share with the advice giver so he/she will understand our/your situation better?** Add this information to the letter.

8. **Which request for advice from our list shall we use to remind the advice giver what we want?** Students may need assistance with this concluding sentence.

> *EXAMPLE:* I need your advice about _____.
> I have a problem with _____.

9. **Let's close with the word sincerely/yours truly.**

> **Thinking about Mechanics:** What should I have done to the first letter in "sincerely"? (capitalize)

> **Thinking about Mechanics:** What punctuation should I put after the closing "Sincerely"? (a comma)

10a. Explain to students that names in an advice column usually contain a feeling word that sums up the writer's emotions. **How shall we "sign" the letter without revealing our real name? What name or "handle" can we use that sums up the situation?**

10b. What feeling word(s) describes the problem? **Praise names and feeling words relevant to the problem. A list of Feeling Words for Problem Letters can be found at the end of this lesson.**

> *EXAMPLE:* Lonely 6th Grader
> Tired of Getting Bullied
> Frantic in New Brunsfield
> Truly Sorry

11. (optional) **Let's add a P.S.—a final thought. What did we forget to say? Considering all of the advice that we might get, which do we absolutely not want?** Praise both interesting and funny ideas.

INDIVIDUAL BRAINSTORMING AND COMPOSING

Suggest students find a private spot in the room to write their problem letter. You may want to institute these two rules:

1. Any spot, even under a desk or lying on the floor, is fine as long as you don't talk or bother a classmate.

2. If you can't handle the freedom, then you may write at your desk.

NOTE: As students compose drafts of their problem letters, consider writing your own problem letter at a private spot somewhere in the room (not at your desk). This will give students some privacy and help you understand how difficult this task is. If you choose this option, alert your students to give you privacy and tell them that you'll assist them during the revising step.

Beginning Writers   Consider giving Beginning Writers the "Seeking Advice" sheet now. Allow short one- or two-sentence problem statements.

> *Problem:* My grandma buys me lots of gifts, but she needs the money for food.
> *Solution:* Ask your grandma to play a game with you or to teach you to cook instead of buying you gifts.
>
> *Problem:* My science partner teases me.
> *Solution:* Ignore her and she'll give up.
>
> *Problem:* My history teacher is unfair. He gives essay tests, not multiple choice.
> *Solution:* Reword the essay question for your first sentence. Work hard and smile at your teacher.

If you have students who choose not to write about personal and relationship problems, perhaps they can write about bicycle, skateboard, motorcycle, or other fix-it problems and solutions or write about beauty/health problems and solutions.

RESPONDING TO STUDENTS' WRITINGS/REVISING

1. As students finish their rough drafts, ask them to self-evaluate their problem letter. Have each student self-edit the following on a Revising Assistant. A copy of this Revising Assistant can be found at the end of this lesson.

Revising Assistant
for Problem Letter

____ Does the problem letter begin with a date?

____ Is there a greeting?
____ Is the name of the advice giver capitalized? Is it followed by a comma?

____ Have I introduced myself and the problem in the opening sentence?
____ Has all necessary information about the problem been included?
____ Has the problem been clearly described?
____ Have I told what solutions I have already tried?
____ Has some useful information about me been included?
____ Does the problem letter make sense to the reader?
____ Have I made a request for assistance?

____ Has the letter been closed with a word like "sincerely"?
____ Has the closing been capitalized? Does a comma follow the closing?
____ Has one or more feeling words been used in the name?

____ Have I checked for capitalization, punctuation, and spelling errors that might hinder the reader in understanding my request for advice?

---

2. After step 1 is completed, require each student to improve his/her request for advice by making at least two improvements to his/her problem letter.

   Suggest students look for one or two words that may be misspelled, circle each one, and check its spelling. (Look at the brainstormed list on the board, look up the word in a personal speller, sound out the word, spell check on the computer.) Explain that this will help the reader focus on the problem and not try to figure out what a misspelled word means.

3. Have Advanced Writers recopy or word process their problem letters on the "Seeking Advice" sheet, which can be found at the end of the lesson.

   Allow Beginning Writers to clean up their draft and use this for publication. Don't insist the request be error-free since this will direct students' attention away from the importance of requesting for help. Growth and improvement will come more quickly with frequent writing experiences, rather than with completing a few almost error-free compositions.

PUBLISHING

Remind students that the advice giver who gets their letter (*audience*) will think about their problem and give some useful advice (*purpose*). Below are two possible publishing formats.

Advice Box

Problem Letter

Problem Letter

Problem Letter

Problem Letter

Advice

Advice

Advice
Place your problem letters here.

Problem Letter

Problem Letter

Problem Letter

Problem Letter

Problem Letter

Problem Letter

Materials:

Shoe or gift box (or other box) with a lid

Directions:

Option 1   To ensure privacy fold your problem letter in half and staple it before placing it in the Advice Box.

Option 2   Fold your problem letter in thirds, place it in an envelope, and seal the envelope before placing it in the Advice Box.

Advice Column

Some teachers publish a class newspaper with problem and solution letters or place them on a class bulletin board. *We've found that public publication inhibits many students from writing from their heart about serious problems.*

If you want to set up a newspaper advice column, have the problems submitted *anonymously by students in another or younger grade*. Find a teacher who would like to have his/her students correspond. Assign each of your students as a columnist for a particular student. Have your students respond privately, but also publish the letters in a public manner, such as in a news column or bulletin board. This can be an ongoing project for several months.

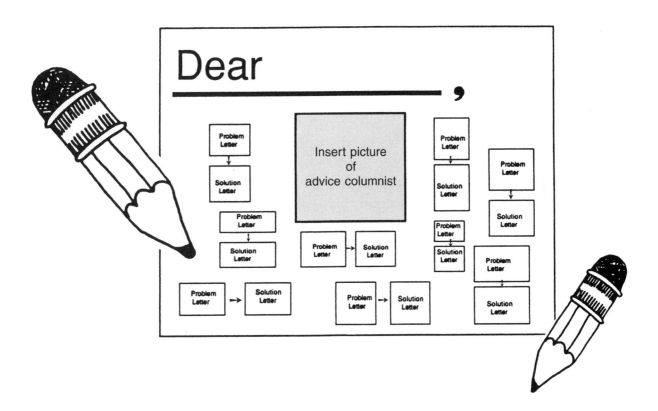

Poll of Common Problems

Please check any of the following problems that you or a friend has had in the last year. If you have time, add any personal and relationship problems that weren't on this poll on the blank lines at the bottom. *Do not write your name on this poll.*

___ 1. You share your _____, but your friend won't share his/her _____ with you.

___ 2. Another student cuts/butts in front of you and grins.

___ 3. You feel lonely, left out.

___ 4. Another student, brother, or sister teases and torments you.

___ 5. You worry about being good, strong, handsome, or attractive enough.

___ 6. You accidentally told a secret that you swore never to tell anyone else.

___ 7. Your mom/dad doesn't keep promises.

___ 8. Someone steals your best friend.

___ 9. No one will listen to your side of the story.

___ 10. Some kids want you to try smoking, alcohol, or drugs for fun.

___ 11. Two friends want you to do different things at the same time.

___ 12. Another student calls you names.

___ 13. You're shy, but you want to make more friends.

___ 14. You ruined something, but it was an accident. Now everyone is mad.

___ 15. Your mom/dad won't listen to you.

___ 16. A bully picks on you after school.

___ 17. Your mom, dad, or teacher embarrassed you in front of the other kids.

___ 18. You made a mistake and everyone laughed at you.

___ 19. No one will listen to your side of the story.

___ 20. You've been blamed for something you didn't do.

___ 21. You heard one of your parents complaining about you.

___ 22. You had a fight with your best friend.

___ 23. Your best friend talks all the time and you never get a chance to share.

___ 24. Someone you know is depressed or angry all of the time.

___ 25. You wonder if it is okay to tell "white lies."

___ _____

___ _____

___ _____

Problem Graphing Sheet

		5	10	15	20	25	30	35
1. You share your ____, but your friend won't share his/her ____ with you.								
2. Another student cuts/butts in front of you and grins.								
3. You feel lonely, left out.								
4. Another student, brother, or sister teases and torments you.								
5. You worry about being good, strong, handsome, or attractive enough.								
6. You accidentally told a secret that you swore never to tell anyone else.								
7. Your mom/dad doesn't keep promises.								
8. Someone steals your best friend.								
9. No one will listen to your side of the story.								
10. Some kids want you to try smoking, alcohol, or drugs for fun.								
11. Two friends want you to do different things at the same time.								
12. Another student calls you names.								
13. You're shy, but you want to make more friends.								

				5	10	15	20	25	30	35
14. You ruined something, but it was an accident. Now everyone is mad.										
15. Your mom/dad won't listen to you.										
16. A bully picks on you after school.										
17. Your mom, dad, or teacher embarrassed you in front of the other kids.										
18. You made a mistake and everyone laughed at you.										
19. No one will listen to your side of the story.										
20. You've been blamed for something you didn't do.										
21. You heard one of your parents complaining about you.										
22. You had a fight with your best friend.										
23. Your best friend talks all the time and you never get a chance to share.										
24. Someone you know is depressed or angry all of the time.										
25. You wonder if it is okay to tell "white lies."										

Brainstorming Assistant
for
Problem Letter

Problems

Description

About Me

Solutions Tried

Requests for Advice

P.S.

Feeling Words
for Problem Letters

Abandoned	Confident	Fascinated	Jealous	Quarrelsome	Terrible
Adamant	Confused	Fearful		Quiet	Terrified
Affectionate	Conspicuous	Flustered	Lazy		Threatened
Ambivalent	Crushed	Foolish	Lonely	Realistic	Thwarted
Angry		Frantic		Reflective	Trapped
Annoyed	Defeated	Frightened	Melancholy	Rejected	Troubled
Anxious	Delighted	Frustrated	Miserable	Relieved	Trusting
Astounded	Despairing	Furious		Resentful	
	Determined		Naive	Responsible	Ugly
Betrayed	Distracted	Grieving	Nervous		Uneasy
Bold	Distraught	Guilty		Scared	Unpredictable
Bored	Disturbed	Gullible	Obnoxious	Searching	Unsettled
Brave	Divided		Obsessed	Self-conscious	
	Dominated	Helpless	Outraged	Sentimental	Vehement
Calm	Dubious	Homesick	Overwhelmed	Shocked	Vulnerable
Capable		Hurt		Sorrowful	
Captivated	Eager	Ignored	Panicked	Startled	Withdrawn
Cautious	Enchanted	Impressed	Perceptive	Stunned	Worried
Challenged	Energetic	Infuriated	Petrified	Sympathetic	
Cheerful	Envious	Inspired	Pitiful		
Clever	Exasperated	Intimidated	Pressured	Tempted	
Competitive	Exhausted	Isolated	Proud	Tense	

© 2000 Cherlyn Sunflower

Feeling Words
for Problem Letters

Abandoned	Confident	Fascinated	Jealous	Quarrelsome	Terrible
Adamant	Confused	Fearful		Quiet	Terrified
Affectionate	Conspicuous	Flustered	Lazy		Threatened
Ambivalent	Crushed	Foolish	Lonely	Realistic	Thwarted
Angry		Frantic		Reflective	Trapped
Annoyed	Defeated	Frightened	Melancholy	Rejected	Troubled
Anxious	Delighted	Frustrated	Miserable	Relieved	Trusting
Astounded	Despairing	Furious		Resentful	
	Determined		Naive	Responsible	Ugly
Betrayed	Distracted	Grieving	Nervous		Uneasy
Bold	Distraught	Guilty		Scared	Unpredictable
Bored	Disturbed	Gullible	Obnoxious	Searching	Unsettled
Brave	Divided		Obsessed	Self-conscious	
	Dominated	Helpless	Outraged	Sentimental	Vehement
Calm	Dubious	Homesick	Overwhelmed	Shocked	Vulnerable
Capable		Hurt		Sorrowful	
Captivated	Eager	Ignored	Panicked	Startled	Withdrawn
Cautious	Enchanted	Impressed	Perceptive	Stunned	Worried
Challenged	Energetic	Infuriated	Petrified	Sympathetic	
Cheerful	Envious	Inspired	Pitiful		
Clever	Exasperated	Intimidated	Pressured	Tempted	
Competitive	Exhausted	Isolated	Proud	Tense	

Revising Assistant
for Problem Letter

____ Does the problem letter begin with a date?

____ Is there a greeting?
____ Is the name of the advice giver capitalized? Is it followed by a comma?

____ Have I introduced myself and the problem in the opening sentence?
____ Has all necessary information about the problem been included?
____ Has the problem been clearly described?
____ Have I told what solutions I have already tried?
____ Has some useful information about me been included?
____ Does the problem letter make sense to the reader?
____ Have I made a request for assistance?

____ Has the letter been closed with a word like "sincerely"?
____ Has the closing been capitalized? Does a comma follow the closing?
____ Has one or more feeling words been used in the name?

____ Have I checked for capitalization, punctuation, and spelling errors that might hinder the reader in understanding my request for advice?

Revising Assistant
for Problem Letter

____ Does the problem letter begin with a date?

____ Is there a greeting?
____ Is the name of the advice giver capitalized? Is it followed by a comma?

____ Have I introduced myself and the problem in the opening sentence?
____ Has all necessary information about the problem been included?
____ Has the problem been clearly described?
____ Have I told what solutions I have already tried?
____ Has some useful information about me been included?
____ Does the problem letter make sense to the reader?
____ Have I made a request for assistance?

____ Has the letter been closed with a word like "sincerely"?
____ Has the closing been capitalized? Does a comma follow the closing?
____ Has one or more feeling words been used in the name?

____ Have I checked for capitalization, punctuation, and spelling errors that might hinder the reader in understanding my request for advice?

Seeking Advice

SECTION 2

Directional Compositions for Young Authors

A directional pattern is useful when writers want to tell or explain how to do a task or project.

- **Simple Directions** Simple directions contain steps given in chronological order.

- **Complex Directions** More complex directions begin with a topic sentence that tells what will be explained, followed by complete and clear steps chronologically ordered. Each direction or step contains a clear, precise action word. The direction begins with a transition word or phrase (such as first, second, next, after that, then, finally) or numbers that signal the order in which the steps must be completed. Most directions include necessary supplies and tools. These may be listed before the directions or within each direction.

Some Forms of "How-to" Writing

Advice
Beauty Tips
Explanations
Game Directions
How-to-do-it Manuals
Instructions
Recipes

Remedies
Rules
School or Neighborhood
   Guides
Survival Manuals
Travel Directions

LESSON 12

Advice to Next Year's Class

OUTCOME Each student will compose a three-paragraph letter of insights for an incoming student about how to succeed in _____ grade.

MOTIVATORS

1. Ask your students what they remember about school this year, what they learned, and what they won't forget. If you have photos or samples of work from the beginning of school, pass them around.

2. Discuss what the incoming students might be like. During the discussion encourage students to fold a sheet of paper in half and draft a picture of a possible incoming student and an outgoing one. Share their pictures.

Incoming Student

Outgoing Student

3. Collaborate with a teacher in a lower grade. Invite a younger class to your room for a tour. Serve treats. Play a game or do an activity together. Encourage younger students to write questions they have about the coming year.

"What do you do in _____ grade?"
"What will I learn?"
"What's difficult?"
"What are the teachers like?"

4. Play the 1999 song "Everybody's Free to Wear Sunscreen," which appeals to young audiences and gives advice in a playful manner. You can listen to the song and print out the lyrics at http://members.xoom.com/tvlive/home.htm.

GROUP BRAINSTORMING

We are going to compose a letter to help incoming students succeed in _____ grade at our school.

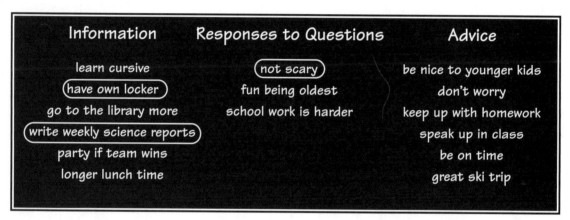

Information	Responses to Questions	Advice
learn cursive	(not scary)	be nice to younger kids
(have own locker)	fun being oldest	don't worry
go to the library more	school work is harder	keep up with homework
(write weekly science reports)		speak up in class
party if team wins		be on time
longer lunch time		great ski trip

Key Questions

Information

1. Write each student's ideas on the group brainstorming board, chart, or overhead under "Information."

   What privileges do we have that the lower grade will soon have?

   What will the students learn?

   What special events will take place?

   What do you like best? least?

   What questions do you wish you had asked last year?

Responses to Questions

   2. Read a question from a lower grade-level student such as:

     Where will we sit in the lunchroom?

     What do you get to do during free time?

How can we answer this question? How can we respond in a way that won't frighten the incoming student? Write students' responses in abbreviated form on the board under "Responses to Questions."

Advice

   3. Write the advice students offer under "Advice."

     What advice should we give to an incoming student to help him/her succeed? What would you do differently if you could start over?

     How can we help the incoming class succeed?

     What can we tell the incoming students to make their first days in grade _____ easier?

GROUP COMPOSING

Tell students they will write a letter to an incoming student (*audience*) to help these students feel comfortable about the coming school year (*purpose*).

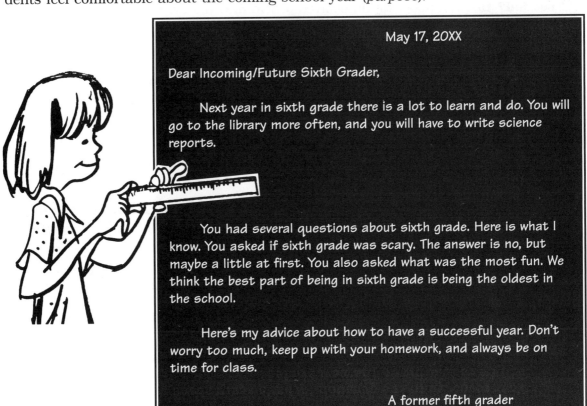

May 17, 20XX

Dear Incoming/Future Sixth Grader,

    Next year in sixth grade there is a lot to learn and do. You will go to the library more often, and you will have to write science reports.

    You had several questions about sixth grade. Here is what I know. You asked if sixth grade was scary. The answer is no, but maybe a little at first. You also asked what was the most fun. We think the best part of being in sixth grade is being the oldest in the school.

    Here's my advice about how to have a successful year. Don't worry too much, keep up with your homework, and always be on time for class.

              A former fifth grader

1. **Let's put the date at the top of our letter. What's today's date?** Choose a student to provide the information. Write the date on the board, overhead, or chart paper.

> **Thinking about Mechanics:** How do we write the date? (month and day, comma, year)

2. **What polite greeting/salutation should we use?** Choose an uninvolved or withdrawn student to select a greeting. Add the greeting to the letter. Ask what punctuation goes after the greeting.

   EXAMPLES: Dear Sixth Grader
   Greetings Future _____ Grader
   Welcome New _____ Grader
   Dear Reader

Paragraph 1: Information

1. **A topic sentence introduces and summarizes a paragraph's topic. What topic sentence can we create to indicate that we are going to give students some helpful information?** Allow time for students to think. Add one topic sentence to the letter.

   EXAMPLES: There is a lot to learn and do in grade _____.
   Here's some info that will be helpful to you next year.

2. **Out of all the information we brainstormed, which ideas shall we include in our letter?** Circle this information. **Which information can we share first? second? third?** Choose an uninvolved or withdrawn student to select one or more ideas. Add this information to the letter.

Paragraph 2: Responses to Questions

1. **What topic sentence can we write to let students know we are answering the questions they sent?** Allow time for students to think. Add one topic sentence to the letter.

   EXAMPLES: You had several questions about _____ grade. Here is what you need to know.
   These are the questions we wish we'd asked last year before entering _____ grade.

2. **Out of all the questions given to us or we generated, which questions do we want to answer?** Choose an uninvolved or withdrawn student to select one or more ideas. Circle or mark two or three questions.

3. **How can we answer this question clearly and honestly? How can we put our answers into sentence form?** Add this information to the letter. Repeat this sequence of questions several times.

Paragraph 3: Advice

1. **What topic sentence can we create to let students know we're going to give them some valuable advice?** Add one topic sentence to the letter.

   EXAMPLES: Here's my advice about how to have a successful year.
   This advice will help you succeed.

2. **Out of all the advice we brainstormed, what would be most helpful for the incoming students?** Choose an uninvolved or withdrawn student to select an idea. Circle five or six pieces of advice that students have decided should be included in the letter. **Which advice can we share first? second? third?** Circle this information.

3. **How shall we word our advice?** Add this information to the letter in complete sentence form.

Closing

1. **What is a supportive way to finish our letter? How can we close on an encouraging note?** Pause to allow students to think. Add one closing. **What punctuation do we need to put after the closing?** Place a comma after the closing.

    EXAMPLES: A friend
                Yours truly
                See you soon
                Sincerely
                Cordially yours
                A former _____ grader
                You will ace it

2. **What will be the last thing you'll add to your letter?** Pause. Sign your name.

INDIVIDUAL BRAINSTORMING & COMPOSING

Ask students to fold a piece of notebook paper in thirds and crease the folds. Open the paper and label the columns "Information," "Responses to Questions," and "Advice." Tell students they may begin brainstorming advice for new students, then write their letters.

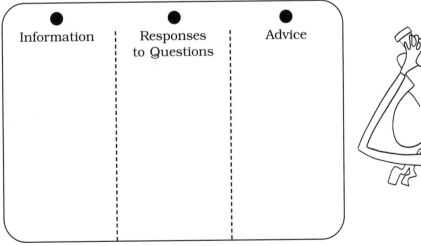

We'll be looking for you!

As students begin brainstorming and composing, circulate around the room praising useful information, clear and comforting responses to incoming students' questions, and valuable, yet nonthreatening pieces of advice.

For example:

- **The information you shared about how incoming students will be involved in a special Science Festival is valuable.**

- **Your response to the question "What's scary about _____ grade?" will be reassuring to the new student.**

- **Incoming students will find your advice to "speak up in class" helpful.**

Ask young writers open-ended questions to stimulate or clarify their thoughts. For example:

- **What information would you have appreciated knowing before you started _____ grade?**

- **How could you respond in a reassuring way to the question "I heard bullies pick on you after school and steal your homework. Is this true?"**

- **What is something valuable you learned this year that helped you be successful with schoolwork or peers?**

RESPONDING TO STUDENTS' WRITINGS/REVISING

As students finish their rough drafts of letters to incoming students, ask each to find a new revising partner with whom he/she has not worked. Have the revising partner read the advice out loud to the writer. Write the following information on the board, a chart, or an overhead to guide students.

- Will the information I provided get the incoming student excited about the new year?
- Did I answer the question in a clear and honest manner?
- Did I reassure any fears the incoming student shared?
- Did I offer advice in such a way that the students (our audience) will appreciate it?

After the peer-revising session is over, ask each young author to reread his/her letter out loud to him-/herself and make at least one or two improvements for the benefit of the incoming student.

Before publishing the letters, pair students with different partners. Trade letters and look for errors that might cause the incoming student to reject the helpful letter because the spelling or punctuation seems juvenile or childish.

PUBLISHING

Explain that the letters to incoming students (*audience*) will advise them so they feel comfortable about the coming school year and help them get started on the "right foot" (*purpose*).

Fold-a-Letter

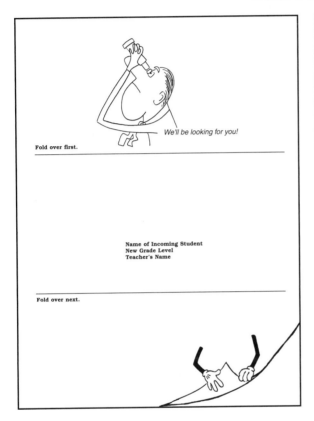
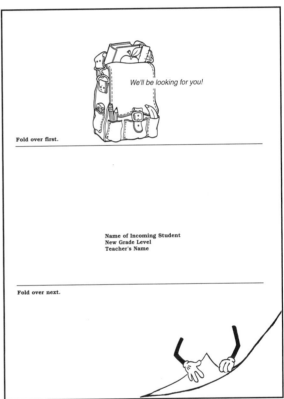

Use school stationery or the Fold-a-Letter reproducibles that can be found at the end of this lesson. Fold in thirds and address the folded letter to a student in the lower grade.

We'll be looking for you!

Fold over first.

Name of Incoming Student
New Grade Level
Teacher's Name

Fold over next.

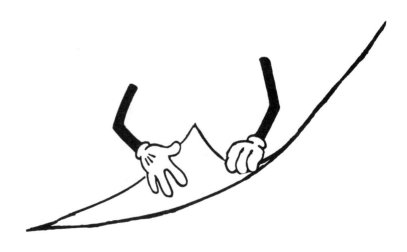

We'll be looking for you!

Fold over first.

Name of Incoming Student
New Grade Level
Teacher's Name

Fold over next.

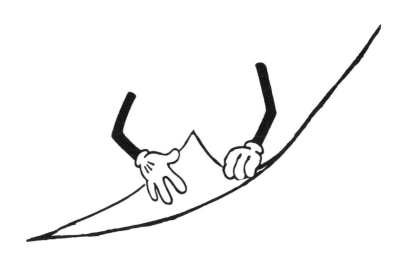

LESSON 13

Treasure Map Directions

OUTCOME Each student will compose instructions for finding a hidden treasure (an object).

MOTIVATORS

1. Share a time when you or someone you know found some money. For example, while my family was entering a water park in Wyoming, my niece Krissy found a twenty-dollar bill on the ground. (She turned it over to the person at the information stand after holding on to it and feeling rich for a while.)

   Ask your students if they know anyone who has found money or a valuable object. Inquire what/how much was found, when, and where it was found. Ask students to imagine how that person felt.

2. Invite a person with a metal detector to search the school grounds and show the "treasures" he/she has found over the years. In large towns check your local phone book for places that sell metal detectors; in small towns call coin dealers who often sell metal detectors. Ask the owner if he/she would do a demonstration. If not, ask for names of people who do metal detecting who might volunteer their time. A number of websites offer information. Try www.treasurenet.com for treasure hunting stories and other information. Another site is www.losttreasure.net.

3. Discuss lost treasure such as the popular *Titanic* or another boat that sunk with jewelry, coins, and other valuables. Inquire what your students would like to look for on land or in water if they could find something valuable.

4. Before class begins put a coin or small item in a resealable bag and hide it in the room.

Explain that students are going to have an indoor treasure hunt. Set up a time limit, such as five minutes. Declare that the first person to locate the treasure will be the winner and will get to keep it. Make this suggestion: "Wouldn't it be nice to have a map to tell us where treasure can be found?"

Now give your students a map with *very poor* directions. You can use this map as a model or make your own poor directions.

Turn left. Then turn right. Go into this corner of the room. Look South. Walk until you reach the treasure. You will find it under something.

Use one or more props (binoculars, eye patch, pirate hat, treasure chest) from motivator 7. Read the treasure map directions to your class.

When you think students are frustrated enough by trying to follow poor directions, show students where the treasure is hidden. Ask students if your directions were helpful. When students chorus "No!" ask them what made the directions so poor. Guide students to see that specific distances, landmarks, and clear directions are necessary. Explain that if your directions were clear and complete, everyone should have found the treasure. State that writing clear directions is both important and quite challenging.

5. Share this story about a teenager who is lost and a neighbor who tries to help. Make copies of this dialogue and ask two students to role-play this quick drama for your class. Encourage students to practice so they can show emotion in their voices.

TEENAGER (*timidly*): Could you help me? I'm trying to find Gary Minor's house.

NEIGHBOR (*eagerly*): I'd be glad to help. Gary lives across the street from me.

TEENAGER (*excitedly*): Terrific! Where do you live?

NEIGHBOR: I told you that already. I live across the street from Gary.

TEENAGER: But where does Gary live?

NEIGHBOR: He lives in the two-story house down the street.

TEENAGER (*impatiently*): Which two-story house? All the houses are two-story!

NEIGHBOR (*puzzled*): Well, Gary's house is the only one besides mine that has a garden in the backyard.

TEENAGER (*getting angry*): I can't see the backyards from here.

NEIGHBOR (*frustrated*): Just look for my house. I told you. Gary's house is the two-story house across from mine.

Ask students to think of a time when they needed directions. Inquire whether the directions offered helped or confused them.

6. Pass out city maps for students to share. Point out the compass rose (or direction symbol) and inquire what these symbols mean. Ask students to find north, west, and so forth on the map. Also direct students' attention to the distance scale. Suggest that these elements would be useful additions on the treasure maps they create.

7. If your students are motivated by the dramatic, use some props: binoculars, eye patch, pirate hat, and/or treasure chest during the lesson.

Binoculars   Use real binoculars or two toilet paper tubes covered with black construction paper. Pretend you are searching for treasure.

Eye Patch Trace the eye-patch pattern onto black construction paper. Cut a two-foot long piece of yarn. Lay the middle of the yarn 1/4 inch from the straight end of the eye patch.

Fold the straight edge over the yarn and glue the yarn in place. When dry, wear the eye patch during the lesson.

Pirate Hat Draw the pirate hat on black construction paper. Lay this pattern on another sheet of black construction paper. Cut out both sides of the hat at the same time. Staple the ends of the hat together so it fits your head. Cover the edges of the hat with a 1-1/2-inch strip of aluminum foil folded in half.

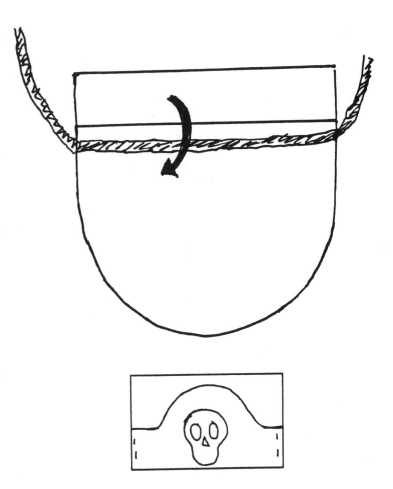

GROUP BRAINSTORMING

Today we will compose directions for locating treasure so we can have our own treasure hunt or run a treasure hunt for a group of younger students.

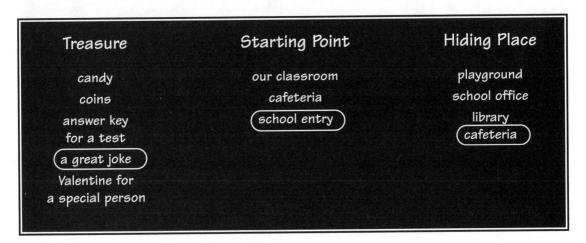

Treasure	Starting Point	Hiding Place
candy	our classroom	playground
coins	cafeteria	school office
answer key for a test	school entry	library
a great joke		cafeteria
Valentine for a special person		

Key Questions

1. **What small object could be the treasure? What small object could be hidden?** Repeat until five to six student ideas have been written on the board under "Treasure." Choose an uninvolved student to select one. Circle it. Request students to locate a "treasure" at home to hide later after they compose their treasure maps.

2. **Where would be a great place to find or hide some treasure? What are some good places where treasure could be hidden in our room, in the school, or on the school grounds? Where is a safe place treasure could be hidden?** Repeat these questions until five to six student ideas have been written on the board under "Hiding Place." Praise interesting or valuable hiding places.

3. **Of all our hiding places, for which one shall we write directions?** Have an uninvolved student select one idea. Circle this idea and use it all the way through group brainstorming and composing.

4. **What might be a familiar starting point? Where might the student begin the treasure hunt?** Repeat these questions until several students' ideas have been written on the board under "Starting Point."

5. **Of all our possible starting points, which one would be logical? Which one is an easy place to find?** Have an uninvolved student select one idea. Circle this idea and use it all the way through group brainstorming and composing.

6. **Now let's write our clues. Which way should the treasure hunter go first? How far should he/she go in that direction? What landmark would be helpful to the treasure hunter?** As students respond, add this information underneath the correct brainstorming categories "Direction," "Distance," and "Landmark." Notice that the board is set up so that information related to one direction can be written across on the same horizontal line. Just capture words or phrases; complete sentences will be composed later in the group composing section of the lesson.

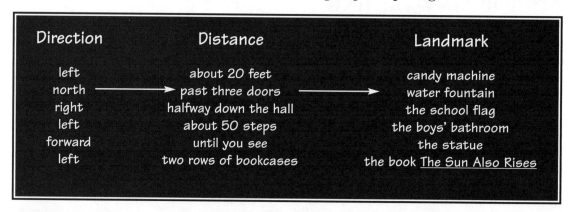

Direction	Distance	Landmark
left	about 20 feet	candy machine
north	past three doors	water fountain
right	halfway down the hall	the school flag
left	about 50 steps	the boys' bathroom
forward	until you see	the statue
left	two rows of bookcases	the book <u>The Sun Also Rises</u>

7. **Which direction should the treasure hunter go now? How far? What is an easy landmark to spot between _____ and _____ ?** As students respond add this information underneath the correct brainstorming categories "Direction," "Distance," and "Landmark." **When should the treasure hunter change directions?** Continue this three-part questioning until the destination is "reached."

GROUP COMPOSING

Now let's create a treasure map and directions for finding the treasure. Ahead of time cut a 4 × 5-foot sheet of light colored butcher paper so that the group composition can be saved and revised during the Revising step.

1. **Let's write a title first: "Treasure Map" by _____.** Add this title to the group composition.

2. (optional) **What date/when did we hide the treasure?**

Treasure Map
by Ms. Landless's 8th graders
20XX

The treasure has been hidden on school grounds. If you want to locate it, follow these directions carefully. Start at the entry of our school _____

The first clue is to follow the left side of the walkway until you can see _____. Then _____

3. **We'll begin our directions so the treasure hunter will know that the directions are for locating hidden treasure. How can we introduce the purpose of our directions?** Praise students' ideas. Choose a quiet student to select one topic sentence. If students are less experienced writers or speakers, share the following topic sentences. Then ask students to choose one topic sentence.

    EXAMPLES: To find your treasure, follow these directions until you reach the X on this map.

    To locate treasure, begin at the star in the circle and keep following these directions.

    If you follow these directions, you will locate the treasure.

Thinking about Mechanics: What should I do to the first word in a paragraph to show that we are going to start a new idea? (indent)

---

4. Comment that the directions need to be clear, complete, and in the correct order so the listener or reader can find the treasure instead of getting lost. **Where did we decide the treasure hunter would begin?** Direct students back to the starting point that was selected earlier.

5. Direct students' attention to the directions, distances, and landmarks brainstormed earlier. **What should we tell the person to do first? What direction? How far? What landmark will the person see to indicate he or she is on the right track?** As students provide this information, add it in sentence form to the group composition on the board. Praise directions that contain direction, distance, and landmark.

> **Thinking about Mechanics:** Which of our landmarks are special names for particular places? How do we show our readers? (capitalize the first letter of each proper noun)

6. How shall we start the next direction? You may want to reproduce and post the "Time Order," "Direction Words," and "Action Words" chart so students can refer to them during brainstorming and later during composing. This chart can be found at the end of Travel Directions, Lesson 15, reproducible 15–2. If the student creating the directions doesn't include a time order word, point to the chart and ask the student to choose a useful word.

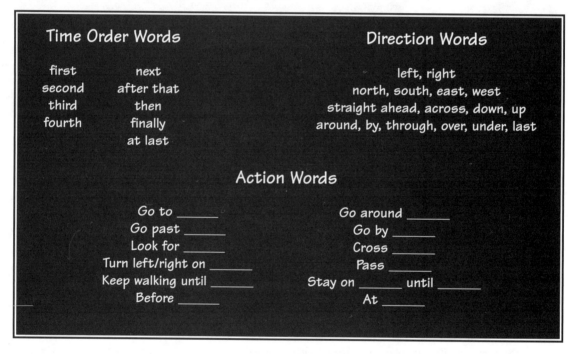

Time Order Words

first	next
second	after that
third	then
fourth	finally
	at last

Direction Words

left, right
north, south, east, west
straight ahead, across, down, up
around, by, through, over, under, last

Action Words

Go to _____
Go past _____
Look for _____
Turn left/right on _____
Keep walking until _____
Before _____

Go around _____
Go by _____
Cross _____
Pass _____
Stay on _____ until _____
At _____

7. How far should the treasure hunter go? What landmark will the treasure hunter see if he or she is on the correct path? As students provide this information, add it in sentence form to the group composition on the board. Praise directions that contain direction, distance, and landmark. **After reaching _____, which direction should he or she go? How far? What landmark is close by?** If the student creating the direction doesn't include a direction word, ask another student for a suggestion.

8. Which way should he or she go next? How far? What landmark can be seen? What is the next thing the treasure hunter should do? Repeat this pattern of questioning until the destination is reached.

NOTE: Don't be concerned at this point about missing, misordered or incorrect directions. This will be addressed in the revising step.

9. **What can we say to indicate that the treasure hunter has reached the location where the treasure is hidden?** Direct students' attention to the hiding place chosen earlier. If students need assistance, share one or two examples of ways to end oral or written directions.

   EXAMPLES: When you see (the landmark) you have reached the X on the map. You may keep it!

   You have reached the location where the treasure is buried. Dig it up and enjoy!

10. (optional) **Next, let's add a compass rose, a distance scale, and a map with the starting place marked with a star in a circle and our hiding spot with a big X.**

INDIVIDUAL BRAINSTORMING & COMPOSING

NOTE: Alert your principal and colleagues to the purpose of this activity. Students will need to walk around your room or leave the classroom to hide their treasures and create their maps. Allow students to choose a partner or prearrange pairs. Have on hand a few extra treasures in case a student forgets to bring one.

Now you and your partner will select a spot to hide your treasure. Once you have selected a hiding spot, write it on a small sheet of paper and show your desired location to me so two teams don't choose the same spot.

library area	special ed. room
entry area	office
locker area	school nurse's area
hallway	counselor's office
art room	principal's office
lunchroom	music room
commons area	gym
janitorial room	

Here is a sample note to school personnel:

Dear Faculty and Staff at _____,

   We are composing a treasure hunt as part of a unit on giving directions. These students would like permission to hide their treasure in your work area.

   Only two students will come to find the treasure and they won't be allowed to touch or move anything in your room. May we have your permission to put our treasure in your area?

   The treasure hunt will take place from _____ on _____ .

                                             Sincerely,

Have students turn a sheet of notebook paper sideways. Direct them to fold the paper in thirds (long and thin), crease the folds, and reopen the paper. Direct students to write "Direction," "Distance," and "Landmark" across the top of the paper.

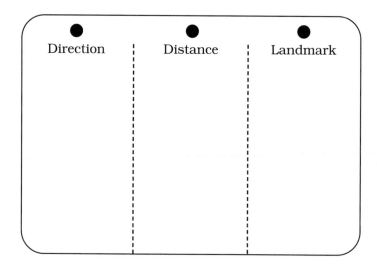

Now sit down and "roughly" draft your directions. Once you have brainstormed directions, distances, and landmarks, contact me before you leave our room to get permission to hide treasure in a particular work area.

Once you have faculty or staff permission to hide treasure in the work area:

   1. Try out your directions,

   2. Take notes, and

   3. Revise your directions until they are clear.

As students begin designing their own directions, be available to assist. Walk around making positive comments about good hiding spots, useful starting points, and clear and complete directions with accurate distances and easy-to-find landmarks. Ask questions to help students organize their directions and evaluate how complete and accurate the directions are. If necessary, assist students in getting permission from school staff.

RESPONDING TO STUDENTS' WRITINGS/REVISING

   1. Pull out the treasure map created earlier by your class during the Group Composing step. Have one or more students read the directions out loud. Ask students to find places where the directions could be more accurate or clearer.

   2. As students finish the rough drafts of their treasure map directions, have one student read his/her treasure map directions aloud to the peer to see if the directions are accurate, have all the important information, and are in the correct order.

3. Pair students with another revising team. Send the treasure map writers with the revising team to try the directions. As the revising team searches for the treasure, the treasure map direction writers should observe their efforts. The treasure hunters should follow the directions *exactly*, not what the other team meant to write.

   Encourage teams to make two to three specific comments on what they like about the treasure map and offer suggestions for (1) how to help make sure the directions can be easily followed and (2) what needs to be added, reordered, or eliminated. After observing and listening to the revising team, require teams to make at least one or two additions and corrections on the rough drafts to improve the treasure map directions.

4. Finally, before publishing their treasure map directions, have students trade treasure map directions and look for punctuation, capitalization, spelling, and other errors that might hinder a treasure hunter in locating the treasure.

PUBLISHING

After students finish revising their treasure directions, explain that they'll publish them on a map (*format*) so that treasure hunters—peers, another grade-level class, or younger students (*audience*)—can locate the treasure (*purpose*).

Map

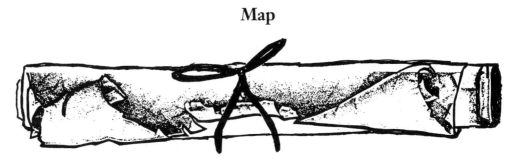

Materials

brown paper grocery bag, scissors, pencil, ruler, yarn or string, (optional) short votive candle, tray or empty tuna can, matches

Directions

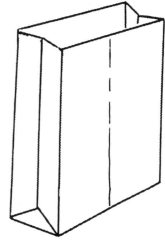

1. Cut off two sides of a brown paper grocery bag. This will create a 12 × 16-1/2-inch area for the directions and map.

   If a larger area (16-1/2 × 36-inch) is desired, cut down the seam at the back of the grocery bag. Then trim off the bottom of the bag.

2. To make the brown paper look old, crumple the paper several times. Then open it and smooth it out. Students who have difficulty crumpling the paper can sit or step on it.

3. (optional) Draw a 1-1/2-inch border around the edge of the brown paper.

4. Cut the edges of the brown paper in an uneven wavy manner, staying outside the border.

5. (optional) **This step will need adult supervision.** Find a metal surface (floor or table). Remove all flammable items. Set the votive candle on a tray or in an empty tuna can to prevent movement and catch ashes. Light the candle.

   Carefully place a small part of the brown paper into the candle flame until it catches fire. Immediately pull the burning edge of the brown paper away and blow the flame out. Repeat until the edges of the whole "parchment" are charred. To help control the flames, dip the paper in water before charring the edges.

NOTE: If you wish to use typing paper instead of grocery bags, dab the edges of the paper with a teabag that has been briefly dipped in steaming hot water. This will make the paper look older and give it a brown stain. After staining, lay the paper on paper towels to speed drying time.

6. Write the directions on the charred or tea-stained paper. If desired, add a drawing (map). If a map will be added, write the directions on the right side or bottom of the map. Draw a star in one corner of the paper and add the direction words north, south, east, west on the points of the star.

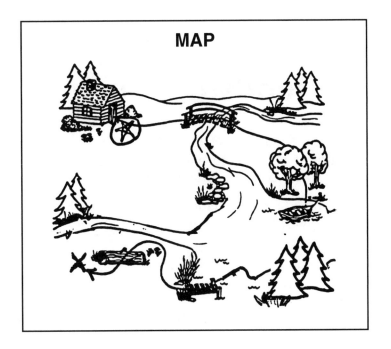

7. Roll the treasure map directions and tie with yarn.

LESSON 14

Friendship Recipe

OUTCOME Each student will create a recipe with ingredients and four to ten instructions for building a great friendship.

NOTE: Other possible nonfood recipes include: Recipe for laughter, a quality world, popularity, wealth, world peace, good citizens, a caring parent, a talented volleyball player, a fair teacher, etc.

MOTIVATORS

1. Ask students what recipes they have followed to prepare a particular food. Share a favorite recipe of yours. For example, my favorite recipe is Chocolate Lovers' Deluxe Brownies, a gift from one of my students.

Chocolate Lovers' Deluxe Brownies

1/3 cup butter	3/4 cup flour
3/4 cup sugar	1/4 tsp. baking soda
1 tsp. vanilla	12-oz. package chocolate chips
2 large eggs	3/4 cup chopped pecans

Blend sugar, butter, and two tablespoons water in a small pan. Heat until it bubbles furiously. Turn off the heat and add half of the chocolate chips and 1 teaspoon vanilla. Mix vigorously to melt the chips.

Use a rubber spatula to remove this yummy, yet hot mixture from the pan and put it in a large bowl. Break open one egg at a time and beat each into the chocolate mixture.

Next, in a separate bowl, stir the flour, baking soda, and salt together. Add this to the chocolate mixture. Fold in the rest of the chocolate chips and all the pecans.

Put this yummy mixture into a nine-inch nonstick baking pan. Spread it evenly so all the brownies will get done at the same time.

Bake the brownies for 25–30 minutes in a 325-degree oven. Beginning at 20 minutes test frequently for doneness. Ovens differ and you don't want to miss out on a good treat. When done let the brownies set until they are cold; otherwise they will fall apart when you try to cut them.

Serves as many people as can "grab" a piece.

Pass out recipes or put one on the overhead. Ask students to identify the parts of your recipe: title, amounts, measurement tools, ingredients, instructions, and so on. Ask what would happen if a particular type of information was left out of a recipe.

2. Bring in a picture of a friend or ask students to bring a picture of one of their friends. Discuss the joys and frustrations that friendships bring. Share a frustration with one relationship. Consider how you keep a relationship growing.

3. Share a friendship recipe you have written and tell why you wrote it. For example, this is one I wrote for my high school friend, Charla.

Recipe for a Long-lasting Friend

From Cherlyn's Heart

For a long-lasting friendship, seriously combine the following ingredients. Pour in at least one quart of togetherness each year. Mix in 10 tsps. assistance and 1 ton patience. Carefully clean up any messes or spills immediately after you make them. Neutralize any sour feelings with honest conversation. Add three cups of commitment. Bake with love. When cool, sprinkle 76 drops of laughter over the top and sides. Enjoy and appreciate every chance we can get.

Serves two.

---

4. Locate some empty cans, plastic containers, and food boxes. Tape on homemade labels such as laughter, patience, trust, loyalty, and honesty. Also bring to class a large bowl and a spoon or electric mixer, measuring cups, eye dropper, etc. If you are so inclined, put on an apron.

Pretend to pour into a bowl a certain amount of each ingredient and stir as you say "These ingredients help make a great friend." Involve students by asking them how much of each ingredient you should add.

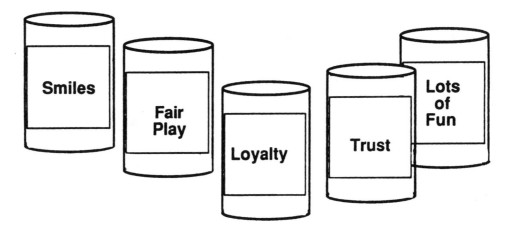

5. Consult your librarian for an attention-getting poem about your lesson the topic.

6. Allow a special occasion such as Valentine's Day, Secretary's Day, Father's or Mother's Day, Grandparents' Day or Bike Safety Week to inspire this lesson.

GROUP BRAINSTORMING

Let's brainstorm ways to build a great friendship or a healthy relationship.

Amounts	Measurement Units	Ingredients/ Qualities	How to Combine
1	cup	sharing	mix
4	tsp.	fun	blend
2	dashes	giving	stir
6	liters/gallon	helping	fold
5	pinches	understanding	pour
8		fair play	
		trust	
		loyalty	

Key Questions

NOTE: The order of the following questions differs from that on the board. Students need to logically choose an ingredient before considering the amount and unit of measurement. Likewise, students choose the action word last so they can think more deeply about what action word is needed for the particular ingredient(s). This modeling matters most for your Advanced Writers who will catch the subtle possibilities that will add depth to their recipes.

1. As you ask the following questions, write students' ideas under the Ingredients/ Qualities column. **What is one ingredient needed for a terrific friendship? What qualities do you need or want in a friend? What ingredients do we need for our recipe? What does a good friend do?**

   What special characteristics do you like most about your current friends? What characteristics does a healthy relationship need? What do you bring to a friendship/relationship?

   (optional) **What spices or seasonings will be needed for a good flavored friendship? What tools are needed?** (such as communication skills)

2. **What units of measurement can we use in this recipe?** (If you want students to use U.S. or metric measurements, point this out before starting.) **What tools do we need to measure the ingredients for our friendship recipe?** Write students' ideas under the Measurement Units column.

Thinking about Mechanics: How do we spell the measurement tool _____?

Volume Measurements: tsp. = teaspoon, tbsp.= tablespoon, cup, pint, qt. = quart, gallon, milliliter, liter

Weight Measurements: oz. = ounce, lb. = pound, microgram, milligram, gram, kilo

Linear Measurements: inch, centimeter, foot, meter, kilometer

Thinking about Mechanics: What punctuation mark needs to be placed after each abbreviation to show that the word has been shortened? (period)

(optional) **What creative words like "sprinkles," "smidgens," "handfuls," or "heartfuls" can we use as measurements?**

3. **How much of each ingredient do we need? How much of a certain quality do you think a friend should have?** Write students' ideas under the Amount column.
What amount of _____ do you think will be needed? What unrealistically large amounts of certain ingredients might a friendship require? What small amounts might be needed? How much is or how many are needed?

4. (optional) **What ingredient can we add that might challenge the relationship? What "negative ingredient" often needs to be dealt with in a friendship? How often?**

   EXAMPLES: Stir in 1 tablespoon misunderstanding for three minutes.
   Carefully clean up any messes or spills immediately after you make them.
   Neutralize any sour feelings with honest conversation.

5. **What action words are used in recipes you know? What action word shall we use to add or combine the ingredients for a great friend?** Repeat these questions until eight to ten action words (verbs) have been captured on the board.
   Post these action words on a wall so students can see them as they brainstorm the directions.

Action Words for Recipes

wash, clean, drain, soak

peel, dice, grate, chop, slice, tear

add, pour, drop, sift, spread, beat, combine, fold in, blend, mix, stir, toss, dissolve, sift, melt, whip, cream, knead, roll, divide, separate, slide, saute, measure

preheat, turn on, brown, steam, simmer, heat, boil, fry, bake, cook, broil, reduce heat, cool, freeze

fill, remove, let stand, wrap, cover, sprinkle, serve

6. (optional) **What needs to be done before starting the recipe?**
How should the ingredients be measured?
How should the recipe be cooled, cooked, or baked?
What temperature?
What can you say about when and how to serve the recipe?
What tips should be remembered by the reader?
What maintenance or clean-up activities could be added to the
instructions for a great friendship or healthy relationship?

7. Keep these brainstormed ideas available to students until after they have composed their rough drafts.

GROUP COMPOSING

Now let's create a Friendship Recipe together.

1. What is the first thing we need to put on a recipe card? What does a recipe's title tell readers? What would be a good title for our friendship recipe? What is our recipe for? Write one title on the board.

(optional) **What could our recipe be about besides friendship? What else might we want to create or maintain?**

Recipe for a Great Friend
from the heart of _____

Making a great friend requires many ingredients. Mix 8 pints sharing and 6 ounces fun in a large bowl for one and a half minutes. Blend in 4 tsp. of understanding; then pick out the negative comments and arguments. Pour in 3 cups giving. Next add 5 pinches thoughtful actions and 1 cup fair play. Stir until lumps (most) are out. Bake frequently for 2 years, then enjoy. Continue to add ingredients as needed. This recipe will help you create a friend for life.

---

2. Out of all of our title ideas, which shall we use? Have a student who doesn't usually participate choose a title. Gently remind students who are disappointed that although their title wasn't selected, they will get to write their own recipe later.

Thinking about Mechanics: What do we need to do to key words in our title?
(capitalize the first letter of each important word)

---

3. We'll add "From the heart of _____." Later you can put your name or skip this part of the recipe under the title. What shall we put for our class recipe? Write this below the title.

4. Next, our recipe needs a topic sentence that tells readers they should follow this recipe. How can we begin our friendship recipe? What shall we say to orient readers who want to develop a great friendship or improve their current relationship? Add one topic sentence to the board.

EXAMPLES: You need the following ingredients to make a great friend.
Making a friend requires lots of hard work.
Keeping or maintaining a friendship is very important.
_____ is my good friend.
For a terrific friendship, combine the following ingredients.
To build an awesome friendship, both people will need to contribute.
This recipe will help you create a friend for life.

5. Let's dream up instructions for each step of preparation. Ask the following questions for each instruction.

a. Which ingredient shall we draft a direction around (first, second, third)? Which ingredient/quality is the most important to include in our friendship recipe? Ask a student who usually doesn't participate to choose an important ingredient.

b. What unit of measurement should we use for this ingredient?

c. What amount do we think is necessary? How much?

d. What action word shall we select to add to or combine with the ingredient needed for a great friend?

e. (optional) **How should this ingredient be added or combined? How should the ingredients be combined? cooled? baked? stored?** (adverbs)

add

a

drop

(optional) **When/How long should this/these ingredient(s) be _____? When should the ingredients be combined? cooled? baked? stored?** (also adverbs)

EXAMPLES: *Slowly* pour in 3 liters of horsing around and mix *carefully.*
Quickly sift the ingredients and bake *until golden brown.*
Vigorously boil 8 drops of challenge and 4 years of activities.
Soak in a gallon of laughter *until all disagreements* have dissolved.
After the mixture gets easy to manage, put it into the refrigerator.

f. How can we put all of these ideas (a–e) into one direction?

g. (optional) **What related ingredient could we add to this direction?**

EXAMPLES: Add 5 pinches of fair play.
Blend in 4 tsp. of understanding, *but* remember to _____.
Pour in 3 cups giving, *yet* _____.

Thinking about Mechanics: What words (coordinating conjunctions) can we use to connect ingredients? (and, but, or, yet, so, nor, for)

6. **Which of our ideas for creating a great friendship should we suggest next?** Repeat each part of step 4 until at least three ingredients are added to the group recipe. **What words can we use to tell readers the order of our directions?**

> **Thinking about Mechanics:** What time order words can we use to help our readers understand the sequence of the instructions? (first, second, third, fourth, fifth, next, then, after that, following that, finally, etc.)

7. **What directions have we left out? What other instructions would be helpful to someone wanting to make or keep a friend?** Add these ideas to the group composition.

8. **Now we need to add a final comment that encourages the recipient to take action. What can we say to encourage the reader to try the recipe? How could we sum up or close our friendship recipe?** If students are beginning writers, offer several examples. Add a final comment to the group composition.

    EXAMPLES: This recipe will help you create a friend for life.
    If you find a person with the above ingredients, you will have a friend for life.
    You are my best friend in the world.
    I'm the luckiest person in the universe because you are my friend.
    If you build a friendship from these ingredients, it will provide you with loving nourishment for many years.

9. **Let's reread our recipe to decide if we have forgotten anything.**

INDIVIDUAL BRAINSTORMING & COMPOSING

Invite students to create their own Friendship Recipe for a friend or potential friend (*audience*) to help develop or maintain a friendship (*purpose*). Encourage students to tailor their recipes to fit their particular readers. Point out that everyone's recipe will be unique because each of us is special. Pass out copies of "Action Words for Recipes." (This reproducible can be found at the end of this lesson.)

Have students begin by choosing the person with whom they want to share their thoughts. Ask students to jot down three or four names of people as you ask these questions: Who is someone you know who might like a friendship recipe? For whom is your recipe?

Beginning Writers   Encourage Beginning Writers to include a title, a beginning or ending sentence, ingredients; but don't require instructions.

Friendship Recipe
from the heart of Jason

For a good friend combine these ingredients.
1/2 tsp. of understanding
2 liters of forgiveness
800 pinches of laughter
3 cups of loyalty
790 pounds of fun
a kilo of fair play
Corey, this recipe will make us pals for life.

Advanced Writers   Advanced Writers can be encouraged to compose more instructions (eight to ten) that create a powerful feeling about true friendship. Ask questions to help students order their instructions thoughtfully.

As students begin brainstorming and drafting their own recipes, walk around the classroom praising healthy ingredients and clear instructions. Ask students to read their friendship recipes aloud to you to see if they are easy to understand and make sense.

RESPONDING TO STUDENTS' WRITINGS/REVISING

1. As each student finishes his or her rough draft, supply a Revising Assistant to support students' revising efforts. The Revising Assistant can be found at the end of this lesson. Instruct students to evaluate each part of their Friendship Recipe and place a check by each point that is present.

Revising Assistant for Friendship Recipe

____ Has a title been placed at the top in the center of the paper?

____ Are the important words in the title capitalized?

____ Has an introduction been included?

____ Does each instruction begin with an action verb?

____ Are you using a variety of verbs to describe how your recipe should be mixed, served, or enjoyed?

____ Does each instruction start with a capital letter and end with a period?

____ Does your recipe include ingredients that make your relationships special?

____ Has an amount and a measurement tool been included for each ingredient?

____ Do the amounts of each ingredient make sense? Do they reflect what is really needed for a good friendship?

____ Has each measurement abbreviation been spelled correctly? Does it end with a period?

____ Has a final comment been added to your Friendship Recipe?

---

2. After step 1 is completed, ask each student to revise and refine his/her recipe.

3. As students finish the self-check, ask them to find a revising partner, exchange recipes, and read one person's recipe aloud to determine if the instructions are clear and helpful for the reader. The partners should tell which (recipe) instructions they liked and offer one or two suggestions regarding how to make the recipe easier to understand. Then switch roles.

    Advanced Writers should consider what to eliminate or add to the recipe and how to improve the introduction and conclusion of their recipes.

4. After the partner check is completed, ask each student to respond by making at least two improvements to his/her recipe. If time allows, ask students to share or show their revising partner the improvements that were made.

PUBLISHING

After students finish revising their Friendship Recipes, explain that they'll publish them on special name border paper (*format*) or inside a folded paper knot (*format*) so that their friends or family members (*audience*) will know how much their friendship means (*purpose*) and how to make the friendship even better (*purpose*). Here are two publishing format ideas; they can be used alone or together.

Name Border Paper

Have students carefully rewrite the revised Friendship Recipe within the borders of the special friendship paper provided at the end of this lesson. Then students can frame their Friendship Recipe by writing the recipient's first name all around the border of the paper.

If you want students to be more precise in how they write the recipient's name, you can give the following directions:

1. Write the first name of the recipient on the line across the top and under the line at the bottom of the Friendship Recipe paper.

2. Turn the paper 90 degrees to the right and write the name on the line across the top and under the line at the bottom. This will put the recipient's name in an easy-to-read position all the way around the border.

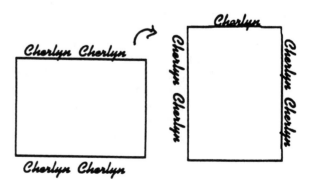

Friendship Knot

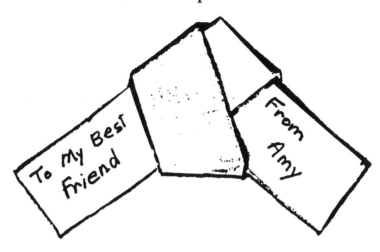

Have students carefully rewrite the revised Friendship Recipe on the special friendship recipe paper provided at the end of this lesson and sign and date it. Then follow these steps:

1. Fold the paper in half vertically and crease.

NOTE: If students want to fold the paper horizontally in step 1, they need to fold the paper in half instead of thirds when they get to step 2. All the other directions are the same.

2. Continue by folding the remaining paper in three equal parts and crease each fold.

3. Fold the remaining paper in half again and crease this fold. This should result in a strip of paper approximately 7/8-inch wide.

4. Now rub the folded strip over the edge of a table or desk to "soften" the strip and make it more flexible.

5. Fold the left and right ends toward the middle. The right end should be longer.

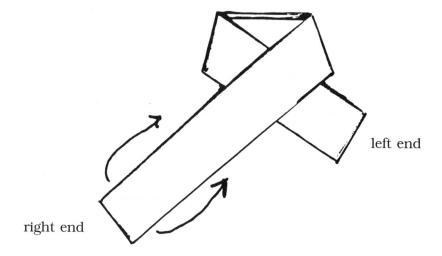

6. Guide the right end backward and up through the hole. Gently tighten the knot by pulling on both ends. Flatten the knot as you pull both ends.

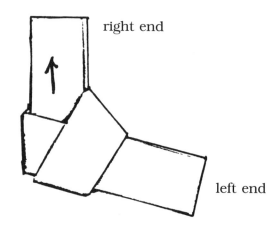

7. Write "To: _____" on one end and "From: _____" on the other end of the friendship knot.

Chocolate Lovers' Deluxe Brownies

1/3 cup butter
3/4 cup sugar
1 tsp. vanilla
2 large eggs

3/4 cup flour
1/4 tsp. baking soda
12-oz. package chocolate chips
3/4 cup chopped pecans

Blend sugar, butter, and two tablespoons water in a small pan. Heat until it bubbles furiously. Turn off the heat and add half of the chocolate chips and 1 teaspoon vanilla. Mix vigorously to melt the chips.

Use a rubber spatula to remove this yummy, yet hot mixture from the pan and put it in a large bowl. Break open one egg at a time and beat each into the chocolate mixture.

Next, in a separate bowl, stir the flour, baking soda, and salt together. Add this to the chocolate mixture. Fold in the rest of the chocolate chips and all the pecans.

Put this yummy mixture into a nine-inch nonstick baking pan. Spread it evenly so all the brownies will get done at the same time.

Bake the brownies for 25–30 minutes in a 325-degree oven. Beginning at 20 minutes test frequently for doneness. Ovens differ and you don't want to miss out on a good treat. When done let the brownies set until they are cold; otherwise they will fall apart when you try to cut them.

Serves as many people as can "grab" a piece.

Action Words for Recipes

wash, clean, drain, soak

peel, dice, grate, chop, slice, tear

add, pour, drop, sift, spread, beat,
combine, fold in, blend, mix, stir, toss,
dissolve, sift, melt, whip, cream, knead,
roll, divide, separate, slide, saute,
measure

preheat, turn on, brown, steam, simmer, heat,
boil, fry, bake, cook, broil, reduce heat, cool, freeze

fill, remove, let stand, wrap, cover, sprinkle, serve

© 2000 Cherlyn Sunflower

Action Words for Recipes

wash, clean, drain, soak

peel, dice, grate, chop, slice, tear

add, pour, drop, sift, spread, beat,
combine, fold in, blend, mix, stir, toss,
dissolve, sift, melt, whip, cream, knead,
roll, divide, separate, slide, saute,
measure

preheat, turn on, brown, steam, simmer, heat,
boil, fry, bake, cook, broil, reduce heat, cool, freeze

fill, remove, let stand, wrap, cover, sprinkle, serve

Revising Assistant for Friendship Recipe

_____ Has a title been placed at the top in the center of the paper?

_____ Are the important words in the title capitalized?

_____ Has an introduction been included?

_____ Does each instruction begin with an action verb?

_____ Are you using a variety of verbs to describe how your recipe should be mixed, served, or enjoyed?

_____ Does each instruction start with a capital letter and end with a period?

_____ Does your recipe include ingredients that make your relationships special?

_____ Has an amount and a measurement tool been included for each ingredient?

_____ Do the amounts of each ingredient make sense? Do they reflect what is really needed for a good friendship?

_____ Has each measurement abbreviation been spelled correctly? Does it end with a period?

_____ Has a final comment been added to your Friendship Recipe?

- -

Revising Assistant for Friendship Recipe

_____ Has a title been placed at the top in the center of the paper?

_____ Are the important words in the title capitalized?

_____ Has an introduction been included?

_____ Does each instruction begin with an action verb?

_____ Are you using a variety of verbs to describe how your recipe should be mixed, served, or enjoyed?

_____ Does each instruction start with a capital letter and end with a period?

_____ Does your recipe include ingredients that make your relationships special?

_____ Has an amount and a measurement tool been included for each ingredient?

_____ Do the amounts of each ingredient make sense? Do they reflect what is really needed for a good friendship?

_____ Has each measurement abbreviation been spelled correctly? Does it end with a period?

_____ Has a final comment been added to your Friendship Recipe?

Friendship Recipe

From the heart of _____

LESSON 15

Travel Directions

OUTCOME   Each student will compose oral or written instructions for getting from a familiar place to an unknown place.

MOTIVATORS

1. Tell students they are going to make a travel directory for new students and visitors to your classroom, school, or city. This way new students (*audience*) can find the places they are looking for more easily (*purpose*).

2. Talk about being lost and how you (or the person) felt.

3. Explain that before there were maps, people had to rely on oral directions. State that giving clear directions is important and quite challenging. Invite students to see if your directions are clear enough to lead them to a particular destination.

    Ask your students to close their eyes. Then give them *very poor* directions for getting from one familiar place to a destination in your school. Here are two examples you can use as models.

Poor Directions:
Leave the classroom and turn left. Walk to the largest hallway and turn right. Go until you reach the doors where a lot of people are going in and out.

Better Directions:
To get to the school office, leave the classroom and turn left. Walk down the hall until you get to the first intersecting hallway. You will see a soda machine, restrooms, and commons area. Turn right and continue down the hall to room 218. Room 218 is on the left, has large double doors, and there are usually many people going in and out. You've reached our school office.

When you finish sharing each example that you created, ask students to guess the destination in your school. Explain that if your directions were clear and complete, everyone should have ended up at the correct location.

Now share your destination. Ask students which of your directions helped and which hindered finding the correct spot/location. Guide students to see that specific distances, landmarks, and clear directions are necessary, especially when the listener or reader is unfamiliar with the area.

4. Lay a city map on the floor and ask students to stand around it to get a "bird's-eye view" of a particular area. Point out the compass rose or direction symbol and ask them what these symbols mean. Ask which way is north, west, and so forth on the map. Also point out the distance scale.

Give small groups of students city maps and ask where local parks, restaurants, businesses, and schools are located and perhaps the approximate distances to various places. Have students use their maps to answer these and other questions.

GROUP BRAINSTORMING

Before you begin this lesson, choose a location for direction-giving based on how sophisticated your writers are and how much working knowledge they have of this area. Usually the easiest location is the classroom because students can see the destination as they write. Next in difficulty is to write directions for your school; students can compose their directions and then try out the directions during revising. More difficult is writing directions for the city or town in which students live. Directions to other places in the state can be even more difficult to compose.

Today, we will be making a travel directory or destination file for new students and visitors to our classroom, school, city, or state so they can find places they want and feel more comfortable here.

Key Questions

1. **What are some destinations in our school/city that a new student might *need* to reach? What is another destination? Where might the person want to go?** Repeat these questions until five to six student ideas have been written on the board. Praise interesting or valuable destinations. Choose one location.

2. **Of all our destinations, for which shall we write directions?** Have an uninvolved student select one idea. Circle this idea and use it all the way through group brainstorming and composing.

3. **Where might the student begin? What might be a familiar starting point?**
Repeat these questions until several students' ideas have been written on the
board. Have an uninvolved student select one starting point. Circle this idea and
use it throughout group composing.

4. **Of all our possible starting points, which one would be logical? Which one is
an easy place to find?** Have an uninvolved student select one idea. Circle this idea
and use it all the way through group brainstorming and composing.

5. **How will the new student get to the destination we chose? What types of
transportation will the new student use? Will the new students walk, bike,
drive, or ride?** Repeat these questions until several student ideas have been written on the board. Have an uninvolved student select one way to travel. Circle this
idea and use it as distances and landmarks are chosen. If students are composing
directions for the classroom or the school, walking/moving slowly may be the only
alternative.

6. **Which way should the person go first? How far should he/she go in that direction? What landmark would be helpful to someone who doesn't know the
way?** As students respond, add this information underneath the correct brainstorming categories: direction, distance, and landmark. Notice that the board is
set up so that information related to one direction is across on the same horizontal line. Just capture words or phrases; complete sentences will be composed later
in the group composing section of the lesson plan.

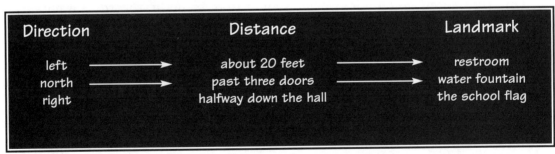

7. **Which direction should he or she travel now? How far? What is an easy landmark to spot between _____ and _____?** As students respond, add this information underneath the correct brainstorming categories: direction, distance, and
landmark. **When should the person change directions?** Continue this three-part
questioning until the destination is "reached."

GROUP COMPOSING

Let's create travel directions to _____ (the destination chosen earlier) **as a group.**

1. **Let's write a title first: Directions for Getting to** _____ **. What is the destination that we chose?** Insert the previously chosen destination in the title.

> ### Directions for Getting to the Moorhead Pool
>
> To get to the Moorhead swimming pool, begin at the Junior High. First go south on 12th Street until you see the Dairy Queen. Next turn right and go straight until you see the high school. It should be about 3 blocks.
>
> When you see the high school, look for the brick path. At the end of the path is Moorhead's swimming pool. Enjoy.

2. **How shall we begin our directions so that the new students and visitors will know both the destination and where to start? Where should the new student or visitor begin?** If students are less experienced writers or speakers, share the following topic sentences. Then ask students what information should be inserted.

   EXAMPLES: To get to your destination, follow these directions.
   To get to _____ begin at _____ and keep following these directions.
   To get to _____ from _____, follow my directions.
   If you like/need _____, follow these directions to _____.

   Before writing a topic sentence on the board, ask students how to start a new paragraph.

   > **Thinking about Mechanics:** What should I do to the first word in a paragraph to show that we are going to share a new idea? (indent)

3. Reproduce or post the "Time Order," "Direction Words," and "Action Words" charts that can be found at the end of this lesson so students can refer to them during brainstorming and later during composing.

4. Comment that the directions need to be clear, complete, and in the correct order so the listener or reader can find the destination instead of getting lost. **Where should we tell the person to go first? What direction? How far? What landmark will the person see to indicate he or she is on the right track?** As students provide this information, add it in sentence form to the group composition on the board. Praise directions that contain direction, distance, and landmark.

   > **Thinking about Mechanics:** Which of our landmarks are special names for particular places? How do we show our readers? (capitalize the first letter of each word)

Words Used in Travel Directions

Time Order Words

first	next	finally
second	then	at least
third	after that	
fourth		

Direction and Location Words

left, right
north, south, east, west
straight ahead, across,
around, by, through,
up, down, over, under, last

in front of, behind, on top of,
outside, inside, in, into,
above, past, beside, below,
beyond, near, between, near,
against, before, beneath

Action Words

Go to _____	Just after _____	Turn left/right on _____
Go around _____	Cross _____	Keep _____ until _____
Go past/by _____	Look for _____	Stay on _____ until _____
Pass _____	Before _____	At _____
Continue _____	Follow _____ to _____	

5. **How shall we start the next direction?** If the student creating the direction doesn't include a time order word, point to the chart and/or suggest one.

6. **How far should the new student go? What landmark will the new student see if he or she is on the correct path?** As students provide this information, add it in sentence form to the group composition on the board. Praise directions that contain direction, distance, and landmark.

7. **After reaching _____, which direction should he or she go? How far? What landmark is close by?** If the student creating the direction doesn't include a direction word, ask another student for a suggestion.

8. **Which way should he or she go next? How far? What landmark?** Repeat this pattern of questioning until the destination is reached. **What is the next thing the person should do?**

9. **What can we say to tell the new student he or she has arrived at the destination?** If students need assistance, share one or two examples of ways to end oral or written directions.

   EXAMPLES: When you see (the landmark) you will be at your destination.
   Your destination will be at the end of the road.

INDIVIDUAL BRAINSTORMING & COMPOSING

Now you will get to select a destination, brainstorm, and then compose your own travel directions. Later, we will gather all the travel directions into a travel directory or destination file for new students and visitors.

As students begin brainstorming their own travel directions, walk around the classroom noting interesting destinations, useful starting points, and clear and complete directions with accurate distances and easy-to-find landmarks. Make sure students brainstorm before beginning to write.

Ask questions to help students organize their directions and evaluate how complete and accurate the directions are.

RESPONDING TO STUDENTS' WRITINGS/REVISING

1. As students finish the rough drafts of their travel directions, ask them to find a revising partner. Have one student read his/her travel directions aloud to the peer to see if the directions have all the important information and if the directions are in the correct order, complete, and accurate. Ask students why the directions need to be clear, complete, and in the correct order. (so the listener or reader can find the destination instead of getting lost)

2. Encourage students to make two to three specific comments on what they like and offer suggestions for how to help make sure the directions can be easily followed and what needs to be added, reordered, or eliminated.

   NOTE: If writing directions for town/city, compose a note asking parents for their cooperation in trying out the travel directions. Ask parents, an older sibling, or a neighbor if they would escort their son or daughter and follow the directions exactly, helping him/her to make additions and corrections on the rough draft.

3. Require each writer to make at least one or two revisions to improve the travel directions before giving them to a new student or visitor to use.

   NOTE: Travel directions do not have to be perfect; they rarely are!

4. Finally, before publishing the travel directions, have students trade compositions and look for punctuation, capitalization, spelling, and other errors that might hinder a traveler in reaching his/her destination.

PUBLISHING

After students finish revising their travel directions, explain that they'll be published in a Travel Directory or Destination File (*format*) to be placed in the school office or library so that new students who need directions to particular locations (*audience*) can get to the right spot without undue stress (*purpose*).

Travel Directory

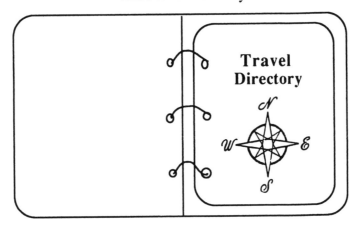

Materials

three-ring notebook, lined paper, hole punch

Directions

1. Print or type the directions or use a word processor.

2. Insert in the binder.

3. Add a cover page and index.

If students are interested and money is available, make copies of the travel directory for each student to use.

Consider allowing students to sell copies to other students and/or members of the community as a way to raise money for future writing projects. Seek approval of school officials before proceeding in any fund-raising activity.

Destination File

Materials

4 × 6-inch or 5 × 7-inch index cards, recipe file

Directions

1. Add a title on a title card.

2. Print or type directions and the title card on index cards and insert in the card file. If students use a computer, have them set margins to fit the index card. Once information has been processed, cut out travel directions and paste on an index card with rubber cement.

3. Have an advanced student type a table of contents on index card(s) for the whole file.

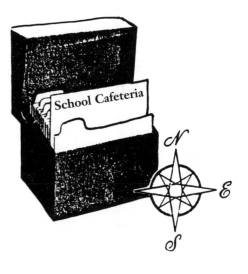

Travel Directions Brainstorming Guide

Destinations	Starting Points	Ways to Travel	Directions	Distances	Landmarks

Lesson 16

Cheer-up Checklist

OUTCOME   Each student will create a checklist for cheering someone who is unhappy, discouraged, or lonely.

Checklists can be made by students for any area of school or personal life. A few ideas include:

- how to orient a new student to the classroom and school

- how to have a safe playground

- steps for getting quietly to a lunchroom

- how to use a microscope correctly

- how to make a graph or divide two-digit numbers

- ways to interview a businessperson in the community about recycling efforts

- how to create survey questions for collecting a neighbor's views on a current issue

These checklists will need brainstorming categories unique for the task.

MOTIVATORS

1. Lead a discussion about feeling sad, discouraged, unhappy, or lonely. Ask questions such as:

     When was the last time you felt sad?
     What do you do when you are discouraged?
     What did you do to cheer yourself up?
     How do you get out of "the dumps"?
     How do you distract yourself from your problems?

2. Invite students to share things they've done for people who felt sad, lonely, or discouraged.

3. Suggest that when sadness continues for a long time or is getting in the way of school and family, the student should discuss those feelings with a trusted adult.

Words Used in Travel Directions

Time Order Words

first   next   finally
second   then   at least
third   after that
fourth

Direction and Location Words

left, right

north, south, east, west

straight ahead, across,

around, by, through,

up, down, over, under, last

in front of, behind, on top of,

outside, inside, in, into,

above, past, beside, below,

beyond, near, between, near,

against, before, beneath

Action Words

Go to _____   Just after _____   Turn left/right on ___

Go around _____   Cross _____   Keep _____ until ____

Go past/by _____   Look for _____   Stay on _____ until _

Pass _____   Before _____   At _____

Continue _____   Follow _____ to _____

GROUP BRAINSTORMING

Let's brainstorm ways to cheer up someone who is sad or discouraged.

Key Questions

1. **Who is someone we know who is feeling "down in the dumps," sad, or "down hearted"? Who needs to be cheered up? Who is feeling discouraged or disappointed?** Repeat these questions until eight to ten ideas have been written on the board under the Who column.

2. **Out of all of these people, for which person do we want to create a cheer-up list?** Have a student who doesn't usually participate choose someone most students know. Circle this person's name and use it all the way through group brainstorming. Gently remind students who are disappointed that although their person wasn't selected, they will get to write their own cheer-up list later.

3. **How is this person feeling? How would you feel if you had this person's problems?** Repeat these questions until four to six ideas have been written on the board.
   If you would like to expand students' vocabulary, a list of words for negative feelings can be found at the end of this lesson. Select several words and ask volunteers to explain what the feeling means. After discussing six to eight, ask students which of these words or new words that came to students' minds "fit" this situation.

Who	Feelings	Do Alone	Do with Someone
flood victims	discouraged	write	have a party
Mrs. Jacks	worried	read	shop
(our principal)	stressed	run	talk
		sing	swim

4. **What healthy things can a person do *alone* to put him or her in a positive mood? What music/musical instrument could you play?** Repeat these questions until five or six students' ideas have been written on the board under the Do Alone column. Point out that suggestions must be appropriate for the person who will receive the checklist or the suggestions won't be used.
   Where could someone go to forget his/her troubles? What is something silly the person could do that would put you in a playful state of mind? Repeat these questions until five or six students' ideas have been written on the board.
   What "crazy" but safe activity could you do to forget your troubles? Repeat these questions until five or six students' ideas have been written on the board.
   What is something inexpensive that our person could purchase to help him/her feel better? Repeat these questions until five or six students' ideas have been written on the board.

5. **What can you do with someone else that would put you in a positive frame of mind? What activities can you do *with someone* to cheer yourself?**

    What game could you play together? What hobby or sport could be pursued with another person? Who could you contact/call? Repeat these questions until about eight students' ideas have been written on the board under the Do with Someone column.

6. **What special activity can we suggest that the reader could do for someone else? What fun but useful activity could the person do for others? What is something a person who is discouraged could say to someone else that would make everyone feel better?** Repeat these questions until about three students' ideas have been written on the board under the Do for Others column.

Do for Others	Say to Yourself
volunteer	I'm O.K. I'm strong enough to handle this
smile	things will get better
do yard work	keep my head up

7. **What is something the reader could say to cheer *him-/herself* up? What silly suggestions could we make that might never happen, but will make the reader smile anyway?** Repeat these questions until about ten students' ideas have been written on the board under the Say to Yourself column.

GROUP COMPOSING

Now let's create a Cheer-up Checklist together.

Cheer-up Checklist for _____

____ 1. Read an exciting poem to one of the kindergarten classes.
____ 2. Go swimming with our class or garage-sale shopping with a friend.
____ 3. Host a pizza lunch for all the teachers and staff. Pig out!
____ 4.
____ 5.

1. **For whom is our checklist?** Add this information to the title.

   Note: To be meaningful introductions need to be written after the suggestions are created in steps 2 and 3.

   > **Thinking about Mechanics:** What do we need to do to people's names or important words in a title? (capitalize the first letter)

2. **Let's number the ideas we brainstormed according to their usefulness. Which suggestion is one that really has the best chance of helping _____ ?** Put a number 1 by it. While students think, write this suggestion after number 1 on the checklist.

3. **Which of our ideas should we suggest next?** Repeat step 2 until at least three to five suggestions are added to the group cheer-up list.

   > **Thinking about Mechanics:** What kind of word should each suggestion begin with? (a verb or action word)

4. **Now we need to create an opening statement or introduction that explains what the recipient should do with the checklist. What feeling words did we think _____ was having?** Direct students to the feeling words generated in step 3 of group brainstorming.

   How can we introduce our suggestions to the reader in a positive way? Add students' ideas to the checklist. If students are Beginning Writers, give an example.

   Examples: Feeling _____ ? No energy? Need a boost?
   There is no reason to stay _____.
   This checklist will help you deal with your problems in a healthy way.

Cheer-up Checklist for Our Principal

If you are feeling sad, discouraged, or in a negative frame of mind, try a few of these suggestions. Check off each idea as you try it. Post this checklist where it is easy to find.

_____ 1. Read an exciting poem to one of the kindergarten classes.

_____ 2. Go swimming with our class or garage-sale shopping with a friend.

~~~~~~

_____ 8. Host a pizza lunch for all the teachers and staff. Pig out!

There is no reason to stay discouraged. Try some of my suggestions NOW. You'll feel much better. Place a star by the ideas that work for you so you can remember them. Post this Cheer-up Checklist where it is easy to find when you need it in the future.

5. **Now we need to add a final comment or conclusion that encourages the recipient to take action. What can we say to encourage the reader to try the suggestions? to take action?** Add these ideas to the checklist. If students are Beginning Writers, suggest a final comment.

   EXAMPLES: There is no reason to stay _____. Act now!
   Start feeling better today. Post this checklist where it is easy to read.
   Try one of our suggestions TODAY! Check them off as you try them.
   Try our suggestions NOW. Don't delay.
   Do one suggestion each day until you feel better.

INDIVIDUAL BRAINSTORMING & COMPOSING

Tell students that now they get to create their own Cheer-up Checklists to help you or someone else who is sad or discouraged (*audience*) to become better/more cheerful (*purpose*). Pass out copies of the Cheer-up Checklist at the end of this lesson or have students compose on their own paper. Remind students to choose the person who they want to cheer before they begin brainstorming.

As students begin brainstorming and drafting their own Cheer-up Checklists, walk around the classroom praising healthy suggestions that are appropriate for the person who will receive the checklist. Encourage "tried and true" suggestions from their own personal experiences (i.e., activities that have cheered them up when they were discouraged). This will encourage students to be kind to others and promote positive self-esteem.

RESPONDING TO STUDENTS' WRITINGS/REVISING

1. As each student finishes his/her rough draft, ask students to self-edit/check their Cheer-up Checklist using the Revising Assistant. A reproducible copy may be found at the end of this lesson.

Revising Assistant

_____ Has the name of the person been placed in the title of the checklist?
_____ Is the name of this particular person capitalized?

_____ Have feeling words been added to the opening sentence comment?
_____ Has the rest of the introduction been included?
_____ (advanced) Have you written your own introduction?

_____ Does each item on the checklist begin with a line or check-off box?
_____ Does a number begin each suggestion? Is the number followed by a period?
_____ Does each statement begin with an action or "doing" verb?
_____ Does each statement start with a capital letter and end with a period?

_____ Has a final comment or conclusion been added to the checklist
      that encourages the reader to take action?
_____ Has one or more feeling words been added to the final comment?

_____
                Signature

---

2. After step 1 is completed, require each student to revise and improve his/her checklist.

3. As students finish the self-edit, ask them to find a revising partner, exchange checklists, and read one person's list aloud to the other person to determine if the suggestions are *healthy* and *cheerful*. The partners should share which suggestions they liked and offer one or two ideas regarding how to make the checklist more helpful or cheerful. Advanced Writers should also consider what to eliminate or add to the checklist. Switch roles and repeat.

4. After step 3 is completed, require each student to respond by making at least two improvements to his/her checklist. Advanced Writers should also review and improve their introduction and conclusion of the checklist.

5. Have Advanced Writers recopy or word-process their revised checklist(s) on a clean sheet of paper and sign and date it before it is published. Allow Beginning Writers to clean up their draft and use this for publication.

PUBLISHING

Allow students time to read and enjoy (*purpose*) each other's (*audience*) cheer-up lists.

NOTE: Some students may want to keep their lists private.

Next, share the Cheer-up Checklists with the selected person, friends, and family members (*audience*) who need to enjoy life (*purpose*). Send the original with the student to share with the person who needs immediate support. Save a copy for the checklist writer (*audience*) for a low moment (*purpose*).

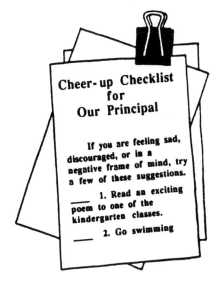

Consider saving one copy of each Cheer-up Checklist in a class book that can be pulled out on a "rainy" or challenging day.

Cheer-up Checklist
for

_____

_____ 1. _____

_____

_____ 2. _____

_____

_____ 3. _____

_____

_____ 4. _____

_____

_____ 5. _____

_____

_____ 6. _____

_____

_____ 7. _____

_____

_____

(Signature of Creator)

Words for Negative Feelings

Afraid
Angry
Annoyed
Anxious
Ashamed
Bashful
Betrayed
Bitter
Bored
Cheated
Crabby
Crushed
Defeated
Disappointed
Discouraged
Disgusted
Embarrassed

Exasperated
Exhausted
Fearful
Frightened
Frustrated
Helpless
Homesick
Horrible
Hurt
Ignored
Irritated
Jealous
Left out
Lonely
Mad
Miserable
Nervous

Outraged
Overwhelmed
Panicked
Pressured
Rejected
Sad
Scared
Stupid
Tense
Terrified
Tired
Ugly
Uncomfortable
Upset
Worried

Revising Assistant

____ Has the name of the person been placed in the title of the checklist?

____ Is the name of this particular person capitalized?

____ Have feeling words been added to the opening sentence comment?

____ Has the rest of the introduction been included?

____ (advanced) Have you written your own introduction?

____ Does each item on the checklist begin with a line or check-off box?

____ Does a number begin each suggestion? Is the number followed by a period?

____ Does each statement begin with an action or "doing" verb?

____ Does each statement start with a capital letter and end with a period?

____ Has a final comment or conclusion been added to the checklist that encourages the reader to take action?

____ Has one or more feeling words been added to the final comment?

_____
Signature

LESSON 17

Medical Guide

OUTCOME Each student will compile ideas and write self-care tips for use by self and peers.

MOTIVATORS

Teach this lesson during the cold and flu season or when a student is ill or has had an accident.

1. Come to class coughing and sneezing and/or limping using a crutch with a bandage on your arm, head, or leg. Bring props such as a box of tissues, a thermometer, cough drops, and a can of chicken noodle soup. Read the poem "Sick" by Shel Silverstein.

   Consider acting out the poem as you read it. For example, shake your head left and right in a "No, No" fashion as you read "I cannot go to school . . ." and hold your back and point to your ankle when you read: "My back is wrenched, my ankle's sprained." Complain of other ailments such as losing your hair, a broken leg, or other problems seeing that prevent you from doing something you don't want to do. (See the list of Health Problems at the end of this lesson for ideas.) Have fun.

2. Ask students to role-play various illnesses/accidents for your class. Put students into teams of two or three. Assign each team an illness or accident. (See the list of Health Problems at the end of this lesson for role-play ideas.) Ask one student from each team to role-play one of these illnesses or accidents and how to treat it. Team members can help by offering suggestions.

   For example, a student could role-play having a headache by putting a hand on his/her head and showing pain on his/her face. Then reach for an imaginary bottle of aspirin, pour out two imaginary pills, fill an imaginary glass with imaginary water, and pretend to swallow the medicine. The actor could continue by holding his/her head and rubbing it until finally he/she demonstrates through facial expressions that he/she is feeling better.

   Challenge the class to guess which illness/accident is being acted out. Repeat until all teams have had a chance.

3. Share that your class is going to create a medical self-care guide of advice and home remedies for use by students in the class or at school so they'll be able to figure out what their illness/injury is and how to get well as soon as possible. Point out that the first rule is "Stay calm, use good judgment, and seek assistance of a responsible adult as soon as possible."

4. Share some home remedies you use personally. For example: "When I have a bad headache, I fill a plastic bag with ice, turn off the lights, lie my neck on a bag of ice, close my eyes, and take a nap." Ask students what they do when they burn their fingers or get hiccups.

Ask how students acquired the information they believe to be useful. Discuss what makes good self-care or useful advice. Comment that since many students will use our Self-Care Guides, we'll need to be careful to give good advice.

- Scaring a person or drinking water upside down, for example, to get rid of the hiccups is very poor advice.

- Here are two useful pieces of advice to stop hiccups. (1) Hold one's breath because it relaxes the muscles in your diaphragm. (2) Breathe into a paper bag held over your nose and mouth. The bag collects carbon dioxide which is discarded by a person's body during breathing. Breathing carbon dioxide causes the malfunctioning nerve in the person's diaphragm to relax.

GROUP BRAINSTORMING

Now, we will brainstorm ideas for a medical self-care guide. Record student responses on the board or overhead for use during group composing. Keep these brainstormed ideas available to students until after they have composed their rough drafts.

Key Questions

1. **What illness or medical problem have you had? What types of illnesses are occurring at this time of year? What injury has someone you know had?** Pause for at least 30 seconds to give students time to think. Write their ideas under the "Health Problems" column. Praise less frequent or interesting problems. After 10–15 health problems are listed, have an uninvolved student choose one and use it throughout the rest of this lesson. If students have trouble generating medical problems, give them the list of health problems.

Health Problems	Symptoms	Treatment	Prevention
flu	bleeding	cold cloths	moisture in winter
chicken pox	broken?	ice	don't pick your nose!
(nosebleed)	frightened	lay head back	
broken arm	weak	pinch nose	
head cold		tell an adult	
		sit up	
		apply pressure to side of nose	
		rest, stay calm	

2. **What symptoms might the person have? How does the person feel? How long has the person been feeling ill? Where would the person hurt/feel pain? How did you know you had _____? were sick/hurt? Which body part(s) would be affected? What should be examined?** After each question, pause for at least 30 seconds to give students time to think. Write their ideas under the "Symptoms" column. Praise valuable symptoms.

3. **How should this illness/injury be treated? What secret cures or home remedies might help? What can a person do/try to make him-/herself feel better or relieve the pain? What would speed up healing? What should be done until help arrives?** Pause for at least 30 seconds to give students time to think. Write their ideas under the "Treatment" column. Praise useful treatments and remedies.

    What do most people have at home to cure this? What common household materials or products are needed? What special food or drink is useful? How should this home remedy be administered? Write students' ideas under the "Treatment" column.

    How long will it take to treat? How long will it be before it will heal? When should the person seek help or see a doctor (immediately or only after symptoms persist or get worse)? What special exercises or physical therapy will help? Write these ideas under the "Treatment" column.

4. (optional) **What caused this illness or accident?**

5. **How could this illness/injury be prevented in the future? What precautions could someone take to prevent future illness or injury? What causes the problem? What early warning signs should be noticed? What lifestyle changes might help?** (eat healthy foods, wear a helmet, exercise, etc.) After each question, pause for at least 30 seconds to give students time to think. Write their ideas under the "Prevention" column. Praise thoughtful prevention ideas.

GROUP COMPOSING

Let's create one entry in our medical self-care guide together. Involve students in choosing ideas from the brainstormed lists and organizing them into paragraphs.

> ### How to Treat a Nosebleed
>
> Nosebleeds are common. You should not be frightened if you get a nosebleed. Stay calm and don't try to blow your nose. Pinch your nostrils shut for five or ten minutes while you breathe through your mouth. Apply cold cloths to your nose. If the nosebleed doesn't stop, you can apply ice to your nose.
>
> If you think you may have broken your nose, see a doctor. Tell your parents. Preventing a nosebleed can be difficult to do.

1. **First, let's choose one illness or accident to write about as a group before you write your own advice.** Choose an illness or accident that might be more difficult to do and circle it.

2. **Our medical advice needs to name the illness or injury about which we'll write.** Explain that we'll use the title *Medical Self-Care Guide*, *Self-Care Tips*, *Get-Well Guide*, or *Heal the Hurt* for the class book, but we need a title for each health problem.

   What should our chapter title(s) be? Pause for at least 30 seconds to give students time to think. Ask a quiet or withdrawn student to select a good title.

   NOTE: The word "best" was not used since it can promote interclass conflict.

   EXAMPLES: How to Treat _____
   _____: A Serious/Minor Health Problem

   > **Thinking about Mechanics:** What should I do to important words in the title? (capitalize)

3. **How can we introduce our health problems? How can each health problem be introduced to the reader?** Explain that the topic sentence should introduce the health problem that will be addressed. After hearing several topic sentences, Advanced Writers can brainstorm their own introductory sentence. Provide several possible topic sentences as examples.

   EXAMPLES: _____ is a common illness.
   An injury such as _____ needs immediate attention.

INDIVIDUAL BRAINSTORMING & COMPOSING

Tell students that they are ready to choose a health problem, then brainstorm and compose self-care advice. Explain that students' medical advice will become a page in the class book titled *Medical Self-Care Guide*, *Self-Care Tips*, *Get-Well Guide*, or *Heal the Heart*.

As you go down the list of illnesses and injuries, ask students to raise a hand to signal which medical problem they want. As students begin choosing illnesses or injuries either from the ideas brainstormed by your class or the list of Health Problems on reproducible 17–1, mark these illnesses and accidents off the master list.

Health Problems

Abdominal Pain	Constipation	Fatigue	Loneliness	Panic
Allergies	Cuts	Fever	Love Struck	Pimples
Anxiety	Depression	Frostbite	Measles	Poison Ivy
Bee Sting	Diarrhea	Headache	Mumps	Rash
Blister	Dizziness	Head Lice	Muscle Ache	Restlessness
Burn	Dry Mouth	Heartburn	Nausea	Sleepiness
Chicken Pox	Ear Infection	Hiccups	Nightmares	Sore Throat
Chills	Eye Injury	Insect Bite	Nosebleed	Speech Delay
Choking		Insomnia	Overeating	Splinter
		Irritability		

Pass out copies of the Brainstorming Assistant, which can be found at the end of this lesson.

As students begin working on their self-care advice, locate students who need assistance or encouragement getting started. Make sure students brainstorm and/or research symptoms, treatments, and ways to prevent the health problem before they begin composing. There are many medical knowledge bases on the web.

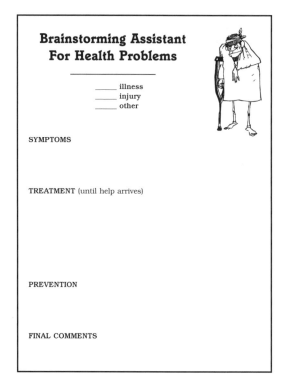

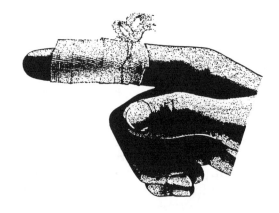

One such site is www.bluecrossmn. com. Then select Health and Medical Information. Or encourage students to choose a search engine and enter their medical problem. Encourage students to locate or create charts, diagrams, and pictures/photographs to include with their self-care advice.

NOTE: You may want to discourage treatments that include over-the-counter medication since many products are not for young children.

As students begin composing a draft, move around the room praising good ideas and asking questions to clarify students' thinking. The following ideas will get you started.

Praise Students' Ideas

Praise an effective title.
Praise particular symptoms or completeness of symptoms.
Praise descriptive words (such as "swollen" ankle or "sunburnt" shoulders).
Praise completeness of remedy.
Praise clear step-by-step directions.
Praise details in treatment (such as "elevate the ankle at least 10 inches").
Praise effective ways to prevent this illness/injury.

Questions to Ask

How can you make your health problem title clearer to readers?

How could you begin your information about your health problem?
Where could you find more information on your illness or accident?
What other symptoms might your readers need to know?
How can you make the symptoms clearer to readers?
How can you introduce your information about symptoms?

What other treatments might you find helpful?
How can you make the treatment clearer to readers?
Which treatments should be tried first? second? as a last resort?
Why might your treatment be dangerous to a person who is ill or injured?
    (Remove it since you don't know who will use your medical advice.)
How could you introduce your information about treatments?

What can a person do to prevent this illness/injury in the future?
How could you conclude your information about _____?

RESPONDING TO STUDENTS' WRITINGS/REVISING

1. As students finish the rough drafts of their medical advice, ask them to find a revising partner. Have one student read the medical advice aloud to the other to see if the advice has all the important symptoms and if the treatment ideas are useful and ordered wisely.

    Encourage students to make two or three specific comments about what they like about the advice. They can offer suggestions to make sure the symptoms are accurate, and the treatment ideas are both valuable and present NO DANGER to the user.

2. After step 1 is completed, require each writer to make at least one or two revisions of the symptoms, treatment, and perhaps prevention parts to improve the medical advice before giving it to someone to use.

3. Before publishing the medical advice, have students trade compositions and look for punctuation, capitalization, spelling, and other errors that might hinder a first-aid giver from giving proper medical attention to an injured party.

4. Ask a health-care provider (such as the school nurse, emergency medical technician, or doctor) to give professional feedback to students on their advice.

PUBLISHING

Explain that students will publish the information so that classmates, other students at school, siblings, parents, and neighbors who are ill or injured (*audience*) can get some immediate medical assistance (*purpose*).

Bound Self-Care Guide

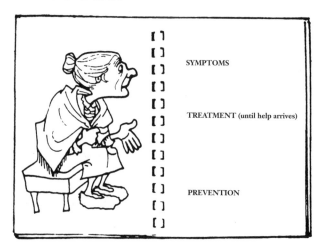

Materials

Illness/Injury sheets, covers, binding machine, plastic binding combs

Directions

1. Stack a cover page, an optional index page, pages of medical advice, and final cover page.

2. Insert the stack into a binding machine and pull the handle down to punch the holes. Lift the handle and remove the stack of paper. (See punch-and-bind machine manual for setting margins, etc.)

3. Place the plastic binding comb on the metal pins at top of the machine, open side facing up.

4. Next, push the handle back to open the plastic comb. Insert your stack of paper into the teeth of the plastic comb and release the handle.

5. Remove the bound Self-Care Guide by lifting it straight up and out of the binding machine.

Layered Self-Care Guide

Self-Care Guide
EMERGENCY PHONE NUMBERS:
Burns
Cuts
Ear Infection
Frostbite
Hiccups
Measles
Nosebleeds
Overeating
Pimples
Splinters

Materials
8-1/2 × 11-inch paper, paper cutter, stapler

Directions

1. Use the Self-Care Guide cover page at the end of this lesson to cut the paper to lengths of approximately 3, 4, 5, 6, 7, 8, 9, and 10 inches.

2. The cover will be 3 inches in length. It will contain the title and any emergency phone numbers the future reader might need.

3. The medical or self-care advice can be printed on 4-, 5-, 6-, 7-, 8-, 9- and a full sheet of 8-1/2 × 10-inch paper. (This means that seven pieces of advice from one student or one piece of advice from seven students will fit into the book. Students can be assigned to bookmaking groups so that the type of medical advice and the amount varies within the group. Students with brief advice can be given the 4- and 5-inch paper, whereas those with longer compositions can be given the 8-, 9-, and 10-inch paper.)

4. Stack the papers from smallest to largest; then staple all the sheets at the title page/cover.

5. Use a black marker to handprint the chapter titles at the bottom of each page. *Be sure to show students ahead of time why to leave this part empty.* If desired, have a student type a list of chapter titles in 48-point Times font.

Health-Care Lessons

Have your students present age-appropriate medical self-care lessons to students in a younger class. Each presentation should include a visual aid to help hold the younger students' attention. Your students should practice their presentations so that they can be done effectively in 2 to 3 minutes.

For excellent information on teaching self-care skills to your students, see "Teaching Self-Care Skills" by S. A. Koblinsky and C. M. Todd in *Teaching Exceptional Children* (Spring 1991), pages 40–44.

Health Column

Perhaps your students would like to write and produce a regular monthly health column of self-care tips. It could be published in paper form or on a website.

Health Problems

Abdominal Pain
Allergies
Anxiety
Athelete's Foot

Back Pain
Bad Breath
Bed Wetting
Bee Sting
Bleeding
Blister
Bloody Nose
Blow to Eye
Boredom
Broken Bone
Broken Tooth
Burn

Chest Pain
Chicken Pox
Chills
Choking
Cold
Confusion
Constant Worrying
Constipation
Cramps
Cuts, Abrasions,
    Lacerations

Depression
Diaper Rash
Diarrhea
Dizziness
Dry Mouth

Ear Infection
Euphoria
Eye Injury
Eyestrain

Fatigue
Feeling Neglected

Fever
Flushing
Foreign Body in Ear/Nose
Frostbite

Gas
Glued to the TV/
    Computer

Headache
Head Injury
Head Lice
Heartburn
Hiccups

Indecision
Insect Bite
Insomnia
Irritability

Loneliness
Loss of Appetite
Loss of Consciousness
Love Struck

Measles
Memory Loss
Motion Sickness
Mumps
Muscle Ache

Nausea
Nightmares
Nosebleed

Overeating
Underweight

Panic
Pimples
Poison Ivy
Poor/Picky Eater
Pupils—dilated/pinpoint

Rash
Reading Problem
Respiration, slow/
    shallow
Restlessness

Screaming
Severe Sadness
Shock
Shortness of Breath
Sinusitis
Skin Blemish
Sleep, unable to
Sleepiness
Slurred Speech
Snake Bite
Sore Throat
Speech Delay
Splinter
Sprained Ankle
Strep Throat
Sweating

Talkativeness
Temper Tantrum
Thumb-sucking
Ticks
Tonsillitis
Toothache

Uncontrollable Crying

Vomiting

Weak Arms
Weakness
Whooping Cough
Won't Eat

Yawning

Brainstorming Assistant
For Health Problems

_____

_____ illness
_____ injury
_____ other

SYMPTOMS

TREATMENT (until help arrives)

PREVENTION

FINAL COMMENTS

Self-Care Guide

EMERGENCY PHONE NUMBERS:

cover

_____

page 1

_____

page 2

_____

page 3

_____

page 4

_____

page 5

_____

page 6

_____

page 7

_____

page 8

_____

page 9

_____

Lesson 18

Advice-Column Solution Letter

OUTCOME   Each student will write advice to another student to help resolve an authentic personal problem or friendship conflict.

MOTIVATORS

1. Pull out the box of problem letters that students wrote in Lesson 11, Advice-Column Problem Letter. Ask students what the box contains and what we plan to do now. (They now have the opportunity to help someone by offering solutions to the problem letters.)

2a. Before writing advice, involve students in determining criteria for good and poor advice by having them decide whether particular advice is good, poor, or debatable. Have students push their desks toward two sides of the room (optional).

2b. Explain that since we want to write advice that is helpful, you'll read some situations with good advice and some with poor advice. Examples of good, bad, and debatable advice can be found at the end of this lesson.

January 4, 20XX

Dear Advice Giver,

   I'm a seventh grader with a very strict dad. He doesn't approve of my friends. Neither does my grandfather. They also dislike kids with purple and green hair.

   A nice boy who just moved here from another country wants to walk to school with me. My dad said I shouldn't be seen with those people. I've avoided Railee by walking to school another way. I feel bad hurting his feelings. I don't agree with my dad. I think it is good being friends with Railee, but I don't want to get in trouble.

   My Social Studies teacher, Mr. Reilly, says we should respect people from other countries and value their differences. What should I do?

Sincerely,
Can't Decide

2c. Now read one problem situation that has clearly good or distinctly bad advice. Explain to your students that as you read the advice, they should silently make a decision regarding the quality of advice.

January 8, 20XX

Dear Can't Decide,

   Talk to your dad. Explain to him that you respect his ideas about Railee, but let him know that you're growing up and you are developing your own values.

   Share why you like Railee. Also explain that you are learning in school to respect people from other countries even though their cultures/ways of doing things are different.

   Offer a compromise. Ask your mom and dad if you can invite Railee over to your house after school to meet them. Perhaps they will see Railee as a person instead of a stereotype.

   If this doesn't work, obey your dad for now—you want his respect and trust, but share your concerns with your Social Studies teacher. He may have some good ideas.

   Don't avoid Railee; talk to him. He may be a little hurt now, but he'll understand better than if you avoid him.

Sincerely,
Your Advice Giver

   Direct students to slowly walk to the front (or the right side) of the room if the advice you read is good. Post a sign saying "Good Advice" at the front of the room. Direct students to walk to the back (or the left side) of the room if the advice you read is poor. Post a sign saying "Poor Advice" at the back of the room.

Good Advice

Poor Advice

2d. Once students are in place and listening, ask two less involved students to explain their reasoning for calling the advice terrific or awful. Repeat this experience several times with different situations and advice. Caution your students that if pushing or running occurs, those students will participate by sitting at a desk.

2e. Next, read a situation to students containing advice that fits in the debatable area. Give students longer to reflect on this situation and its accompanying advice before asking them to take a position in the room.

   Some students may object to two choices. When this occurs, indicate that there is lots of space in the room between the "Good Advice" and the "Poor Advice" signs.

Good Advice		Poor Advice

2f. Allow time for movement, then ask everyone to stand still and quietly look around to see where their peers are standing. Again ask several students in various parts of the room to explain their reasons for drawing these conclusions. Praise a variety of logical reasons.

2g. Repeat with another situation containing debatable advice. If students need encouragement to listen to each other's reasons, make the rule that potential speakers must first repeat the previous speaker's reasons before giving his/her own.

2h. Finally, request that students return the room to normal as they think about good/terrific advice and bad/awful advice. When everyone is seated, ask your class "What is good advice?" "How do good and poor advice differ?"

    As volunteers share their criteria, write their ideas on a sheet of butcher paper. This criteria will be used later when students compose their own advice. You want students to generate some agreed-upon criteria, like the following.

> - Respects the advice seeker and everyone involved in the situation.
> - Shows empathy for the advice seeker's problem. Avoid cruel or flippant advice.
> - Encourages kind or nonviolent responses and problem-solving behavior to resolve problems. Don't suggest harm to anyone. Initiate compromise when possible.
> - Makes advice seeker aware of school and community resources, and refer him/her when the problem is truly serious.

    No matter how sophisticated students' criteria is, the most important part is that they have agreed to the criteria generated by the group and that it belongs to them, not to the teacher.

3. Reread the problem letter generated during the group brainstorming and group composing sections of Lesson 11 to your class. If you have an uneven number of students, you can carefully preselect a real problem letter from the Advice Box. Challenge students that each real problem must be addressed sympathetically.

GROUP BRAINSTORMING

We will brainstorm some ideas to help this person with his/her problem.

Restate Problem	Restate Feelings	Solutions Tried
face bully	lost patience	report to parents tell him to stop ignore him

NEW Solutions	Steps	Helpful Resources
get to know kid trying to get attention ask what likes to do get him some help tell him you won't be his friend	find out his name ask what he likes to do	teacher school counselor principal

Key Questions

1. **What problem is this person facing? How can we show the person we understand what his/her problem is before we start giving advice? What is he/she really wanting from us?** Pause to give students time to think. Write students' ideas under the "Restate Problem" column. Encourage students to be sensitive in restating the person's problem.

2. **When the person wrote this letter, how was he/she feeling?** (hurt, angry, confused, or sad) The goal here is to pave the way for students to empathize with the writer and eventually show warmth and empathy. **When have you felt similarly? Why did you feel _____?** Pause for at least 30 seconds to give students time to think. Write their ideas under the "Restate Feelings" column.

3. Reread the letter to students so they can listen for the solutions that the advice seeker has tried. **What solutions has the person already tried? How has the writer already attempted to solve the problem?** Write these ideas under the "Solutions Tried" column.

4. **What more effective solutions/suggestions can we offer? What kind of help do you think the person really needs? What is a new method for solving this problem? What can we advise that might truly fix the problem?** Pause for at least 30 seconds to give students time to think. Praise thoughtful ideas and write them under the "NEW Solutions" column. If students come up with poor advice, have the class reread the list of criteria generated during the good, bad, debatable advice activity to evaluate the advice.

5. **Considering the criteria we generated during brainstorming, which two suggestions are the most helpful? Which are the best solutions? Which ones help the advice seeker assume responsibility for his/her problem?** Circle these ideas on the the board.

6. **How can we explain exactly what to do? What is the first step to solving this problem? What should be done next? After that what must the advice seeker do?** Repeat until three to five steps are listed on the board.

   NOTE: Even though eventually we want students to order the steps, list them without commenting about their order. Chronological order will be dealt with during group composing. If a student comments about steps being incorrectly ordered, ask where the step fits and draw an arrow to where this student thinks it should go. Praise this student for his/her insight and continue brainstorming steps.

7. (optional) **Why should the advice seeker follow our advice? What favorable consequences might the advice seeker experience if he/she acts on the suggestions? What could happen if the advice seeker doesn't follow our advice?**

   EXAMPLES: If you follow my advice, you will be
   amazed with the results.
   The advice I am giving you should help
   solve your problem.

8. **Who can the advice seeker go to for help if our suggestions don't work or don't achieve the desired results? If a suggestion doesn't work, who should he/she turn to next?** Put under "Helpful Resources" column. List hot lines and resource people available in your area.

GROUP COMPOSING

Now we are advice columnists. Let's organize our ideas into a powerful letter to the advice seeker full of useful and helpful advice. Put the group composition on butcher paper so it can be saved and used in the Revising step.

> April 29, 20XX
>
> Hi Sad and Lonely,
>
>   Dealing with a bully can be a big problem no matter what grade you are in. It seems as though you've lost patience with the locker slamming and shoving. I'm going to give you two suggestions.
>
>   First, this kid is trying to get your attention and get you "riled up" by slamming the locker and shoving you in the hall. Like you stated, it is hard to ignore his actions. One solution is to get to know the kid. Maybe he is tormenting you because he doesn't know how to be a friend. Find out his name and ask him what activities, sports, or movies he likes.
>
>   If this doesn't work or if he suggests you do something illegal, tell him you won't be his friend. Then talk to your teacher, school counselor, or principal and ask for help. The locker slamming and shoving are dangerous and this kid may need some serious help.
>
> Sincerely,
> Class of 20XX

1. **What is today's date?** Add this information to the board or overhead.

> **Thinking about Mechanics:** What punctuation should I put between the day and year? (a comma) Why? (so the numbers don't run together and confuse the reader)

2. **How could we greet _____?** Insert advice seeker's "name" or "handle" from his/her letter.

> **Thinking about Mechanics:** What should I have done to the letter "d" in "Dear _____"? (capitalize)

> **Thinking about Mechanics:** What do we do to the first letter of a person's name? (capitalize the first letter of each part of the name)

> **Thinking about Mechanics:** What punctuation should I put after the name? (a comma)

3. **What was the advice seeker's problem? How can we acknowledge the problem in one sentence?** Praise one-sentence responses that capture the problem. Add one to the letter of advice.

> **Thinking about Mechanics:** What do we need to do to this first word in this sentence to show it is the beginning of a new idea? (indent)

4. **What was the advice seeker's predominant feeling? How can we acknowledge the writer's feelings in one sentence? What can we say to the advice seeker to let him/her know we understand? How could we acknowledge the person's pain or frustration in one sentence?** Praise one-sentence responses that capture the feeling. Add one to the letter of advice.

5. **Now let's get to the heart of our letter. Which suggestions did we decide were best?** Encourage students to choose useful advice from the brainstormed list. Add these to the letter of advice.

> **Thinking about Mechanics:** What do we need to do to this first word in this sentence to show it is the beginning of a new idea? (indent)

6. **What should we advise as the first step in implementing the suggestion? What is the first thing the advice seeker should do? second step? third?** Encourage students to choose steps for implementing the selected suggestion from the brainstormed list. Add these to the letter of advice.

7. (optional) **Why should our advice be followed? What will happen if the suggestions aren't pursued? What may be the consequences if the advice isn't followed?** Encourage students to choose thoughtful consequences from the brainstormed list. Add these to the letter of advice.

8. Repeat steps 5, 6, and 7. Ask Advanced Writers to describe two or three solutions, each one containing a suggestion, several steps, and reasons for following the advice. Add one or more to the letter of advice.

9. **Where did we decide the advice seeker could go for assistance? If all else fails, to whom could the advice seeker go for help?** Add this to your letter.

10. **How can we close our solution letter?**

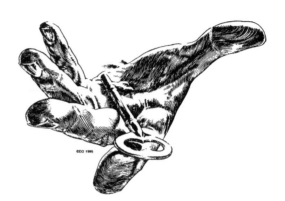

> *EXAMPLES:* Yours truly—a friend
> From another advice seeker
> Genuinely yours

Thinking about Mechanics: What do we do to the first letter of the closing? (capitalize each part of the name)

Thinking about Mechanics: What punctuation should I put after the name/closing? (a comma)

INDIVIDUAL BRAINSTORMING & COMPOSING

Give each student a letter and time to read and reflect on it. Explain that this is an opportunity to help another person. Pull out the brainstormed sheet of criteria from the motivation step. Remind students of the agreed-upon criteria, and point out that any request for help must be honored in a serious manner.

NOTE: Caution your students that severe problems put even more responsibility on the advice giver. Explain that if a student gets a letter that has a problem he/she doesn't feel comfortable or qualified to handle, he/she may see you.

As students begin to brainstorm and write, walk around the room and converse with students who need individual guidance coming up with helpful suggestions.

Allow less skilled writers to include the date, greeting, restatement of the problem, a suggestion, and a closing. Allow them to skip restating the feeling, steps, and consequences, since these parts are more difficult to express.

RESPONDING TO STUDENTS' WRITINGS/REVISING

1. Ahead of time make an overhead of the "Hi Sad and Lonely" group composing letter from this lesson or use your own class's solution letter composed earlier.

2. Pass out the Revising Assistants, found at the end of this lesson. Point out that students will use these Revising Assistants to build even stronger and more effective responses for the person needing their help.

Revising Assistant: Solution Letter
(Ideas & Mechanics)

Revising Team	– Needs Work	+ Works	* Is Strong	Teacher
_____	1. Has the date been placed at the top of the letter?			_____
_____	2. Is the name of the advice seeker used in the greeting?			_____
	Is the advice seeker's name capitalized?			_____
_____	3. Are the writer's problem and feelings identified in the opening sentence?			_____
_____	4. Is sensitivity shown to the advice seeker?			_____
_____	5. Has at least one helpful solution or piece of advice been offered?			_____
_____	6. Are the steps needed for the solution stated clearly and logically?			_____
_____	7. Have you told why the advice should be followed?			_____
_____	8. Have you offered at least one resource to the writer?			_____
_____	9. Have you signed your solution letter?			_____

Show students how to use the Revising Assistant by evaluating the solution letter you chose for an example. Give students several minutes to reread the solution letter to themselves. Then read question 1 on the Revising Assistant aloud and ask your students whether the writing task has been met. Have students silently decide if the solution letter "Needs Work," "Works," or "Is Strong." Allow some discussion, then ask students to independently rate question 1.

Instruct students to use the "Needs Work" mark if in doubt. Explain that everyone will get a chance to change a "Needs Work" to a "Works" after improvements have been made. Demonstrate how easy it is to change a minus sign to a plus.

3. Walk through the whole Revising Assistant evaluating the solution letter item-by-item. Then explain that you will do the final check before the advice letters go to the advice seeker. Point out the spot on the right side of the Revising Assistant where you'll evaluate the elements of their solution letters. Give students 15–20 minutes to evaluate and improve their solution letters.

4. After students finish revising their advice letters, collect them so that you have a chance to read each letter. Be alert to any hurtful remarks and confer with students who may need to write their letters in a more respectful manner. Depend on the self- and peer-revising process to handle other issues.

5. Return the solution letters so students can rewrite legibly or word-process them on the special "Advice" paper provided at the end of this lesson. Point out to your students that the advice seekers need to focus on the advice, not on trying to figure out the advice givers' handwriting.

PUBLISHING

Plan a quiet time to distribute the solution letters (*format*) so the advice seekers can open their letters in private (*audience*) and reflect on the advice they received (*purpose*).

1. Pull blinds (or shades) to reduce light. Play some soft music to aid reflection.

2. To keep the identity of the writer anonymous, set letters out on a table and allow students to go to the table one at a time to find their letters.

3. Some students will want to guess the identity of the advice giver; instead, focus attention on considering the advice.

4. Ask students to evaluate the advice they receive before choosing to act. Assure them that they don't have to take the advice. Perhaps you'll want to suggest that students be true to their own hearts and feelings.

5. Suggest that if students handle the exchange in a healthy manner, an Advice Box and time to write will be organized on an ongoing basis.

Seeking Advice

January 4, 20XX

Dear Advice Giver,

I'm a seventh grader with a very strict dad. He doesn't approve of my friends. Neither does my grandfather. They also dislike kids with purple and green hair.

A nice boy who just moved here from another country wants to walk to school with me. My dad said I shouldn't be seen with those people. I've avoided Railee by walking to school another way. I feel bad hurting his feelings. I don't agree with my dad. I think it is good being friends with Railee, but I don't want to get in trouble.

My Social Studies teacher, Mr. Reilly, says we should respect people from other countries and value their differences. What should I do?

Sincerely,
Can't Decide

Good Advice

January 8, 20XX

Dear Can't Decide,

Talk to your dad. Explain to him that you respect his ideas about Railee, but let him know that you're growing up and you are developing your own values.

Share why you like Railee. Also explain that you are learning in school to respect people from other countries even though their cultures/ways of doing things are different.

Offer a compromise. Ask your mom and dad if you can invite Railee over to your house after school to meet them. Perhaps they will see Railee as a person instead of a stereotype. If this doesn't work, obey your dad for now—you want his respect and trust—but share your concerns with your Social Studies teacher. He may have some good ideas.

Don't avoid Railee; talk to him. He may be a little hurt now, but he'll understand better than if you avoid him.

Sincerely,
Your Advice Giver

Seeking Advice

January 4, 20XX

Dear _____,

I'm a good student with a terrible problem. My mom makes me do my homework after school, but my brain is tired then. When I'm at my dad's apartment, I get all of my homework done in the morning before school.

I like doing my homework in the morning before school. My work and grades are just as good as when I do my homework in the afternoon at Mom's house. I'm not really procrastinating. I'm just tired.

My mom and I usually agree except for this one area. How can I make her change her mind?

Sincerely,
Tired of Arguing

P.S. Don't tell me to do my homework after supper. I have chores to do.

Bad Advice

January 8, 20XX

Dear Can't Decide,

Tell your mom to "bug off." It's your homework and as long as you get it done, it's none of her business when you get it done. You worked all day at school and should get to have some fun after school.

Sincerely,
Your Advice Giver

Seeking Advice

January 4, 20XX

Dear _____,

I feel lonely a lot. Sometimes I wish I could just go away and be alone forever. I can't talk to my parents about being lonely because my brother had an accident and is very sick and they only have time to pay attention to him. Sometimes I wish I were sick like my brother.

What can I do to get my mom and dad to do neat things with me like we used to do?

Sincerely,
Sad at Home

P.S. Don't tell me to talk to my parents. I've already tried to tell them.

Debatable Advice

January 8, 20XX

Dear Sad at Home,

You seem to have lost the company of your brother and your parents. It's okay to be sad and alone since your brother is sick and both your parents seem to have forgotten about you. Your mom and dad are probably so upset about your brother's illness that they may be in pain, too.

Since you haven't been able to get your parents to listen, talk to a favorite teacher, a relative, a coach, a counselor at school, your minister or priest, or older friend. Talking about your problems won't make them go away, but it will make you feel better and sometimes this person can help you make a plan for dealing with the problem.

Meanwhile, ask some of your friends to take you along when they do neat things with their family. Make some new friends who seem to understand about your brother's illness and who can get you out of the house and have some fun.

Sincerely,
Your Advice Giver

Seeking Advice

January 4, 20XX

Dear _____,

I'm a sixth grader with glasses and asthma. I like helping other people. After school I work at the community center helping kids from 5th through 10th grade with their homework. I want to keep doing this.

Every day about five o'clock when I leave the center, an eighth grader from the middle school picks on me. Yesterday he tore my book bag and pushed me down. One time he broke my glasses. Another time he pushed me in the mud and my coat was ruined. It was my only good coat.

I've tried to run away, but I start coughing.

I told him to stop it, but he just laughed. He told me if I report him, he'll beat me up. I don't want to quit my job helping the other kids. What should I do?

Sincerely,
Scared

P.S. Don't tell me to sock him. My family doesn't believe in physical violence.

Debatable Advice

January 8, 20XX

Dear Scared,

You sound like a wimp. If this kid tries to push you around, smack him in the nose. If he gets you on the ground, bite his leg. Don't be a crybaby. Show that kid you can stand up for yourself. Then he won't bother you any more.

If that doesn't work, call the police.

Sincerely,
Your Advice Giver

Brainstorming Assistant
for
Advice-Column Solution Letter

Restate Problem   **Solutions Tried**

Restate Feelings

NEW Solutions   **Consequences**

Steps   **Resources**

Revising Assistant: Solution Letter
(Ideas & Mechanics)

Revising

Team   – **Needs Work**   + **Works**   * **Is Strong**   **Teacher**

_____ 1. Has the date been placed at the top of the letter?   _____

_____ 2. Is the name of the advice seeker used in the greeting? _____
Is the advice seeker's name capitalized?   _____

_____ 3. Are the writer's problem and feelings identified
in the opening sentence?   _____

_____ 4. Is sensitivity shown to the advice seeker?   _____

_____ 5. Has at least one helpful solution or piece of advice
been offered?   _____

_____ 6. Are the steps needed for the solution stated clearly
and logically?   _____

_____ 7. Have you told why the advice should be followed?   _____

_____ 8. Have you offered at least one resource to the writer?   _____

_____ 9. Have you signed your solution letter?   _____

Revising Assistant: Solution Letter
(Ideas & Mechanics)

Revising

Team   – **Needs Work**   + **Works**   * **Is Strong**   **Teacher**

_____ 1. Has the date been placed at the top of the letter?   _____

_____ 2. Is the name of the advice seeker used in the greeting? _____
Is the advice seeker's name capitalized?   _____

_____ 3. Are the writer's problem and feelings identified
in the opening sentence?   _____

_____ 4. Is sensitivity shown to the advice seeker?   _____

_____ 5. Has at least one helpful solution or piece of advice
been offered?   _____

_____ 6. Are the steps needed for the solution stated clearly
and logically?   _____

_____ 7. Have you told why the advice should be followed?   _____

_____ 8. Have you offered at least one resource to the writer?   _____

_____ 9. Have you signed your solution letter?   _____

Advice

LESSON 19

Stress Diet

OUTCOME Each student will create a humorous three-meal, two-snack menu of scrumptious high-calorie foods along with realistic information to encourage healthier living.

MOTIVATORS

1. Bring in a delicious snack and share it with your students or have your students help you make a yummy recipe at school.

2. Share your own strong food temptations when tired, angry, bored, lonely, or under stress. For example, I am tempted by ice cream, homemade cheesecake, cheese danish, and cream cheese frosting. When I'm exhausted my mind says I just need some sugar and fat to give me some energy. I'm really not hungry; I just need some sleep.

   Ask students which foods tempt them.

3. Invite students to share which feelings move them to deal with stress by unhealthy eating. Ask students when do they find themselves overeating. Write students' ideas on chart paper for use later. If students aren't able to identify their feelings, allow them to choose from these: afraid, angry, awkward, confused, depressed, desperate, frustrated, guilty, helpless, humiliated, hurt, jealous, lonely, resentful, sad, self-doubt, rejected, ridiculed, unattractive, not appreciated, unfairly treated.

Allow reluctant students to select feelings they believe motivate a friend or family member to overeat. Respect privacy by deleting names. Discuss realistic/healthy eating habits and the joys and terrors of unrealistic/unhealthy eating habits.

4. Read a sample Stress Diet. Encourage students to make fun of some of the unhealthy eating choices in this diet.

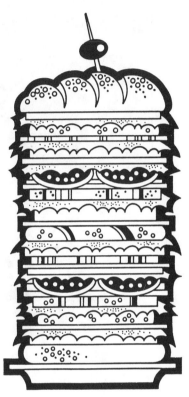

Stress Diet for a Boring Day
Afternoon Snack

1 small hamburger
6 cheese danish pastries
5 large glasses of milk
10 bowls of delicious old-fashioned vanilla ice cream
    smothered with 1 cup cherries and 3 cups pecans

Tips
1. If you eat a danish pastry piece by piece, the calories will drop off.
2. Milk is a healthy food so it doesn't matter how much you consume.
3. If you eat ice cream out of the container, it doesn't count; you won't gain weight.

---

5. Challenge students to create a special menu for stressful or boring days so their friends (*audience*) will see how foolish eating as a stress-reduction technique is unhealthy (*purpose*).

GROUP BRAINSTORMING

Let's brainstorm tempting foods that might be contained in a "Stress Diet."

NOTE: To assist with composing, the ingredients are brainstormed before the serving sizes and amounts, even though the board is set up as follows.

Key Questions

1. **What high-calorie treats make your mouth water? What sweets tempt you the most? Which sweets or beverages would tempt almost anyone to adopt unhealthy eating habits?**

> **Thinking about Mechanics:** What do we need to do to signal brand-name foods and/or beverages? (capitalize the first letter)

2. **Which healthy foods/beverages in too-large portions do you crave when you are stressed, tired, or depressed?** Repeat these questions until eight to ten ideas have been written on the board. (optional) **Which meats? Which side dishes? Which salads? Which appetizers? Which breads? Which desserts?** Add these ideas to the board.

Amounts	Serving Sizes	Healthy Foods & High-Calorie Treats
4	giant platters	chicken fried steak and BBQ ribs
whole	box	cherry pie topped with whipped cream
10	bowls	ice cream with chocolate sauce
7	mouthfuls	chips with sour cream dip
3	bags	popcorn oozing with butter
15	cans	soft drink

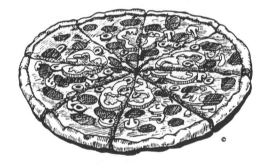

3. **What kind of _____ (ingredient)? How can we describe the _____?** As ingredients are given, inquire about descriptors before writing the ingredient on the board.

Thinking about Mechanics: What kind of foods? What kind of beverages? (Add adjectives and prepositional phrases to describe the food.)
   EXAMPLES: Change frosting to dark chocolate frosting.
   Change ice cream to ice cream covered with pecans and strawberries.

---

4. **What enormous-size serving shall we use for _____?** Repeat these questions until four to six ideas have been written on the board. What not quite-so-large amount could we suggest?

5. **What amount of _____ shall we put into our menu? What is another enormous amount? What smaller amount could we suggest?**

6. Repeat questions 5 and 6 until at least six to eight sets of students' ideas have been written on the board.

7. (optional) **What ridiculous tips for overeating have you heard?** Give several examples of your own or one or two of the following. **What wisecrack/teasing statement can be added to the stress diet that will make people laugh?** Add students' ideas to the board.

Tips for Using this Stress Diet:

1. If you drink a diet soda, you can eat twice as many candy bars.
2. If you break a chocolate chip cookie in half, the calories will drop out or fall off.
3. If you eat buttered popcorn with a friend, you won't gain weight since the calories are divided in half.
4. If you smother BBQ ribs with BBQ sauce, the fat is covered up.
5. Foods you eat when you are ill don't count.
6. When you put a scoop of ice cream into a Coke, the calories cancel each other out.
7. When eating a whole pizza, cut it into eight pieces instead of six so you won't gain so much.

GROUP COMPOSING

Now we'll create a tempting stress diet (menu) for a full day together so that we can remind our friends and family members how ridiculous food temptations can be.

1. **We'll create our title first. When will we want to eat a ridiculous amount of food? When could our stress diet be eaten? On what special occasion will the stress diet be served?** If students need assistance coming up with stressful situations, offer a few suggestions such as before a test, on a rainy holiday, when moving to a new city, going out on a date, or after a fight with a friend.

> **Thinking about Mechanics:** Which words do we need to capitalize in our title? (the important words) What do we need to do to people's names, names of holidays, names of a town or city? (capitalize the first letter)

2. **Let's create our breakfast menu first.**

   For our breakfast menu which scrumptious-sounding food, treat, beverage item shall we put first? While students think, write this suggestion under "Breakfast" on the stress diet, leaving room for amount and the measurement tool.

   Which of our amount of this food, treat, or beverage should we suggest as healthy/unhealthy?

   Which serving size could be used with this food or treat?

   Repeat step 2 until at least three to five suggestions are added to the breakfast menu.

Stress Diet for _____

Breakfast	Lunch	Afternoon Snack	Evening Meal	Bedtime Snack

3. Next apply this pattern of questioning to create a lunch menu, an afternoon snack, a dinner or supper menu, and a bedtime snack. For each meal encourage students to consider in what order readers should consume the healthy and unhealthy food/treats.

   (optional) Suggest that Advanced Writers start the day's menu with nutritious foods and gradually progress to poorer choices on their menus.

EXAMPLES: Breakfast: grapefruit, cereal, milk
       Lunch: salad, double cheese pizza, garlic bread sticks, diet soda
       Dinner: whole roasted chicken, mashed potatoes & gravy, fresh rolls,
       2 milkshakes, whole pumpkin pie with real whipped cream

4. Now we need to create an introduction that explains our philosophy about the stress diet. Direct students to the feeling words generated in the motivation step. **What reasons were given for overeating earlier? What feelings tempted us to gorge our faces to avoid the real problems? What is our philosophy about eating to avoid stress? How can we introduce our fanciful diet for stress?**

NOTE: To be meaningful, introductions need to be written after the suggestions are created in steps 2 and 3. If students are Beginning Writers, give an example.

EXAMPLES: This menu of high-calorie foods may taste great, but it won't make you feel better.

The next time you feel worthless, sad, or hurt and have a food attack, you can have a good laugh instead.

Feeling hungry? No energy? Depressed? Remember, eating to solve your problems WON'T help you.

Our Stress Diet might make your mouth water, but your tummy will suffer. It causes tremendous weight gain and won't make you feel accepted and lovable.

Stress Diet for Lonely Weekend

If you are feeling sad, discouraged, or in a negative mood and are about to have a food attack, consider what these menu suggestions will do for you. Tape this stress diet on your refrigerator and read it the next time you need to laugh. Remember how disgusting you'll feel if you eat the whole thing.

Breakfast	Lunch	Afternoon Snack	Evening Meal	Bedtime Snack

There is no reason to overeat or stuff yourself with fat and sugar. Skip the empty-calorie treats, too. Instead go for a walk or call me.

---

5. Now we need to add a final comment that encourages the recipient to resist temptations and consider a healthier choice. What healthy choice could the person under stress make instead of eating? What can we say to encourage the reader to choose a reasonable alternative to food? If students are Beginning Writers, suggest a final comment.

EXAMPLES: Instead of trying to solve your problems by stuffing your face, call your best friend.

Skip the high-calorie treats and explore your thoughts/feelings in a journal.

Take care of yourself. Eat three nutritious meals a day and get some exercise.

Ask yourself these questions: Am I tired? If so, go for a walk or take a nap. Am I lonely? If so, call a friend. Am I really hungry? If so, eat a balanced meal. Keep portions small. Act now!

Other people will respect you when you solve problems in a healthy manner. Kick the food habit.

Turn your compulsion to eat-eat-eat into building new relationships.

Substitute positive self-talk for food. I'm not really hungry; I ate a nutritious dinner. I may be lonely, but I don't have to stuff my face. I can do something good for myself.

INDIVIDUAL BRAINSTORMING & COMPOSING

Now tell students that they get to create their own diet to remind themselves, friends, and family members how foolish it is trying to relieve stress by eating. Before they begin brainstorming, pass out the Brainstorming Assistant: Stress Diet for _____ (found at the end of this lesson) to assist in brainstorming and composing.

As students begin brainstorming and drafting their stress diets, walk around the classroom praising healthy foods with reasonable amounts and high-calorie foods with ridiculous amounts.

Advanced Writers   Encourage Advanced Writers to choose foods from each food group in their breakfast, lunch, and dinner menus.

EXAMPLES: BREAD GROUP: 3 loaves of sourdough bread covered with 3 cups of butter and garlic

VEGETABLE GROUP: 7 carrots cooked in brown sugar

MEAT GROUP: 25 slices of sugar-cured bacon

DAIRY and FRUIT GROUP: 5 bowls of peaches and cream with 8 fudge cookies

BEVERAGE: 1 diet soda

RESPONDING TO STUDENTS' WRITINGS/REVISING

1. As each student finishes his or her rough draft, ask him/her to self-edit. Stress that each question on the Revising Assistant (found at the end of this lesson) needs to be answered thoughtfully so that readers will clearly understand the message behind the Stress Diet.

Revising Assistant: Stress Diet

____ Has the occasion or place been placed in the title of the Stress Diet?
____ Does this occasion or place start with a capital letter?

____ Has an introduction been included? Does it reflect a healthy philosophy towards dealing with food and stress?
____ Does each sentence in the introduction start with a capital letter?
____ Does each sentence end with a period?

____ Are at least three (healthy & unhealthy) breakfast foods listed?
____ Are at least four (healthy & unhealthy) foods for lunch listed?
____ Are at least two (healthy & unhealthy) afternoon snacks listed?
____ Are at least five (healthy & unhealthy) dinner or supper foods listed?
____ Are at least two (healthy & unhealthy) bedtime snacks listed?
____ Does each name brand food start with a capital letter?
____ Will your tips promote a smile or laughter? Are ridiculous eating beliefs pointed out to the reader?

____ Has a final comment been added to the Stress Diet that encourages the reader to think?
____ Does each sentence in the conclusion start with a capital letter and end with a period?

2. After step 1 is completed, require each student to revise and improve his/her stress diet.

3. As students finish the self-edit, ask them to find a revising partner, exchange Stress Diets, and read one person's Stress Diet aloud. The partner should share which ideas they liked and offer one or two suggestions for making the Stress Diet more outrageous and entertaining. Switch roles.

4. After step 3 is completed, require each student to respond by making at least two improvements to his/her stress diet.

Beginning Writers   Clean up their draft and use this for publication.

Advanced Writers   Consider (a) what to eliminate or add to the Stress Diet, (b) how to improve their introduction so it gets readers' attention, and (c) evaluate the conclusion to see if it gives an alternative to unhealthy eating. Have Advanced Writers recopy or word-process their revised stress diet(s) on a clean sheet of paper, then sign and date it before it is published.

PUBLISHING

Share the stress diets with the selected person, friends, and family members (*audience*) who may be in a stressful situation and need to reflect on more healthy ways to relieve stress (*purpose*).

Before students take their stress diets home, make a copy and staple them together for a class book so the other students (*audience—peers*) can read and enjoy (*purpose*) each other's ideas. Suggest students use two refrigerator magnets to post their stress diets on the refrigerator at home close to the handle to assist (*audience—self, friends, and family*) in times of stress (*purpose*).

Refrigerator Magnet Display

Materials

typing paper, two heavy-duty round magnets (Radio Shack, pkg. of 5 for $1.79) per student, glossy magazine pictures, glue

NOTE: The material that covers many refrigerators requires a strong magnet.

Directions

1. First, strengthen the paper on which the Stress Diet is written by gluing it to a blank sheet of typing paper. Let dry overnight.

2. Find food pictures in a glossy magazine and cut them out.

3. Glue one food picture to each magnet.

4. Use the two magnets to post the Stress Diet on a refrigerator close to the handle.

Class Ring Book

Materials

paper, 4 × 6-inch or 5 × 7-inch index cards, hole punch, 2-inch ring

Directions

1. Punch a hole in the top left corner of each index card.

2. Write one meal or snack on each 4 × 6-inch index card. If you want students to put a whole day's menu on one card, have students type the Stress Diet on the computer and glue it on the front and back of a 5 × 7-inch index card.

3. Add a title on the first index card: Stress Diet for _____ .

4. Insert the ring through the cards and close it.

Stress Diet
for a
Slow Weekend

1 small hamburger
6 cheese danish pastries
5 large glasses of milk
10 bowls of delicious old-fashioned vanilla ice cream
1 cup cherries and 3 cups pecans

Brainstorming Assistant: Stress Diet for _____

Introduction

Breakfast

Lunch

Afternoon Snack

Evening Meal

Bedtime Snack

Tips

Final Comments

Revising Assistant: Stress Diet

____ Has the occasion or place been placed in the title of the Stress Diet?
____ Does this occasion or place start with a capital letter?

____ Has an introduction been included? Does it reflect a healthy philosophy towards dealing with food and stress?
____ Does each sentence in the introduction start with a capital letter?
____ Does each sentence end with a period?

____ Are at least three (healthy & unhealthy) breakfast foods listed?
____ Are at least four (healthy & unhealthy) foods for lunch listed?
____ Are at least two (healthy & unhealthy) afternoon snacks listed?
____ Are at least five (healthy & unhealthy) dinner or supper foods listed?
____ Are at least two (healthy & unhealthy) bedtime snacks listed?
____ Does each name brand food start with a capital letter?
____ Will your tips promote a smile or laughter? Are ridiculous eating beliefs pointed out to the reader?

____ Has a final comment been added to the Stress Diet that encourages the reader to think?
____ Does each sentence in the conclusion start with a capital letter and end with a period?

Revising Assistant: Stress Diet

____ Has the occasion or place been placed in the title of the Stress Diet?
____ Does this occasion or place start with a capital letter?

____ Has an introduction been included? Does it reflect a healthy philosophy towards dealing with food and stress?
____ Does each sentence in the introduction start with a capital letter?
____ Does each sentence end with a period?

____ Are at least three (healthy & unhealthy) breakfast foods listed?
____ Are at least four (healthy & unhealthy) foods for lunch listed?
____ Are at least two (healthy & unhealthy) afternoon snacks listed?
____ Are at least five (healthy & unhealthy) dinner or supper foods listed?
____ Are at least two (healthy & unhealthy) bedtime snacks listed?
____ Does each name brand food start with a capital letter?
____ Will your tips promote a smile or laughter? Are ridiculous eating beliefs pointed out to the reader?

____ Has a final comment been added to the Stress Diet that encourages the reader to think?
____ Does each sentence in the conclusion start with a capital letter and end with a period?

SECTION 3

Persuasive Compositions for Young Authors

A persuasive pattern is useful when writers want to persuade, convince, or entice the reader toward a particular point of view.

- **Simple Directions** A simple persuasive composition consists of one or more opinions or a list of reasons.

- **Complex Directions** A complex persuasive composition includes one opinion supported with reasons, facts, and/or evidence that clearly support the opinion. These reasons are ordered so that they achieve the desired result; often the most powerful or convincing reason is placed first or last. Many writers repeat their opinion or make a final plea for the reader to act at the end of the composition.

Some Forms of Persuasive Writing

Advice Columns
Apology Notes
Book Jackets
Campaign Speeches
Classified Ads
Commercials (Radio
    or TV)
Complaint
Congratulations
Consumer Reports

Debate Notes
Editorials
Excuses
Letters to the Editor
Letters to Public Officials
Letters of Request
Movie Reviews
Petitions
Political Speeches

Propaganda
Protest Letters
Rebuttals
Recommendations
Requests for Financial Aid
Requests for Forgiveness
Restaurant Reviews
Sales Pitches
Thank-you Letters

LESSON 20

Apology/Apology Note

OUTCOME   Each student will express regret for having hurt, angered, or disappointed another person.

MOTIVATORS

1. Tell students about a time when your feelings were hurt and how it felt. Then lead a visual imagery. Close your eyes and ask students about times when their feelings were hurt. **When did you get hurt? How did it happen? Who was involved? What happened?** Open your eyes. Ask students to share. Accept all responses.

2. Share an oral or written apology you have written.

> April 14, 20XX
>
> Dear Terence,
>
> I heard you were disappointed that you weren't included in our kickball game last Saturday. I understand how you might feel. You are a terrific kicker and a fast runner. We have great kickers and other guys who can run fast, but no one else does both as well as you.
>
> I'm sorry that nobody told you about the game. We want you on our team. Our next meeting is this Saturday. Would you like to walk with me?
>
> Your friend and coach,
> Daniel

3. Explain that one way to solve the problem of hurting another person's feelings is to make an oral or written apology. Say that many times we don't mean to hurt someone, but we do. An apology is a way to say that you are sorry and still want to be friends. Ask students if they've ever received an apology, from whom, and why. Accept all responses.

4. Ask students to think of someone who is owed an apology. If students need guidance coming up with a person to whom they (as a group) owe an apology, preselect this person and gently remind your students of that situation.

GROUP COMPOSING

Instead of group brainstorming first, a group apology will be written. Place a 5-foot wide × 4-foot tall piece of light colored butcher paper on the board. Use a dark wide-tipped colored marker. Later students can be given the opportunity to sign the apology.

Let's create a group apology to _____.

1. **How do we start this apology letter?** Write "dear _____," on the chart paper so all the students can see. **To whom are we writing an apology?** Insert the given name after the "dear."

> **Thinking about Mechanics:** What should I have done to the letter "d" in "dear _____"? (capitalize)

> **Thinking about Mechanics:** What punctuation should I put after the person's name? (a comma)

2. **What happened?** Accept several ways to state this information, but do not write it on the chart. **When did it happen?** Accept several ways to state this information, but do not write it on the chart.

Sept. 2, 20XX

Dear Mr. Lopez,

    We are sorry we made a muddy mess in the hall yesterday. The playground was very wet, and we didn't pay attention when we came in from recess. You should not have to clean up after us. We will remember to wipe our boots better next time.

                              Sincerely,
                              Mrs. Atkin's class

Amy   Daniel Lenard CRISSY   LAURIE ☺
Crystal   Noah Mark Bruce   Steve   S. on ya! Linda
*   Sarah   Jason Helene   Carol*
PAUL Kimberly   Bev   Joey   Gary L.

---

3. Explain that a good opening sentence in an apology might contain what we did to hurt or anger the person and when it happened. **How can we combine those two ideas in one sentence?** Pause to give students time to think. Accept several students' suggestions for creating this sentence before choosing one to begin the apology. Write this sentence on the chart paper. If students need assistance with this task, display one or two examples and fill in the blanks.

   EXAMPLES: Do you remember last _____ when _____?
                      On _____ we _____ and _____.

4. Explain that often in an apology a statement about being sorry goes next. **How do we feel about what we did?** Pause to give students time to think. Add this information to the chart paper. If students need assistance, write one of these examples on the chart paper and ask various students to insert the appropriate information.

> *EXAMPLES:* I am sorry for _____ and _____.
> I regret that I _____.
> Causing you extra work was _____.
> It wasn't fair to you to have to _____.

5. **Why are we sorry? What went wrong? Why did it happen?** Pause for at least 30 seconds to allow students time to reflect on their actions. Praise insight. Add this information to the group apology on the chart paper. If a student blurts out something like "terrific," suggest that he or she rethink what happened.

> *EXAMPLE:* This happened because _____.

6. **What can we do to make things better in the future? How could we hope to correct the problem?** Pause for at least 20 seconds to allow students time to consider which ideas to offer. Praise effective solutions. Add students' ideas to the group apology on the chart paper.

> *EXAMPLE:* I'll remember to _____ from now on.

7. **What final comment/plea could we say to let _____ know that we won't ever do this again?** Pause for at least 30 seconds to allow students time to reflect on their actions. Praise thoughtful final comments. Add this information to the group apology on the chart paper.

> *EXAMPLES:* I won't ever _____ again.
> Please forgive me for _____.
> I'll do my best to make sure it doesn't happen again.

8. **How shall we close the group apology?** Add this to the apology on the chart paper. Praise the students' apology and all the thought, honesty, and effort that went into creating this apology.

9. Encourage students to sign their names to the group apology. Later, two students can roll it up, tie it with yarn, and deliver it to the proper person.

Brainstorming Assistant
for
Apology

Who   **When**   **Where**

What Happened

Reasons for Apology

Possible Resolutions

INDIVIDUAL BRAINSTORMING

Now you will get the opportunity to write personal apologies to someone you have hurt or offended. Give each student a copy of the reproducible Brainstorming Assistant to help them generate ideas. The Brainstorming Assistant can be found at the end of this lesson. Explain that for the next 10–15 minutes everyone will need to be thinking and writing, not sharing.

Key Questions

1. **To whom do you need to apologize? Who have you hurt, angered, or disappointed lately?** Pause for at least two minutes to give students plenty of time to think and to privately write their ideas under the "Who" column on their individual brainstorming sheet.

2. **To which of these people do you want to write your apology?** Tell students to circle the name of this person on their brainstorming assistants.

3. **When did this unfortunate event occur? Where did it happen?** Pause for at least 30 seconds to give students time to think and to privately write their ideas under the "When" and "Where" columns.

4. **What happened? What did you do to this person that hurt, angered, or disappointed him/ her? What are you sorry for?** Pause for at least two minutes to give students plenty of time to think through what happened and to write their ideas under the "What Happened" column. Remind students that a person can be sorry for something that wasn't his/her fault or that they had little control over.

5. **A person has been hurt. How do you feel about what happened now? Why are you sorry about it? Why were you in the wrong?** *or* **What part of the problem was your fault? Consider this honestly.** Pause for at least two minutes to give students time to think and to write their ideas under the "Reasons" column.

6. **What could you do to make things better? How do you hope to solve your part of the problem?** Pause for at least two minutes to give students plenty of time to think and to privately write their ideas under the "Possible Resolutions" column.

7. Ask students to raise their hands to indicate they are ready for individual composing. Instruct students that they will use their notes to help them compose their apologies. Share that students will publish their finished apologies on special triangular notepaper. (The triangular notepaper can be found at the end of the lesson.) Having a special format often helps motivate students to put more thought into their apologies.

    Confirm that students have brainstormed three or four ideas for each column before they move to individual composing.

INDIVIDUAL COMPOSING

As students use their notes to write their apologies, walk around the classroom. Note productive starts regarding what happened or how the student feels. Make positive comments on students' sincere ideas or genuine comments.

    Ask questions to help students include when and where, what happened, reasons for apologizing, and solutions. Also help writers order their thoughts more effectively in their apologies.

RESPONDING TO STUDENTS' WRITINGS/REVISING

Every group of writers contains large differences in reading, writing, and intellectual abilities. For this lesson mentally place your students into two groups. Ask your Advanced Writers to work independently while you meet with the Beginning Writers.

Beginning Writers

1. Give each student a copy of an apology such as the one below. Explain that "Sara" knows she was in the wrong and she really wants "Ms. Lucerno" as a customer. Therefore she wants her apology to be clear and to sound contrite. Encourage students to find both mechanical and grammatical errors, as well as errors in reasoning. Once problems are identified, ask for solutions orally.

September 9, 20XX

dear Ms lucerno

I'm sorry that I have been missing your home when I deliver my newspapers. I caught the flu over laborday weekend and I've been unable to ride my Honda ever since. I must have spaced out when I came to your street. I will make sure that you get your newspaper from now on.

your news carrier
Sara

---

2. Pull these writers together for a group revising session. Ask each Beginning Writer to read his/her apology to the small group. Find at least one positive thing to say about each student's apology.

3. Since most of these beginning writers have labored long and hard just to write their rough drafts, consider moving them directly to publishing. Don't even require a clean copy. *The rationale for this is that you don't want students to forget the reason for their composition.*

   Growth and improvement will come more quickly with frequent writing experiences, rather than a few almost-perfect compositions. If a student wants to make a correction, praise his/her efforts.

Advanced Writers   As Advanced Writers finish their rough drafts, ask them to find a revising partner.

1. Ask one partner to read the other's apology aloud to see if it sounds contrite and if the reasons make sense. Encourage these students to do one of the following:

   • Make two to three specific comments on what he or she likes about the apology.

   • Ask questions to expand or clarify the writer's ideas.

   • Share one or two suggestions for how to improve the apology.

2. After completing step 1, ask the Advanced Writers to make one or two revisions to improve the apology. Ideas and suggestions can be written directly on the composition so students can refer to them as they rewrite their apologies on special paper.

3. Ask revising partners to trade compositions and look for punctuation, capitalization, spelling, and other errors that might hinder the reader in understanding the apology. Don't insist the apology be perfect since this may direct students' attention away from the meaning of the apology.

PUBLISHING

Share that you are proud of each of your students for sharing feelings that may have been difficult to consider and expressing them in writing. Privately, you may want to ask selected students how writing the apology made them feel.

You will publish your apologies on special triangular notepaper so that the people receiving the apologies (*audience*) **will understand how sincere you are** (*purpose*).

Triangular Note Paper

Materials

triangular apology notepaper, scissors, tape or glue stick, crayons or colored markers

Directions

1. Fold the sheet of paper diagonally and crease the fold.

2. Cut off the excess at one end.

3. Draw your own cover or cut out the words "Please Accept My Apology" with the picture. Two different pictures with text can be found at the end of this lesson. Tape or glue them to the cover of your apology paper.

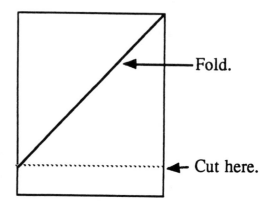

4. Lift the cover and write your apology on the inside at the bottom. If more room is needed, flip the triangular apology notepaper over and write on the back.

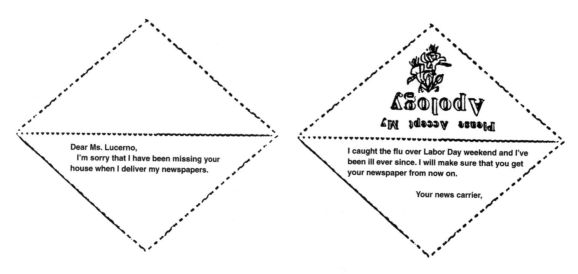

5. Add color to the cover of your apology with crayons or colored markers.

6. Give your written apology to the person you hurt or angered.

Brainstorming Assistant
for
Apology

Who   **When**   **Where**

What Happened

Reasons for Apology

Possible Resolutions

Please Accept My
Apology

- -

Please Accept My
Apology

LESSON 21

Travel Brochure

OUTCOME   Each student will create a brochure advertising the best qualities of his/her town to potential visitors.

MOTIVATORS

1. As you inquire in which towns and states students have lived, have the student point these out on a state, province, or country map. Ask several students to briefly describe towns in which they've lived or visited. Lead the students to share how the former town and the town/state/country where they now live are similar and different.

2. Have your students study brochures for your town or state that you have gotten from the State Department of Tourism, the Chamber of Commerce, and/or the Convention and Visitor's Bureau.

   Inquire if any of your students have visited the sites mentioned in the brochures. Ask how those brochures entice readers to visit or move to a particular place.

WELCOME to MOORHEAD

Moorhead is a great place to live.

- terrific playgrounds
- great bike trails
- 12 ice hockey teams
- hot summers & cold winters
- good teachers
- a museum with a huge boat
- great for elderly and handicapped
- lots of ice cream stands
- a skateboard farm

Come visit us!

---

3. Suggest students check tourism websites. (A list of websites can be found at the end of this lesson.)

GROUP BRAINSTORMING

Now we will brainstorm some ideas for our state. Students will brainstorm together for a state brochure; later they will brainstorm individually to write a brochure for their town(s).

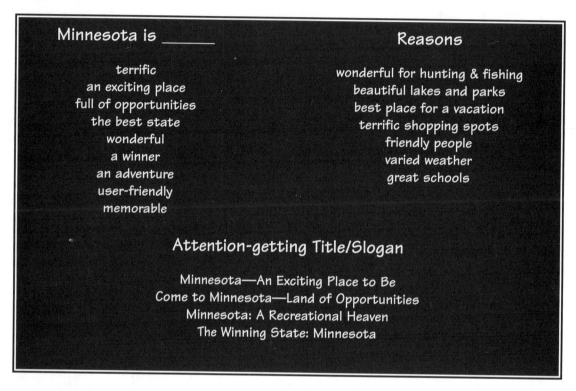

Minnesota is _____	Reasons
terrific	wonderful for hunting & fishing
an exciting place	beautiful lakes and parks
full of opportunities	best place for a vacation
the best state	terrific shopping spots
wonderful	friendly people
a winner	varied weather
an adventure	great schools
user-friendly	
memorable	

Attention-getting Title/Slogan

Minnesota—An Exciting Place to Be
Come to Minnesota—Land of Opportunities
Minnesota: A Recreational Heaven
The Winning State: Minnesota

Key Questions

1. **What are some opinions about our state that will draw people? What positive feeling of (our state) do you have?** Pause for at least 30 seconds to give students time to think. Write their opinions under the "Minnesota is _____" column.
   What is another opinion you have that may entice brochure readers to come to _____?

   NOTE: Less experienced writers often want to offer facts, instead of opinions. (In truth, many opinions are seen as facts to some people and vice versa. Your goal is to keep the opinion column general enough so that students can support their opinions without significant research.)

   When brainstorming opinions, if a "fact" is offered, respond in a positive manner and write it under the "Reasons" column. Comment that the idea will be useful later, then repeat an opinion question.

2. **Out of all our opinions which one shall we prove first?** Choose a quiet or withdrawn student to select one opinion. Circle this idea and use it throughout the lesson. If other students object that their opinion wasn't chosen, remind them that they get to choose and develop their own ideas later. (optional) **Out of our remaining opinions which one shall we prove second? third?**

3. What reasons can we give to support our opinion that (Minnesota) is (an exciting place) to visit/live? Insert your town or state and your students' opinion into this question. Praise each reason that supports the opinion and write the reasons under the "Reasons" column.

NOTE: Develop your students' sense of the audience. If you want students to focus on a particular audience (children, teenagers, parents, businesspeople, retired citizens), design your questions so they include your target audience.

EXAMPLES: Why would children, teenagers, parents, businesspeople, retired citizens want to visit or move here to live?
What do (insert the audience you selected) **need to know about** (insert the name of your state) **to convince them to visit or move here?**

Why is our state such a great place to live? What are _____'s positive qualities? What do we have that will attract interesting people to our state? What do we have to offer? Why visit or come here to live? Pause for at least 30 seconds to give students time to think. Write their ideas under the "Reasons" column.

NOTE: In this persuasive composition factual information is a reason.

If students need more specific questions to generate reasons, try some of these.

- **What attractions will readers want to know about?** (movie theaters, zoos, water slides, arts and craft shows, river tours, health clubs, speedways, state fairs)

- **What entertainment do we have?**

- **What in-town recreation is available?** (playgrounds, picnic shelters, biking trails, golf courses, softball fields, ice rinks)

- **What state-wide recreation is available?** (parks, beaches, lakes, hiking trails, camping opportunities, scenery)

- **What art galleries and museums do we have?**

- **What night life is available?**

- **What professional and personal sports are available?**

- **How are the restaurants? fast-food places? hotels?**

- **What shopping opportunities do we have? shopping malls?**

- **What medical facilities, churches, etc., are bonuses for those who live in** (insert the name of your state)**?**

- **What is the weather like? climate? average daily temperature?**

- **What employment opportunities are available?**

- **What educational opportunities can we offer?**

- **What are the people like?**

- **What transportation is available?**

4. Next select four to six uninvolved students to each choose one strong reason. Circle each reason on the board.

5. (optional) Choose one of the selected reasons. **What example can we give to illustrate this reason? What is the name of this place? Where is it located? What is its address? How can we describe this place?** (type of establishment, hours, cost, phone number for further information)

6. **What other needs could people have?** (phone numbers such as recorded time/weather information, road conditions, local entertainment ticket outlet)

7. **What kind of attention-getting title can we have for our brochure? How can we interest potential readers in reading our brochure?** Write these ideas under the "Attention-Getting Title/Slogan" column.

GROUP COMPOSING

Before class begins cut two large rectangular pieces of folded butcher paper to illustrate the parts of the group brochure. Then tape newspaper to the wall if you think markers may bleed through. Next tape the 15 × 24-inch sheet to the newspaper-covered wall; it will represent the cover of the brochure. Fold the 30 × 24-inch sheet in half to represent the inside of the brochure. Then open it and tape it on the wall.

We are going to write one possible brochure together for our state. Later you'll get to create your own brochures to advertise the benefits of our state.

1. **Let's start our brochure by arranging our attention-getting title on the cover of the brochure. How could we space the words of our title?** Choose a creative student to add the title to the cover of the brochure. If this student is a poor speller, select a good speller to assist.

> **Thinking about Mechanics:** What do we do to show the name of a state or town? (capitalize the first letter of each word in the name)

2. Open the folded brochure. Point out to students that the left side of the enlarged brochure will contain a picture or photograph related to our state/town.
   (optional) **How can we use the size and style of the letters, color, and art work/pictures to attract and hold readers' attention?**

3. Point to the right side of the enlarged brochure. Explain that this page will begin with a friendly greeting and a hope that the reader will visit/move to our state. **Class, what state will our brochure advertise?** Praise the correct response.
   How can we greet the reader in a friendly manner? How can we let readers know they will enjoy our state?

4. **Class, all together, what opinion of our state did we choose to direct our brochure?** Praise their correct response and write this information on the brochure for the topic sentence.
   Ask students why this topic/opinion sentence was placed first in the brochure. **How does it help future readers? Next, ask students how they will begin their brochures about their towns. What town will be used? Whose opinion will be used?**

5. **Of all our reasons, which ones did we select to convince readers to come to our state?** As the chosen reasons are renamed, ask students to think about how to order them in the brochure.

6. **How can we order our reasons? Which ones do you feel are the strongest? Which of our reasons for coming to our state do you feel will appeal the most to our future readers?** Allow students to discuss with their neighbors before making a decision. As students reselect reasons, number them from strongest (1) to good (8).

7. **How can we close our travel brochure? What can we say to urge readers to visit or move here? How do we get them to act? Who can the reader contact for further information? Finally, let's wish our future readers a pleasant visit or best wishes for their future in our state.** Praise all reasonable suggestions, then choose one and add it to the brochure on the sheet.
   EXAMPLE: Try Minnesota. There's so much to see and do.

Motivator for Switching to Town Brochures

Before switching from composing a group state brochure to composing town brochures, organize students to gather some data.

This experience enables your students to see people value different aspects of their town and provide a valuable oral language experience. (For example, children may appreciate the zoo; teenagers might enjoy the activities by the river and the varied sports; parents may appreciate the good schools; businesspeople may like the new civic center; and the elderly may enjoy the transportation system and the social groups.)

1. Have your students carry out an informal survey asking friends, family, neighbors, and businesspeople what they like about your town/city or what these people are proud of in their town. Define "survey" for students. (*Survey*—a set of oral or written questions asked of a representative sample of the population to gather opinions on a current issue.)

2. Give students copies of the Town or State Survey you'll find at the end of this lesson. Explain that when people are approached, they must be told the name of the sponsor and reason for the survey.

Town or State Survey

	What do you like about _____?	What makes you proud?
Friend		
Parent		
Neighbor		
Business-person		

Information collected by

3. Carry out the interview with friends, family, neighbors, and businesspeople.

4. Place the data from surveys on chart paper or a tally sheet. Tabulate and summarize the results.

5. Discuss the survey results. Draw conclusions about the reasons people like their town.

INDIVIDUAL BRAINSTORMING & COMPOSING

Point out that now students will get to create their own town brochures. As students begin to brainstorm and write, walk around the room and converse with students who need individual guidance expressing their thoughts and feelings.

Beginning Writers Allow Beginning Writers to write a brochure for your *town* or *state* from the lists of ideas generated during the group brainstorming. Encourage students to include a title, their own opinion sentence, and bulleted facts in list form (incomplete sentences, instead of paragraphs). See this example.

**WELCOME
to
MOORHEAD**

Moorhead is a great place to live.

- terrific playgrounds
- great bike trails
- 12 ice hockey teams
- hot summers & cold winters
- good teachers
- a museum with a huge boat
- great for elderly and handicapped
- lots of ice cream stands
- a skateboard farm

Come visit us!

Advanced Writers   Suggest Advanced Writers tailor their brochures for one particular audience (such as teenagers or parents) and focus their reasons on convincing that audience. Encourage the use of descriptors to help the people considering the town to really visualize what it has to offer.

Another possibility is to encourage Advanced Writers to compose three paragraphs each supporting a different opinion. *For example:*

- **Introductory Paragraph:** Moorhead is a wonderful place to live and visit (*the overall opinion*). We have great parks, wonderful entertainment, friendly people. Consider us.

- **Second Paragraph:** Moorhead has outstanding parks (*the first opinion*). Describe 2–4 examples.

- **Third Paragraph:** Another reason for coming to Moorhead is the entertainment (*the second opinion*). Describe 2–4 examples.

- **Fourth Paragraph:** A third reason for moving to Moorhead is the friendly people (*the third opinion*). Describe 2–4 examples.

- **Conclusion and Request for Readers to Act:** Moorhead is a wonderful place to live and visit. We're known for our parks, entertainment, and friendly people. Don't pass us by.

RESPONDING TO STUDENTS' WRITINGS/REVISING

As students complete their own brochure, ask them to find a partner and read the message aloud to see if it is convincing and provides useful examples. Write the following information on the board or overhead to guide your students' revising.

Town Brochure Revising Assistant

_____ 1. Does it sound like an interesting place to move to or visit?

_____ 2. Does the town brochure contain lots of useful information (details)?

_____ 3. Is my information accurate?

_____ 4. What is the best part of this brochure?

_____ 5. Which words have I used that are worn out? What specific vibrant words could I choose to replace each worn-out word?

PUBLISHING

Ask students to rewrite their town drafts in a brochure advertising your town to share with people who are interested in visiting or moving to your town (*audience*) so they can learn about your town/state and see what residents are proud of (*purpose*).

Brochure

Materials

white paper, colored markers, picture(s), paste or tape

Directions

1. Fold an 8-1/2 × 11-inch sheet of paper in half or in three equal parts.

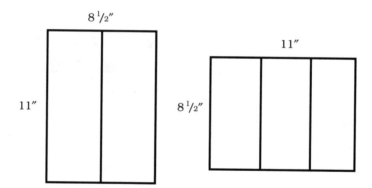

2. Consider how to arrange your title/slogan on the front cover. Add some color.

3. Open the brochure and paste or tape the picture you selected to attract visitors or potential citizens on the left side.

4. On the right side and back of the brochure, write or paste your advertisement. Use an attractive style of the letters, color, and art work/pictures to attract and hold readers' attention.

Town or State Survey

What do you like about _____?   **What makes you proud?**

Friend		
Parent		
Neighbor		
Business-person		

Information collected by

- -

Town or State Survey

What do you like about _____?   **What makes you proud?**

Friend		
Parent		
Neighbor		
Business-person		

Information collected by

Websites for State Tourism Offices

- Alabama: www.touralabama.org (or call 800-252-2262)
- Alaska: www.alaskanet.com/tourism (or call 907-465-2010)
- Arizona: www.arizonaguide.com (or call 800-842-8257)
- Arkansas: www.1800.natural.com (or call 800-628-8725)
- California: www.gocalis.ca.gov (or call 800-862-2543)
- Colorado: www.colorado.com (or call 800-265-6728)
- Connecticut: www.state.ct.us/tourism/ (or call 800-282-6863)
- Delaware: www.state.de.us.com (or call 800-441-8846)
- District of Columbia: www.travel.org/IC.html
- Florida: www.goflorida.com (or call 800-488-5607)
- Georgia: www.gomm.com (or call 800-847-4842)
- Hawaii: www.hawaii.gov/tourism/ (or call 800-464-2924)
- Idaho: www.visitid.org (or call 800-635-7820)
- Illinois: www.enjoyillinois.com (or call 800-223-0121)
- Indiana: www.state.in.us/tourism/ (or call 800-289-6646)
- Iowa: www.state.ia.us (or call 800-345-4692)
- Kansas: www.kansascommerce.com (or call 800-252-6727)
- Kentucky: www.kentuckytourism.com (or call 800-225-8747)
- Louisiana: www.louisianatravel.com (or call 800-334-8626)
- Maine: www.visitmaine.com (or call 800-533-9595)
- Maryland: www.mdisfun.org (or call 800-543-2937)
- Massachusetts: www.mass-vacation.com (or call 800-447-6277)
- Michigan: www.michigan.org (or call 800-543-2937)
- Minnesota: www.exploreminnesota.com (or call 800-657-3700)
- Mississippi: www.mississippi.org (or call 800-927-6378)
- Missouri: www.missouritourism.org (or call 800-877-1234)
- Montana: http://www.visitmt.com (or call 800-541-1447)
- Nebraska: www.visitnebraska.org (or call 800-228-4307)
- Nevada: www.travelnevada.com (or call 800-638-2328)
- New Hampshire: www.visitnh.gov (or call 800-386-4664)
- New Jersey: www.state.nj.us/travel (or call 800-537-7397)
- New Mexico: www.newmexico.org/ (or call 800-545-2040)
- New York: www.ILoveNY.state.ny.us (or call 800-225-5697)
- North Carolina: www.visitnc.com (or call 800-847-4862)
- North Dakota: www.ndtourism.com (or call 800-435-5663)
- Ohio: www.ohiotourism.com (or call 800-282-4393)
- Oklahoma: www.travelok.com (or call 800-652-6552)
- Oregon: www.traveloregon.com (or call 800-547-7842)
- Pennsylvania: www.experiencepa.com (or call 800-847-4872)
- Rhode Island: www.visitrhodeisland.com (or call 800-556-2484)
- South Carolina: www.sccsi.com/sc/ (or call 800-346-3634)
- South Dakota: www.state.sd.us (or call 800-732-5682)
- Tennessee: www.state.tn.us/tourdev (or call 800-836-6200)
- Texas: www.state.tx.us/travel (or call 800-452-9292)
- Utah: www.utah.com (or call 800-538-1030)
- Vermont: www.travel-vermont.com (or call 800-837-6668)
- Virginia: www.virginia.org (or call 800-847-4882)
- Washington: www.tourism.wa.gov/ (or call 800-544-1800)
- West Virginia: www.westvirginia.com (or call 800-225-5982)
- Wisconsin: www.tourism.state.wi.us (or call 800-432-8747)
- Wyoming: www.wyomingtourism.org (or call 800-225-5996)

NOTE: Websites change frequently. If an address doesn't work, try entering the name of the state, a plus sign (+), and the word "tourism" in a search engine such as Webcrawler.

A valuable website for a complete list of tourism sites can be located at: http://www.destinationmag.com/state.html.

LESSON 22

Personal Decision-Making

OUTCOME Each student will create pro/con lists to aid making a good decision about a current problem he/she is facing.

MOTIVATORS

1. Read these personal problem *dilemmas*. Ask students what each problem is, what decision(s) must be made, and what choices the person has in each dilemma.

Annie accepts an invitation to a skating party with Carrie, but realizes two days before the skating party that her family is planning a surprise birthday dinner for Annie's elderly grandmother, Tess. Annie would rather go to the skating party, but she knows her grandmother would be very disappointed if she didn't attend the family gathering.

Jeff studies hard for a difficult algebra exam and is relieved to score a B-. As he is leaving the classroom, he overhears a classmate bragging that she got an A on the test without studying; she had stolen the answers out of the teacher's desk the day before! There is another important algebra test in two weeks.

> Emily's friend Kelly asks her to try out for a part with her in a play at the community theater. Emily doesn't know if she wants to be in the play, but goes along with Kelly anyway. The tryouts turn out to be a lot of fun, and Emily does her best when it's her turn to read the lines. Three days later, Emily finds out that she got a part in the play, but Kelly didn't. Kelly says that if Emily is a true friend, she will not take the part.

2. Share a tough decision that you have faced. Explain how you went about making your decision.

3. Talk about the differences among morals, ethics, and laws. For example, give students examples of inappropriate behavior. Ask students what makes the actions poor decisions. Share a poor decision you made as a child. Ask students what poor decisions they made at a younger age.

> Moral Question: disrespect for your parents, taking money out of your dad's wallet

> Ethical Question: cheating on a test, lying to your best friend

> Legal Question: stealing the school flag, painting red and orange graffiti on the city library

GROUP BRAINSTORMING

Let's use brainstorming to help us make a decision. Plan ahead so that you can keep the list of ideas generated by the group available on the board or on chart paper until students have composed their rough drafts.

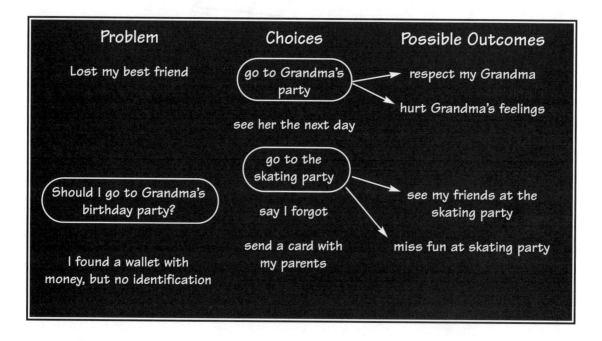

Key Questions

1. **What is an important personal problem you currently face? What future conflict might you have to solve?** Repeat these questions until eight to ten student ideas have been written on the board.

2. **Out of all these problems, which one do you want us to solve together?** Choose a student whom you want to be more involved to select a problem. Circle this idea. Gently remind students who are disappointed that although their problem wasn't selected, they will get to choose their own problem to solve later.

3. **What choices do you have? What options might you consider as you make up your mind? What healthy alternatives do you have? What other positive or wise alternatives might you consider?** Repeat these questions until five to six student ideas have been written on the board.

4. **Out of all these choices, which two do you want us to deliberate? What are our two best choices?** Ask two quiet students who usually don't participate to select one idea each. After circling each choice that was selected, ask each student why his/her idea is a good choice. Use these two ideas throughout the rest of the lesson.

GROUP COMPOSING

Now we'll evaluate these choices using a pro and con decision-making technique. Later, you'll use a pro/con list to make one or more important personal decisions.

Key Questions

1. **What are the reasons (PROS) for selecting Choice #1? Why should you do this? What are the benefits or gains of making this decision?** Point out the "Possible Outcomes" on the group brainstorming board. **How will your choice affect others: friends, family, other people?** Repeat these questions until two or three students' ideas have been written on the board under PROS.

2. **What are the reasons (CONS) against Choice #1? Why shouldn't you do this? What objections may your teacher, family, or friends have? What are the costs of making this choice/decision?** Repeat these questions until two or three student ideas have been written on the board under CONS.

Choice/Decision #1

Go to your grandmother's party and skip the skating party.

PROS	My grandmother is cool and I don't want to hurt her feelings.	CONS	I'll miss skating with that cute new boy, Frederick.

Choice/Decision #2

Skip your grandmother's party and go to the skating party.

PROS		CONS	
	My grandmother will understand if I explain the importance of the skating party.		I see my friends at school every day, but my grandmother is elderly.

I may not have a chance to celebrate many more birthdays with her. |

---

3. Repeat steps 1 and 2 for Choice #2.

4. Let's study our PRO and CON lists and evaluate this information. Allow students time to silently study the PRO and CON chart.

5. Which of these choices look the best? Which is the better/more responsible decision? Which will help you and not hurt anyone else? Allow students some quiet time to study the PRO and CON chart. Wait until the next day if it is a difficult choice.

6. Ask students to discuss these choices in pairs. **What is your decision? What did you conclude this person should do? What is a responsible choice?** Call on students one at a time to state their conclusion(s) and tell why they made/would make that choice.

7. (optional) **If you select Choice #_____, what resources will you need?** Encourage students to share ideas orally.

8. (optional) **If you select Choice #_____, what obstacles will you face in achieving it? How can you overcome these obstacles?** Encourage students to share ideas orally.

Decision-Making Assistant

My Personal Problems

Choice #__   PROs
              CONs

Choice #__   PROs
              CONs

Choice #__   PROs
              CONs

Choice #__   PROs
              CONs

I have decided to_____

_____

_____
                Signature

INDIVIDUAL BRAINSTORMING & COMPOSING

Explain that students will now get to consider a personal problem or civic responsibility and make a decision regarding it.

Pass out copies of the Decision-Making Assistant. This brainstorming assistant can be found at the end of this lesson.

Comprehension Check

Before students start to work, do a comprehension check. This will cut down on "What do I do?" questions once students begin.

1. **What do you need to brainstorm first?** (Brainstorm a list of personal problems I face.)

2. **What must you do now?** (Choose one problem.)

3. **Then what do you need to brainstorm?** (Brainstorm possible choices.)

4. **Next, what do you need to do?** (Brainstorm at least two possible outcomes for each choice.)

5. **After that what do you need to do?** (Write out one or two pros and one or two cons for each of the two choices.)

6. **Finally, what do you do?** (Study the information and make a responsible decision.)

7. **If you choose, what option can you take?** (Consider my resources and what obstacles I'll face.)

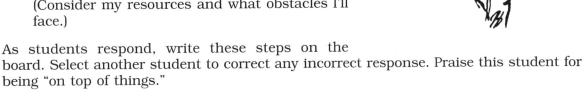

As students respond, write these steps on the board. Select another student to correct any incorrect response. Praise this student for being "on top of things."

RESPONDING TO STUDENTS' WRITINGS/REVISING

1. As students finish their rough drafts, ask them to choose a revising partner wisely. Explain that confidentiality MUST be respected. Have each student read aloud his or her problem in a whisper, the decision that must be made, and each choice with its pros and cons. Ask your revising partner whether the decision appears to be a healthy and responsible choice. Switch roles.

2. After step 1 is completed, ask each student to review his/her list to see if there are other choices that weren't considered earlier and if additional pros and cons should be considered.

3. Now require every student to talk with an older family member before coming to a final decision. In some situations, it might be wise to require the input of a responsible adult. If the student has no one, you could offer to accept this role of wise elder or brainstorm responsible adults from whom the student could seek advice.

PUBLISHING

After students make a decision for themselves (*audience*), ask them to fill in the "I decided to _____" portion of the Decision-Making Assistant with their decisions, and add their signatures at the bottom. Suggest students find a special or private place to post their lists to help them remember the decision (*purpose*). Allow students time to reflect privately or to share their decision with peers.

Decision-Making Assistant

My Personal Problems

Choice #___

PROs

CONs

Choice #___

PROs

CONs

Choice #___

PROs

CONs

Choice #___

PROs

CONs

I have decided to _____

_____

Signature _____

LESSON 23

Movie/Video Review

OUTCOME   Each student will write a dynamic review of a recent video or movie he/she has seen.

MOTIVATORS

1. Read some current reviews of popular movies from your local paper (especially the Sunday paper) to your students. Get some "Movie Reviews in Brief" as well as longer reviews that go into more detail. Reviews can be located using a search engine online with the key words "movie reviews," or search using the name of the movie. There are also websites like Movie Critic that will recommend movies/videos the reader might like (http://www.moviecritic.com/).

   Ask students if they read movie/video reviews. Then inquire why we read a review. (They help us decide which movies or videos we want to view.) Ask students where they would go to find a review.

2. Make overheads of reviews of several current or popular movie reviews. Ask students what information an effective review contains (title, quality rating such as four stars, brief story line with names of key actors, strengths, weaknesses, and perhaps a viewer rating such as G, PG-13, R).

3. Pass out one napkin or paper towel to each student. Then close the classroom door and window blinds.

   Direct students to place the napkin on their desk and close their eyes. Place a few kernels of freshly popped popcorn on each paper towel. Instruct students to breathe in and imagine they are in a movie theater or at home in front of the television ready for the movie/video to begin. Before moving to group brainstorming, give each student a small cup of popcorn to eat as they think.

GROUP BRAINSTORMING

Let's brainstorm ideas for movie/video reviews and what aspects of the movie/video we liked or disliked.

Key Questions

1. **What movies have you seen lately? Which videos do you own or rent frequently? What was the name of the movie/video?** Pause for at least 30 seconds to give students time to think and to privately write their ideas under the "Movie/Video Name" column. Accept all responses. Repeat these questions until six to eight movies have been written on the board.

Movie/Video Name	Opinions	Information
The Speeder	appealing	Africa
The Long Walk	sad	info—"western"
Young Guns	thrilling	real life
A Chimp Called Goldie	spellbinding	Jason Durant
Black Eagle	smashing	slaughtering elephants

2. **Which movie/video shall we review?** Ask an uninvolved student to choose one movie/videotape. Circle this idea and use it all through the lesson.

3. **What was your opinion of this movie/video? In your opinion would this movie/video be worthwhile for others to see? Why or why not? What was the overall effect of this movie/video on you? What will you tell your friends?** Accept everyone's opinions and write them on the board under the "Opinions" column. If other students reject a student's opinion, remind them that they will choose and develop their own opinion later to use in the movie review.

4. **Which opinion(s) shall we focus on in our review?** Choose a quiet or withdrawn student to select one opinion. Circle this idea and give reasons for it though the lesson.

5a. Now we need some information about the story and other information to support our opinion. Repeat the following questions until three or four ideas have been written on the board for each question. Praise each idea. Place all responses under the "Information" column.

5b. What was this movie about? What can we say happened without giving away the story? (plot or storyline) **What was the most memorable scene?**

5c. Who was the main character (stars) in the movie/video? How can we describe the main character? What did the actor do?

5d. Where did the story take place? How can we describe the setting? What special effects were used?

5e. What type of movie was it? (comedy, science fiction, romance, mystery, animated)

5f. What did you like the most/least about this story? What were your favorite/worst parts? Which part was the most exciting/boring? What made the movie/video a success or a failure? Why do you feel this way?

Reasons	Audience	Rating Systems
funny jokes	not for children	Must See—Skip this one
too violent	people who like suspense	Go—Don't go
made me cry		Interesting—Boring
excellent music		Terrific—Don't waste your time

6. Who would be a good audience for this movie/video? (kids 4–6 years old; teenagers 10–11 years old; old folks) Praise appropriate audiences and add students' ideas to the board.

7. What kind of rating systems have you seen?
Share these systems if students lack knowledge of standard rating systems.

> * to ****
> 1, 2, 3, 4, 5
> entertaining—boring
> see—don't see
> thumbs up—thumbs down

What other rating systems could we use?
Praise interesting rating systems and add students' ideas to the board.

GROUP COMPOSING

Now we will compose a movie/video review together. Later you'll get to choose your favorite movie or video to review.

The Long Walk

The video <u>The Long Walk</u> was spellbinding. The lead character, played by Sam Johnson, was a tough wrangler. He made us hate and adore him. The African desert setting and the eerie music added to the drama of the foreigners slaughtering the rhinoceros for their horns. At first the story was difficult to follow because there were so many twists and turns in the plot, but the ending made it worth it.

Teens and adults will find this movie entertaining and quite effective at nudging their consciousness to care about what is happening to the rhinoceros in Africa. I wouldn't recommend this movie to children because they might vomit when they see how the rhinoceros were treated, but it is quite effective at nudging their consciousness to care about what is happening. Overall I give <u>The Long Walk</u> the "thumbs up" award. Be sure to see it.

Reviewed by _____

---

1. **Which movie/video have we chosen to review?** Insert the name of the movie/video at the top of the sheet for the title.

> **Thinking about Mechanics:** What should I do to important words in a title? (capitalize)

2. **What was our opinion of _____?** Write this information in the opinion sentence "The movie/video <u>The Long Walk</u> was _____."

> **Thinking about Mechanics:** What should I do to the first word in a paragraph to show the beginning of a new idea? (indent)

3. **Next, let's give a brief summary of the plot without giving away the story. How shall we describe the plot? What information can we include about the actors/actresses?** Praise effective ways to summarize the plot and add this information to the review.

4. **Which information about the setting supports our opinion about the movie or video? How can you put that in a sentence?** As students provide information about the setting, add it to the movie/video review on the board.

5. **What type of story is it? Who would be a good audience?** As students provide information about the type of story and who the audience is, add it to the review on the board.

6. **Based on our comments, how shall we rate this movie/video for the audience? What would be a good way to summarize its overall effectiveness?** Add this information to the review. Have students read the review aloud. Praise their review.

INDIVIDUAL BRAINSTORMING & COMPOSING

Now you get to select your own movie or video to review.

As students begin brainstorming their ideas about the movie/video they are reviewing, walk around the classroom noting the inclusion of opinions; information such as plot, characters, settings, type of story; other reasons for the opinion(s); audience; and a rating system.

Encourage students to use descriptive language to make the review interesting for their readers. Praise students for solid information and reasons to back their opinions about the movie review. Ask students questions to help them organize their thoughts so that readers will get *a clear and accurate idea whether to view the movie or not.*

Beginning Writers   Some Beginning Writers find it easier to brainstorm their thoughts in two columns:

	(movie or video title)
Positive Opinions	Negative Opinions

RESPONDING TO STUDENTS' WRITINGS/REVISING

1. As students finish the rough drafts of their movie or video reviews, ask them to find a revising partner who has *not seen* the movie/video. Have writers read their reviews aloud to their revising partners. The revising partner is responsible for helping the reviewer to think of important details the writer may have left out that the reader might want to know.

2. Encourage students to make two to three specific comments on what they like and to offer suggestions for improving the movie/video review.

3. Next request/require the writers to make at least one or two revisions to improve their reviews.

4. Before publishing, have students trade compositions and look for punctuation, capitalization, spelling, and other errors that might hinder a reader from understanding the review and using its information.

PUBLISHING

Now that you have revised your movie/video review, we'll share our reviews with our classmates, the other classes and their teachers, family, and neighbors (*audience*) **so they can make good decisions about which movies/videos to view** (*purpose*).

Class Book

Compile students' reviews in a class book and add a dated cover using the illustration at the end of this lesson.

    Repeat monthly during the year. By the fourth time most students will only need a motivator (seeing the movie or video), individual brainstorming and composing, revising, and publishing. As students' reviews become stronger, consider placing them on your school website. Students' illustrations can be scanned in.

Our
Movie and Video
"Picks"

Lesson 24

Request for Financial Support

Outcome Each student will write a letter requesting financial support for a worthy cause or to solve a particular problem.

MOTIVATORS

1. Ask your students if they know Percy Ross (or feature another philanthropist you know). Percy Ross is a trillionaire, philanthropist, and newspaper columnist who has given encouragement and money to people in need for 17 years. Percy Ross "earned a fortune and a wealth of knowledge during his lifetime" and chose to share both with others. His vow was to help people until he gave away all his money. His motto is "He who gives while he lives . . . also knows where it goes."

2. Explain that the class is going to continue the legacy of philanthropists by caring about others and raising financial support for worthy causes in the community. Ask students what groups they have raised money for and their purpose for raising the money.

3. Before doing motivators 4, 5, and/or 6, choose two students to use ribbon or heavy yarn to divide a bulletin board in two parts—"Funds Granted" and "Funds Refused"— so students can reread the letters and corresponding responses that are discussed.

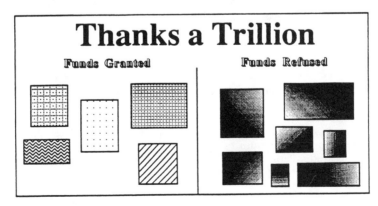

4. Give two pairs of students "preselected" clippings from the news column "Thanks a Million" by Percy Ross or use these clippings. (A reproducible can be found at the end of this lesson.) Past copies from the "Thanks a Million" news column can be obtained from Percy Ross, c/o Midweek Plus, P.O. Box 39000, Minneapolis, MN 55439. Preview letters to make sure topics are suitable for your students.

Allow time for students to rehearse reading their column aloud. One student in each pair should take the role of the advice seeker and read the first part of a clipping. The second student should take the role of the financial philanthropist/donor.

When students are ready, have one pair slowly read their request letter to the class. Ask your class what the letter contained. (pleas from people facing tragedies and misfortunes who needed financial aid) Inquire why these people asked for money and how might this affect the philanthropist's response. Also ask about the tone of the letter. Next, have the partner read the response that was received. Repeat with the other request letter and its response.

To: Someone who cares about the small guy From: Lazy Max I'm writing because I need money to support my two-pack-a-day cigarette habit. I've tried to get a job, but I always get fired within a week. They want me to work hard, but I don't really enjoy hard work. They don't like my back talk. Could you help me? I really like the nicotine. Be considerate. It will make my day. Besides, you have lots of money. Be nice and share it. Make my day.	To: Someone who cares From: Sara School starts in two weeks. We need your help. Mom and Grandma died last year in a car accident. Dad promised my sister and me that he'd buy us clothes, coats, books, and shoes for school. He loves us a lot, but he lost his job and our car was stolen. He misses Mom and has to work and raise us too. He tries hard, but can't seem to make ends meet. Would you help our family? We can buy some clothes and coats at the thrift shop, but we also need underwear, shoes, and school supplies. My teacher's name is Mrs. Talbert. Her phone number at school is 1-512-233-8424.

5. If students haven't commented on the responses, point out that one response was serious and/or compassionate while the other response was pointedly critical. Ask your students why they think that certain requests for money are supported and why others are not. Praise students' insightful responses regarding tears for the "needy" and laughter at the "greedy." Post copies of these letters/responses on the bulletin board under "Funds Granted" and "Funds Refused."

To: Lazy Max From: Someone who cares You deserve what you get. Nothing! Stop smoking and get a job. You'll need the health insurance when you get lung cancer. Stick a lollipop in your mouth instead of a cigarette. Perhaps it will help keep you from opening your mouth inappropriately at work.	To: Sara From: Someone who cares A check is on its way to pay for school clothes, shoes, and school books. I talked to your teacher. She will take you and your sister shopping before school starts. Give your dad lots of hugs. I'm sure he'll appreciate them as he tackles the job of two parents. Work hard in school and someday help someone in need.

6. Invite students to consider the credibility of the writers who ask for funds. Put the following real request on an overhead or make copies for each student. A reproducible can be found at the end of this lesson.

Nov. 17, 20XX

Dear Pet Food Manufacturer,

My name is Judith. I'm a seventh grader at Fargo Middle School. I've been working as a volunteer at the Humane Society for three years. Every winter we have hundreds of dogs and cats dropped off at our door. We try to get them all placed in good homes as soon as possible, but in the meantime they must stay in an old unheated dairy barn. It is very cold and many of the cats and dogs get sick before we can find them a home. These dogs and cats are put to sleep because medicine is costly. As a pet lover I know you won't want this to happen.

The other workers have put out announcements on our three radio stations for blankets for warmth, but we need money to buy enough straw to cover the animals. I talked with three farmers. They will sell us straw at half price. It will cost $350 to pay for the straw. If you want to see if I'm telling the truth, you can call the director of our Humane Society. His phone number is 1-718-HELP-NOW. Next year we'll plan ahead so we can get the straw donated. Will you please send us $350 to pay for the straw? Do you care about keeping these unwanted pets alive as much as we do? Please help us. We need your assistance.

Yours truly,

Judith

Judith, a dog lover

First, ask students if they think this letter received financial support. Then ask why or why not. List students' impressions under "Reasons $$$ Is Requested." List students' reasons on chart paper so these ideas can be revisited during Group and Individual Composing.

Second, ask students if the writer seems credible. If students think the writer is credible (or not credible), ask why these conclusions were drawn. List students' conclusions under "Credibility of Writer."

Reasons $$$ Is Requested	Credibility of Writer
homeless cats and dogs	volunteer for 3 years
straw to keep them warm	can call director Humane Society
so homeless pets won't be put to sleep	phone number is provided
	researched price of straw

Third, if you desire, this discussion can be followed by analyzing other clippings for the reasons people ask for money and the credibility of the writers.

NOTE: This student, whose name was changed, did receive $100 to help pay for straw.

7. Restate that students are going to raise financial support for worthy causes in the community. Share several current worthy causes in your school or community of which you are aware.

NOTE: Students can be guided to one cause, or they can brainstorm many worthy causes during group brainstorming. While students relate better to helping specific individuals in need, perhaps staff from the United Way, March of Dimes, American Heart Association, Multiple Sclerosis, Big Brother/Big Sister Organization can share with your class specific examples of people in need.

GROUP BRAINSTORMING

Now we are going to compose a letter requesting financial support for a worthy cause.

People in Need/Worthy Cause

school needs new bike rack
Mrs. Claude, our janitor, needs new glasses
Coats for Kids needs new containers
my brother Jason needs winter boots
our school needs new computers
a girl in scouting program needs $ to go to camp
the homeless

Reasons

6 computers for 300 students
money for computers used for school roof
students need to be ready for 21st century

Possible Donors

business owners
parents
students
alumni
computer companies

Plans

continue bake sales, etc.
develop websites & sell to businesses
buy discounted computers online
send out letters to alumni for $$$

Credibility

our teacher Mr. Platte
supports our fund-raising plan

show computer savings account
many alumni will know us

Key Questions

1. If the cause was not selected in the motivation step by the teacher, then brainstorm many worthy causes here. **Who is someone you know who needs financial assistance? What group needs money for a worthy cause?** List these ideas under the "People in Need/Worthy Cause" column. Praise sincere ideas.

2. If the need wasn't identified in responses to question 1 (only the group), inquire further. **What is the person's/group's problem? What goal does the person or group want to achieve? What dream does the person or group hope to fill?** List ideas under the "People in Need/Worthy Cause" column across from the person's or group's name.

    (optional) **What is a stronger way to state this need/worthy cause?** Modify each response before writing it on the board. Praise valuable improvements.

    EXAMPLES: Initial Response: "needs glasses"

    Stronger Response: "needs glasses so she can continue reading to the first graders at our elementary school"

3. **Out of all the people or groups, which one deserves help the most? Which one do we believe really deserves a financial boost? Which one shall we choose to support?** Circle the chosen person or group under the "People in Need/Worthy Cause" column.

4a. **How can we convince someone to donate money? What reasons can we give to convince the financial donor to give support? What is an even stronger reason for giving support?** Insert information under the "Reasons" column.

4b. **How can we vividly describe the problem so the reader will understand and respond to the need? What true examples can we give? What facts do we need to give to justify the need for a donation?** Insert information under the "Reasons" column.

4c. **What can we say to convince the reader that this is a worthy cause, one that will make a difference? How will the donation help the receiver or the community? How will a particular amount of money make things better? For example, what will $10 buy or accomplish? $100?** Insert information under the "Reasons" column.

    EXAMPLES: If you contribute $5, this will provide a week of hot meals for a homeless child.

    If you donate $2 a week, three dogs or cats will receive medical attention for a year.

4d. How will the financial donor benefit from the contribution? Insert information under the "Reasons" column.

5. **Out of all our reasons, justifications, and/or examples, which ones are our strongest? most convincing? Which justifications will be appealing to the possible financial donor?** Circle this information under the "Reasons" column.

6. **What amount of financial support is needed? How can we determine this? Who would know?** Insert suggested amounts under the "Plans" column. Praise realistic dollar amounts.

7. **What is our plan for accomplishing the goal once the money is received? What people, materials, and/or equipment are needed? How/When/Where will they be used?** Insert information under the "Plans" column.

8. **Who might be a donor? Who might sympathize with our worthy cause enough to donate money? Who could benefit from this problem being fixed or this goal being reached? Who might be willing to help solve this problem?**

   Most students will need assistance coming up with possible donors. This background information will help you. Besides contacting individuals as possible donors, consider approaching local businesses and national corporations as well as foundations. A list of charities can be found on the web at http://www.guidestar.org.

   Most businesses and corporations set aside money in their budgets for community causes. Foundations are established solely to collect donated money and

distribute it to worthy causes. Foundations are usually run by volunteer boards that review requests for funds, grant those requests, and evaluate the progress of worthy causes that received their donations. Requests are often in the form of "grant applications." Grant applications require information similar to the information generated in this lesson.

   It is important to research possible donors to determine whether your worthy cause is one they might support. *For example:* A dairy company might give to a cause that benefits children or pregnant mothers. A health club or hospital might be interested in supporting something that benefits physical health. A software company might support an educational cause.

9. **What can we tell the financial donor about us that will establish our credibility and trustworthiness? What are our motives for raising funds for this project? What qualifications/knowledge/skills do we have that will increase the financial donor's faith that we can carry out the plan successfully?** Insert information under the "Credibility" column. Praise insightful ideas.

GROUP COMPOSING

Now let's organize our ideas into a letter to _____ (or another financial donor that you've selected).

January 5, 20XX

Dear South High Alumnus,

    We are juniors and sophomores at South Junior High. We'll be attending South High soon. We are writing to you because we have a problem that we hope you can help us solve.

    Each semester, over one hundred students sign up for computer classes at South High. Yet there are only six old computers for students to use in our school so the time available on these computers is very limited.

    The school district earmarked funds for new equipment, but we had a bad storm that damaged the school roof so badly that we couldn't use the building unless the roof was fixed.

---

1. **What is today's date?** Write this information on the board or overhead.

> **Thinking about Mechanics:** What punctuation should I put between the day and year? (a comma) Why? (so the numbers don't run together and confuse the reader)

2. **How can we greet the reader? Write "dear** _____ **," on the board so all the students can see.**

> **Thinking about Mechanics:** What should I have done to the letter "d" in "dear _____ " ? (capitalize)

   To whom are we writing our request for financial aid? Who is our potential donor? Insert the potential donor's name after the "dear."

> **Thinking about Mechanics:** What should I do to the donor's name? (capitalize)

> **Thinking about Mechanics:** What punctuation should I put after the donor's name? (a comma)

3. Explain that a good opening sentence in a letter requesting financial support might contain who the writer is, who the person/people in need is/are, and the problem or worthy cause. **Let's start our request for financial aid by introducing ourselves and the cause and the need.**

3a. Direct students' attention to the "Credibility" part of the brainstormed information. **Out of all of the ideas we brainstormed, how shall we introduce ourselves? Which ideas should we share about ourselves to establish the trust of the financial donor?** Accept one or two ideas orally.

3b. Direct students' attention to the "People in Need/Worthy Cause" part of the brainstormed information. **Which worthy cause did we choose to write on behalf of/is the worthiest? Which person/group did we decide needs financial aid the most? How can we explain this need in a way that catches the reader's attention?** Accept one or two ideas orally.

3c. How can we combine these two ideas (a and b) **for our introduction? What might we say?** Accept ideas. Choose one you want to use and add it to the letter.

> **Thinking about Mechanics:** What do we need to do to this first word in this sentence to show it is the beginning of a new idea? (indent)

CAR WASHES

>   We are trying to raise money through bake sales, car washes, and a school carnival, but we have only been able to raise $250 so far. This is only enough for one computer and a printer. We are sending you a copy of our "computer savings account" to show you how hard we've worked to raise money.
>
>   We are writing to you because you graduated from South High. We hope you will donate money to help us buy computers. Could you donate $150, $50, $25, or even $10 to help us reach our goal of twenty computers? The money you donate will be used to purchase discounted computers from the On-Line Computer Store @ $150 each. If you help us, we can learn new skills so we (and future South High students) can work on school projects (like developing and selling web pages to area businesses), learn new skills, and prepare for the 21st century.
>
>   Send your check to South High, attention Mr. Platte, our Physics teacher. Help us continue the South High tradition of excellence.
>
>   Sincerely,
>
>   Sophomores & Juniors of South Jr. High

4. **What are our main points we need to make? Which reason, justification, or example shall we put first? second? third? Why?** Pause to give students time to choose. Add at least three reasons to the group composition.

5. **What final comment or emotional plea could we make? How can we sum up our ideas and end our letter in a way that appeals to the reader's own needs, hopes, and dreams? How can we request action in a memorable, but polite manner?** Pause to allow students time to reflect. Praise thoughtful final comments. Choose one and add this information to the group request for financial support.

6. **How shall we sign our group financial aid letter?** ("Sincerely," and name)

7. Praise your students' financial aid letter and all the thought, effort, and caring that went into creating it. Encourage students to sign their names to the group financial aid letter. Later, mail it, if appropriate.

INDIVIDUAL BRAINSTORMING & COMPOSING

Tell students that they now get the opportunity to write a letter requesting financial support for a cause of their choice. Point out that our only *tools* for getting financial support for our/their worthy causes are our written WORDS. Explain that because the written words are so critical to accomplishing their goals, we need to make the words powerful and effective.

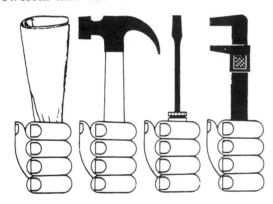

Explain that for the next 20–45 minutes everyone will need to be thinking and writing. Consider pairing Beginning Writers who are good idea generators with Advanced Writers. Give each pair an individual brainstorming sheet to help them generate and organize their ideas. A Brainstorming Assistant can be found at the end of this lesson.

As students brainstorm their requests, walk around the classroom.

1. Praise students for choosing worthy causes or sincere interest in helping someone in need.

NOTE: If a student has chosen to write about his/her own personal need, inquire further. Some students with emotional and/or behavior disorders will be hurting inside so much that they may not be able to think about the needs of others.

If this occurs either (a) try to redirect the focus of the letter to a family member's needs or (b) accept their "worthy cause" and push for strong reasons and credibility of the writer.

2. Ask questions to help students include:

- accurate information about the person/people in need and the worthy cause

- relevant background of the writer

- logical order

- convincing reasons

- effective examples (advanced)

- realistic plans

- a strong ending plea for financial assistance

3. Request letterhead stationery for each student from your school office. Explain why you want students to rewrite their final drafts on the school letterhead.

RESPONDING TO STUDENTS' WRITINGS/REVISING

Remind your students that our only *tools* for getting financial support for our worthy causes are our written WORDS. Explain that since they will want to locate funds for their worthy causes, they will need to revise until their request for financial support letters are convincing and credible, and nothing hinders the possible donor in understanding their plea for money. Tell students that they will have the assistance of two or more peer readers.

Peer Readers

Assign preselected students (your Advanced Writers) as Idea and Mechanics Readers. They can begin their jobs as peer readers after they finish and revise their own letters. At that time give each peer reader a headband with philanthropic "dollars" glued to it. This will help peer readers be easily identified in an active room.

Ahead of time have two students who could benefit from a hands-on task make simple headbands from two large cereal boxes and the money patterns at the end of this lesson. First, flatten a cereal box and use scissors to cut 2-inch wide strips across the middle of the box. This will create an average-sized headband. Add a spacer or shorten as needed. Cut out and glue the money patterns to the headband. Since the headband signals excellence, peer readers in grades 4–6 respond positively to wearing them. Students in grades 7–9 often enjoy the change of pace.

Assign one half the peer readers to review ideas and one half to review mechanics. Impress upon peer readers that their first responsibility is to find at least three specific positive things to say to the writer about his/her letter requesting financial support. Next, review the Ideas or Mechanics checklist. Caution peer readers that the financial aid letters do not need to be "perfect" since this may direct students' attention away from the meaning of writing for a worthy cause. When instructions are clear, give peer readers a package of philanthropic dollars to distribute.

1. As peer readers make positive comments to students, ask them to make a check on the appropriate line of the Revising Assistant.

2. If a student needs to revise something, the peer reader should put a small dot on that/those lines and explain why. The student should then return to his/her seat and make revisions.

3. Direct the peer reader to give philanthropic dollars when a student's letter is "convincing and credible" or "mechanically clear and easy to understand."

Whole Class

Give each student an Ideas and a Mechanics Revising Assistant. The Revising Assistants can be found at the end of this lesson.

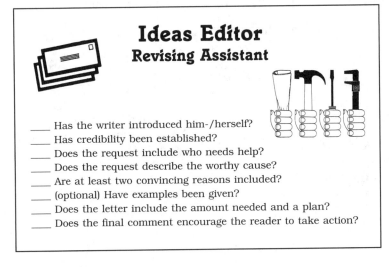

Ideas Editor
Revising Assistant

____ Has the writer introduced him-/herself?
____ Has credibility been established?
____ Does the request include who needs help?
____ Does the request describe the worthy cause?
____ Are at least two convincing reasons included?
____ (optional) Have examples been given?
____ Does the letter include the amount needed and a plan?
____ Does the final comment encourage the reader to take action?

Mechanics Editor
Revising Assistant

____ Does the letter start with the date?
____ Is there a greeting? Does it begin with a capital letter?
____ Is the name of this particular person capitalized?
____ Does the greeting end with a comma?
____ Is the first paragraph indented?
____ Does each sentence begin with a capital letter?
____ Does each sentence end with appropriate punctuation?
____ Is there a closing followed by a comma?
____ Has the writer signed his/her name?

Write the following suggestions on the board for your students:

1. Evaluate the effectiveness of your own letter requesting financial support before going to one of the peer readers. Make revisions.

2. Go to the Ideas Revising Assistant for assistance.

3. Make improvements. Repeat steps 2 and 3, if necessary.

   • When your letter is convincing and credible, you will receive two "dollars."

4. Go to the Mechanics Revising Assistant for assistance.

5. Make improvements. Repeat steps 4 and 5, if necessary, so nothing hinders the possible donor in understanding and hopefully supporting your plea for money.

   • When your letter is easy to understand, you will receive another dollar.

6. Go to the teacher for a final reading before publishing.

   When a student comes to you, comment individually about how much the student's request was improved through revisions. Consider requesting that students bring each of their drafts with them so that you can see their progress and growth.

   • When a student's request for financial support is convincing and credible, and nothing hinders the possible donor in understanding the plea for money, give him/her a final "dollar" as a go-ahead for publishing.

PUBLISHING

Share that you are proud of each of your students for choosing a worthy cause and for the effort they put into writing convincing, credible, and easy-to-understand requests for financial support. Shake each writer's hand as you declare, "Thanks a Trillion for helping people in your community."

School Letterhead

Distribute one sheet of school letterhead stationery to each student, so final drafts can be written or word-processed on it. The letterhead stationery adds an extra stroke of credibility to each letter.

NOTE: Don't require a final clean copy from Beginning Writers since it may direct their attention away from requesting money for a worthy cause.

Next, tell students that you'll mail their letters with a brief cover letter explaining that the worthy cause(s) detailed in the letters are real—not made up just for a writing lesson. Include your school phone number. Mail the letters to a funding organization or a philanthropist (*audience*) to consider funding your worthy cause(s) (*purpose*). Perhaps the letters can be mailed by your school office in one large package.

Caution students that they may not get a response.

Funds Granted	Funds Refused

Here is a situation in which we received a welcome response. One of our families couldn't afford bikes for their seven children. Six of these students attended our school. We wrote to several bike companies requesting assistance in getting a new or used bike for these children to share.

Three months later we were astounded when our principal received a call from the VP of a major bike company alerting us that seven new bikes could be picked up at a local bike shop *and* that special handle bar covers and sparklely things for the wheels were being shipped to our school for these children.

My homeroom students were amazed at the power their writing had. All of us learned an important lesson.

P.S. Our students' proud parents were able to see the fourth graders' very persuasive letters in the Sunday edition of our local paper. Oh yes, the generous vice president asked that the bike company not be identified.

To: Someone who cares about the small guy

From: Lazy Max

I'm writing because I need money to support my two-pack-a-day cigarette habit. I've tried to get a job, but I always get fired within a week. They want me to work hard, but I don't really enjoy hard work. They don't like my back talk.

Could you help me? I really like the nicotine. Be considerate. It will make my day. Besides, you have lots of money. Be nice and share it. Make my day.

To: Lazy Max

From: Someone who cares

You deserve what you get. Nothing! Stop smoking and get a job. You'll need the health insurance when you get lung cancer.

Stick a lollipop in your mouth instead of a cigarette. Perhaps it will help keep you from opening your mouth inappropriately at work.

To: Someone who cares

From: Sara

School starts in two weeks. We need your help. Mom and Grandma died last year in a car accident. Dad promised my sister and me that he'd buy us clothes, coats, books, and shoes for school. He loves us a lot, but he lost his job and our car was stolen. He misses Mom and has to work and raise us too. He tries hard, but can't seem to make ends meet.

Would you help our family? We can buy some clothes and coats at the thrift shop, but we also need underwear, shoes, and school supplies. My teacher's name is Mrs. Talbert. Her phone number at school is 1-512-233-8424.

To: Sara

From: Someone who cares

A check is on its way to pay for school clothes, shoes, and school books. I talked to your teacher. She will take you and your sister shopping before school starts.

Give your dad lots of hugs. I'm sure he'll appreciate them as he tackles the job of two parents.

Work hard in school and someday help someone in need.

Nov. 17, 20XX

Dear Pet Food Manufacturer,

My name is Judith. I'm a seventh grader at Fargo Middle School. I've been working as a volunteer at the Humane Society for three years. Every winter we have hundreds of dogs and cats dropped off at our door. We try to get them all placed in good homes as soon as possible, but in the meantime they must stay in an old unheated dairy barn. It is very cold and many of the cats and dogs get sick before we can find them a home. These dogs and cats are put to sleep because medicine is costly. As a pet lover I know you won't want this to happen.

The other workers have put out announcements on our three radio stations for blankets for warmth, but we need money to buy enough straw to cover the animals. I talked with three farmers. They will sell us straw at half price. It will cost $350 to pay for the straw. If you want to see if I'm telling the truth, you can call the director of our Humane Society. His phone number is 1-718-HELP-NOW. Next year we'll plan ahead so we can get the straw donated. Will you please send us $350 to pay for the straw? Do you care about keeping these unwanted pets alive as much as we do? Please help us. We need your assistance.

Yours truly,

Judith

Judith, a dog lover

Brainstorming Assistant
for
Financial Support

Person in Need/Worthy Cause

Possible Donors

Reasons

Plans

Credibility

Ideas Editor
Revising Assistant

____ Has the writer introduced him-/herself?

____ Has credibility been established?

____ Does the request include who needs help?

____ Does the request describe the worthy cause?

____ Are at least two convincing reasons included?

____ (optional) Have examples been given?

____ Does the letter include the amount needed and a plan?

____ Does the final comment encourage the reader to take action?

Mechanics Editor
Revising Assistant

____ Does the letter start with the date?

____ Is there a greeting? Does it begin with a capital letter?

____ Is the name of this particular person capitalized?

____ Does the greeting end with a comma?

____ Is the first paragraph indented?

____ Does each sentence begin with a capital letter?

____ Does each sentence end with appropriate punctuation?

____ Is there a closing followed by a comma?

____ Has the writer signed his/her name?

Money Patterns for Headbands

Money Patterns for Peer Conferences

LESSON 25

Sympathy Message

OUTCOME Each student will compose a genuine note or letter to someone during a time of illness, accident, misfortune, pain, loss, or tragedy to help the person cope.

MOTIVATORS

1. Talk about a person students know who is ill. Bring to class a newspaper article about a family devastated by tragedy, or a town that has been destroyed by fire, floods, tornado, etc. Examine how the person/family may feel: awful, upset, depressed, afraid, out-of-control, irritable, shocked, etc.

   Ask students how they would feel in a similar situation. What helped you? What do you think the person needs? What helped you? Awaken students' awareness of the pain experienced by this person.

2. Share a personal message that you have received and why it was special to you. Here is a very special card one of my students wrote to me 29 years ago. Ask students to share why I found this note so special.

> Dear Miss Sunflower,
>
> I hope you get better and kome bak to skool soon. John is sick and we onle got 5 boys and 10 girls in ire class today. I took atendense to the ofice. 15 were abcent. I feel sic to I had the floo for 4 days. Kome back soon.
>
> love Marc

3. Perhaps you'd like to share one of many sympathy messages that were written by sixth and seventh graders after a child named Jacob Wetterling was abducted. These messages were sent to the child's parents in hopes that it would help ease their pain. This child is still missing. Show a flyer of a missing child from your area.

Dear Wetterling Family,

I really hope you find your son, Jacob, soon. I know you love him very much. I am sad to hear what happened to Jacob. I have been watching CNN and reading our newspaper everyday. The police are working hard to find Jacob. I hope they catch the man who took him and give him a life sentence.

Don't give up because our whole country is trying to find him. I saw that the World Series players' had Jacob's initials on his bat. The Minnesota North Star players are wearing Jacob's on their uniforms to remind everyone to keep looking.

I found this poem on the sidewalk. I thought you might like it as much as I did.

> Mom and Dad I know you feel blue,
> I'm watching for Jacob too,
> I hope he has quarters just a few,
> Enough to escape and call you.
> (writer unknown)

Keep your spirits up. Jacob might even come home on his own. I'll watch for him.

Yours truly,
Amy

Discuss which parts of this sympathy letter students like and why. Ask your young writers how they think this child's parents felt when they received letters like this from all around the country. (For more information on locating lost children, contact the Jacob Wetterling Foundation at 800-325-HOPE.)

4. Share that a personal message is more special and helpful than a purchased card, but that we can get ideas from commercial cards. Read several messages in commercial "get well," "condolence" and other cards that you've received or purchased. Explain that it is natural to feel tongue-tied and that any kind of genuine/heartfelt empathy is usually welcome.

GROUP BRAINSTORMING

Now we will brainstorm some ideas for a sympathy message. As you ask your students these questions, write the ideas on the board. Encourage students to generate many ideas before asking the next question.

Key Questions

1. **What happened? How could we acknowledge the person's pain or tragic news?**
   Pause for at least 30 seconds to give students time to think. Write their ideas under the "Acknowledge" column.

   EXAMPLES: Losing your (favorite dog) is terrible.
   When (your parents separated) it really hurt.

2. **How can we express sympathy? What can we say to show our sadness or regrets at the tragic news? How do you feel _____? How can we show that the grief-stricken person is not alone? share the sorrow?** Pause for at least 30 seconds to give students time to think. Write their ideas under the "Sympathy" column. If students need help putting their feelings in words, give them an example.

   EXAMPLES: I was sorry to hear that _____.

                 I felt _____ when I heard _____.

                 I'm thinking of you as you face _____.

Acknowledge	Sympathy	Wishes or Memories	Assistance
dog died broken foot Carol's stolen bike lost basketball game	I'm sorry We're worried That's awful!	Hope you feel better soon Wish you get a new bike Perhaps your parents have insurance	help you look for bike help you carry your books give you a ride to school I'm a good listener

3. **If illness or bad fortune occurred, what good wishes do you have?** Pause for at least 30 seconds to give students time to think. Praise good ideas and write them under the "Wishes or Memories" column. If students need help putting their feelings in words, give them an example.

   EXAMPLES: We hope _____.

                 I wish _____.

                 During this difficult time _____.

     If a death occurred, what good qualities of the deceased or good memories can you share that you had with the departed (person or pet)? How will you remember the grief-stricken person in your thoughts (and/or prayers)? Pause for at least 30 seconds to give students time to think. Praise good ideas and write their ideas under the "Wishes or Memories" column. If students need help putting their feelings in words, give them an example.

   EXAMPLES: _____ was _____.

                 I will always remember the time _____.

                 I want you to know _____.

4. **What kind of help do you think the person needs? What would you need? What assistance/support can you offer the person during this difficult time? In what small ways can you help? What small acts of kindness are you willing to do?** Pause for at least 30 seconds to give students time to think. Praise thoughtful offers of help and write them under the "Assistance" column. If students don't know appropriate kinds of assistance, give them several examples.

The Internet offers resources for loss, tragedy, and death. Here are a few examples for the loss of one's pet:

Cornell University Pet Loss Support Hotline at http://web.vet.cornell.edu/ public/petloss/

Iowa State University College of Medicine Pet Loss Hotline at http://www. vm.iastate.edu/support/

Association for Pet Loss and Bereavement at http://www.aplb.org

If your students want to offer assistance in the form of a website in their sympathy notes, they should search for an appropriate site and then surf to that site to see if it is (1) still working and (2) appropriate for the situation.

GROUP COMPOSING

Now we are going to write a sympathy note to _____ to show _____. Choose a real child, adolescent, or adult who has experienced illness, accident, misfortune, or loss.

> April 29, 20XX
>
> Hi Jesse,
>
> We heard that your bike was stolen over the weekend. That's awful! We will be thinking about you. We hope your parents have insurance. Meanwhile we will give you a ride home after school until you get a new bike.
>
> Your friends,

1. **What is today's date?** Add this information to the board or overhead.

2. **How could we greet an unhappy or deeply sad person?** Choose one suggestion and add it to the sympathy message on the board.

> **Thinking about Mechanics:** How do you show proper respect when addressing an adult? (Mr., Mrs., Ms., or a professional title such as Dr.)

3. **How can we acknowledge _____'s loss, misfortune, or illness? What happened to this person?** Praise all responses. Then choose one suggestion and add it to the sympathy message on the board.

4. **How can we express our sympathy for _____? What words of comfort can we say to _____?** Explain that it is best to allow the person privacy, not to ask questions. This would not be "in good taste" since it might hurt the person. Also avoid explanations. In a sympathy message focus on the person, not on yourself. Praise all responses. Then choose one suggestion and add it to the sympathy message on the board.

5. **What good wishes do we have for _____? or What good qualities/memories can we share about the deceased?** Praise all suggestions. Then choose one suggestion and add it to the sympathy message on the board.

6. **What assistance can we offer?** Praise all suggestions, then choose one and add it to the sympathy message on the board.

7. **How can we close our sympathy message?** (Your friend, With love, Thinking of you, With affection, and so on) Praise all suggestions, then choose one and add it to the sympathy message on the board.

INDIVIDUAL BRAINSTORMING & COMPOSING

Point out that now students will get to write their own sympathy message(s). As students begin to brainstorm and write, walk around the room and converse with students who need individual guidance expressing their thoughts and feelings.

Ask less-skilled writers to include the date, greeting, acknowledgment, good wishes, and a closing. Allow them to skip sympathy and assistance since these parts of a sympathy message include emotions that are more difficult to express.

RESPONDING TO STUDENTS' WRITINGS/REVISING

As students complete their personal sympathy messages, ask them to find a partner and read the message aloud to see if it makes sense and sounds sincere/heartfelt. Next, have partners reread the message to see if it expresses comfort and support.

Write the following information on the board or overhead to guide your students.

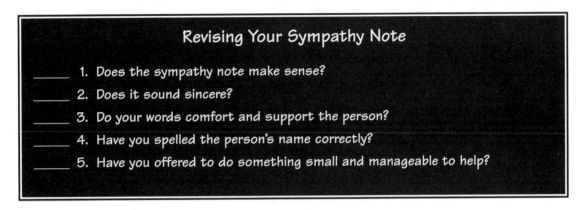

Revising Your Sympathy Note

_____ 1. Does the sympathy note make sense?

_____ 2. Does it sound sincere?

_____ 3. Do your words comfort and support the person?

_____ 4. Have you spelled the person's name correctly?

_____ 5. Have you offered to do something small and manageable to help?

PUBLISHING

Rewrite the sympathy note on a handmade card clearly enough for the person in pain (*audience*) to understand your thoughts and feelings (*purpose*). You can also use copies of the two prepared cards at the end of this lesson or have students make their own crayon-resist cards.

Prepared Cards

Crayon-Resist Cards

Materials
white paper, scissors, white crayons, watercolors, glass of water, paintbrush

Directions
1. Fold the white paper in half the long way.

2. Write a brief message on the cover of the card using a white crayon. (Inspect commercial cards for other brief messages [such as those below] to write on the cover.)

Get Well   **With Deepest Sympathy**
We Care   **In Your Time of Sorrow**
Thinking of You   **A Message of Sympathy**
We Miss You   **Words of Comfort**
Hang in There   **You Are in Our Thoughts**
Wishes for Improved Health

3. Write the sympathy message on the inside lower part of the card. If more room is needed, close the card, turn it over, and write the rest on the back.

4. Wet the brush and paint over part of the white crayon message with the watercolors to make the message appear. Wash the brush, get another color of paint on it, and brush over a different part of the message. Keep the area of paint limited to the message; otherwise, the paper will become too saturated and take longer to dry.

5. Give or mail your sympathy note to the person in pain. (Caution students ahead of time that a person in mourning will often hurt so much that they won't seem to respond. Assure your students that the sympathy note *will* matter.)

You Are in Our Thoughts

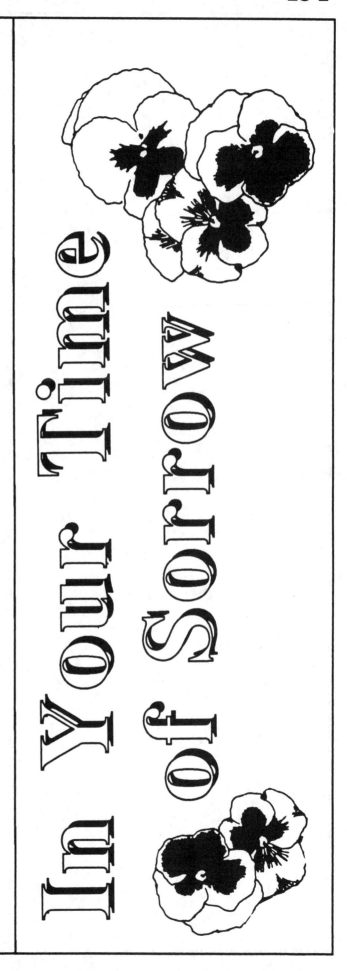

In Your Time of Sorrow

LESSON 26

Compliments

OUTCOME Each student will compose a genuine compliment for a classmate or a person (such as the janitor, school librarian, bus driver, principal, or a secret pal), and actually say the compliment orally and in writing to this person.

MOTIVATORS

1. Share that there are many special gifts people have to give. (The following list of gifts is adapted from an e-mail titled "Eight Gifts" sent by Kathy Sutterfield.)

The gift of laughter—time to relax and really enjoy life.
The gift of a favor—when someone goes out of their way to do something kind.
The gift of a cheerful disposition—when someone projects a positive attitude.
The gift of listening—when someone really listens to you.
The gift of solitude—when we allow another to be alone.
The gift of a compliment—taking time to share a genuine positive feedback with someone.

Explain that we all have special gifts we can share with others. Then share a real compliment that you have received lately. Here is an example:

"At work yesterday Ms. Tyson, our principal, told me that I was doing a terrific job teaching science and math and she appreciates all the creative ideas I bring to school. I was so pleased that Ms. Tyson noticed my hard work that I felt good all day."

2. Demonstrate the simple "Let's Go" cheer, then teach it to your students:

> Let's go <u>(insert student's name)</u>.
> Let's go.

(If you or your students are music fans, you'll realize the Let's Go cheer is a takeoff of the song "Let's Go" by a group named the Ventures.)

Next, teach the beat of this encouraging cheer. Write the following information on the board. Ask students to clap with the word(s) each time they see an X. Have students clap fast when they see two Xs close together. Demonstrate.

> Let's go <u>(insert student's name)</u>.
> X   X   X
>
> Let's go.
> X   X

Now choose a student to lead the Let's Go cheer. This student gets to choose who to cheer. The person who was cheered then leads the next cheer and chooses the next individual to be given encouragement.

3. Give a less-deserving student a compliment.

NOTE: Write the compliment ahead of time so it can be genuine and sound natural. Direct the cheerleader from motivator 1 to lead the class in the Let's Go cheer for this student. Repeat this sequence three or four times, selecting students who need honest praise and encouragement.

Now inquire what you gave each student. (a compliment) Discuss what a compliment is.

Share that many people believe a compliment is something positive, true, and new. (Rachel Benson, grade 2, Lincoln Elementary, Fargo, ND)

Give a put-down and ask how it differs from a compliment. (Select a confident student ahead of time and ask permission to give a put-down during instruction.)

Inquire how students felt when they were given the compliment. Then ask why it is important to notice positive behavior and give compliments. After hearing students' thoughts, explain that later each student will compose a compliment for a classmate and a special person such as the school janitor, the school librarian, the bus driver, the principal, a parent, or a secret pal.

4. Give each student or pair of students an old magazine or newspaper. Check the magazines to make sure they include positive descriptors. Have your students cut out describing words (words that express positive opinions), such as *wonderful, terrific, awesome, thoughtful,* etc. Explain that the positive cut-outs will help students generate ideas for brainstorming compliments about people they know.

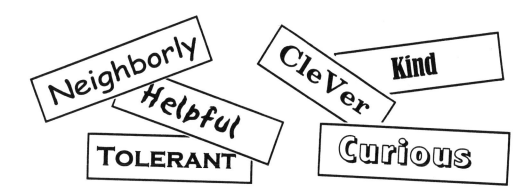

After about ten minutes, ask students to share positive opinions they have found. Write these positive descriptors on a chart as students share. This chart will be used in the game in motivator 5, and during group and individual brainstorming. The reason for putting positive descriptors on the chart is to prevent "smart" remarks or negative descriptors during the game and to aid recall of positive descriptors during brainstorming.

Have each student fold a sheet of notebook paper in half the long way, write his/her full name on the paper, then place their cut-outs between the folds. If desired, the sides of the paper can be paper clipped or stapled. Collect the cut-outs to use during publishing.

5. Teach your students a version of the truly ancient game "Smile If You Love Me." The modern version is called "Smile If You Are <u>Awesome</u>." Explain that while this activity is funny, they will learn how to give and receive positive feedback and to notice how it feels to lift each other up instead of exchanging negative remarks (put-downs).

NOTE: Positive comments stated sarcastically are also put-downs.

Feel free to insert another positive descriptor for "Awesome" that is currently popular with your students. Have your students form a circle. If your class is too large for one circle, have students count off by threes. Have the ones sit on chairs. Direct the twos and threes to stand behind the chairs. Explain that they will be rotated as time permits. Choose an "active" student who needs lots of positive

attention to be IT. Direct this student to get inside the circle.

The student who is IT should choose another person and kneel in front of him/her, then look into that student's eyes while saying, "If You Are <u>Awesome,</u> Smile."

The chosen person must reply "I'm awesome, but I can't smile." The student who is IT has three chances to make the chosen person smile. The statement can be repeated three times using normal volume, but any tone of voice.

The student who is IT must not touch the chosen person and must keep both knees on the floor. If desired, you can provide a pillow on which students can kneel.

If the chosen person keeps a sober face, the student who is IT must go to a different individual in the circle. If the chosen student cracks a smile or laughs, he/she must enter the circle of students and help the student who is IT make people smile.

The other students (or the students standing behind the chairs) get to decide whether the chosen person smiled. The game is over when everyone is laughing and feeling good.

A more advanced version of this game differs only slightly. The student who is IT gets to select a positive descriptor from the positive words collected and posted on the chart earlier and use this descriptor in place of the word "Awesome."

brave	curious	tolerant	delicate	cautious
peaceful	optimistic	cool-headed	appealing	excited
enthusiastic	skillful	helpful	elegant	open
delightful	handsome	smart	relaxed	fair
watchful	confident	serious	graceful	interesting
amusing	agreeable	amazing	kind	clever
witty	respectful	steady	determined	honest
careful	grateful	lucky	neighborly	eager
thoughtful	daring	gorgeous	careful	charming
strong	bright	compassionate	reasonable	stunning

GROUP BRAINSTORMING

Now we will brainstorm some ideas for complimenting someone we all know and appreciate.

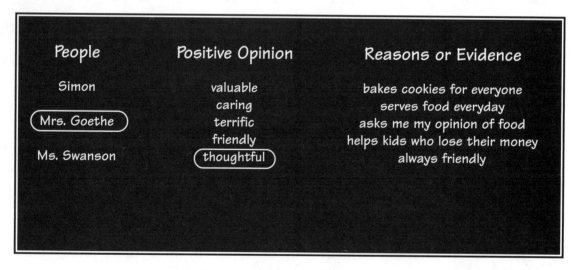

People	Positive Opinion	Reasons or Evidence
Simon	valuable	bakes cookies for everyone
Mrs. Goethe	caring	serves food everyday
	terrific	asks me my opinion of food
	friendly	helps kids who lose their money
Ms. Swanson	thoughtful	always friendly

Key Questions

1. **Who is someone all of us would like to compliment? Who is someone who makes us feel good? Who has helped us recently? What politician or person in the news would we like to compliment?** Pause for at least 30 seconds to give students time to think. Write their ideas under the "People" column.

2. **Out of all these people, whom shall we choose to compliment?** Choose a student who needs encouragement or inclusion to select a person. Circle this idea and use it all through the lesson. If other students object that their person wasn't chosen, remind students that they get to choose and develop their own idea for a compliment later.

3. **Which of the words we cut from newspapers conveys our opinion of _____? What is one word that describes _____? What is a positive opinion of _____ that we could support with evidence?**
Pause for at least 30 seconds to give students time to think. Praise and write students' ideas on the board under the "Positive Opinion" column. Ignore negative opinions.
   Repeat these questions until six to eight ideas have been written on the board. If a student persists with a negative opinion, tell the student that negative opinions go in letters of complaint and that if he/she wants to write a complaint, they can brainstorm ideas for that letter.

4. **Out of all these positive opinions, which opinion shall we choose?** Choose a student who needs encouragement or inclusion to select an opinion. Circle this idea and use it all through the lesson. If other students object that their opinion wasn't chosen, remind students that they get to choose and develop their own opinions later.

5. **What evidence can we give for how we feel? What is some evidence that this compliment is true? What reason(s) could we give so that _____ knows we aren't just "flattering" him/her? What is another reason he/she deserves a compliment?** Pause for at least 30 seconds to give students time to think. Praise all responses that support the opinion. Write students' ideas on the board under the "Reasons or Evidence" column. Repeat these questions until six to eight ideas have been written on the board.

NOTE: Choosing reasons/evidence will take place in group composing so students can get some mental distance from them. This will help students select ones that support the positive opinion instead of just choosing ones they like.

GROUP COMPOSING

We are going to organize our ideas and write a compliment to _____. Write on chart paper, instead of the overhead or board, so that later the compliment can be given to the person.

April 29, 20XX

Dear Mrs. Goethe,

    You are thoughtful. You always bake enough cookies for everyone. You helped Max when he lost his lunch money, and you asked us if the roast beef sandwiches were good. You're great!

        Your friends,
        Mr. Conroy's Class

1. What is today's date? Add this information to the group composition on chart paper.

> **Thinking about Mechanics:** What punctuation is needed between the date and year? (a comma) Why?

2. How could we greet the person? Choose one suggestion and add it to the compliment.

> **Thinking about Mechanics:** What do we do to the first letter in a greeting? (capital letter)

3. To whom are we writing a compliment? Add the name to the greeting.

> **Thinking about Mechanics:** How do you show proper respect when addressing an adult? (Mr., Mrs., Ms., or a professional title such as Dr.)

> **Thinking about Mechanics:** What should I have done to the person's name? (capitalize the first letter)

> **Thinking about Mechanics:** What punctuation should I have placed after the person's name? (a comma)

4. Which positive opinion did we choose earlier? Choose an uninvolved student. **How can we put this word/phrase in a complete sentence?** Ask the uninvolved student to create a sentence from the positive opinion.

> **Thinking about Mechanics:** What should I do to the beginning of our paragraph? (indent and use capital letter)

5. **Let's choose our best two or three reasons that support our opinion.** Number the reasons as you ask students why they want a particular reason first, second, or last. **Which reason/evidence shall we place first in the compliment? Second? Last?** Number the reasons.

6. **What can we say about our first reason or evidence?** Ask a student to create a complete sentence from reason 1 and add it to the compliment. Continue with the other reasons. **What is our second reason? our next reason? our last reason?**

7. **What final comment can we make?** Add one or two suggestions to the compliment.

8. (optional) Start a new paragraph. Choose a new opinion and support it with two or three reasons. Repeat for a third paragraph using questions 4–7.

9. **How can we close our compliment?** Praise all suggestions such as sincerely, truly, your friend, etc., then add it to the compliment.

Thinking about Mechanics: What should I do to the first letter in "sincerely"? (capitalize)

Thinking about Mechanics: What punctuation should I put after the word "sincerely"? (a comma)

---

10. **Let's sign our compliment _____'s class of 20_ _.** Allow time for students to sign the group compliment on the chart.

INDIVIDUAL BRAINSTORMING & COMPOSING

Ask students to choose someone and write a real compliment to him/her. As students begin to brainstorm and write, walk around the room and converse with students who need individual guidance.

If students are having trouble getting started, direct them to review the complimentary words listed on the board. Also assist students in identifying reasons and evidence that support the compliment. Guide students as they order the ideas in their compliments.

Alternative Composing: Strength Bombardment

Choose one or two students a week to receive compliments from the rest of the class. Continue until all students have had a full week of "Strength Bombardment."

Start by choosing students with low self-confidence. When preparing your class to write compliments for low-achieving or challenging students, prep your class by group brainstorming for this particular student. Some teachers compile each student's compliments in a book titled "Compliments to [student's name]" by ___'s Classmates and the date.

This is such an ego-boosting activity that even adults will glow afterward. It is great for any teachers' meeting. (I still have the compliments I received eight years ago taped to my bathroom mirror!)

RESPONDING TO STUDENTS' WRITINGS/REVISING

As students complete their compliments, ask them to find a partner and read the compliment aloud to see if it makes sense and sounds sincere. As students work with partners, have them use the Revising Assistant (found at the end of this lesson).

Ask the students to individually evaluate their compliments using the Revising Assistant to make their compliments even more effective. Direct students to check off each item on the Revising Assistant that is present and correct. Next, students should revise and improve their draft before bringing it to you for a final look.

Revising Assistant:
Making Your Compliment Effective

Writer   **Teacher**

_____ 1. Has the date been included?   _____
_____ 2. Is there a friendly greeting?   _____
_____ 3. Is the person's name spelled correctly?   _____
_____ 4. Does your compliment begin with a positive
            opinion?   _____
_____ 5. Have you supported your positive opinion with
            at least two reasons/evidence?   _____
_____ 6. Does your compliment make sense?   _____
_____ 7. Does your compliment sound sincere?   _____
_____ 8. Have you included a closing?   _____
_____ 9. Have you signed your compliment?

PUBLISHING

After students finish revising their compliments, explain that they'll publish them on cubes (*format*) so that the special person (*audience*) can look at the cube and feel good about him-/herself (*purpose*). Since compliments should be written frequently, three publishing methods have been included to give variety.

Compliment Cubes

Materials

cube pattern, manila folder (1 per student), pencil, scissors, positive cut-outs, transparent tape

Directions

1. Place the two cube patterns (found at the end of this lesson) on a manila folder with half the pattern on each side of the fold. Tape the pattern in place and trace around it.

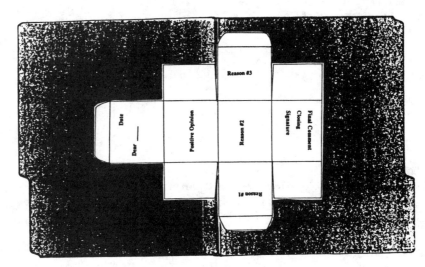

2. Carefully cut out the cube.

3. Write the compliment on the cube pattern as follows:

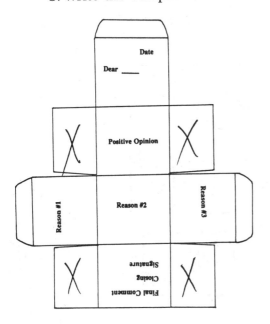

Place the **"Date" and "Dear _____,"** on the top flap with tab.

Place the **"Positive Opinion"** on the side between the two Xs.

Place one **"Reason"** on each three sides.

Place the **"Final Comment," "Closing,"** and compliment giver's **"Signature"** on the last side of the cube between the two Xs.

4. Fold on the dotted lines and crease the folds.

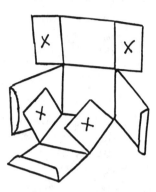

5. Construct the cube with the "X"ed flaps inside.

6. Fold the two longer sides over the flaps and tape in place.

7. Insert the cut-outs in the cube and tape the lid shut.

8. Say your compliment to the person as you give him/her the cube.

(Caution students ahead of time that some people may be embarrassed and try to deny that he/she deserves it or react by making a joke. Assure your students that their compliment *will* matter.)

Positive Cut-outs Card

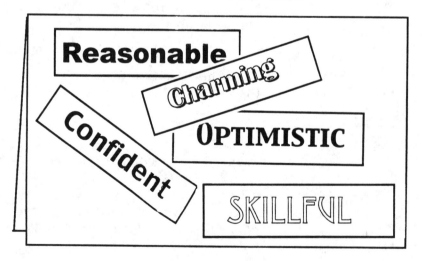

Materials

white paper, glue, positive cut-outs, colored markers, large envelope

Directions

1. Fold the paper in half and crease the fold.

2. Carefully write the compliment on the inside at the bottom half of the card and on the back.

	SKILLFUL / Confident / OPTIMISTIC / Charming / Reasonable
April 29, 20XX Dear Mrs. Goethe, You are thoughtful. You always bake enough cookies for everyone. You helped Max	when he lost his lunch money, and you wanted to know if the roast beef sandwiches were good. You're great!
Front	**Back**

3. Close the card. Place a scrap of paper in the folded card to prevent glue from sealing the card shut. Glue your positive cut-outs to the front of the card.

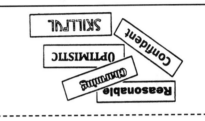

4. Lay the card open to dry.

5. Say your compliment to the person as you give him/her the card. (Caution students ahead of time that some people may be embarrassed and try to deny that he/she deserves it or react by making a joke. Assure your students that their compliment *will* matter.)

Compliment Card

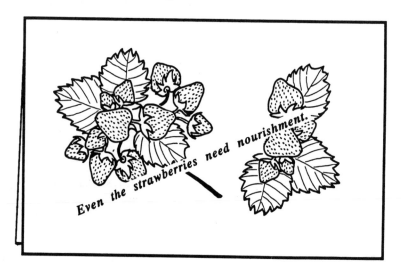

Make copies of the cards found at the end of this lesson. Fold in half and write the compliment inside the card. Add color to the cover with crayons or colored markers. If colored markers are used, insert a blank sheet of paper inside to keep the markers from bleeding through the cover.

Revising Assistant:
Making Your Compliment Effective

Writer   **Teacher**

_____ 1. Has the date been included?

_____ 2. Is there a friendly greeting?

_____ 3. Is the person's name spelled correctly?   _____

_____ 4. Does your compliment begin with a positive
            opinion?   _____

_____ 5. Have you supported your positive opinion with
            at least two reasons/evidence?   _____

_____ 6. Does your compliment make sense?   _____

_____ 7. Does your compliment sound sincere?   _____

_____ 8. Have you included a closing?   _____

_____ 9. Have you signed your compliment?   _____

- -

Revising Assistant:
Making Your Compliment Effective

Writer   **Teacher**

_____ 1. Has the date been included?

_____ 2. Is there a friendly greeting?

_____ 3. Is the person's name spelled correctly?   _____

_____ 4. Does your compliment begin with a positive
            opinion?   _____

_____ 5. Have you supported your positive opinion with
            at least two reasons/evidence?   _____

_____ 6. Does your compliment make sense?   _____

_____ 7. Does your compliment sound sincere?   _____

_____ 8. Have you included a closing?   _____

_____ 9. Have you signed your compliment?   _____

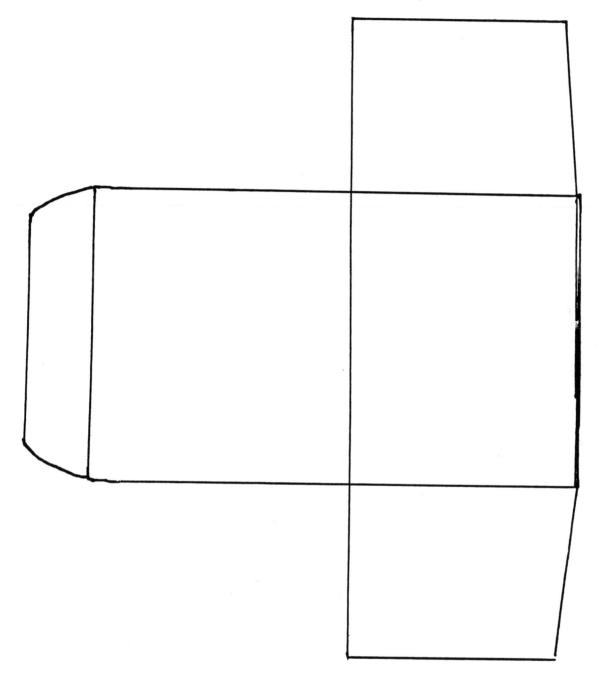

Place this edge of the cube pattern on the fold of the file folder.

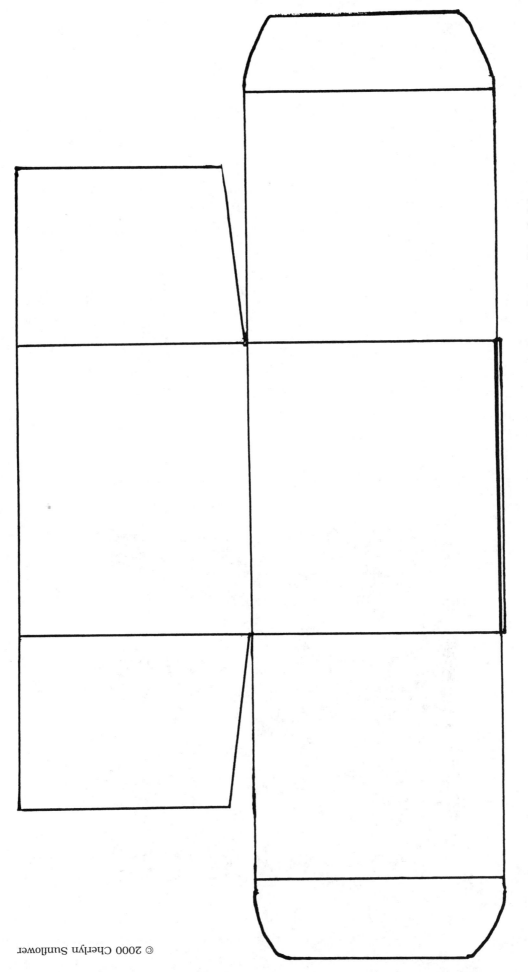

Place this edge of the cube pattern on the fold of the file folder.

Even the strongest oak needs to be watered.

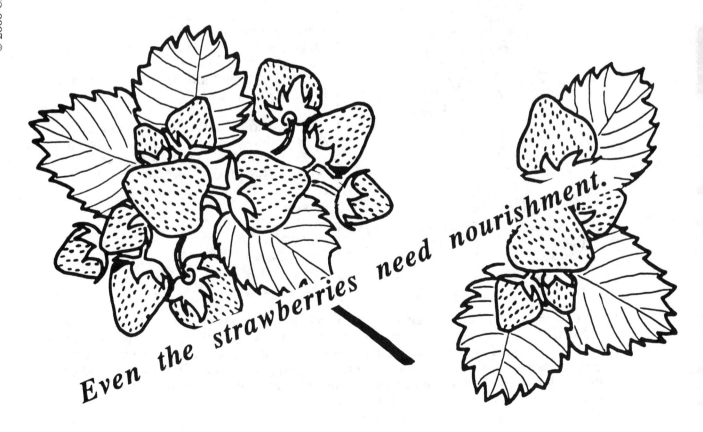

Even the strawberries need nourishment.

LESSON 27

Letter of Complaint

OUTCOME Each student will compose a genuine oral or written complaint about a product, service, or policy. The complaint will include a request for the reader to take action.

MOTIVATORS

1. Share a problem you had with a product such as restaurant or grocery store food, clothes, electronic equipment, a household appliance that you bought or received as a gift. Discuss why you took the product back to the store before you contacted the company by letter, phone, in person, or e-mail. Here's a real complaint that a fourth grader wrote. Ask why it is important to be clear.

January 23, 20XX

Dear Mr. Timms,

I am disappointed that the model airplane, Tygen Flyer Model AF25, lacked one wing. I worked all day to put the plane together and then could not finish it or fly it.

Please send me either the missing part or a whole new kit. I tried to get a replacement piece at the store where I bought the plane (Joe's Hobby Hut), but they said I have to write to the company.

Sincerely,
Jason Baker
Jason Baker

2. Share a complaint about a service you received and what you did. Here's a complaint written by a ninth grader who shared her thoughts with the manager over the phone. When the oral complaint failed, she sent her letter. Ask students what the purpose of Jason's and Amy's letters were. Although both their attempts failed, the students felt better. Inquire why Amy felt better even though she didn't get what she wanted.

November 14, 20XX

Dear Ms. Gamberger, Manager of StarMax,

I have tried to have my computer fixed at StarMax three different times and it still doesn't work. My next-door neighbor came over last night and fixed the problem in ten minutes.

I would like you to refund the $35.00 I paid for the repairs done by StarMax since you never fixed the problem.

Sincerely,
Amy Henrickson
Amy Henrickson

3. Share a complaint about a policy of the school, family, or government. Here are two complaints written by groups of students. Inquire if the letters are pleasant and courteous and what makes them so.

May 26, 20XX

Dear Principal Littoral,

We, the students of Lincoln Middle School, are writing to protest the uniform policy. We are tired of wearing the same thing day after day. You encourage imagination, but make all of us wear the same clothes!

If you won't repeal the policy, then please meet with us to discuss a compromise. Perhaps we can settle on a policy that makes everyone happy.

Sincerely,
Your Students
Students of Lincoln Middle School

May 26, 20XX

Dear Mayor Danielson,

We, the seventh-grade students at Harwood Junior High, are writing to protest the dumping of garbage close to the city softball park. The wind catches the paper and blows it all over the field while we are playing. Also there is a definite smell coming from the garbage. Would you investigate the problem and come to our class to visit with us about alternatives. We would appreciate prompt action since our team is leading.

Sincerely,
Your Future Voters
Seventh Graders
at Harwood Junior High

4. Role-play a polite and effective way to voice a complaint and a negative attacking complaint. Choose two students to read the two approaches to complaints provided below. Give the students time to practice in the hall before reading to the class. When the students are ready, have them take turns reading their complaints. Ask your class which complaint is more effective.

Mr. Manske

What were you thinking?
Can't you do anything right?
Do it NOW! And do it right this time or you will be sorry.
I'll tell all of the other kids how awful a job you do at Manske's Bike Repair.

Mr. Manske

The brakes on my 10-speed bike were not repaired correctly. When I use my right-hand brake, nothing happens. Earlier both brakes were faulty. Having the left brake work helps, but I need both brakes to work smoothly before Saturday when my bike club rides to Somerville.
Will you do this for me?

Discuss what made each approach more or less effective. Jot this information on the board for use later. If students need help, inquire which approach is more effective—attacks, sarcasm, offensive language, and personal slurs **or** pleasant, courteous, tactful manner, sticking to the facts. Then ask why sticking to the point and not offending the reader is likely to get better results. Be prepared for some students to comment strongly that it feels good to attack someone for the inconvenience. This value conflict can be handled effectively by agreeing that strong negative feelings are natural. Suggest that these feelings are valuable to write about in one's journal. Then ask the class what response is more effective for the audience of our complaint. Why?

5. This motivator is fun and especially effective with younger or less mature writers. Read the story *Old Hat New Hat* by Stan and Jan Berenstain to your class. The main character in this story has an old hat and wants a new one. As he/she tries on hats, they are quickly evaluated as "too big," "too small," "too heavy," "too fancy," "too pointed," until one is found that is just right.

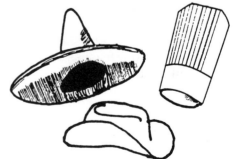

If you don't want to use the book, role-play the situation of complaining about a piece of clothing, shoes, or some object with which you are unhappy. For example, my swimsuit is too small so I need a new one. When I find one, it is too large. The next one has too many polka dots. The next is too bare (shows my tummy), has too thin of fabric, is too leathery. This continues until I found one just right.

You can use any object that is appropriate for your audience and for which you can find multiple items. My students loved so much to assist with the complaints that we often ended up laughing.

GROUP BRAINSTORMING

Now we will brainstorm some ideas for a complaint.

Complaint	Facts/Reasons/Evidence	Action
food was cold	promised March delivery	give discount on equipment
(equipment wasn't delivered)	lost $ on fund raiser	you should pay for late set-up
having exams all in one week		withhold payment

	Feelings	Deadline
	worried about losing funds	A.S.A.P.
	anxiety because equipment schedule was delayed	within two weeks
	concerned about safety with unassembled equipment laying around	

Key Questions

1. **About what are we unhappy? What is our/your complaint? What is wrong? What is the problem from your point of view?** Pause for at least 30 seconds to give students time to think. Praise students' ideas and write them under the "Complaint" column.

2. **Out of all these complaints, which one shall we choose?** Choose a low-achieving or uninvolved student to select one complaint. Circle this idea and use it all through the lesson. If other students object that their idea wasn't chosen, remind students that they get to develop their own complaints later.

3. **What feelings do we have about this problem?** Pause for at least 30 seconds to give students time to think. Praise students' ideas and write them under the "Feelings" column.

4. **Which of these feelings is appropriate to share?** Allow discussion on pros and cons of sharing certain feelings before choosing a low-achieving or uninvolved student to select one feeling. Circle this idea.

5. **Now let's support our complaint with facts, reasons, and evidence.**

    What are the facts? How can we describe the problem? Pause for at least 30 seconds to give students time to think. Praise students' ideas and write them under the "Facts/Reasons/Evidence" column.

    If complaining about a product, what is the brand name? Model number? When was it purchased? Where? Pause for at least 30 seconds to give students time to think. Praise students' ideas and write them under the "Facts/Reasons/Evidence" column.

    NOTE: Enclose a copy of the receipt or proof of purchase.

    What occurred? When? Where? Witnesses? Why is it a problem? What have we done to solve the problem? Pause for at least 30 seconds to give students time to think. Praise students' ideas and write them under the "Facts/Reasons/Evidence" column.

    Has a previous complaint been made? To whom? What was the result? Pause for at least 30 seconds to give students time to think. Praise students' ideas and write them under the "Facts/Reasons/Evidence" column.

6. **What do we want done? What reasonable action are we requesting? What solution do we desire? What suggestions do we have to remedy the situation?** Pause for at least 30 seconds to give students time to think. Praise students' ideas and write them under the "Action" column.

7. **How soon do we want the problem resolved? By when do we need this done?** Pause for at least 30 seconds to give students time to think. Praise students' ideas and write them under the "Deadline" column.

GROUP COMPOSING

Now, let's organize our ideas into a letter of complaint that is thorough, concise, and polite, yet firm. As information is generated, add it to the group composition on the board or overhead. The letter format can be block or modified block.

Carol Grim
406 West Andrew Rd.
Grand Forks, ND 58201
March 3, 20XX

Ms. Carmen
Valley Playground Equipment
Vienna, NJ 07880

Dear Ms. Carmen:

I am writing to complain about a promise that was made and not kept by your company. You promised to deliver our new playground equipment in March so we could have it installed in time for our annual fund-raising carnival May 1. The cost of the equipment was $3,041.

We were all quite distressed when our equipment was delivered April 30. Because of this late delivery, our playground wasn't ready for the annual carnival in May. We estimate almost $300 was lost at this year's carnival due to not being able to use our equipment.

Our student organization has decided that the $300 we lost at the carnival should be deducted from the amount we owe on the equipment. We will withhold payment until we hear from you regarding a satisfactory settlement. Please call within the week. Speak to our principal at 453-299-6767.

Sincerely,

Carol Grim

Carol Grim

---

1. **What is our return address?** Add this information to the board.

> **Thinking about Mechanics:** What needs to be capitalized? (proper nouns—names of people, streets, cities, and states) Why is our address important?

2. **What is today's date?** Add this information to the board.

> **Thinking about Mechanics:** What needs to be capitalized? (the month) What punctuation is needed? Where? (a comma between the day and the year)

3. **Where will we be sending our complaint? What information should we include in the inside address?** (inside address: name of person, title, name of company, company's address) Add this information to the board.

> **Thinking about Mechanics:** Where can we look up the name of the person, the person's title, and name of the company so we can spell it correctly? Why is it important to spell names correctly?

4. **How could we greet _____?** Choose one suggestion and add it to the complaint on the board.

5. **To whom should we complain?** It is important to send the complaint to a specific person, and preface this name by Mr. or Ms., not Dear Sir or Dear Madam.

> **Thinking about Mechanics:** How do you show proper respect when addressing an adult? (Mr., Ms., or a professional title such as Dr., Manager, V.P., President)

> **Thinking about Mechanics:** What punctuation do we put after the person's name in a formal letter? (comma)

6. Direct students' attention to the complaint selected earlier. **How shall we politely and clearly state our complaint in one sentence?** Praise all responses that are effective topic sentences. Then choose one suggestion and add it to the complaint on the board.

> **Thinking about Mechanics:** What do we need to do to the first sentence in a paragraph? (indent, capitalize first word)

7. Direct students' attention to the feelings selected earlier. **What feeling shall we share in our letter of complaint?**

8. Direct students' attention to the fact/details generated earlier. **Which details/facts will the reader need to know to resolve our problem?** Praise concise, yet complete information and add it to the complaint.

9. **Of our list of desired actions, which of these is a fair and reasonable request? Which request do we want to use?** Choose a low-achieving or uninvolved student to select a desired action. Circle this idea and use it all through the lesson.

10. **What positive statement can we make regarding the company, their products, employees, etc.? How can we politely conclude this letter?** Since this can be a difficult task, choose bright, thoughtful students to generate a positive statement. Circle this idea and add it to the complaint.

11. **How can we close our complaint?** ("Yours truly" or "Sincerely" followed by a comma)

12. **Now let's add our signature.** (signature of person complaining)

13. Tell students when they compose their complaints, they will also type their full name below their signature.

INDIVIDUAL BRAINSTORMING & COMPOSING

Point out that now students get to compose their own complaint(s). As students begin to brainstorm and write, walk around the room and converse with students who need individual guidance expressing their thoughts and feelings without anger, accusations, put-downs, or name calling.

Beginning Writers   Beginning Writers can list their complaints and request in the body of the letter. See this example from a seventh grader who was a Beginning Writer and a weak reader. Consider writing the inside address for these students to ensure a correct address in case a response is forthcoming.

> James Dill
> 102 44th Street
> Clarmore, Texas 76834
>
> February 23, 20XX
>
> Regional Manager
> Hamburger City
> 1102 Dicier Ave.
> Clarmore, Texas 76834
>
> Dear Ms. Clamber,
>
> I have some complaints about my dinner at your restaurant, Hamburger City.
>
> - The waiter was too rude.
> - The food took a long time to come.
> - My hamburger was cold.
> - The manager wouldn't listen to my complaints.
>
> Please send me a refund or a coupon for another meal. My receipt is enclosed.
>
> Sincerely,
> *James Dill*
> James Dill

RESPONDING TO STUDENTS' WRITINGS/REVISING

1. As students complete their letters of complaint, ask them to find a partner and read each letter aloud to see (a) if it is clear and to the point and (b) if the facts and evidence are used to prove their point, instead of anger, name calling, accusations, or put-downs.

2. Write the "dear Mr. Dummy brown" letter on the board or overhead. Explain that soon students will revise their own letters of complaint, but since it is easier to find the problems with other people's letters, we'll warm up by looking at two real letters written a year or two ago.

   Ask a good reader to read this true letter left for a principal by an angry student. Give students time to consider how to revise and edit the "dear Mr. Dummy brown" letter. (A reproducible copy can be found at the end of this lesson.)

yesterday

dear Mr. Dummy brown

we should be allowed to chew gum any where we want to. it is stupid to have rules that say no gum in school. if we can eat sticky suckers when we bring our lunch then only a dumb principal would try to stop us from chewing gum we are going to make your life terrible if you don't I have a right to chew gum at school if you don't want us to chew in the computer room that's okay and i would not mind if you prohibited us from blowing bubbles.

snap to it and tell me this week or else I'll start sticking gum up under the lunchroom tables.

Unhappy Joe

Inquire how effective students think this letter was. (It wasn't, and the fifth-grade student's parents were called to school for a conference.)

Then ask why it wasn't effective. (Anger, name calling, rude, threats, or poor mechanics that discredit the writer and make it hard to understand.)

3. Pass out a Revising Assistant to guide your students. (One can be found at the end of this lesson.) Demonstrate how to use the Revising Assistant by involving students in using it to evaluate and rewrite the above letter.

NOTE: There are several effective parts to the letter, such as an opinion sentence and two compromise offers.

4. Write the earlier "Dear Ms. Clamber" letter on the board or overhead. You may want to add a few mechanical errors. Ask a good reader to read this true letter written by an angry student. Inquire how effective this letter is compared with the "dear Mr. Dummy brown" letter. Then ask why it is more effective.

Finally, brainstorm how the "Dear Ms. Clamber" letter can be even more effective.

Revising Assistant:
Making Your Complaint Effective

Writer   **Teacher**

_____ 1. Have you included your address?

_____ 2. Has the date been included?

_____ 3. Have you included the inside address?

_____ 4. Have you included the salutation?

_____ 5. Have you spelled the person's, the company's, and/or the product's name correctly?

_____ 6. Have you clearly stated your complaint?

_____ 7. Does it include all the important details/facts?

_____ 8. Have you made a fair and reasonable request?

_____ 9. Does your complaint get to the point? Is it clear?

_____10. Is it tactful and courteous? Have you avoided attacks, accusations, put-downs, and name calling?

_____11. Is your letter concise? Have you removed unnecessary comments?

_____12. Have you included a formal closing?

_____13. Have you signed your letter?

PUBLISHING

Tell students they'll give or mail their complaints (*purpose*) to the person who needs to take action (*purpose*). Encourage students to word-process the complaint about a service, product, or policy so that it looks professional and effectively presents their thoughts. Here are two possible publishing methods.

Personal Stationery

Type or print a large letter representing the first letter in the student's last name in the top left side of the paper or cut out and paste on the letter from a magazine. Avoid getting letters from newspapers because the ink bleeds when glued onto the stationery. (See the reproducible at the end of this lesson.)

Cut Title

Cut around three sides of each letter in the special complaint stationery found at the end of this lesson.

Revising Assistant:
Making Your Complaint Effective

Writer   **Teacher**

1. Have you included your address?

2. Has the date been included?

3. Have you included the inside address?

4. Have you included the salutation?

5. Have you spelled the person's, the company's, and/or the product's name correctly?

6. Have you clearly stated your complaint?

7. Does it include all the important details/facts?

8. Have you made a fair and reasonable request?

9. Does your complaint get to the point? Is it clear?

10. Is it tactful and courteous? Have you avoided attacks, accusations, put-downs, and name calling?

11. Is your letter concise? Have you removed unnecessary comments?

12. Have you included a formal closing?

13. Have you signed your letter?

yesterday

dear Mr. Dummy brown

we should be allowed to chew gum any where we want to. it is stupid to have rules that say no gum in school. if we can eat sticky suckers when we bring our lunch then only a dumb principal would try to stop us from chewing gum we are going to make your life terrible if you don't I have a right to chew gum at school if you don't want us to chew in the computer room that's okay and i would not mind if you prohibited us from blowing bubbles.

snap to it and tell me this week or else I'll start sticking gum up under the lunchroom tables.

Unhappy Joe

COMPLAINT

LESSON 28

Restaurant Review

OUTCOME Each student will use the data collected on his/her checklist to compose a review of a restaurant.

MOTIVATORS

1. Choose a popular restaurant or fast-food spot. Duplicate copies of the checklist with the name of this restaurant on it. This checklist was created in Lesson 8, Restaurant Review Checklist. Ask students to quickly rate the restaurant based on past experience. See completed checklist below.

Share ratings. Draw conclusions about the restaurant. Encourage students with different viewpoints to share them. If there is time, compile the information on a tally sheet. See Lesson 5, Consumer's/Buyer's Guide, for ideas.

Point out that to get the best information, data from several visits should be collected and averaged.

Gary's Ribs

Criteria	Poor	Good	Excellent	Comments
1. Food Quality	1	2	③	great BBQ sauce, lots of meat on ribs, fresh baked breads
2. Amount	1	2	③	all-you-can-eat
3. Decor	1	②	3	Old West look, interesting objects on walls
4. Service	1	2	③	friendly and efficient
5. Cost	1	2	③	terrific quality for price
6. Accessibility	1	②	3	easy to get into restrooms
7.				

2. Search for restaurant reviews on the Web. One informally written restaurant review site is Steven Shaw's New York Restaurant Review and Food Guide at http://www.shaw-review.com/reviews.htm. The reviews are divided by topics such as burgers, pizza, franks, steak, deli, etc. By clicking on a topic, 10–30 restaurant reviews can be found.

GROUP BRAINSTORMING

We'll use information from the restaurant we just evaluated to create a fictitious restaurant review. Later you'll write your review on the restaurant you selected and observed.

	Food Quality	Amount	Decor	Service
Data:	3	3	2	2
Comments:	yummy	lots	booths	friendly
	hot BBQ	as much as	low lights	okay
		you can eat	western	fast
		plates full	live plants	rude

	Cost	Accessibility	Overall Opinion
Data:	2	2	
Comments:	expensive	parking	great place for ribs/BBQ
	$10.95	bathroom	crowded and noisy
	plus salad bar	too crowded	delicious, but expensive
			best meal in town

Key Questions

Note: Use the criteria from the checklist your class created in Lesson 8, Restaurant Review Checklist.

1a. What data did we get on food quality? Write the data about food quality on the board, overhead, or chart paper under the brainstorming category "Food Quality" across from data.

1b. What information did you get from the comments? Write the information from comments on the board, overhead, or chart paper under the brainstorming category "Food Quality" across from comments.

2a. What data did we get regarding the amount of food? Write the data under "Amount."

2b. What information did we get from the comments? Write comments about amount of food on the board.

3a. What data did we get on the decor? Write the data under "Decor."

3b. What information did we get from the comments? Write comments about decor on the board.

4a. What data did we get on the service? Write the data under "Service."

4b. What information did we get from the comments? Write comments about service on the board.

5a. What data did we get on the cost? Write the data under "Cost."

5b. What information did we get from the comments? Write comments about cost on the board.

6a. What data did we get on the accessibility? Write the data under "Accessibility."

6b. What information did we get from the comments? Write comments about accessibility on the board.

7. Now we need to determine our overall impression of this restaurant. Based on the data and comments we've compiled here for the restaurant, what overall statement is appropriate? What is the overall impression we had? Write students' ideas under "Overall Opinion."

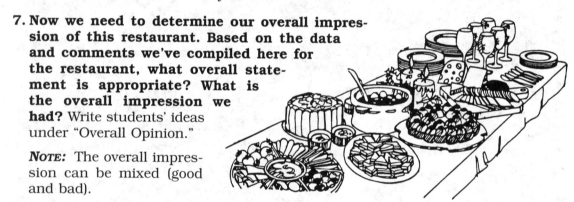

NOTE: The overall impression can be mixed (good and bad).

GROUP COMPOSING

Now let's create a restaurant review for our restaurant.

> ## Gary's Ribs
>
> Gary's Ribs is a great place to eat BBQ. The food was delicious, and you can have all you can eat. The decor was simple. Although it was crowded and noisy, the service was good. The cost was reasonable, and the restaurant is accessible to people in wheelchairs. If you are hungry, eat at Gary's Ribs. We highly recommend it. It's the best rib place in town and it has great steaks, too!

1. **What is the name of our restaurant?** Place the restaurant's name at the top of the review.

> **Thinking about Mechanics:** What do we need to do to the name of a specific restaurant? (capitalize the first letter of each important word in the name of a specific place)

2. **We came up with many different overall statements that are true about our restaurant. Which overall statement best fits this restaurant? How can we put that into a sentence?** Begin the review with this topic or opinion sentence.

   EXAMPLES: _____ is a _____ eating establishment.
   Dine at _____ for a truly delicious meal.

3. **In our review we can order the information we share in many ways. Which criteria shall we describe first in our review? second? third?** Number the criteria. Explain that when students compose their own restaurant reviews, they will choose which criteria to describe first. Share that often writers start with the good points and then describe the weaker points.

4a. **Since we chose to discuss (decor) first at our restaurant, let's write a topic sentence about the (decor).**

4b. **Considering the rating and comments, what is our overall opinion about the decor at this restaurant? Write this in the review.**

   EXAMPLES: The decor at the restaurant we reviewed was _____.
   The food at the restaurant we reviewed was _____.
   The service at the restaurant we reviewed was _____.
   The cost at the restaurant we reviewed was _____.

4c. **What comments did people make about the decor that we could use? How can we summarize the comment(s)?** Add this information to the review.

4d. **What describing words can we add to enhance or clarify our information? What adjectives and/or adverbs can we use to help our readers understand more clearly what we are saying?** Add descriptors to the review.

5. Repeat 4 b, c, and d for each criteria students generated.

6a. **Now let's end our review with a conclusion, suggestion, and/or final recommendation.**

Final Statements	Suggestions
recommend/don't recommend	eat here when you are in the mood for loud music
eat there/skip this one	take along some stomach medicine
go on weekday to avoid the crowd	go when you have plenty of time
best ribs in town	don't look any further for ribs

6b. Would we recommend this restaurant? How could we say this? What can we say to sum up our review? As students brainstorm write their ideas somewhere they can be easily seen.

6c. What suggestions can we make to help the reader have a good experience at the restaurant? As students brainstorm write their ideas somewhere so they can be easily seen.

6d. What descriptive words (adjectives and/or adverbs) can we add to enhance or clarify our recommendation(s) and/or suggestions? Add students' descriptive words to final statements and suggestions in the review.

7. Which of our final statements shall we use? Which suggestions should we include for readers? Circle this information and add it to the review.

8. (optional) Tell students that reviews often use symbols in their reviews. The more symbols (stars, thumbs up, smiling faces, pizzas), the better the rating. **What symbol shall we give this restaurant? How many?** (One symbol means poor, two symbols mean fair, three mean good, and four mean excellent. Or design several different symbols and choose one for each restaurant.)

INDIVIDUAL BRAINSTORMING & COMPOSING

Now you will use the information on your checklist to write a restaurant review. Do a comprehension check to remind students of the task ahead and determine which students understand what to do. Make sure students have their restaurant or other checklist(s) in front of them.

Comprehension Check

1. What goes in the title of your review? (name of restaurant or service)

2. How do we want to open the review? (an overall impression or opinion)

3. Which criteria might you want to discuss first? How could you order the information? (often criteria that supports the opening statement or good points are discussed first, then the weaker ones)

4. Once we have decided on a particular criteria, what do we need to do to help the reader understand what we'll discuss first? (topic sentence)

5. **What information/details do we have to support our topic sentence?** (rating and comments)

6. **Are describing words appropriate in this kind of genre? Why?** (yes, describing words help clarify the writer's opinions for the reader)

7. **After we draft our ideas for one criteria, what goes into the review next?** (paragraphs for the other criteria)

8. **How will you end your review?** (conclusion, suggestions, and a final recommendation)

9. **Would you want to make crude or offensive remarks in a review?** (no) **Why not?** (It is rude to the restaurant owner and readers will dismiss your valuable ideas.)

RESPONDING TO STUDENTS' WRITINGS/REVISING

1. Display several restaurant reviews on the overhead. The following are reviews written by sixth, seventh, and eighth graders. (A master of these reviews can be found at the end of this lesson.) Ask students which review is strongest, then ask why students feel this way. Inquire what strengths each review has and how each review could be strengthened.

Sample Restaurant Reviews

Amber's Restaurant

Amber's is a great place to eat. The food is terrific and it has a variety of dishes from which to choose. The service is good. The decor looks inviting and the plates and glasses are clean or you can ask for a new one. It is a little expensive, but the food is so good you won't mind. Please give Amber's a try.

Amber's Restaurant

Amber's is the best place to eat out in Rapid City. I should know because my family eats there every Saturday night. The food is delicious. The price is fair considering the all-you-can-eat tastebud-melting steaks and fries. The salad bar is huge. The atmosphere is great too. The servers are friendly and wear welcoming smiles. They are always helpful. Amber's is situated on the edge of a beautiful lake. A fire is always going in the fireplace. Even the bathrooms are clean and they smell fresh.

Amber's Restaurant

Amber's is a terrible place to eat. The food tastes like shoe polish. The service is slow. The waiter was a moron. The table cloths are always dirty. So, don't eat there. Oh yes, it is too expensive.

2. Write these four sentences on the board or overhead. Ask students which statement in each pair is accurate, yet gracious. Ask why they will want to avoid crude/offensive remarks in their reviews. **Which of the following is more accurate and gracious?**

> The restaurant stunk.
> The restaurant had an odor that we couldn't identify.

> The waitresses were ugly left-handed pigs.
> The new waitresses accidentally spilled my drink all over my new jacket and then laughed.

3. Have students reread their restaurant reviews to see if they are accurate, graciously stated, and avoid crude or offensive remarks.

   Next, encourage students to evaluate the following. Especially focus on adjectives and adverbs that make their points clearer or help convince readers.

   ___ title
   ___ overall opinion
   ___ five or more criteria
   ___ recommendation
   ___ suggestion
   ___ adjectives and adverbs
   ___ spelling
   ___ capitalization and punctuation

PUBLISHING

Explain that we'll post the restaurant reviews around the school under the banner "Tips on Where to Eat" so friends and other students (*audience*) will have information before making a decision (*purpose*). Also publish copies in a book titled "Restaurant Guide." A sample cover can be found at the end of this lesson, or publish the restaurant or other service reviews on your website.

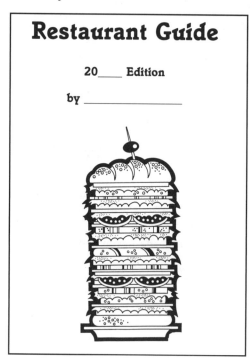

Restaurant Guide

20____ **Edition**

by _____

Sample Restaurant Reviews

Amber's Restaurant

Amber's is a great place to eat. The food is terrific and it has a variety of dishes from which to choose. The service is good. The decor looks inviting and the plates and glasses are clean or you can ask for a new one. It is a little expensive, but the food is so good you won't mind. Please give Amber's a try.

Amber's Restaurant

Amber's is the best place to eat out in Rapid City. I should know because my family eats there every Saturday night. The food is delicious. The price is fair considering the all-you-can-eat tastebud-melting steaks and fries. The salad bar is huge. The atmosphere is great too. The servers are friendly and wear welcoming smiles. They are always helpful. Amber's is situated on the edge of a beautiful lake. A fire is always going in the fireplace. Even the bathrooms are clean and they smell fresh.

Amber's Restaurant

Amber's is a terrible place to eat. The food tastes like shoe polish. The service is slow. The waiter was a moron. The table cloths are always dirty. So, don't eat there. Oh yes, it is too expensive.

Restaurant Guide

20_____ Edition

by _____

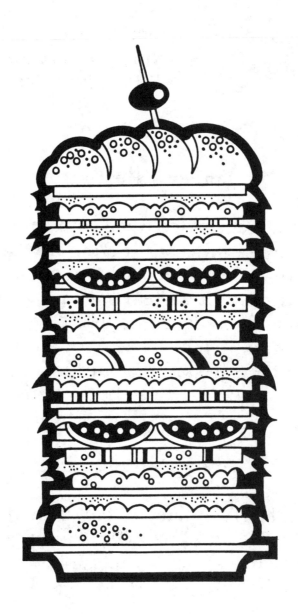

LESSON 29

Bill of Rights

OUTCOME Each student will contribute to a class bill of rights and then create his/her own document of rights and responsibilities for a group of children/teenagers/people who work or play together.

MOTIVATORS

1. Review the Declaration of Independence and the reasons why the American colonies broke away from Great Britain. To stimulate discussion, read this excerpt from the Declaration of Independence line by line and discuss each sentence.

> **Declaration of Independence**
> (excerpt)
>
> When in the Course of human Events, it becomes necessary for one People to dissolve the Political Bands which have connected them with another, . . .
>
> We hold these Truths to be self-evident, that all Men [and Women] are created equal, that they are endowed by their Creator with certain unalienable Rights, that among these are Life, Liberty, and the Pursuit of Happiness—That to secure these Rights, Governments are instituted among Men [and Women], deriving their just Powers from the Consent of the Governed, that whenever any Form of Government becomes destructive of these Ends, it is the Right of the People to alter or abolish it, and to institute new Government, . . . [Following this introduction is a long list of complaints against the King of Great Britain.]

If you want a complete copy of the Declaration of Independence, check an American History or American Government textbook or search the web.

2. Explain that even though we are free, problems in our classroom, at school, and in our community still exist. Explain that freedom (rights/privileges) results in responsibilities and limits, and not everyone acts responsibly. This causes problems.

Ask students what problems they might face in the classroom. What problems do they face in school? in the community? List problems under the correct heading. This information will be used during group brainstorming.

Classroom	School	Community
kids talk out of turn	bullies	litter in park and on roadway
others don't pay attention	fights in hallways	speeding cars
too much homework	teachers who don't care	homeless people
some kids do all the work	vandalism	theft

3. Ask students what our country's Bill of Rights is. (the first ten amendments to the United States Constitution) For a copy of the complete Bill of Rights, see: http://www.lawcornell.edu/constitution/constitution.table.html#preamble.

Ask students what freedoms are preserved by the Bill of Rights. Focus on the following freedoms:

- **Freedom of Assembly** (freedom to gather and protest, but the responsibility to be nonviolent)

- **Freedom of Speech** (freedom to say what we think and feel, but the responsibility to not lie or slander someone)

- **Freedom of the Press** (freedom to print the news, but the responsibility to report both sides honestly and fairly)

- **Freedom of Activity** (freedom to do the things we want and go where we choose, but the responsibility to not hurt other people or their property)

- **Freedom of Religion** (freedom to worship however we want or to not worship, but the responsibility to respect the values of others)

- **Freedom to Petition** (freedom to be heard by the leaders of the community, but the responsibility to follow the rules about how to circulate a petition)

- **Freedom from Fear** and other rights such as **Due Process; Seek Counsel; Search and Seizure; Jury Trial; Cruel and Unusual Punishment; Vote; Rights not Denied Due to Race, Disability, or Gender**

After these freedoms are recalled, inquire what each one means. Ask for everyday examples of our freedoms. That is, what are you/we free to do in our country? To save time, briefly jot down a word or phrase representing each student's idea for a particular freedom, not a whole sentence.

Rights	Examples
Activity:	I can choose my hobbies. I can pick my own friend(s).
Assembly:	I can go to the mall. I can go to a huge football game as long as we are nonviolent.
Speech:	I can disagree with school policy. I can give my opinions about who to elect for governor.
Press:	I can publish my thoughts on recycling. I can write a letter to the editor telling how unhappy I am about a new law.
Petition:	If I don't like a government policy, I can get people who agree with me to sign a document requesting a change be made.
Religion:	I can discuss my religious beliefs as long as I don't force others to believe as I do.

4. Share examples of other Bill of Rights. Here are a few brief excerpts from some Bill of Rights I've encountered. If you want to make copies to share with your students, a reproducible can be found at the end of this lesson.

Teenager's Rights

Teenagers are people too. They should have rights like adults.

- Teenagers should have the right to be valued for who they are, not what we think they should be.
- Teenagers should have the right to voice their opinions to their parents in a respectful manner.
- Teenagers should have the right to be treated with courtesy and respect.
- Teenagers should have the right to make reasonable choices and to be responsible for those decisions.

A Dog's Bill of Rights

As a living creature, I have rights too.

- I have the right to give and receive unconditional love . . .
- I have the right to be trained so that I do not become the prisoner of my misbehavior . . .
- I have the right to special time with my people . . .

(Excerpted from http://www.geocities.com/Petsburgh/3241/billofrights.html)

A Car Buyer's Rights

I have some important rights any time I buy something.

- The car buyer has the right to know how much the car lot paid for the vehicle.
- The car buyer has the right to the background and warranty of the vehicle.
- The car buyer has the right to know whether the vehicle has been in an accident.
- The car buyer should know the correct mileage of the vehicle.

GROUP BRAINSTORMING

Now we are going to brainstorm ideas for our own bill of rights.

Rights	Responsibilities
talk while we work	get our work done don't disturb other students
be respected by teachers	be on time
teacher should understand if I'm late	come in and sit down without disturbing class have a reasonable excuse
be heard in class	raise hand before speaking listen to others
be safe in hall	don't bully other kids tell an adult if you see a bully hurting someone
good food for lunch	

Key Questions

1. Have students review the problems generated earlier during motivator 2.

2a. To help us brainstorm rights, let's consider the different parts of the school day. Allow plenty of time after each question for students to think.

2b. **What rights should you have before school starts?** List each possible right on the board in an abbreviated form. **Why?** Ask the student why it should be a right. To save time do not write reasons on the board. Praise good ideas based on students' point of view. Realize that students' thinking will mature as they have more useful life experiences.

    If a student says "because" or "I want it" for a reason, seriously ask your class why it should be a right. If no one can give a reason, explain that without a reason you must put a question mark next to the possible right for now. This action will signal that serious thoughts are being requested. Do not erase the "right" because another student may use this idea to build a better one. Continue questioning.

2c. **What rights should you have as school is starting?** List each possible right on the board. **Why?** Ask the student why it should be a right. To save time do not write reasons on the board. Praise good ideas based on students' point of view.

2d. **What rights should you have during class?** List rights on the board. **Why?** Ask the student why it should be a right. Praise good ideas based on students' point of view.

2e. **What rights should you have at free time?** List rights on the board. **Why?** Ask the student why it should be a right. Praise good ideas.

2f. **What rights should you have when working in cooperative groups?** List rights on the board. **Why?** Ask the student why it should be a right. Praise good ideas.

2g. **What rights should you have in the halls?** List rights on the board. **Why?** Ask the student why it should be a right. Praise good ideas.

2h. **What rights should you have at lunch?** List rights on the board. **Why?** Ask the student why it should be a right. Praise good ideas.

2i. **What rights should you have while on school grounds?** List rights on the board. **Why?** Ask the student why it should be a right. Praise good ideas.

2j. **What rights should you have after school?** List rights on the board. **Why?** Ask the student why it should be a right. Praise good ideas.

3a. **What is the difference between a right and a privilege?** (a privilege is earned) Which of these are rights and which are privileges?

a safe school building (right)	club membership (privilege)
pizza party (privilege)	driver's license (privilege)
loving parents (right)	clean air (right)
knowing what is expected on a project (right)	a library card (privilege)
	allowance (privilege)

When differences occur, allow time for students to discuss.

NOTE: The concept of privilege is constantly changing. For example, I may believe that clean air is a right, but at some point in the future it may well become a special treat.

3b. Now let's review our list of proposed rights to determine which are rights and which are privileges. Point to each idea on the brainstormed list and evaluate each idea to determine whether it is a right or a privilege. If there is doubt whether an idea is a right, allow your class to decide. It is their bill of rights.

4. Out of all our proposed rights, which ones do you believe are important rights? As students offer ideas, circle or star these rights. Repeat until five or six rights are selected.

5. Now let's consider responsibilities for each right. If we select this right (point to one right), **what corresponding responsibilities will we have? What must everyone do so our rights aren't infringed upon? What can we do to assure that everyone benefits from this right?** Repeat until two or three responsibilities are selected for each right.

GROUP COMPOSING

Now that we have considered what rights we should have and the corresponding responsibilities, let's compose our bill of rights together.

A Bill of
Rights & Responsibilities

We, the students in _____ class/school, on this _____ day of _____ propose/declare the following rights and responsibilities in order to improve life in our class/school.

The Right to _____
1. All students have the right to _____
and the corresponding responsibility to _____

The Right to _____
2. All students have the right to _____
and the corresponding responsibility to _____

The Right to _____
3. All students have the right to _____
and the corresponding responsibility to _____

The Right to _____
4. All students have the right to _____
and the corresponding responsibility to _____

The members of this class/school are responsible for ensuring those rights are received and these responsibilities are followed. If problems occur, we agree to _____.

SEAL

signatures of writers and others who agree to support these rights and responsibilities

1. **The words "Bill of Rights" should be in our title. Whose Bill of Rights is it?** Insert a word or phrase such as "Our" or "Seventh Graders," etc.

2. To save time and to keep students' attention have the preamble written on chart paper or the board before class. Feel free to modify this suggested preamble as you see fit. **Next, to make our Bill of Rights sound official, we'll use a modification of the preamble of the Constitution of the United States of America for our introduction.** Have students read with you the chosen preamble.

> We, the _____ students in _____, in an attempt to help everyone get along, avoid angry moments, promote a friendly classroom/school, and to secure liberty for us and our friends, hereby on _____ ordain and establish these student-designed guidelines for _____.

or

> We, the students in _____ class/school, on this day of _____ propose/declare the following rights and responsibilities to improve life in our class/school.

3a. **What word or phrase can we place in the first blank to describe us? What kind of students?** Insert this descriptor in the preamble.

3b. **In the next blank we need to tell people which group, class, or school this bill of rights is for. Who is our bill of rights for?** Insert the group in the second blank of the preamble.

3c. **To make this document legal, we must insert today's date. What is today's date? What is the date that we will sign this document?** Insert the date after the words "hereby on _____."

3d. **Finally, for whom are we establishing these guidelines?** Insert this information.

4. **Which right shall we put first? Why?** Choose an uninvolved or withdrawn student to select a right. Add this right to the bill of rights.

5. **Out of all the corresponding responsibilities for this right, which ones are the most important to place in our Bill of Rights?** Choose a student who needs encouragement or inclusion to select the responsibility. Add this responsibility to the bill of rights.

6. (optional) Ask Advanced Writers for reasons the right should be granted.

7. Repeat steps 4 and 5 for other rights and responsibilities.

8. **What will we do if problems occur?** Choose several students to offer ideas. Ask the class to select one idea. Add this idea to the bill of rights.

9. Allow time for students to sign the class bill of rights. Post it where students can reread it as needed.

INDIVIDUAL BRAINSTORMING & COMPOSING

Tell students that now it is their job to generate a list of rights they believe everyone in the class/school or another group should have and the corresponding responsibilities and obligations. Pass out copies of the Brainstorming Assistant, which can be found at the end of this lesson.

Brainstorming Assistant for Bill of Rights

Rights   corresponding   **Responsibilities**

1. _____   _____

2. _____   _____

3. _____   _____

4. _____   _____

As students begin brainstorming rights and responsibilities, walk around the classroom praising unique rights and responsibilities students have brainstormed. Read back each young writer's bill of rights so he/she can hear what he/she has written so far.

- Make positive comments about important rights and their corresponding responsibilities.

- Ask questions that assist students to clarify what they mean regarding certain rights and/or to sharpen the responsibilities.

- Ask Advanced Writers questions to sharpen reasons why rights should be granted.

If a young author is having difficulty getting started, ask him/her what problems he/she is currently having at home, school, or other. Together sort out the student's rights in this situation.

As students begin to organize their thoughts into a bill of rights draft, support the inclusion of a title, preamble, a list of rights and responsibilities, a statement addressing what will be done when problems occur, space for a seal, and space for the signature of the writer and supporters.

Beginning Writers These young authors can use the simplified bill of rights brainstorming form at the end of this lesson.

Advanced Writers These young authors can create their bill of rights around a theme concept like genetic engineering of food crops or the right to life.

Another variation for Advanced Writers is the Bill of NO Rights. One of your students might enjoy using this useful "NO Rights" pattern. Here's an excerpt that demonstrates this "do not" pattern:

ARTICLE I:

You do not have the right to a new car, a big-screen TV, or any other wealth. More power to you if you can legally acquire them, but no one is guaranteeing anything.

(http://belle/pcpros.net/~grandma/billofrights.html)

RESPONDING TO STUDENTS' WRITINGS/REVISING

As students finish their rough drafts of the bill of rights, tape them to a wall somewhere in the room at eye level for others to read and consider: "Are your rights necessary or unnecessary?" "Are responsibilities fair/unfair?" Encourage students to respond using these symbols:

☆☆—**necessary right**   NN—**not a necessary right**
☆—**fair right**   NF—**not a fair right**

Ask students to add suggestions on sticky notes and attach to the draft. Mingle with the students. Direct students so that each draft has a similar number of readers. You may want to display the drafts for a day or two. Once students have had time to respond, ask each young writer to take down his/her bill of rights and reflect on the feedback he/she received before composing a rough draft.

If you want students to further evaluate their bill of rights, list the following on the board, overhead, or chart:

----- Does my preamble tell who the rights are for and the date they begin?
----- Did I write at least five rights?
----- Does each right have a corresponding responsibility?
----- Does each sentence begin with a capital letter?

Before word-processing and publishing, ask each young author to reread and look for punctuation, grammar, and spelling errors that might hinder a reader from understanding and supporting his/her bill of rights.

PUBLISHING

Explain to students that since their Bills of Rights are such important documents, we'll add a seal to each one and then publish them in three ways.

1. Post them on their desks or in their personal notebooks so they (*audience*) can recall their rights and responsibilities (*purpose*).

2. Share the rights with classmates by posting the rights on the wall outside your room so that peers and the other classes and their teachers (*audience*) can respect our rights (*purpose*) and add their signatures if they support these rights.

3. Roll up each Bill of Rights and tie it with string or a ribbon. Send this copy home, to the principal, to family, and to neighbors (*audience*) so they will understand the students' beliefs and feelings (*purpose*).

Bill of Rights Examples

Teenager's Rights

Teenagers are people too. They should have rights like adults.

- Teenagers should have the right to be valued for who they are, not what we think they should be.
- Teenagers should have the right to voice their opinions to their parents in a respectful manner.
- Teenagers should have the right to be treated with courtesy and respect.
- Teenagers should have the right to take reasonable choices and to be responsible for those decisions.

A Dog's Bill of Rights

As a living creature, I have rights too.

- I have the right to give and receive unconditional love . . .
- I have the right to be trained so that I do not become the prisoner of my misbehavior . . .
- I have the right to special time with my people . . .

(Excerpted from http://www.geocities.com/Petsburgh/3241/billofrights.html)

A Car Buyer's Rights

I have some important rights any time I buy something.

- The car buyer has the right to know how much the car lot paid for the vehicle.
- The car buyer has the right to the background and warranty of the vehicle.
- The car buyer has the right to know whether the vehicle has been in an accident.
- The car buyer should know the correct mileage of the vehicle.

Brainstorming Assistant for Bill of Rights

Rights

corresponding

Responsibilities

1.

2.

3.

4.

A Bill of
Rights & Responsibilities

We, the students in _____ class/school, on this _____ day of _____ propose/declare the following rights and responsibilities in order to improve life in our class/school.

The Right to _____

1. All students have the right to _____

and the corresponding responsibility to _____

The Right to _____

2. All students have the right to _____

and the corresponding responsibility to _____

The Right to _____

3. All students have the right to _____

and the corresponding responsibility to _____

The Right to _____

4. All students have the right to _____

and the corresponding responsibility to _____

The members of this class/school are responsible for ensuring those rights are received and these responsibilities are followed. If problems occur, we agree to _____.

SEAL

_____   _____

_____   _____

_____   _____

_____   _____

_____   _____

_____   _____

_____   _____

signatures of writers and others who agree to support these rights and responsibilities

LESSON 30

Eulogy

OUTCOME Each student will write a eulogy to say goodbye to someone, something, or somewhere they remember and miss.

MOTIVATORS

1. Capture students' feelings just after your students have experienced a common loss. This loss could be due to the death of a student, teacher, principal, a president; a popular person who is leaving; failure to achieve a cherished goal such as victory in an important sporting event; or a natural disaster.

2. Share at least two eulogies. Use one of the following and perhaps a eulogy that you wrote/gave to honor a loved one or friend.

Toby

Toby was a silver and black Pekingese who loved life. Toby was my best friend. He protected me through my divorce. Toby was only a dog, but he stayed up all night licking my tears during the first six months of my divorce.

He loved the long walks we took in the park. He rode in my canoe and slept in my tent during outings and even was allowed to sit beside me during outdoor church and board meetings.

Toby even forgave the neighborhood kids who shaved all of his hair and whiskers off and left him shivering from fear on my front porch. I remember putting him in a soft sweater, rocking and talking to him all night until he licked my cheek as if to say, "I'm okay now. It's time for you to go to work."

Toby always joined me in our garden; he was a super gardener. I just had to point where I wanted to plant tomatoes and he dug the hole. And while he loved tomatoes, he never stole our tomatoes, although he did bring a few home from my neighbor's garden.

Toby was a terrific and loyal friend. I was lucky to have him in my life.

Eulogy
for
My Blue Devil

My bike disappeared off my front porch last week. I looked and my heart broke when I realized I probably would never see it again.

It was the first bike I ever owned. I wanted a blue bike since I was eight. All my friends had them. My dad bought it for me on my 14th birthday. My dad worked overtime for five months so he could afford it. When I first got it, I couldn't even balance it because I was so tall and I had never ridden a bike before.

My bike was metallic blue with red racing stripes. I can still close my eyes and see it now. I will always remember how smooth it rode at the bike park. I felt like I was flying! When I rode my Blue Devil there were no rules; no one scolding me. I felt so free and alive. All the other kids admired my bike.

I'll always remember my blue racing bike.

Eulogy
for
My Dad

My dad was hard to get to know. Sometimes he came home from work and wouldn't speak to anyone. He would fix a drink or grab a beer and go to his room and turn up the radio so loud my head hurt. Other days he was so friendly. We arm wrestled and told jokes. When he was feeling good we went for long walks. He was a great listener. Dad taught me important stuff like how to ask a girl out on a date and how to fix the lawn mower.

Our family never went out together because we didn't know when Dad would blow up at someone. When Dad was down, he seemed to pick on Mom and me. He would yell all the time about how we were to blame for his problems and if he didn't have a family, he could move to Detroit or Chicago. Many nights Mom and I had to carry my dad to bed. Even during the bad times I knew he loved me.

The police arrested Dad for driving while drunk and striking an officer with a broken bottle. The judge gave him a choice of jail or detox. Dad went to detox for three months. The house seems empty now that Dad has gone. I wonder what he'll be like when he gets out. The judge told mom that she didn't have to put up with his abuse.

Close your eyes and visualize or draw the image of a loved one you lost. Think about the good times you had. What was your relationship to the person? How does he/she look? What is he/she doing? What was one good time you had together? What does the loved one want to say to you?

3. Ask students what a eulogy is and why we have eulogies. Give students time to think.

   A eulogy is a way to say goodbye to someone who has died, a remembrance of the good qualities of that person, a celebration of the person's life, and a sharing of good times with others in honor of a loved one. Share that an eulogy helps the writer/speaker and others cope with grief. Writing and talking with others about the person who died helps us accept the reality of the loss. It gives us a chance to grieve, helps us and others feel a little better about the loss, and allows us to keep the loved one alive in our hearts. A eulogy is usually said aloud to friends and family in honor of a lost loved one, but is thought about carefully and written before it is read or said aloud at the funeral.

4. If the lost one was a fellow student or someone known by most students, invite a counselor to come to your class to help students express the grief and cope with the loss they have had. Depending on how close the student was to the deceased, normal feelings include sadness, confusion, denial, fear, anger, guilt, and unfairness.

5. When a classroom pet has died, many students respond well to reading a very special book, *The Tenth Good Thing About Barney* by Judith Viorst (New York: Macmillan/Aladdin, 1987).

GROUP BRAINSTORMING

We are going to compose a eulogy for _____. Later you'll have the opportunity to write your own eulogy for a pet or family member who died, a friend who moved away, or something important you have lost. For the sake of this example, we'll use Ida, the school cook who recently died at our school. Design your lesson around a real person or other actual loss students' have had.

Description	Memories	Feelings
bright smile huge colored aprons thoughtful greeting	always cool very patient made special cakes	left many friends would like to be as well liked admire her

Key Questions

1. Pause for at least 30 seconds to give students time to recall. Record students' responses on the board or overhead under the "Description" column.

> **What did he/she/it look like?**
> **How can we describe _____?**
> **What were his/her unique/special qualities?**
> **What was his/her/its good traits?**
> **What are some important facts about _____?**
> **How can we describe _____'s character?**
> **What was special or unique about him/her/it?**

2. Pause for at least 30 seconds to give students time to recall. Record students' responses on the board or overhead under the "Memories" column.

> **What happy memories do you have of _____?**
> **When you close your eyes and think of _____, what is he/she/it doing?**
> **What special adventures or events took place in _____'s life?**
> **Who did he/she help?**
> **Who will he/she be remembered by? For what?**
> **What was special or important about this person/pet's life?**
> **What funny moment was shared?**
> **What is something this person/pet did that was special or unique?**
> **What were his/her special accomplishments for family/friends/school/community?**
> **What did he/she/it know all about?**
> **What did he/she care about?**
> **What was he/she dedicated to?**
> **What did he/she believe?**

3. Pause for at least 30 seconds to give students time to recall. Record students' responses on the board or overhead under the "Feelings" column.

> **How do you feel about _____? Why?**
> **Why was he/she/it important?**
> **How did _____ influence others?**
> **How did he/she/it change our lives?**
> **Why did we like/admire _____?**
> **How did _____ make us feel?**
> **What will he/she be remembered for _____?**
> **How did he/she change our lives?**
> **What impact did _____ have on us? What was an example of this?**

GROUP COMPOSING

Now we will compose a eulogy for _____ together. Later you can choose who or what you want to eulogize.

Ida

Ida was our school cook. She had to retire when she got sick, but she kept coming back to our school to visit until she died. We will always remember Ida in her brightly colored aprons that she always wore—along with her bright smile. Every time I saw Ida, she smelled like fresh baked bread and she made awesome, melt-in-your-mouth cinnamon rolls for our school breakfast program.

We admired Ida because she was always cool when the cafeteria became a "loud and crazy" place. I still remember the day the principal's office caught fire. It was Ida who grabbed the fire extinguisher and put out the burning carpet. On the day we planted trees, Ida . . .

I was very sad when I heard that Ida had died. She gave of herself to all of us. And I'll always think of her when I smell fresh cinnamon rolls.

Opening

1. Introduce the departed friend, family member, person, or animal.

Who/What died? Who or what has been lost? Who was _____? What was our relationship to/with _____? Add this information to the eulogy in sentence form.

2. How shall we let people know the areas we'll discuss in our eulogy for _____? Pause to let students think. Share an example. Add one or more students' ideas to the board, overhead, or chart paper.

EXAMPLE: I want to share with you how I'll remember _____, some of the moments we shared, and my feelings about _____.

> **Thinking about Mechanics:** How can we show our readers that we are beginning the eulogy? (indent)

Paragraph 1

1. **Out of all the ideas we listed under description, which ideas shall we choose to include in our eulogy?** Choose an uninvolved or withdrawn student to select three. Circle these descriptive phrases.

2. **Which description shall we write about first? second? third?** Number these ideas.

3. **How can we put our first idea into a sentence to help our audience understand that we're remembering _____'s image?** Insert statement(s) into eulogy. Repeat with second and third descriptive phrases.

Paragraph 2

1. **Out of all the ideas we listed under memories, which memories shall we choose to include in our eulogy?** Choose a student who needs encouragement or inclusion to select three memories. Circle these memories.

> **Thinking about Mechanics:** How can we show our readers that we are changing the topic to "memories"? (indent)

2. **Which of our memories shall we write about first? second? third?** Number these memories.

3. **How can we put our first memory into a sentence to help our audience understand that we're reflecting some of our most powerful memories of _____?** Insert statement(s) into eulogy. Repeat with second and third memories.

Paragraph 3

1. **Which of our feelings shall we choose to include in our eulogy?** Choose a low-achieving or uninvolved student to select three feelings. Circle these feelings.

> **Thinking about Mechanics:** How can we show our readers that we are changing the topic to "feelings"? (indent)

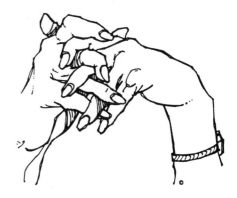

2. **Which of our feelings shall we share first? second? third?** Number these ideas.

3. **How can we put our first feeling into a sentence or two to help our audience understand that we're reflecting some of the most powerful feelings we had for _____?** Insert statement(s) into eulogy. Repeat with second and third feelings.

4. **How shall we end our eulogy? What final words can we say about _____?** Add these thoughts to the eulogy.

   EXAMPLES: The memory of ___ will always stay with me/will last a lifetime.
   His/her untimely death is a tragedy for all who knew him/her.
   We'll never be the same without _____.
   I'll miss you. Goodbye.

GROUP REVISING

Ask students to read the eulogy silently to themselves to see what was left out and which of the thoughts might work better in another place. Add and delete thoughts. Use arrows to move information. Look for trite or overused words. Draw a line through these words. Ask a question such as "What is a more powerful word or one that will make a more vivid image?" Replace the overused word with a more powerful one.

If students were close to the deceased, this may be a time many students become quiet and reflective. Allow time for this and don't push group revising. Other groups may deal with their pain by wanting the group composition to be very precise. Go with the flow.

INDIVIDUAL BRAINSTORMING & COMPOSING

Select one of the following choices for your students:

1. Have students individually brainstorm and compose about the person in question. Remove the Group Brainstorming and Group Composing boards/overheads before students start so they won't be tempted to use that information. If a student asks to see one of the charts, suggest that he/she can do a much better and more personal eulogy.

2. Help students choose an emotional loss such as a death, a dying grandparent, a friend who is moving/has moved away, a divorce or the loss of a parent, a broken toy or a stolen bike, a lingering illness, a wrecked car, a natural disaster that destroyed their home, a boy-/girlfriend choosing someone else, a lost sporting event, a place that the student misses.

   NOTE: Strongly suggest to students that it will be easier to write a eulogy about someone or a situation they know well.

Once the painful subject has been chosen, have students individually brainstorm and compose. Ask students who want assistance to visit you one at a time.

RESPONDING TO STUDENTS' WRITINGS/REVISING

After students complete their eulogies, wait a day or two before asking them to silently reread what they have written, meditating on the person or thing that was lost. Ask young writers to consider these:

- Have I captured the essence of the person/thing I've lost?

- What is something personal or negative I may want to leave out?

- What area have I missed that I may want to include?

- What part may I want to reword? What is a better word to use at this point?

- Did I say goodbye to this person/pet/thing? If not, how can I word this part?

PUBLISHING

We'll publish our eulogies so we can celebrate the memories of _____'s life and express our feelings of loss (*purpose*) **by sharing fond memories of lost loved ones with others** (*audience*)**.** Allow students to read their eulogies aloud at a classroom funeral or other memorial gathering or choose one or more of the following methods.

Oral Sharing with Peers

Depending on your students and the situation, ask them to read their eulogies to each other. This can be very therapeutic.
   Suggestions:

1. Invite your school counselor and other well-liked school staff.

2. Put a note on your door and alert the office that you should not be bothered.

3. Bring plenty of tissues.

4. Have students make a circle with their chairs. This will facilitate mourning.

5. Ask students to support all their peers by looking at the person and listening to his/her pain.

Memorial Wall (Public Memorial)

Materials

a public wall or fence (over 100,000 people put messages and favorite items on a fence after the horrible bombing in downtown Oklahoma City in 1995)

Directions

1. Write the eulogy on stiff paper.

2. Add a photo, illustration, or a small memorial object.

3. Laminate the message or cover it with clear self-stick vinyl to help preserve it from moisture.

4. Use tape to affix it to a public wall. Use the wire from paper clips to affix the message to a nearby fence. To increase the length of time the message will last in the open, punch a small hole in each corner of the laminated document and insert grommets (purchased from a leather store such as Tandy Leather Company) before inserting wire and attaching to a fence.

Stand-up Frame

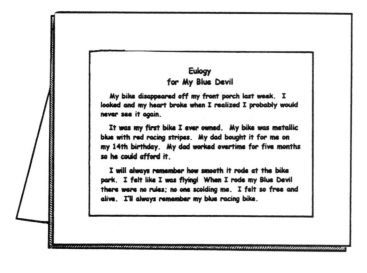

Materials

frame pattern, back pattern, two 8-1/2 × 11-inch pieces of cardboard (the backs of cereal boxes are a good thickness), scissors, glue, newspaper, (optional) 2 rubber bands, (optional) ribbon, tape

Directions

1. Cut around the frame pattern. Use scissors to poke a hole in the center and cut it out so the eulogy can show through. (If a student wants an oval center, draw one on the pattern. It will need to be somewhat larger than the rectangular center in order to hold the eulogy.)

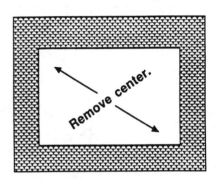

2. Next, cut out the back pattern. Cut on the two sides of the stand. Fold the stand on the short dotted line.

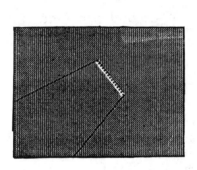
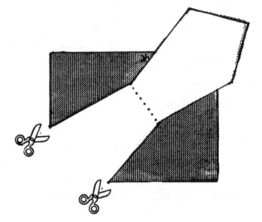

3. Place each pattern on a sheet of cardboard and trace around them. Then cut out the cardboard front and the back of the frame. Lift the stand part of the pattern to trace around it. If a student wants to construct a larger frame, use a matte knife to cut both the front and back of the frame from corrugated cardboard. (Plan for proper supervision if students use the matte knife.)

4. To keep glue off the desk or table during the assembling of the frame, lay the eulogy face down on a sheet of newspaper.

5. Spread glue evenly over three sides of the back, but keep the glue off the stand. This will keep the stand from becoming glued to the body of the frame. Center the back of the frame over the back of the eulogy and press down. Smooth out any wrinkles.

6. Next, spread glue over the front of the frame. Center the frame over the front of the eulogy and press down.

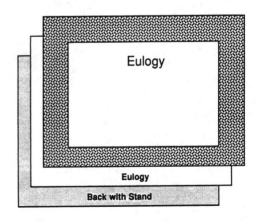

7. Stand up the completely framed eulogy to dry. If the glued parts of the frame try to curl or separate, place two rubber bands around the frame (but not the stand) until it dries correctly.

8. (optional) If a stand tries to collapse, tape a 1/4-inch wide × 1-1/2-inch long strip of ribbon or cloth to the back of the framed eulogy and to the stand. This will keep the complete frame in a standing position.

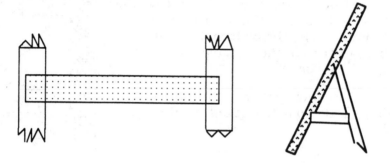

9. (optional) If desired, there are a number of ways to decorate the front of the frame *after it dries.*

   • Glue stamps, tissue paper, yarn, cloth, wallpaper, comics, pieces from photos, colorful advertisements, cardboard shapes, or wrapping paper to the frame.

   • Hot glue buttons, pennies, shells, keys, small stones, starburst macaroni, or crumpled aluminum foil to the frame. (If one of these heavier decorations is used, the back of the frame and the stand may need to be constructed from heavier cardboard.)

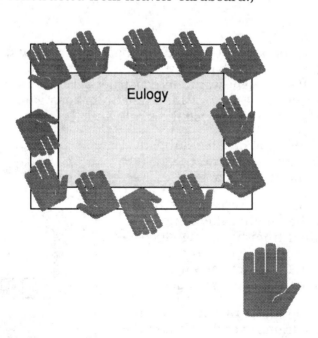

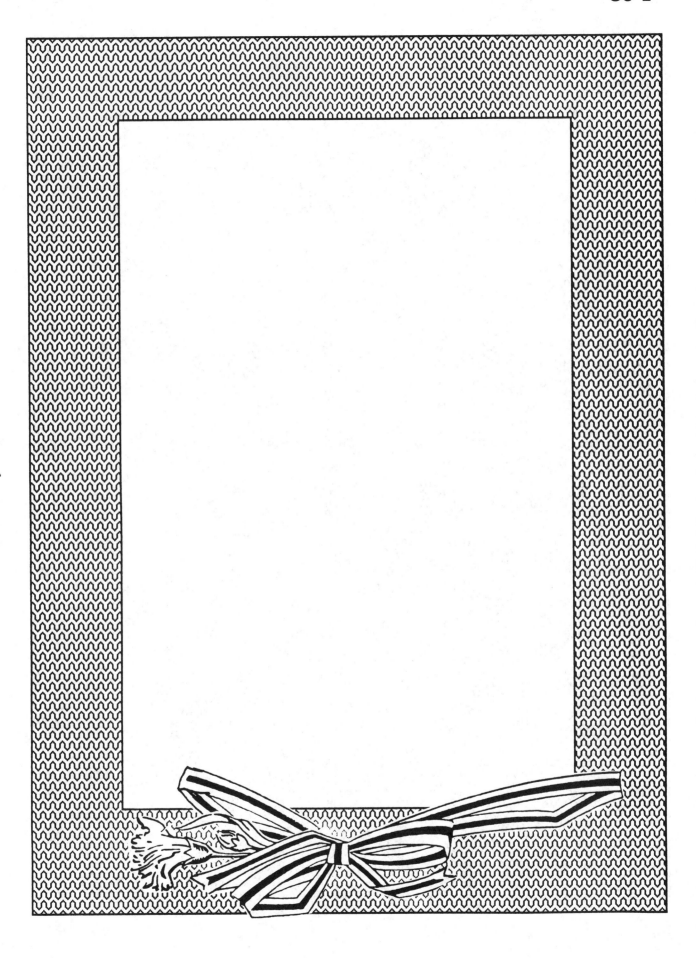

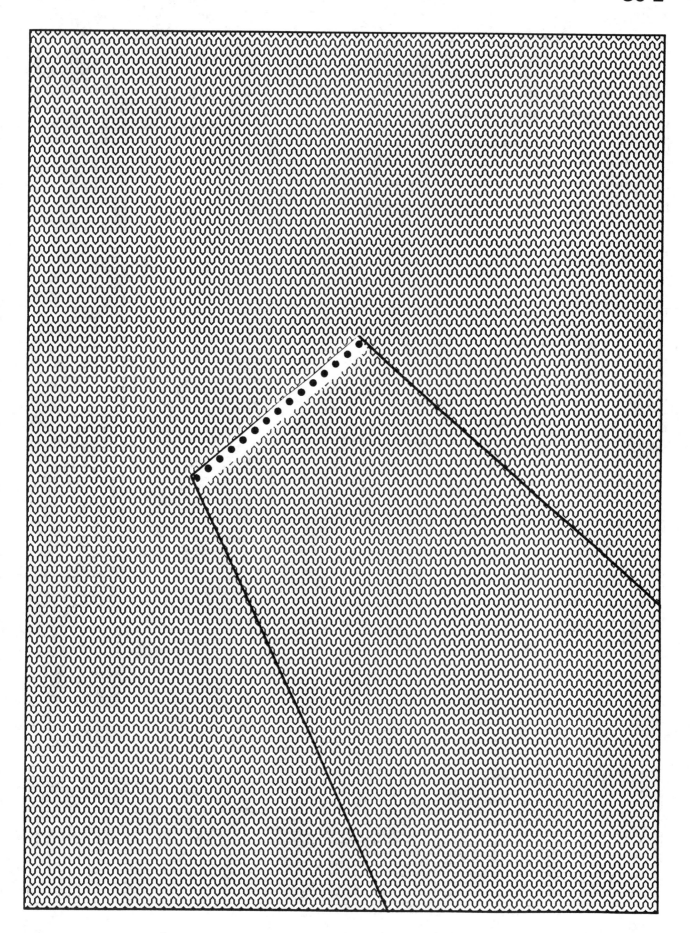

LESSON 31

Letters to Our Troops

OUTCOME Each student will write a letter to a member of the Armed Forces to boost morale and to let the soldier know people back home care.

MOTIVATORS

1. Discuss a current conflict or disaster that has been in the news. Show a map of the area of the world where the conflict is occurring. Show pictures from magazines and newspapers such as *Newsweek* and *Time*.

   Explain that our country often works with the United Nations and other countries on peace-keeping missions to prevent war or protect innocent people who live in a war-torn area. Soldiers are also sent to help after natural disasters, such as earthquakes and floods.

2. Explain that many of our service men and women must be away from their homes for long periods of time. Some leave behind a new spouse, a new baby, or work/school when they go somewhere to serve our country. Mail is the link to home that boosts the soldiers' morales, eases their loneliness, and makes life bearable. A soldier can never get too much mail. Letters from students let the soldier know that he/she is appreciated.

3. Ask students if any of their relatives are members of the Armed Forces. Let students tell the class about the service person and where he/she is stationed.

GROUP BRAINSTORMING

We will brainstorm ideas for a letter to a service person.

About Us	News from Home
6th grade Mr. Schmidt	Beach Boys played at dome water polo game against the Tigers fund raiser for families of service members
Questions	**Support**
What do you eat? Do you sleep in a tent? What do you do all day?	appreciate you fighting for our country we feel safe because you are protecting our country

Key Questions

1. Pause for at least 30 seconds after each question to give students time to think. Write students' responses on the board or overhead under the heading "About Us." Praise each idea.

   What would the service person want to know about us/you?
   What grade are you in?
   Where do you live (state/city)?
   What are your interests?
   What have you done recently with your class? family?
   About what else might the service person be curious?

2. Pause for at least 30 seconds after each question to give students time to think. Write student responses on the board or overhead under the heading "News from Home." Praise each idea.

   What is some news from home?
   What is happening here in our town? our state? city? country?
   What politics are in the news?
   What's the weather doing?
   What is going on in sports? What games has our school team played lately?
   What music are people listening to?
   What is the hometown gossip?

3. Pause for at least 30 seconds after each question to give students time to think. Write students' responses on the board or overhead under the heading "Questions." Praise each idea.

What can we say to ask how he/she is doing?
What do you want to know about the service person?
What do you want to know about where he/she is living?
What is he/she eating?
What does he/she do during free time?
How old is he/she?
What do you want to know about the service person's family back home?

4. Pause for at least 30 seconds after each question to give students time to think. Write students' responses on the board or overhead under the heading "Support." Praise each idea.

How can we tell him/her we appreciate the service people protecting us and
    our country?
How can we show him/her to show we remember what he/she is doing to
    serve our country?
What other supportive thoughts can we share?

GROUP COMPOSING

Now we will compose a letter to a service person as a class, then you will write your own letter to "any member of our armed services."

> February 23, 20XX
>
> Dear Service Member,
>
> We are in Mr. Schmidt's 6th-grade Social Studies class. We live in Kansas City. It is a huge town with a lot to do. We have been studying the Mideast. We've learned a lot about the history and geography of Iran and the surrounding countries.
>
> This year we have had 18 inches of snow. Normally we only get a few inches and it melts and looks muddy. This year we have been ice skating during lunch. After school we go to the dike and slide down the snow bank on cardboard boxes.
>
> Where are you? Do you live on a ship or in a tent? We would like it if you would write back to us and tell us about yourself and your job.
>
> Remember that we appreciate the job you are doing to keep our country safe. Keep up the good work. Take care.
>
> Come home safely,
> Mr. Schmidt's Class

1. **What is today's date?** Ask students about mechanics (capital letter on the month and comma between day and month). Then place this date on the letter.

2. **What respectful greeting should we use to address the service member?** Add this information to the letter.

Introductory Paragraph

3a. Direct students' attention to the brainstorming category "About Us." **Now let's begin our paragraph about us. The first thing we need to do is tell the reader who we are. How can we say this?** Add this information to the letter.

    EXAMPLES: We are in Mr. Gonzales' fifth-grade homeroom.
               I am a ninth grader from Boulder, Colorado.

> **Thinking about Mechanics:** How do we indicate the beginning of a new idea? (indent)

3b. **Of all the ideas we brainstormed about us, which will the service person want to know?** Circle two or three personal pieces of information to share.

3c. **Which of our brainstormed ideas shall we share first?** Add this personal information to the letter. **second?** Add this personal information to the letter. **third?** Add this personal information to the letter.

"News from Home" Paragraph

4a. **Now let's begin our paragraph of news from home. How can we let the service member know what this paragraph will contain?** Pause to allow time for students to think. Praise good topic sentences. Add one topic sentence to the letter.

    EXAMPLES: I thought you'd like to know what's happening back home.
               There are lots of things happening here.

> **Thinking about Mechanics:** How do we indicate the beginning of a new idea? (indent)

4b. **Of all the ideas we brainstormed about news from home, which shall we include in our letter?** Circle two or three pieces of news.

4c. **Which of our brainstormed ideas shall we share first? second? third?** Add this news from home to the letter.

"Questions We Have" Paragraph

5a. **Let's begin our paragraph of questions. How can we let the service member know what this paragraph will contain?** Pause to allow time for students to think. Praise good topic sentences. Add one topic sentence to the letter.

    EXAMPLES: We have many questions to ask you.

               I'm really excited. I have so many
               questions to ask you.

5b. Of all the questions we brainstormed, which shall we include in our letter? Circle two or three questions.

5c. Which of our brainstormed ideas shall we share first? second? third? Add these questions to the letter.

Closing Paragraph

6. **Of all the ideas we brainstormed about support, which of our brainstormed ideas shall we share?** Circle one or two ways to close the letter.

7. **How shall we close our letter?** (Adios, A friend, Later, Thinking about you, and so on.) Ask students about mechanics and then add one closing to the letter.

8. **How shall we sign our letter?** Praise students' ideas. Add one to the letter.

INDIVIDUAL COMPOSING

Since writing to a complete stranger is very difficult, leave the Group Brainstorming lists on the board to build students' confidence. Do, however, remove the class's group composition. Walk around the classroom making positive comments and asking questions about the student, news from home, questions the student wants to ask, and words of support. Especially praise ideas that are original and information that sounds friendly. Encourage students to write from the heart. Do not require topic sentences, since this may sound too formal.

RESPONDING TO STUDENTS' WRITINGS/REVISING

1. Make overheads of these two real letters written by students. Direct students to read both letters. Ask which sounds friendlier and which will be more interesting to a service member. Praise insightful observations. Then ask how each letter could be improved. These letters can be found at the end of the lesson.

> January 24, 20XX
>
> Dear Enlisted Soldier Brian,
>
> Hi, my name is Bill. We got your address from our teacher. He is a retired officer in the Air Force.
> I am in the 8th grade at Walker Middle School. My favorite sports are football, basketball, and ice hockey. My favorite football teams are the Vikings and the Giants. Spring Break will be here soon. My Dad and I will take our three-wheelers out of storage and drive around.
> How are you doing? I heard that you are a long way from home. What do you guys do at night? Is it hot in the desert? It is cold here. It was 20 degrees below zero last night. We went sledding down a huge hill and crash landed. Have you ever driven a tank? We saw lots of them on the news.
> Well I have to go now. Write back as soon as you can. I'll be thinking of you.
>
> Bill P.

November 21, 20XX

Dear Service Member,

   Hi, my name is Sherry. I'm in the 6th grade. My favorite subject is Math. I love kickball and ice skating.

   How are you doing? Is it hot or cold there? Do you have to drink a lot of water? What do they let you eat? Do you ever get a Mountain Dew or a candy bar? What kind of music do you like? What do you do in your free time? How old were you when you enlisted in the Navy? I have a boy friend. His name is Terri. Sherry and Terri rhyme. He is smart. My dad says to catch a smart one because he'll earn lots of money when he grows up. Do you have a wife at home?

   I hope you come home soon.

                                    Sherry

P.S. Please write back as soon as you can.

2. As students finish the rough drafts, ask them to find a revising partner. Have each read his/her letter aloud to the other person to see if it sounds friendly and makes sense. Write the following on the board for peer teams:

- Make two or three specific comments on what they like about the letter, such as information about the student, news from home, questions the student wants to ask, and words of support.

- Ask questions to expand details regarding information about the student, news from home, questions the student wants to ask, and words of support.

- Make one or two suggestions about how to make the letter sound friendlier or be more interesting to a stranger.

   After this is completed, ask each writer to make at least one or two revisions to make his/her letter better for the service member.

   Most service members will be so pleased to receive the letters that punctuation, capitalization, spelling, handwriting, and other errors will only add to the personality. Therefore, consider limiting revising to the heartfelt meaning of the letters.

PUBLISHING

Explain that students will publish their letters on special pop-up stationery (*format*) so that the service members (*audience*) can enjoy letters from home which boost their spirits (*purpose*).

Letters can usually be sent to:

> Any Service Member (Army, Air Force, or Marine Corps personnel ashore)
> Any Service Member (Navy or Marine Corps personnel on ship)

Check with your local post office for addresses.

V-Fold Pop-up Stationery

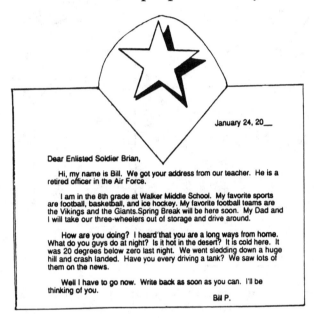

January 24, 20___

Dear Enlisted Soldier Brian,

   Hi, my name is Bill. We got your address from our teacher. He is a retired officer in the Air Force.

   I am in the 8th grade at Walker Middle School. My favorite sports are football, basketball, and ice hockey. My favorite football teams are the Vikings and the Giants. Spring Break will be here soon. My Dad and I will take our three-wheelers out of storage and drive around.

   How are you doing? I heard that you are a long ways from home. What do you guys do at night? Is it hot in the desert? It is cold here. It was 20 degrees below zero last night. We went sledding down a huge hill and crash landed. Have you every driving a tank? We saw lots of them on the news.

   Well I have to go now. Write back as soon as you can. I'll be thinking of you.

                                                  Bill P.

Materials

typing paper, scissors, school or magazine picture, glue, markers

Directions

1. Fold the stationery in half.

2. Fold the top left corner of the stationery down. Crease this fold. Refold the other direction. Open the stationery.

Thoughts from Home

3. Cut out a blank pop-up. Also cut out a magazine or school picture that can be cut to fit into the pop-up area. Glue the picture on the blank pop-up (or use one of the pop-ups found at the end of this lesson).

4. Open the stationery so the V-fold lies flat. Glue the pop-up to the empty V-fold area. Use the glue sparingly. Allow to dry.

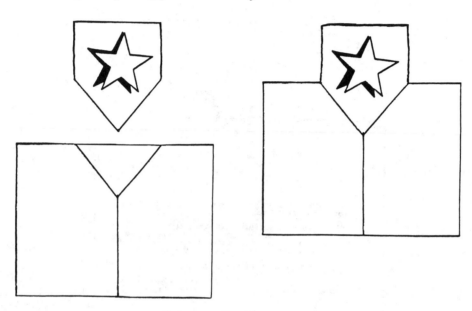

5. Now as you close the stationery, poke in the pop-up with your left finger. If necessary, pinch the V-fold with your right hand at the same time. Recrease the V-folded pop-up.

6. Write your letter on the inside and on the back of the stationery. If you want, place a small souvenir, photo, or drawing inside the letter before mailing it.

January 24, 20XX

Dear Enlisted Soldier Brian,

Hi, my name is Bill. We got your address from our teacher. He is a retired officer in the Air Force.

I am in the 8th grade at Walker Middle School. My favorite sports are football, basketball, and ice hockey. My favorite football teams are the Vikings and the Giants. Spring Break will be here soon. My Dad and I will take our three-wheelers out of storage and drive around.

How are you doing? I heard that you are a long way from home. What do you guys do at night? Is it hot in the desert? It is cold here. It was 20 degrees below zero last night. We went sledding down a huge hill and crash landed. Have you ever driven a tank? We saw lots of them on the news.

Well I have to go now. Write back as soon as you can. I'll be thinking of you.

Bill P.

November 21, 20XX

Dear Service Member,

Hi, my name is Sherry. I'm in the 6th grade. My favorite subject is Math. I love kickball and ice skating.

How are you doing? Is it hot or cold there? Do you have to drink a lot of water? What do they let you eat? Do you ever get a Mountain Dew or a candy bar? What kind of music do you like? What do you do in your free time? How old were you when you enlisted in the Navy? I have a boy friend. His name is Terri. Sherry and Terri rhyme. He is smart. My dad says to catch a smart one because he'll earn lots of money when he grows up. Do you have a wife at home?

I hope you come home soon.

Sherry

P.S. Please write back as soon as you can.

Thoughts from Home

Thoughts from Home

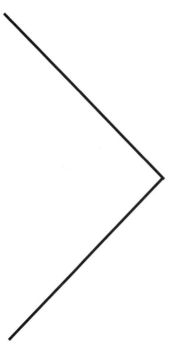

LESSON 32

Petition

OUTCOME Each student will create a petition based on a real school, community, state, or national concern and collect signatures of supporters.

MOTIVATORS

1. Tie this lesson into a current event going on in your school, city, state, or country, or to a topic in Science or Social Studies that you are studying.

2. Bring news articles and/or editorials to class about problems in your community, state, or nation such as homelessness, pollution, or violence.

3. Ask students to close their eyes and visualize this problem or share a problem about which you are familiar. Here is a problem/opportunity our community just faced.

City of Gofar

Ten years ago, the city of Gofar built a beautiful building for concerts, basketball games, and hockey games. The citizens of Gofar paid $200 million for the facility from a five-cent city sales tax. Everyone really likes having the building, and the citizens have almost paid for it.

Now, some leaders want to declare another city sales tax to build a building just for hockey. City leaders want the new hockey center, but thousands of people who live in Gofar and who supported the other building do not want to pay more sales tax. These citizens wrote a petition and asked neighbors to sign it. Since so many people signed the petition, the mayor and other city leaders decided against building a new hockey facility. Because of the petition citizens of Gofar won't have to pay additional sales tax and they'll have money for things they really want.

---

4. Point out that the right to be heard by leaders of the community is one of the freedoms guaranteed by our Bill of Rights (see Lesson 29). Explain that a petition is a way to carry our voices to government officials. Inform students that there are rules about how to file a petition, what a petition must include, who can sign it, and how to present the petition to the government. The clerk at your local city hall can assist you if you desire more information.

GROUP BRAINSTORMING

Let's brainstorm some of our concerns.

Concern	Reasons	Request/Solution	Why
the environment	increasing crime	more lights	be safe outside
litter	poor lighting	extra patrol officers	cross streets safely
bad lunch food	cars go too fast	more stop signs	so can visit friends
(safe neighborhood)			(to discourage crime)
required stay outside			
during cold weather			

Key Questions

1. (if you do not select the concern) **What are we concerned about? What is something in our school, city, state, or nation that upsets you? What are some issues about which you are concerned?** Pause for at least 30 seconds to give students time to think. Praise thoughtful concerns. Write student responses on the board or overhead under "Concern."

2. (if you do not select the concern) **Out of all our concerns, which one is important to most of our class? About which of these ideas should we write a petition?** Have an uninvolved student select one concern. Circle it. Assure students that they will select their own problems later.

3. **Why is this a concern or problem? What information do we have to support our opinion? What examples can we give?** Pause to give students time to think. Praise important reasons. Write student responses on the board or overhead under "Reasons."

You Can Make a Difference!

4. **What do we want to happen? What are we respectfully requesting? pleading?** Write student responses on the board or overhead under "Request/Solution."

5. **Why are we requesting this? What evidence do you have that the solution will work?** Write student responses on the board or overhead under "Why."

GROUP COMPOSING

Now let's create a petition so we can get other people involved in solving this problem.

1. **Let's start our petition "We, the undersigned citizens and future voters of the State of _____ and the city of _____, are concerned about _____."** (Have this information written on the board or overhead.)

   EXAMPLE: We, the citizens of _____ County, are concerned with _____.
   We, the seventh graders at _____ Middle School, are unhappy about _____.

   We, the visitors and residents of _____, have seen an increase in _____.

2. **How can we complete the first sentence of our petition? What is our state?** Insert this. **What is our city?** Insert this. **What did we select as our concern?** Add the concern to the petition.

Petition

We, the undersigned citizens and future voters of the State of California and City of Los Angeles, are concerned about our safety in the north side of our city. We have seen an increase in crime in recent years in our area. We believe it is due to the beet plant and other industries in this area. The workers go home in the evening to their families so nobody is around. It is dark. Also, cars are going too fast.

We are requesting more street lights in the area, and a police officer, to discourage crime. We believe there should be at least three stop signs on Center Avenue to slow traffic. We want to be safe in our neighborhood and we want the north side of town to be safer so we can visit friends.

Date	Name	Phone # or e-mail
_____	_____	_____
_____	_____	_____
_____	_____	_____
_____	_____	_____
_____	_____	_____
_____	_____	_____

Sponsors

_____

_____

State of California
County of Los Angeles

I, _____,
promise that each signature on this petition represents a genuine signature of a real person at my school or in my neighborhood.

_____
signature of circulator

_____
date

3a. Which of our reasons shall we share first? second? third? Place a number by each reason as it is selected. Praise thoughtful ordering.

3b. How shall we state our first reason? How can we put this idea in a sentence? Add the reason to the petition. Encourage students to use transition words to signal a shift to a new piece of logic.

BEGINNING REASONS	FOLLOW-UP REASONS	RESTATING THE MAIN IDEA
One important idea is	Some more evidence is	Therefore
First of all	In addition	Thus
The best proof is	The next piece of evidence is	As a result
The strongest evidence	Finally	In summary
To begin	Similarly	Since
	Besides	In conclusion
	Nevertheless	Otherwise
	Also	In view of these
	Furthermore	For these reasons
	Accordingly	It is evident
	Another reason	Unless

4a. What are we requesting be done? What do we hope this petition will accomplish? Add the request to the petition.

4b. How can we explain why we believe this solution will be effective? Which piece of evidence shall we offer first? Insert this. **Next?** Add evidence to the petition.

5. Repeat steps 3 and 4 for the second and third reasons.

6. (optional) Suggest students address a viewpoint that opposes the ideas presented in their petition. Give proof that the viewpoint is faulty.

WORDS SIGNALING AN OPPOSING POINT OF VIEW		
But	However	Unless
While	On the other hand	Yet
Although	In contrast	Conversely

7. Now let's conclude our statement.

- *Beginning Writers:* **Let's repeat our original request.** Add this to the petition.

- *Advanced Writers:* **How can we state our concern and request so it sticks in people's minds? What is our final plea?** Add this to the petition.

8. Involve students in helping complete the rest of the group petition. See sample petition.

9. Encourage students, who wish, to sign the class petition.

INDIVIDUAL BRAINSTORMING & COMPOSING

1. Direct students to choose a concern for his/her petition. Walk around the classroom as each student brainstorms concerns. If a student is having difficulty choosing a concern, brainstorm together. Allow plenty of time for students to choose and commit to a concern. Many students will need a day or two to decide. Comment positively about significant concerns.

2. Once students are committed to a concern, give them a Brainstorming Assistant. One can be found at the end of this lesson. Ask students to complete it before they begin writing their petitions.

3. Circulate around the room praising powerful reasons people should support the petition, clear requests, good evidence to back the solution, and a strong final plea. Ask open-ended questions to help students generate stronger reasons, clearer requests, and better evidence to support their requests.

RESPONDING TO STUDENTS' WRITINGS/REVISING

As students finish the rough drafts of their petitions, ask them to find a revising partner. Have each read his/her petition aloud to the other person to see if it sounds clear and convincing.

- Encourage peers to make two or three specific comments on what they like about the petition.

- Ask the revising partner to particularly comment on the concern addressed in the petition, the reasons given to convince people to support it, the request or solution, and the final plea.

After this is completed, ask each petition writer to make at least one or two revisions to make his/her petition clearer and/or more convincing.

Before publishing the petitions, direct revising partners to trade petitions and look for punctuation, capitalization, spelling, and other errors that might keep a reader from deciding to sign the petition.

PUBLISHING

Explain that each student must try to get ten signatures on his/her petition in order to influence government officials to change policy or take action (*purpose*). They can get classmates, other students, neighbors, and/or family members (*audience*) to sign. Suggest that students take along clipboards and pens when they are collecting signatures. This should be done in free time, before class, after school, or on the weekends. Explain that petitions completed with at least ten valid signatures by the deadline will be sent to the appropriate governmental official. Caution students that if petitions are circulated during instruction, they'll be collected.

Petition Package

Materials

one petition form, the signature page, one colored sheet of paper, stapler, (optional) yarn, pen, hole punch

Directions

1. Make copies of the petition and signature page provided at the end of this lesson, or allow students to create their own pages on a word processor.

2. Have students complete the petition form using their final draft.

3. Fold the top edge of a colored sheet of typing paper over about 3/4 inch.

4. Slide the petition and signature page face-up into the fold.

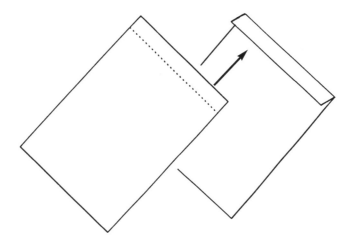

5. Staple twice on the fold.

6. (optional) Punch a hole in the left corner of the petition. Use a 15-inch length of yarn to tie a pen to the petition holder.

7. Role-play how to ask people to sign the petition. Model this interaction for students before they role-play.

   a. Hi, my name is _____. I'm circulating a petition to (insert purpose) . Will you lend your support for this cause by signing our petition?

   b. Hand petition and pen to potential signer.

   c. Allow person to read the information and decide to sign or choose not to sign.

   d. If the person decides to sign, thank him/her for the support for improving conditions in the community.

   e. If the person doesn't want to sign, politely ask the person how he/she feels this problem should be solved. Listen to his/her ideas. Thank the person for his/her concerns. Jot down good ideas on a scrap piece of paper.

Petition

We, the undersigned citizens and future voters of the State of

_____ and City of _____, are concerned

Date	Name	Phone # or e-mail

Sponsors

_____

_____

State of _____

County of _____

I, _____,
promise that each signature
on this petition represents a
genuine signature of a real
person at my school or in my
neighborhood.

_____
signature of circulator

_____
date

Brainstorming Assistant
for
Petition

Concerns

Reasons for Your Selected Concern

Respectful Request or Solution

Evidence that the Request will Solve the Problem

LESSON 33

Weekly/End-of-Year Evaluation

OUTCOME   Each student will give feedback to his/her teacher's weekly or end-of-year evaluation using responsibly stated "I" statements.

MOTIVATORS

1. Ask students what they remember about the week/year. If you have pictures taken during the time period, share them.

2. Explain that all of us are going to evaluate the week/unit/year. Show a sample weekly, unit, or yearly evaluation. One can be found at the end of this lesson. Discuss the purpose of an evaluation. (Open or maintain lines of communication.) Explain how the information will help you. Assure students that all their thoughts are helpful.

Unit Evaluation

Before the 6th-grade teachers plan the next interdisciplinary Science unit, I want to know how this last month worked for you. You can help by answering the following questions.

1. In this last interdisciplinary unit, which subject did you learn the most: Language Arts, Science, or Math? Why? _____
2. Out of all the activities, which were the most useful to you? Why? _____
3. Did you feel the final project assessed what you learned in this unit? Why or why not? _____
   _____
4. What else would you like to share? _____

GROUP BRAINSTORMING

Let's brainstorm some ideas about this week/year.

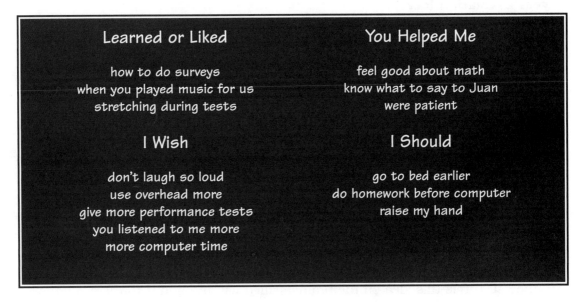

Learned or Liked

how to do surveys
when you played music for us
stretching during tests

You Helped Me

feel good about math
know what to say to Juan
were patient

I Wish

don't laugh so loud
use overhead more
give more performance tests
you listened to me more
more computer time

I Should

go to bed earlier
do homework before computer
raise my hand

Key Questions

1. **What did you learn this week/year? What did you like?** Ask students to be specific. **What is an example of what you learned?** Praise students' responses and write them on the board, overhead, or chart paper under the "Learned or Liked" column.

2. **What was something I (your teacher) did that helped you succeed? When did I (your teacher) help you learn something?** Ask students to be specific. **What is an example of this?** Praise students' responses and write them on the board, overhead, or chart paper under the "You Helped Me" column.

3. **What do you wish you would have learned? What do you wish I (your teacher) would do (would do more of)? What do you wish I (your teacher) wouldn't do? What could I do to help you learn better? What shouldn't I (your teacher) do?** Ask students to be specific. **What is an example of what I (your teacher) could do?** Praise students' responses and write them on the board, overhead, or chart paper under the "I Wish" column.

4a. **What should you do to learn better?** Ask students to be specific. **What is an example of what you could do to improve your schoolwork?** Praise students' responses and write them on the board, overhead, or chart paper under the "I Should" column.

4b. **What should you do to get along better with other students?** Ask students to be specific. **What is an example of what you could do to improve your relationships with peers?** Praise students' responses and write them on the board, overhead, or chart paper under the "I Should" column.

GROUP COMPOSING

Now we're going to compose a response based on our earlier end-of-week or end-of-year evaluation ideas.

> ## End-of-Year Evaluation
>
> I learned/liked <u>when you played music for us.</u>
>
> You helped me <u>feel good about math.</u>
>
> I wish you <u>wouldn't laugh so loud.</u>
>
> I should <u>raise my hand more often.</u>

1. **Out of all our brainstormed ideas about what you learned or liked, which one do you want us to put on this evaluation?** Ask a student to choose one idea from the list. Circle this idea on the brainstormed list and add it to the evaluation form.

2. **Which idea on the "You Helped Me" list is the most important to you?** Ask a student to choose one idea from the list. Circle this idea on the brainstormed list and add it to the evaluation form.

3a. **Let's think about how to word criticism. Raise your hand if you have had your feelings hurt by something someone has said. Since it is important on an evaluation to share honestly, let's think about how to word critical feedback.** Here are some examples you can share with students. Write the three sets of honest responses on the board or overhead. Ask students which they would rather receive as feedback. Ask students which ways of giving feedback hurt less/help more.

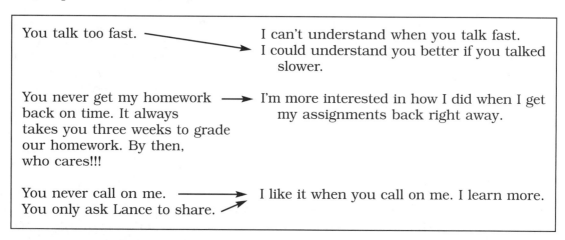

You talk too fast. ──────➤ I can't understand when you talk fast.
I could understand you better if you talked slower.

You never get my homework ──➤ I'm more interested in how I did when I get my assignments back right away.
back on time. It always takes you three weeks to grade our homework. By then, who cares!!!

You never call on me. ──────➤ I like it when you call on me. I learn more.
You only ask Lance to share. ──➤

After hearing students' ideas, confirm that "I" statements are less threatening to the receiver when giving critical feedback than "you" messages. We are going to word our ideas as "I" statements.

3b. Based on this information, how can we word our critical feedback from the "I Wish" list? Out of all the things you wished, which one do you wish? Ask an uninvolved student to choose one idea from the list. Add this to the evaluation form.

4. **Which idea on the "I Should" list is something you should really do?** Ask an uninvolved student to choose one idea from the list. Add this idea to the evaluation form.

Thinking about Mechanics: What should I do to the first letter in a sentence? (capitalize) How should I end this sentence? (with a period or exclamation point)

NOTE: You can change the brainstorming categories. Some teachers like to ask about the textbook, schedule, special projects, tests, and other things that interest them.

INDIVIDUAL BRAINSTORMING & COMPOSING

Put away the Group Brainstorming/Group Composing charts so students must reflect on their own thoughts.

Now, it is your turn to personally evaluate this week/our year. It is important to write your own thoughts, both your good and bad feelings about the week/year. This will help me know what helped you learn so I can be an even better teacher next week/year. As you share, pass out your evaluation form.

I want to know your thoughts. When I read them, I won't know who wrote the evaluation because no one will put his/her name on the evaluation.

Explain that while they write, you'll work at your desk, also evaluating this week/year instead of circulating around the room like you usually do. This will give students some privacy. Let students know whether or not you are open to students coming to your desk or private space.

RESPONDING TO STUDENTS' WRITINGS/REVISING

1. Before sending students to revise, have them look with you at some comments from your old or another teacher's evaluations to determine whether those students put their ideas across clearly and kindly. Write these comments on the board, a chart, or overhead, but *do not attach the labels* UNCLEAR, NO EXAMPLE, etc.

I didn't learn anything in Science. It was disgusting.

I learned about 2-digit multiplication

I didn't learn anything in Science. It was disgusting.
UNCLEAR   NO EXAMPLE

I learned about 2-digit multiplication.
CLEAR

I didn't learn anything. Working in groups every day in Social Studies was disgusting. Sometimes I like to work by myself. All the three girls in my group did were talk, talk, talk.
CLEAR   EXAMPLE

Class was fun.
UNCLEAR   KIND   NO EXAMPLE

When you told me that my Eulogy for my cat made tears come to your eyes, I realized that you understood how sad and lonely I felt.
CLEAR   KIND   EXAMPLE

I wish you would drop dead.
UNKIND   UNCLEAR   NO EXAMPLE

Mr./Ms./Mrs. _____, I don't think you like me. I work really hard and you NEVER say "Good Job _____" or notice the neat things I do.
CLEAR   EXAMPLE

I shouldn't do anything different, but my teacher should!
UNKIND   UNCLEAR   NO EXAMPLE

Ask students what makes a statement unclear. (Doesn't answer the question.) Next, ask students what makes a statement unkind or mean/cruel. (Puts someone down or blames another person.)

Next, inquire how to reverse each negative or unclear statement. Praise responses that were improved enough so they would help you understand the students' thinking. Especially praise critical feedback that is stated kindly so students will see that it is safe to share negative feelings too.

2. Since thoughts on an evaluation are private, explain that students will reflect privately on each of their weekly or end-of-year responses.

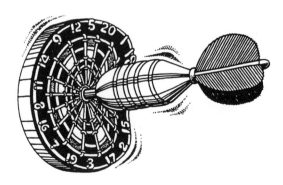

   • Have I said what I believe? Is the information true?

   • Should I explain something more completely so it will be understood?

• Have I included at least one example for each question?

• Have I stated my ideas kindly?

• Can my handwriting be read easily?

Make clean copies of the evaluation form available for those who choose to rewrite parts of their evaluations.

PUBLISHING

Direct students to fold their evaluation in half. Have two students collect the evaluations. Thank students for their honesty. Assure them that you'll (*audience*) use the information to help them/other students and improve learning (*purpose*).

Take time later to read the evaluations and jot down notes about what you'd like to recall later.

Weekly/Unit/Yearly Evaluation

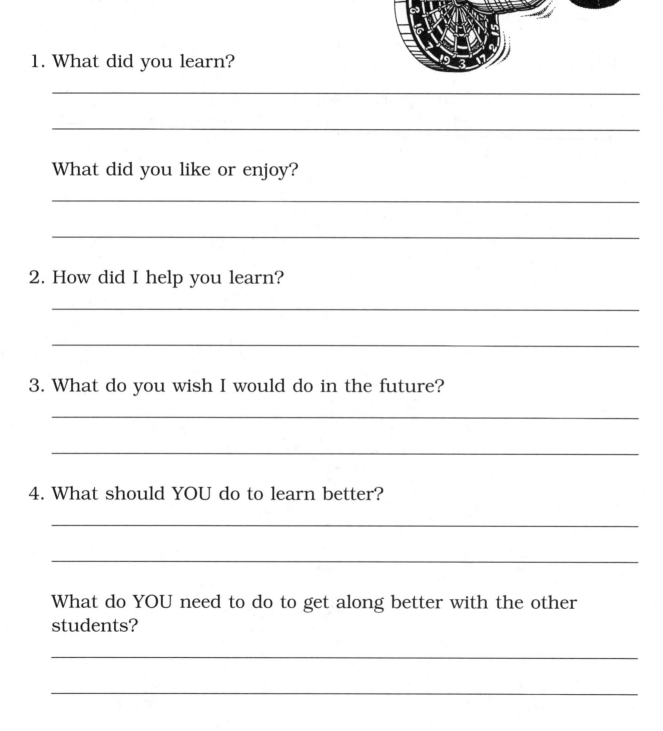

1. What did you learn?

_____

_____

What did you like or enjoy?

_____

_____

2. How did I help you learn?

_____

_____

3. What do you wish I would do in the future?

_____

_____

4. What should YOU do to learn better?

_____

_____

What do YOU need to do to get along better with the other students?

_____

_____

SECTION 4

Narrative Compositions for Young Authors

A narative pattern is useful when writers want to tell a story that may or may not have happened.

- **Simple Narrative**   A simple narrative consists of at least three events in chronological order: a beginning, a middle, and an end. When writing a story, writers often use transition words and phrases such as "Long, long ago," "Suddenly," "A short while later," and "At last" to show time order.

- **Complex Narrative**   A complex narrative consists of a longer and more complicated sequence of events. Complex stories often have both good characters (heroes/heroines) and bad characters (villains). Usually each main character has a well-developed personality. The hero/heroine confronts one or more problems and often makes a series of unsuccessful attempts to solve each problem. Finally a solution is found. Complex narratives may also include a setting, descriptions, characters' feelings, dialogue, and a moral to the story.

Some Forms of Narrative Writing

Adventure Stories
Autobiographies
Biographies
Cartoon/Comic Strips
Chain-of-Events
   Stories
Choose-the-Ending
   Stories
Cliffhangers
Creative Story
   Retellings
Fables
Fairy Tales

Family Histories
Fantasies
Folktales
Friendly Letters
Ghost Stories
Good News/Bad News
   Stories
Historical Novels
Jokes
Legends
Memoirs (Memories)
Movie Scripts

Mysteries
Myths
Novels
Play Scripts
Science Fiction
Short Stories
Slide-show Scripts
Spooky Stories
Surprise Endings
Tall Tales
Television Scripts
Timelines

LESSON 34

Good News/Bad News Tale

OUTCOME   Each student will write either a happy tale—composed of a series of bad events resolved by good events, or a tragedy—composed of a series of good events ruined by unfortunate events.

MOTIVATORS

1. Share a good news/bad news story that has occurred to you or one that you've heard. Here is a true tale I wrote while composing this lesson plan.

My Good News/Bad News Tale

The bad news is I have pneumonia for three weeks.
> The good news is the doctor gave me some strong antibiotics.

The bad news is it will take five days before I feel better.
> The good news is I don't have to go to work, fix meals, wash dishes, or take out the trash. I can snooze and watch television.

The bad news is the TV shows are really boring and I don't have HBO.
> The good news is a friend rented eight great action videos for me.

The bad news is I'll have to pay the rent on them.
> The good news is that these videos were on a 2-for-1 special at Sunmart.

The bad news is I go back to work next Friday.
> THE GOOD NEWS IS I'll be healthy in time to go ice fishing with my friend, Dan!

2. Introduce your class to one or both of these good news/bad news books. Also read these tales written by other students:

Fortunately/Unfortunately by Remy Charlip (Four Winds Press, 1980)
That's Good, That's Bad by Joan M. Lexau (Scott Foresman, 1971)

<table>
<tr><td>

My News

My good news is I have new juicy gum, but the bad news is it got stuck in my hair.

My good news is I can cut it out, but the bad news is I'll have lopsided hair.

My good news is I was planning on a new haircut anyway, but the bad news is my appointment is next month.

My good news is I can wear my new floppy hat to cover the bald spot, but the bad news is we can't wear hats in class.

My good news is next week is VACATION! No school ALL WEEK!

</td><td>

Jeffrey's Good News

The good news is my brother left for college yesterday.

The bad news is I'll miss him.

The good news is I get to have Sam's bedroom and his old CD player.

The bad news is he left a bunch of old clothes and junk in the room.

The good news is I can move his stuff into the basement.

The bad news is now that I've cleaned the room, it looks so very very empty.

The good news is my dad said he'd take me shopping for some new stuff. Dad did. Now my room looks great!

</td></tr>
</table>

Interject that good news/bad news tales are entertaining (*purpose*) for both the composer and the listeners/readers (*audience–peers*). Good news/bad news tales make fun at the series of everyday misfortunes and tragic events the character faces—indeed we all face each day.

Point out that good news/bad news tales can be happy tales composed of a series of bad events that result in wonderful events, or they can be tragedies composed of a series of great events ruined by unfortunate events.

A Happy Tale				**A Tragic Tale**	
Bad News				Good News	
	Good News				Bad News
Bad News				Good News	
	Good News				Bad News
Bad News				Good News	
	Good News				Bad News
Bad News				Good News	
	Good News				Bad News
Bad News				Good News	
	Good News!				Bad News!

The questioning in this lesson follows the more difficult task of seeing good develop from the bad or of having a positive attitude when things go wrong—finding the bright side of a dark day, searching for the silver lining. Impress upon students, however, that it is acceptable to write either type of tale.

3. Ask students what bad events have happened lately to them or other people they know. As a bad event is shared, ask the group to think of a positive event that could result. The only stipulation/requirement is the person who shared the bad event must agree that the suggested event is indeed positive. If the sharer considers the suggestion negative, then the group must come up with a different piece of good news.

   Be prepared for the sharing to become both creative and somewhat silly. The point is to get students conceptualizing something good coming from a bad event. Even adults have difficulty with this form of positive projecting. We're better at worrying how something good may turn to something bad.

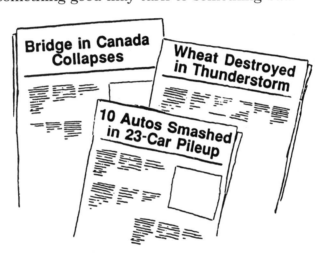

4. Bring in the front section of 15 newspapers; they need not be current. Pair students. Give each pair a large piece of butcher paper. Direct students to fold the butcher paper in half. Use markers to label the left side "Bad News" and the right side "Good News." As bad news is found, cut it out and tape or glue it to the left side under "Bad News."

BAD NEWS	GOOD NEWS
Wheat Destroyed in Thunderstorm	*The good news is we have surplus of wheat this year.*
Unemployment Reaches All-Time High	*The good news is I have a job.*
10-Car Pileup	*The good news is no one died.*
Bridge in Canada Collapses	*The good news is the bridge was an old two-laner. Now we can build a modern 4-lane bridge.*

Both students are responsible for cutting out or listing the bad news that the team finds. Give students ten minutes and challenge them to find the most bad news events. Suggest students number the news events as they are found. When time is up, ask teams to report their total number of bad events.

Next, direct students to circle their five favorites. Finally, challenge students to turn each of these five bad events into a good event. Give students about 8–10 minutes to write their ideas opposite the bad news under the "Good News" column. When the teams are finished, ask each pair to share their best Good News/Bad News Report with your class.

NOTE: The term "report" is used here because the story consist of just two events, not a sequence of events.

5. Challenge students to collect short or long good news/bad news stories from friends and parents and bring them to class to share. This can be a first-rate learning experience for everyone.

GROUP BRAINSTORMING/GROUP COMPOSING

Let's brainstorm our ideas for a Good News/Bad News Tale. In this lesson the group brainstorming and the group composing steps alternate back and forth.

Story Set-up

Key Questions

1. **Who can be our main character? Who is someone we all know about whom we could write a Good News/Bad News Tale?** Repeat these questions until three ideas for characters have been written on the board next to "Character."

2. **Out of all these characters, around which shall we build our Good News/Bad News Tale?** Choose a low-achieving or uninvolved student to select one character. Circle this character and use it throughout the tale.

3. **What could be the initial or main problem? What bad news could start this tale?** Repeat these questions until three student ideas have been written under the "Bad News" column.

4. Around which of these problems shall we build our Good News/Bad News Tale? Choose a withdrawn student to select an initial or starting problem. Circle this problem.

CHARACTER   a scuba diver   (teenager)   Sarah

BAD NEWS   GOOD NEWS

Mom's car broke down   if I keep trying I'll figure it out
no $ for lunch   (a manual was included)
(don't know how operate new computer game I bought)   I'm not dumb, just computer disabled

5. (optional) **What time period shall our story cover? How long will our narrative last? an hour? a day? a week? a month? a year?** Listen for a group consensus. Write this decision under a "Time Period" column.

Creating a Good News/Bad News Tale

Now let's compose a Good News/Bad News Tale together. Direct students' attention back to the initial brainstorming of the character and bad news generated earlier.

1. Which character and bad news did we choose for our tale? How shall we combine these ideas to open our tale? Praise your students' ideas that include at least character and problem. Insert the necessary information to make a complete sentence on the Good News/Bad News board.

> **Thinking about Mechanics:** Every sentence needs someone or something (a subject) and what is occurring, did occur, or will occur (present, past, future tense). If students don't notice the missing sentence parts, ask questions such as "What word(s) do we need to add to tell the subject?" or "What word(s) do we need to add to complete the verb/predicate?"

(Encourage students to add details.) **Where did the problem occur? When? With whom? How? Why? What kind of or how many _____?** Add this information to the tale.

Examples: on Friday night at the scouting camp out at Clear Lake . . .
shortly after nine P.M. at the mall . . .
while I was returning from the movies . . .
yesterday at soccer practice . . .

2. Now let's add the phrase "The bad news is" to the bad news that we chose for our story.

Thinking about Mechanics: What should we do to the first word in this sentence? (capitalize)

Thinking about Mechanics: How should we signal the end of this sentence? (period)

CHARACTER   *a scuba diver*   (teenager)   *Sarah*

BAD NEWS   GOOD NEWS

Mom's car broke down   if I keep trying I'll figure it out
no $ for lunch   (a manual was included)
(don't know how operate new computer game I bought)   I'm not dumb, just computer disabled

Set 1

doesn't have pictures   hire a tutor
(I can't understand the manual)   Dad will help me when he gets back
(the manual is written in Chinese)   (go to store & talk to cute guy/gal who sold it to me)

Set 2

she/he won't be working then   _____
(I feel stupid if I ask for help)   it is intelligent to learn new things
I'll need a car to get to the shopping center   _____

Set 3

3. Now let's reread the bad news sentence to see if it makes sense. If it doesn't make sense, ask students what we need to change.

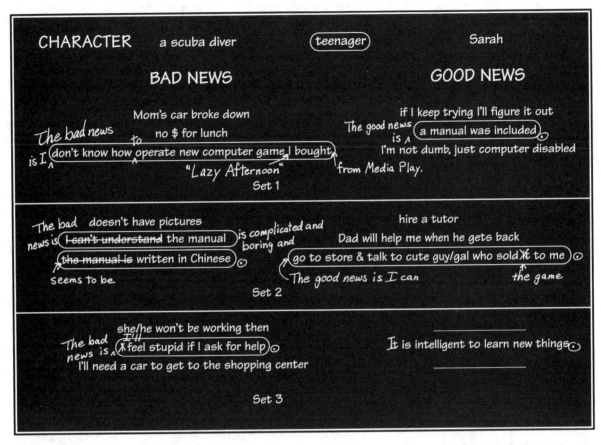

CHARACTER   a scuba diver   (teenager)   Sarah

BAD NEWS   **GOOD NEWS**

The bad news   Mom's car broke down   if I keep trying I'll figure it out
to   no $ for lunch   The good news (a manual was included)
is I (don't know how operate new computer game I bought,)   is ∧   I'm not dumb, just computer disabled
            "Lazy Afternoon"   from Media Play.
               Set 1

The bad   doesn't have pictures   hire a tutor
news is (I can't understand the manual) is complicated and   Dad will help me when he gets back
            boring and
(the manual is written in Chinese)   (go to store & talk to cute guy/gal who sold it to me)
seems to be   The good news is I can   the game
               Set 2

The bad   she/he won't be working then   _____
news is ∧ (I'll feel stupid if I ask for help)   It is intelligent to learn new things.
I'll need a car to get to the shopping center   _____

               Set 3

4. **What interesting, terrific, good news could occur as a result of the bad news? next? What exciting, wonderful, or important event could occur in spite of this bad news?** Repeat these questions until three ideas have been captured on the board. Write them under "Good News."

5. **Out of all this good news, which shall we choose?** (optional) **Which good events are the direct result of the bad news?** Choose an uninvolved student to select a good event that results from the bad news. Circle the good news.

6. (optional) Ask students to expand the chosen statement by adding the phrase "The good news is," the subject, and what happened in order to create a complete sentence. Also encourage students to add optional details (such as when, where, how, why, with whom, what kind of, and/or how many). **Where did the problem occur? When? With whom? How? Why? What kind of or how many _____?** Use arrows to add this information to the tale.

> **Thinking about Mechanics:** What should we do to the first word in this sentence? (capitalize)

> **Thinking about Mechanics:** How should we signal the end of this sentence? (period)

7. **Now let's reread our Good News/Bad News Tale to see if it makes sense so far.** If it doesn't make sense, ask students what needs to be done to improve it.

8. Now repeat this sequence of questioning. **What bad news could occur next? What awful, terrible, unhappy, disastrous event could result from the good news? could spoil the fun? What awful "jam" or problem could occur?** Repeat these questions until three bad events have been written on the board.

9. **Out of the bad news, which shall we choose? Which bad news is the direct result of the good news?** Choose an uninvolved student to select a bad event that results from the good news event. Circle this bad news.

10. Ask students to reread the Good News/Bad News Tale aloud to see if it makes sense and is interesting to listen to/read. Where necessary ask students to expand the chosen statement by adding the phrase "The good news is," the subject, and what happened in order to create a complete sentence and optional details (such as when, where, how, why, with whom, what kind of, and/or how many) so that it makes a complete sentence.

11. Repeat this sequence of questions several more times. **Which good news happens next? Which bad news results?**

12. Ask students whether they want the group tale to end happily or end in tragedy. **How shall we have our Good News/Bad News Tale end? How will this day/week/year result?** Invite students to end on a good note. **What positive, yet unexpected, dramatic, or surprise ending can we dream up?** Repeat these questions until three students' ideas have been written on the board under the "Good News" column.

13. **Out of the good news, which shall we choose to end our tale?** Choose an uninvolved student to select a good news event. Circle this final good or bad news.

INDIVIDUAL BRAINSTORMING & COMPOSING

Tell students that now they will get to write their own Good News/Bad News Tales to entertain their friends, classmates, and families. Provide each student or pair of students a copy of the Brainstorming Assistant (found at the end of this lesson) to help them generate ideas and organize their thoughts.

Good News/Bad News Tale
Brainstorming Assistant

Character

--------------------------------   --------------------------------   --------------------------------

Bad News   **Good News**

Consider letting students brainstorm their own titles. (If students need a reminder, ask them what they should do to the important words in the title.) Here are a few ideas:

_____'s Tale
News Report of _____'s Day
_____'s Good News/Bad News Story
The Latest News

Instruct students that they need at least five sets of events. Each set includes a good and bad event. Advanced Writers should be expected to have a connected sequence of bad events resulting in good events. Beginning Writers need not have a connected sequence of events, Five separate events that are ordered bad followed by good are enough; the events need not be related.

Allow some Advanced Writers to choose their own "set" of opposites instead of good/bad. Opposites (such as creative/destructive, legal/illegal, safe/dangerous, healthy/unhealthy, modern/obsolete) make interesting stories. Try this pattern before you ask students to do it; it is harder than it looks. Here are two brief examples modeled after the book *That's Good! That's Bad!* by Margery Cuyler (Holt, 1991). The words "creative/destructive" have been used instead of "good/bad."

A Creative Action	**A Destructive Reaction**
I noticed the inline skates in the driveway and took time to put them away. Boy, that was creative and smart.	Later that day, I saw two kids by a pile of leaves. They were striking matches and starting small fires. I yelled, "Go for it!" Boy, that was destructive and dumb.

As students begin brainstorming and composing their own Good News/Bad News Tales, walk around the classroom commenting positively upon interesting characters, settings (when or where), related bad and good events, relevant details, connected sequence of events, dramatic or surprise endings, and intriguing Good News/Bad News titles.

RESPONDING TO STUDENTS' WRITINGS/REVISING

1. As students finish the rough drafts of their Good News/Bad News Tales, pass out copies of the three unrevised tales ("Football," "alien attack," and "The Sub Report") and the Good News/Bad News Tale Revising Assistant which can be found at the end of this lesson.

> **alien attack**
>
> The good news is I bought a new computer game - alien attack at best buy.
>
> The bad news is I read the directions but I can't figure how to play it.
>
> The good news is I can ask my cute next door neighbor to help me but then she'll know I'm not a computer whiz.
>
> The good news is she wears dirty jeans and braces and I like her.
>
> she told me about alien attack her brother plays it all the time

Walk your students through the "Football" tale which contains many mechanical errors, a content or format problem, and no title. Demonstrate on the board or overhead how to put – for missing or weak, + for present, and * for excellent by each item on the Revising Assistant checklist. Let students work for ten minutes either independently or in pairs to evaluate and revise the "alien" and "Sub Report" tales. Both contain many mechanical errors and content or format problems.

Pull the students back together to share item by item how they rated the "Alien" and "The Sub Report" tales (–, +, *), your students' reasons for these ratings, and what improvements your students made to each tale.

NOTE: It is important for peers to hear these evaluations and mentally compare them with their own ratings/reasons and changes. Select one or two teams to read their improved versions. Encourage peers to clap to show their approval. Add your own praise for "the power of revision."

Good News/Bad News Tale
Revising Assistant

Revising Team	- Needs Work	+ Works	* Strong	Teacher
____	1. (optional) Is my title intriguing?			____
____	2. Have important words in the title been capitalized?			____
____	3. Is my character interesting?			____
____	4. Do I tell the setting (when or where)?			____
____	5. Do I tell five unfortunate, tragic, or disastrous events?			____
____	6. Are my good events interesting to the reader?			____
____	7. Is the sequence of five events connected?			____
____	8. (optional) Is each set of bad and good events related?			____
____	9. Does my story make sense and can it be easily followed?			____
____	10. Is my ending dramatic or a surprise for the reader?			____
____	11. Is there a capital letter at the beginning of each sentence?			____
____	12. Is there a period at the end of each sentence?			____

---

2. Next ask each young writer to find a revising partner. One student should read his/her Good News/Bad News Tale aloud to the other to see if the Good News/Bad News Tale makes sense, is interesting, and can be easily followed. Ask each writer to make at least one or two revisions to improve the Good News/Bad News Tale.

   Ask revising partners to complete the left-hand side of the Revising Assistant as a team to identify areas of their own Good News/Bad News Tales needing improvement. Ask students to look for problems that might hinder a reader from understanding and enjoying the tale. Explain, if you choose, that later you'll evaluate and grade their Good News/Bad News Tales using the same form. Finally, invite each writer to make at least one or two revisions to improve their Good News/Bad News Tale.

PUBLISHING

After students finish revising their Good News/Bad News Tales, explain that they'll publish them in a flap book (*format*) so that other students/peers (*audience*) who need a little humor in their lives (*purpose*) can enjoy the series of everyday misfortunes and tragic events the character encounters—and we all face each day in our lives.

Two-part Flap Book

Materials

9 × 12-inch tagboard or cardboard foundation page, 10 blank strips for news, Good News and Bad News cover patterns, scissors, stapler

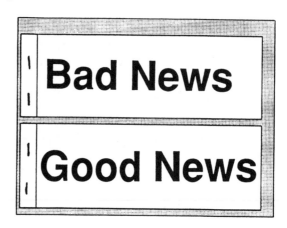

Directions

1. Cut out the two covers and ten blank strips. (optional) Students with poor handwriting may benefit from having lines added to their blank sheets or they can word-process their stories and glue one good news/bad news statement per page.

2. To assemble, lay the foundation page on the table. Stack five blank strips horizontally across the top of the foundation page.

3. Top these strips with a Bad News cover and staple along the left margin to hold the pages in place.

4. Repeat with the Good News cover and five blank strips. Staple these strips along the left margin to hold them in place.

5. Alternately write a bad news statement on a strip under the bad news cover and then write the corresponding good news statement under the good news cover.

6. Encourage students to illustrate the events in their Good News/Bad News Tales. Drawings can be placed on the back of the previous page so that they can be seen opposite the writing while the person reads the written strip.

7. To read the flap book, alternately read a bad news statement and its corresponding good news statement. Continue in this manner.

NOTE: The size and arrangement of the flap book can be varied to meet the needs of the writer. A larger foundation page can be used to provide room for a title. For longer or more permanent books, use a spiral-binding machine instead of stapling the pages.

Good News/Bad News Tale

Brainstorming Assistant

Character

- -

Good News

Bad News

34-2

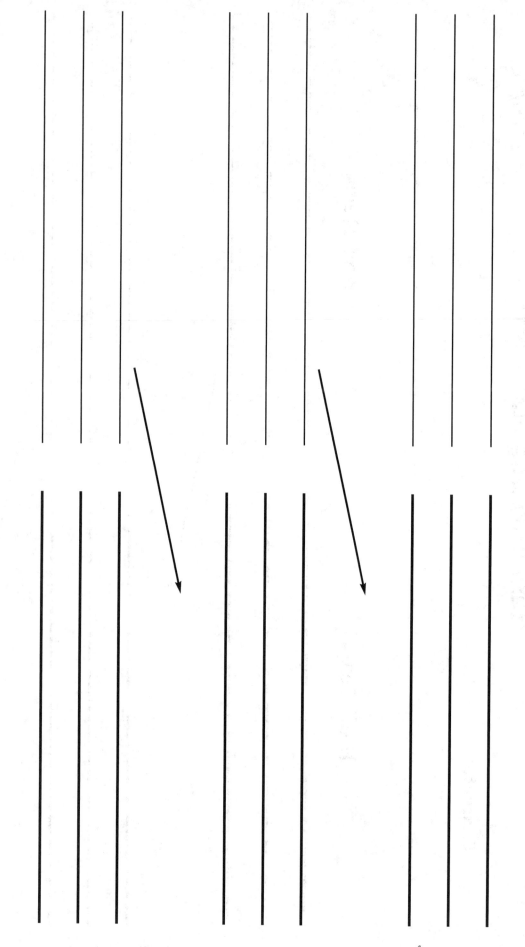

| alien attack | | The Sub Report |

The good news is I bought a new computer game - alien attack at best buy.

The bad news is I read the directions but I can't figure how to play it.

The good news is I can ask my cute next door neighbor to help me but then she'll know I'm not a computer whiz.

The good news is she wears dirty jeans and braces and I like her.

she told me about alien attack her brother plays it all the time

The bad news is our team lost last year.

the good news is I made the team.

the bad news is I'm the smallest member our football team.

the good news is my best friend plays on the team. He is huge and he is a defensive player

I get to play defense too, but I'm not good at dodging or mowing down the other team

the bad news is we may lose again this year

The good news is our teacher is on vacation this week.

The bad news is we have a substitute.

The good news is this sub is Awesome. We get to do lots of neat stuff.

The bad news is our principal always drops by to check on us.

He might not like it if we are having fun while we learn.

The good news is ???

© 2000 Cherlyn Sunflower

Good News/Bad News Tale
Revising Assistant

Revising

Team	- Needs Work	+ Works	* Strong	Teacher

____ 1. (optional) Is my title intriguing? ____

____ 2. Have important words in the title been capitalized? ____

____ 3. Is my character interesting? ____

____ 4. Do I tell the setting (when or where)? ____

____ 5. Do I tell five unfortunate, tragic, or disastrous events? ____

____ 6. Are my good events interesting to the reader? ____

____ 7. Is the sequence of five events connected? ____

____ 8. (optional) Is each set of bad and good events related? ____

____ 9. Does my story make sense and can it be easily followed? ____

____ 10. Is my ending dramatic or a surprise for the reader? ____

____ 11. Is there a capital letter at the beginning of each sentence? ____

____ 12. Is there a period at the end of each sentence? ____

© 2000 Cherlyn Sunflower

- - - ✂ -

Good News/Bad News Tale
Revising Assistant

Revising

Team	- Needs Work	+ Works	* Strong	Teacher

____ 1. (optional) Is my title intriguing? ____

____ 2. Have important words in the title been capitalized? ____

____ 3. Is my character interesting? ____

____ 4. Do I tell the setting (when or where)? ____

____ 5. Do I tell five unfortunate, tragic, or disastrous events? ____

____ 6. Are my good events interesting to the reader? ____

____ 7. Is the sequence of five events connected? ____

____ 8. (optional) Is each set of bad and good events related? ____

____ 9. Does my story make sense and can it be easily followed? ____

____ 10. Is my ending dramatic or a surprise for the reader? ____

____ 11. Is there a capital letter at the beginning of each sentence? ____

____ 12. Is there a period at the end of each sentence? ____

Bad News

Good News

LESSON 35

Mystery/Whodunit

OUTCOME Each student will compose an intriguing mystery with a suspenseful search for clues to find out who is responsible.

MOTIVATORS

1. Tell students that mysteries are fun (*purpose*) for the reader (*audience–peers*) because they draw the reader into solving a problem. Ask students with what mysteries they are familiar and the names of mystery writers they know.

   One website to explore is the online Nancy Drew mysteries for children and adults at http://www.nancydrew.com. Check these weekly episodes. Another site to consider is http://www.thecase.com/kids. One bookstore hosts a variety of weekly interactive mysteries such as See-n-Solve, Vote-n-Solve for older students and adults. It is located at http://www.MysteryNet.com.

2. Read several short mysteries or whodunits to your students. See your librarian for grade-level choices. Ask students to identify important parts of each mystery.

3. Set up a mysterious event in your room such as (a) strange footprints on the floor, walls, and ceiling or (b) an unusual message left on the blackboard or unusual items (unopened soft drink, eyeglasses left on a student's desk, and/or dirt on the floor). Ask your students what they think occurred. What might these clues tell us about the mystery?

4. If you want to focus your students' attention on detective stories, invite a local police detective to your class. Ahead of time ask the detective to share unsolved mysteries in your area and how police officers collect and use evidence in their investigations. Particularly point out that in order to write their detective stories, students will need information on how evidence is collected from the crime scene, how leads are followed up, and how statements are taken from witnesses/victims.

GROUP BRAINSTORMING

Let's brainstorm some ideas for a mystery or whodunit.

Key Questions

Plan ahead so you can keep the brainstormed ideas available to students until after they have composed their rough drafts. Since there are so many ideas that must be generated, consider writing your students' brainstormed ideas on chart paper.

1. **What mysterious thing could happen? If you were a detective, what kind of mystery would you like to solve? Who or what is missing? What unsolved problem do the characters encounter? What clever crime could have been committed? What unusual occurrence might be interesting to figure out?**

   NOTE: In a mystery someone is usually missing property or harms another. Praise interesting mystery ideas that are not killing/crime oriented. Repeat these questions until five to six student ideas have been written on the chart.

2. **Which of our possible mystery ideas shall we use for our class mystery?** Select an uninvolved student to choose an interesting mystery idea. Circle this idea and use it all the way through group composing. If other students object that their idea wasn't chosen, remind them that they get to choose and develop their own idea for a mystery later.

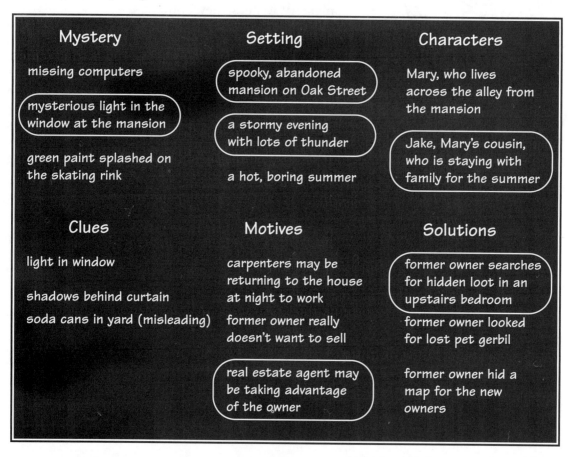

3. **How would you describe the scene? When did the mystery or unexplained event occur?** (weather, sounds, time of day, etc.) **Where did the crime take place?** Accept all responses. Repeat these questions until eight to ten ideas have been written on the chart.

4. **What characters do we need?** (a mystery solver, an inspector, or a detective; suspects and the one who caused the mystery/criminal; witnesses; and perhaps a victim) If students don't come up with all the characters, ask questions such as the following.

Who will investigate the mystery?
What is the name of problem solver or detective?

Who are the suspects?
What caused the mystery?
Who did it?
Who committed the crime?

Who saw/heard it happen?
Who were the witnesses?

Repeat these questions until five to six student ideas have been captured on the chart for each.

5. **How can we describe the mystery solver? What unique physical traits does he/she have? What special personality traits does he/she have?**

   NOTE: The hero/heroine in a mystery must outwit the one who caused the mystery/criminal by observations and intelligent guesswork/reasoning about clues and motives. Praise unusual or unique descriptors. Repeat questioning for the other characters as time allows.

6. **What clues (pieces of information) were left behind? What evidence was found that will help the reader solve the mystery, but doesn't give it away? What disguise, if any, was used? What did the witness see/find?** Praise intriguing clue ideas. Repeat these questions until six to eight clues have been written on the chart. **Which clues shall we use in our group mystery?** Select an uninvolved student or nonparticipator to choose the clues. Circle the clues as they are chosen.

   (optional) **Which clues will be correct? Which clues will we use to mislead readers?** For more complicated mysteries, mark selected clues with + for correct clue and – for incorrect clue.

7. (optional) Ask only Advanced Mystery Writers these brainstorming questions. **What questions should be asked of the witness(es)? the suspects? How will the alibi of each suspect be checked? What hunches does the detective investigate?** Add each student's question ideas on a special chart under "Questions for Witnesses" column, "How to Check Alibi" column, and "Detective's Hunches" column.

8. Share that the problem solver or inspector/detective tries to determine who had motive, opportunity, and means by finding clues (including misleading clues). Suggest that suspense builds as each clue and suspect is investigated until the crime is solved/the solution is found. **Why did the suspect do it? What was his or her motive? What was the person's reason for committing the crime?** Write students' ideas in the "Motive" column.

9. **How will the mystery or unexplained event be solved? What proof will be used in solving the mystery?** Write students' ideas under the "Solutions" column.

GROUP COMPOSING

Now let's compose an exciting mystery together. Involve students in choosing ideas from the brainstormed lists and organizing them into at least parts of a group mystery/whodunits.

The Case of Hidden Loot

As thunder roared and lightning flashed across the sky, Jake saw a mysterious light in the window of the abandoned mansion that stood across the street from his uncle's home. As he looked more closely, a shadow could be seen. Jake didn't realize how exciting and full of mystery his summer with his aunt, uncle, and cousin Mary would be . . .

. . . so Mary and Jake, after questioning all the suspects, decided to go to the library to research the rumors about suspected bank robbers who once lived in the mansion. They spent several hours looking through old newspaper articles until Jake said, "I think I've found a clue!". . .

The bank robbers' loot was finally found: just six old, empty locked boxes. The mystery of the light in the window was solved, but the rumor of money hidden in the old mansion lived on.

---

1. **Let's write the title first. The title for a mystery is often phrased like "The _____ _____ Mystery" or "The Case of the _____ _____."** Ask students to review ideas listed under "Mystery" and "Solutions" columns before choosing the title. The title should reflect the main idea of the mystery.

   EXAMPLES: The <u>Stolen</u> <u>Skateboard</u> Mystery
   The Case of the <u>Green</u> <u>Paint</u>

   Thinking about Mechanics: What should I do to important words in the title? (capitalize)

2. Explain that mysteries can begin in many ways. It is up to us, the writers, to decide how to "set the stage." Ask students to look back at the "Mystery," "Setting," and "Clue" columns of the group brainstorming. **How can we begin the mystery? Where (time and place) is the main character and what is he/she doing as the story begins?** Pause to allow students to consider how to begin the group mystery. Accept several ideas, then choose the one you think is best.

3. Suggest that suspense builds as each clue or suspect is investigated and until the crime is solved/the solution is found. **How can we describe the intriguing search for clues/evidence that were left behind by the guilty party? What will the mystery solver do first, second, third?** As students provide information, add it to the group composition on the chart.

4. What shall we have the mystery solver do next? Praise your students' ideas. As students provide information, add it to the group composition on the chart. Here are other advanced questions that can be asked.

Which clue(s) shall the mystery solver find at this point? Where is the clue found?

What information did the witness reveal?

What questions did the mystery solver ask during the interrogation of the suspect?

What conclusion does the mystery solver draw from the clue? What conclusions were drawn from the interrogation of the witness(es)?

Where does this information lead?

What does this clue tell the reader about "how the unexplained event occurred," "who did it," and "why"?

Repeat this sequence of questions several times as the search continues. As students provide information, praise each reasonable idea and add it to the group composition on the chart. The quality and quantity of this portion will depend on both your students' level of writing expertise and their knowledge of mysteries.

Post the Time Order Word Chart so students can refer to it now and later during composing.

Time Order Word Chart	
first	next
second	after that
third	then
fourth	finally
	at last

5. Suggest to students that suspense builds in a mystery as each clue and each suspect is investigated and until the crime is solved or the solution is found. **When should we introduce new evidence/clues, a witness, or new suspects? Where does each new clue lead? How can we show the motives of each suspect?** As students provide information, add it to the mystery on the chart.

     (optional) **Which clues that we brainstormed can we delete or only touch on lightly so we do not give away the guilty party?** Ask students if they want to give their future readers enough clues to help them solve the mystery themselves. If not, ask question 6.

6. **What serious, dramatic, or surprise ending might work in our mystery?** Repeat this pattern of questioning until students reach an oral consensus on a dramatic ending. **How shall we reveal the solution to the mystery? Who will reveal the solution? What will this person say about who/what did it, how it was done, and why the action was committed? How will everyone hearing the solution react?** Add this information to the group mystery.

INDIVIDUAL BRAINSTORMING AND COMPOSING

Tell students that now they will get to write their own mysteries/whodunits to entertain their friends, classmates, and families. Give each student or pair of students a copy of the Brainstorming Assistant to help them generate ideas and organize their thoughts. It can be found at the end of this lesson.

Brainstorming Assistant: Mystery/Whodunit

Mysteries	Settings	Characters	Descriptors
	Location	Mystery Solver or Detective	Physical Traits
			Personality Traits
	Time	Suspects	Physical Traits
			Personality Traits
	Weather	Other Characters	

As students begin brainstorming their own mysteries, walk around the classroom commenting positively upon the following:

_____ intriguing problems (mysteries)
_____ novel settings
_____ interesting characters
_____ thoughtful clues
_____ clear, well-built motives
_____ useful witnesses

Encourage Advanced Writers to make use of misleading clues or ways to add to the suspense.

As students begin composing their own mysteries, comment positively upon descriptive language that helps the reader to visualize the mystery. Ask questions about each of the above areas to get students to think more deeply about particular points in their mysteries.

_____ a beginning that captures readers' attention
_____ a search that is easy to follow
_____ multisensory details that help the reader visualize the setting, clues,
          the mystery solver, and the suspects
_____ a dramatic ending that makes sense

RESPONDING TO STUDENTS' WRITINGS/REVISING

1. As students finish the rough drafts of their whodunits, ask them to find a revising partner. One student should read his or her whodunit aloud to the other to see if the mystery/whodunit makes sense and the sequence of clues can be easily followed.

   Give each set of partners a copy of the reproducible Revising Assistant from the end of this lesson. Ask revising partners to complete the left-hand side of the Revising Assistant to identify areas of their mysteries needing improvement. (optional) Explain that later you'll evaluate and grade their mysteries using the same form.

Revising Assistant
for
Mystery/Whodunit

The purpose of this checklist is to assist you in evaluating and improving your mystery.

Revising Team	Content & Style	Teacher
_____	1. The beginning captures reader's interest.	_____
_____	2. The sequence of search is easy to follow, not excessively gory.	_____
_____	3. Many multisensory details help the reader visualize the setting, clues, the mystery solver, and the suspects.	_____
_____	4. The ending is dramatic and makes sense.	_____
_____	5. Grammar, usage, spelling, and mechanics aid reader.	_____
_____	6. The writer used all steps of writing process.	_____

2. After step 1 is completed, require each writer to make at least one or two revisions to improve the Mystery/Whodunit.

3. Before publishing the whodunits, have students trade compositions and look for punctuation, capitalization, spelling, and other errors that might hinder a reader from understanding and enjoying the mystery.

PUBLISHING

After students finish revising their mysteries, explain that they'll publish them in a class book so that other students/peers (*audience*) who need to relax and have some fun (*purpose*) can read their mysteries.

Students may illustrate one or more events from their mystery. Construct a class book using a 3-ring binder with index pages to separate the mysteries. Consider asking students to illustrate key events or characters on the title page or on each chapter page. Caution young authors not to give away the solution, of course.

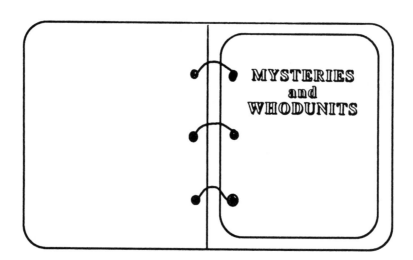

Brainstorming Assistant: Mystery/Whodunit

Mysteries	Settings	Characters	Descriptors
	Location	Mystery Solver or Detective	Physical Traits
			Personality Traits
	Time	Suspects	Physical Traits
			Personality Traits
	Weather	Other Characters	

Revising Assistant

for

Mystery/Whodunit

The purpose of this checklist is to assist you in evaluating and improving your mystery.

Teacher ___ ___ ___ ___

Revising Team

Content & Style

1. The beginning captures reader's interest.

2. The sequence of search is easy to follow, not excessively gory.

3. Many multisensory details help the reader visualize the setting, clues, the mystery solver, and the suspects.

4. The ending is dramatic and makes sense.

5. Grammar, usage, spelling, and mechanics aid reader.

6. The writer used all steps of writing process.

Overall Comments:

MYSTERIES and WHODUNITS

SECTION 5

Poems and Songs for Young Authors

Poem and song patterns are useful when writers want to express feelings or entertain.

Poems There are four basic kinds of poems: rhythm, pattern, rhyming, and free verse.

- In rhythm poems, new words of the same part of speech and the same number of syllables can be substituted for words in the original poem to recreate the beat.

- In pattern poems, specified types of words, phrases, and sentences go into each line of the poem pattern.

- In rhyming poems, the end words in particular lines must rhyme.

- In free verse, there is no particular form or pattern in which thoughts and feelings can be placed.

While writing poems can be an exciting and powerful way to put thoughts into words, many people are frightened of poetry. The poems in this section have been selected because they allow every young writer to feel successful. Working with poetry is important because the knowledge young writers gain can be transferred to narrative, persuasive, and descriptive compositions. While writing poetry, young writers can learn rhythm, structure, imagery, and figurative language such as similes and metaphors.

Some Forms of Poetry

Acrostics	Diamantes	Nursery Rhymes
Bio Poems	Drawn Poems	Rhymed Poems
Cheers	Five-Word Poems	Rhythm Poems
Cinquains	Free Verse	Sensory Poems
Color Poems	Haiku	Shape Poems
Concrete Poems	Jump Rope Rhymes	Tanka Poems
Couplets	Limericks	Three-Line Poems

Songs   Songs are really poems or stories put to music. Sometimes a songwriter writes the words (lyrics) first, and other times the music or melody is created first. Almost any song, from "Mary Had a Little Lamb" to a popular song, can be used as a pattern for students' ideas. When lyrics are rewritten for an old melody, the desired rhythm has already been established. The writer need only choose words and phrases that fit the rhythm to communicate his or her thoughts and feelings.

Some Forms of Songs

Anthems	Hymns	Nursery Rhymes
Ballads	Jingles	Popular Song Lyrics
Chants	Lullabies	Raps
Folk Songs		

LESSON 36

Simple Chant

OUTCOME   Each student will compose and clap four-line chants.

MOTIVATORS

1. This writing is appropriate for days when students need to release some stress and have fun. Ask students to clap and chant several of the following chants with you or make up some other chants that will appeal to your students. (For a copy of these chants, see the sheet of "Student-Created Chants" at the end of this lesson.)

Student-Created Chant

Mud
Mud (*slap legs*) between my (*clap hands*) toes (*snap fingers*),
Mud (*slap legs*) between my (*clap hands*) toes (*snap fingers*),
      Slimy (*slap legs*), grimy (*clap hands*)
Mud (*slap legs*) between my (*clap hands*) toes (*snap fingers*).

Peanut Butter
Peanut butter (*slap legs*) on my (*clap hands*) fingers (*snap fingers*),
Peanut butter (*slap legs*) on my (*clap hands*) fingers (*snap fingers*),
      Yummy (*slap legs*), gooey (*clap hands*)
Peanut butter (*slap legs*) on my (*clap hands*) fingers (*snap fingers*).

Bees
Bees (*slap legs*) down my (*clap hands*) shirt (*snap fingers*),
Bees (*slap legs*) down my (*clap hands*) shirt (*snap fingers*),
      Buzzing (*slap legs*), tickling (*clap hands*)
Bees (*slap legs*) down my (*clap hands*) shirt (*snap fingers*).

Canoe
Canoe (*slap legs*) in the (*clap hands*) river (*snap fingers*),
Canoe (*slap legs*) in the (*clap hands*) river (*snap fingers*),
      Swift (*slap legs*), lonely (*clap hands*)
Canoe (*slap legs*) in the (*clap hands*) river (*snap fingers*).

Darkness
Sounds (*slap legs*) in the (*clap hands*) dark (*snap fingers*),
Sounds (*slap legs*) in the (*clap hands*) dark (*snap fingers*),
      Thumping (*slap legs*), bumping (*clap hands*)
Sounds (*slap legs*) in the (*clap hands*) dark (*snap fingers*).

Motorcycle
Motorcycle (*slap legs*) on the (*clap hands*) road (*snap fingers*),
Motorcycle (*slap legs*) on the (*clap hands*) road (*snap fingers*),
      Smooth (*slap legs*), fast (*clap hands*)
Motorcycle (*slap legs*) on the (*clap hands*) road (*snap fingers*).

2. Chants can also be written about Science, Social Studies, and other topics.

---

* This simple chant format is an adaptation of the old jump rope rhyme "Jello in the Bowl" compiled by Carl Withers (1967) in the book *A Rocket in My Pocket*.

419

GROUP BRAINSTORMING

Now we'll brainstorm some ideas for our own chants.

1. **About what would you like to write? What is your favorite object or animal? About whom would you like to compose a chant? About what activity could we write?** Pause for at least 30 seconds to give students time to think. Accept only one-word topics and write them under the "Topic" column.

2. **From all our terrific topics, about which of these shall we write a group chant?** Choose a low-achieving or uninvolved student to select one topic.

3. **Where could _____ be? Where might we find a _____? What is an unusual place where we don't usually find _____?** Pause to give students time to think. Write their ideas under the "Location" column.

4. **Of all the locations we brainstormed, which place shall we use?** Circle chosen location.

5. **What is one word that describes _____? What kind of _____?** Pause to give students time to think. Write their ideas under the "Descriptors" column.

6. **Of all the descriptors for _____, which one shall we use?** Circle the chosen descriptor. **What is another one?** Circle the chosen descriptor.

GROUP COMPOSING

Now that we brainstormed such good ideas, we just need to place the ideas we've chosen in the chant format.

1. **Which subject/topic did we choose for our group chant?** Tell students that this word will become our title. Write it at the top of the paper.

> **Thinking about Mechanics:** How do we let people know this is the title? (capitalize)

2. Which lines contain the topic? At the beginning of which lines does our one-word subject go? Insert this information at the beginning of lines 1, 2, and 4.

> **Thinking about Mechanics:** How do we show this word starts a new line? (capitalize)

3. Which location word did we select? Where does this location word go in our chant? Insert this information at the end of lines 1, 2, and 4.

> **Thinking about Mechanics:** What punctuation needs to be placed after the location word to show it is the end of this line of the poem? (a comma)

4. Share with students that the word that introduces the location word is called a preposition. Explain that a preposition is "anywhere a cat can go" such as *on, under, at, with, to, behind, in, about, between, inside, outside, around, by.* Allow students to change the preposition if a different preposition would work better. If needed, provide a list of prepositions from which students can choose.

5. Let's clap the first and second lines of our chant to see how they sound. What do you think we need to add, delete, or change to make the lines sound better? Add, delete, and/or change words to make the chant sound better to students. Avoid making your own suggestions and hold all urges to criticize at this point. If you think students are on the wrong track, ask them to clap and listen again.

NOTE: The number of syllables in each line of the chant will change the way it sounds.

> **Football**
>
> Football in the snow,
> Football in the snow,
> Sliding, colliding
> Football in the snow.

6. Which of our describing words shall we place first? second? Insert students' choices.

> **Thinking about Mechanics:** What punctuation needs to be placed between the two describing words in line 3? (a comma)

7. **Let's clap our whole chant to see how it sounds.** Clap the completed chant. **What words do you think we need to add, delete, or change to make it sound better?** Make suggested changes. Then ask the students to clap the chant as a group and evaluate it again.

> **Thinking about Mechanics:** What punctuation needs to be placed at the end of the first two lines of our chant? (a comma)

INDIVIDUAL BRAINSTORMING AND COMPOSING

Tell students that now they'll write some chants on their own topics. Ask students to compose four to ten chants. Explain that later, they'll select their best chants and add hand motions and share their chants with each other during break or with a class of younger students.

As students write, walk around the room and converse with those who need individual guidance.

Beginning Writers   These young authors may profit from paper with lines for particular parts of the chant.

Advanced Writers   Challenge Advanced Writers who finish ten or more good chants to experiment with a new chant format. Here are a days-of-the-week or months-in-the-year or time-of-day chant formats. Students can create chants for each day of the week and/or each period of time throughout the day (morning, noon, afternoon, evening).

<table>
<tr><td>

Time for Computer

Wednesday, Wednesday
Computer on Wednesday
Get in line for the computer.

</td><td>

Speeding

Noon, noon
Speeding through lunch at noon
So I can go outside.

</td></tr>
</table>

Invite more Advanced Writers to compose a series of chants that tell a story with a beginning (one or more chants), middle (several chants), and an end (one or more chants).

RESPONDING TO STUDENTS' WRITINGS/REVISING

As students complete one or more chants, ask them to read the chant out loud to a partner. Write the following on the board or overhead so students can evaluate.

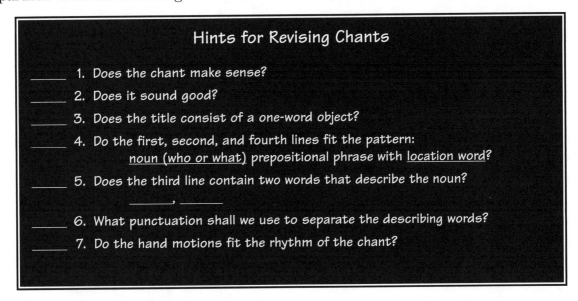

Hints for Revising Chants

_____ 1. Does the chant make sense?

_____ 2. Does it sound good?

_____ 3. Does the title consist of a one-word object?

_____ 4. Do the first, second, and fourth lines fit the pattern:
        <u>noun (who or what)</u> prepositional phrase with <u>location word</u>?

_____ 5. Does the third line contain two words that describe the noun?
        _____ , _____

_____ 6. What punctuation shall we use to separate the describing words?

_____ 7. Do the hand motions fit the rhythm of the chant?

Students will modify the chant pattern to fit their thoughts. Accept and praise new creations that have a workable rhythm. For example:

Fun
Baseball in my mitt, Baseball in the mitt, Catch it, Throw it Baseball in the air.

Friends
Friends at school, Friends at school, Caring, sharing Those outrageous friends of mine.

PUBLISHING

Explain that motions will be added to the chants before they are performed for their peers' or younger students' (*audience*) enjoyment (*purpose*). Involve students in reading the chant "The Lonely Puppy" using the suggested motions.

The Lonely Puppy

Puppy	behind the	fence,
(*slap legs*)	(*clap hands*)	(*snap fingers*)
Puppy	behind the	fence,
(*slap legs*)	(*clap hands*)	(*snap fingers*)
Lonely,	frightened,	
(*slap legs*)	(*clap hands*)	
Puppy	behind the	fence.
(*slap legs*)	(*clap hands*)	(*snap fingers*)

Next ask students to suggest other motions such as flapping arms and stamping feet that can be used to accent the rhythm. Finally allow students in pairs to experiment with these and other motions.

Choral Readings

Choral reading a chant is fun to do and exciting for the audience. Assign students to three- or, if necessary, four-person teams.

Write the following on a board, chart, or overhead so that each group will know what to do next. Explain that each group should:

1. Break their chant into a number of parts. Perhaps two students can read/say lines 1, 2, and 4. The other student(s) can read/say line 3. Encourage students to be creative.

2. Decide which parts to read softly/loudly and which parts of the chant to read slowly/quickly so that an overall mood can be created. For example, in "The Lonely Puppy" the word "lonely" could be said softly and slowly and the word "frightened" could be said quickly and loudly.

3. Experiment with hand motions for each part of the chant(s). Choose the three best motions.

4. Practice the chant with motions before performing it.

5. Type the chants on the word processor. Invite students to draw an illustration to accompany each chant.

6. Collect these pages and staple them in a class book to be shared with peers.

Consider allowing your students to read and teach their chants to a class of younger students.

Student-Created Chant

Mud

Mud (*slap legs*) between my (*clap hands*) toes (*snap fingers*),
Mud (*slap legs*) between my (*clap hands*) toes (*snap fingers*),
    Slimy (*slap legs*), grimy (*clap hands*)
Mud (*slap legs*) between my (*clap hands*) toes (*snap fingers*).

Peanut Butter

Peanut butter (*slap legs*) on my (*clap hands*) fingers (*snap fingers*),
Peanut butter (*slap legs*) on my (*clap hands*) fingers (*snap fingers*),
    Yummy (*slap legs*), gooey (*clap hands*)
Peanut butter (*slap legs*) on my (*clap hands*) fingers (*snap fingers*).

Bees

Bees (*slap legs*) down my (*clap hands*) shirt (*snap fingers*),
Bees (*slap legs*) down my (*clap hands*) shirt (*snap fingers*),
    Buzzing (*slap legs*), tickling (*clap hands*)
Bees (*slap legs*) down my (*clap hands*) shirt (*snap fingers*).

Canoe

Canoe (*slap legs*) in the (*clap hands*) river (*snap fingers*),
Canoe (*slap legs*) in the (*clap hands*) river (*snap fingers*),
    Swift (*slap legs*), lonely (*clap hands*)
Canoe (*slap legs*) in the (*clap hands*) river (*snap fingers*).

Darkness

Sounds (*slap legs*) in the (*clap hands*) dark (*snap fingers*),
Sounds (*slap legs*) in the (*clap hands*) dark (*snap fingers*),
    Thumping (*slap legs*), bumping (*clap hands*)
Sounds (*slap legs*) in the (*clap hands*) dark (*snap fingers*).

Motorcycle

Motorcycle (*slap legs*) on the (*clap hands*) road (*snap fingers*),
Motorcycle (*slap legs*) on the (*clap hands*) road (*snap fingers*),
    Smooth (*slap legs*), fast (*clap hands*)
Motorcycle (*slap legs*) on the (*clap hands*) road (*snap fingers*).

Cat

Cat (*slap legs*) in the (*clap hands*) tub (*snap fingers*),
Cat (*slap legs*) in the (*clap hands*) tub (*snap fingers*),
    Wet (*slap legs*), angry (*clap hands*)
Cat (*slap legs*) in the (*clap hands*) tub (*snap fingers*).

Friends

Friends (*slap legs*) at (*clap hands*) school (*snap fingers*),
Friends (*slap legs*) at (*clap hands*) school (*snap fingers*),
    Caring (*slap legs*), sharing (*clap hands*)
Outrageous (*slap legs*) friends of (*clap hands*) mine (*snap fingers*).

LESSON 37

Five-Line Poem

OUTCOME   Each student will compose a five-line poem about an academic topic or topic of his/her choice.

MOTIVATORS

1. Use this lesson as a get-acquainted activity. Share a five-line autobiographic poem with your students. One pattern for a five-line poem is: the person's/pet's name, three things the person/pet likes, and the describing words.

   Krissy
   Parks
   Frogs
   Waterfalls
   Very cautious

   Invent your own autobiographic poem pattern such as this three-line pattern: name, what likes to do, and where; or a four-line pattern: name, what likes to do, when, and what kind of person.

   Gary   Kimberly
   Fish   Roses
   Deep river   Spring
                   Assertive

2. Use this lesson as a culminating activity for a unit in Science or Social Studies. The pattern for these five-line poems is the topic; three people, places, objects, events, or ideas related to the topic; and a word that describes the topic (adjective).

GROUP BRAINSTORMING

Today we'll brainstorm ideas about the American Revolution and then organize our ideas into a poem. Insert your own topic in the blank throughout the lesson.

Topic	People/Places/ Objects/Events/Ideas	Describing Words
American Revolution Civil War Western Movement	George Washington Philadelphia Cannons War Freedom from England Taxes	revolutionary frightening angry protective

Key Questions

1. **Since we've been studying the American Revolution , we'll think of people, places, events, objects, and ideas that come to mind when we think of the American Revolution .** Insert your own topic.

2a. **First, let's brainstorm some people, places, objects, events, and ideas about our topic.** Pause to give students time to think. Praise useful ideas. Place students' ideas under the "People/Places/Objects/Events/Ideas" column.

2b. **What famous people come to mind when you think of the American Revolution ?**

2c. **What famous places do you think about when you think of the American Revolution ?**

2d. **What objects do you visualize when you think of the American Revolution ?**

2e. **What events do you think about when you think of the American Revolution ?**

2f. **What ideas come to mind when you think of the American Revolution ?**

3. **From our list "People/Places/Objects/Events/Ideas" we need to choose five words that characterize the American Revolution . Which words best capture the American Revolution ?** Choose a low-achieving or uninvolved student to select an idea. Circle three ideas.

4. **What words describe the American Revolution ? What kind of American Revolution ?** Pause to give students time to think. Praise useful ideas. Write students' ideas under the "Describing Words" column.

5. **What feelings did the people have/do you have about the American Revolution ?** Pause to give students time to think. Praise useful ideas. Write students' ideas under the "Describing Words" column.

GROUP COMPOSING

Now, let's compose a five-line poem about the American Revolution together.

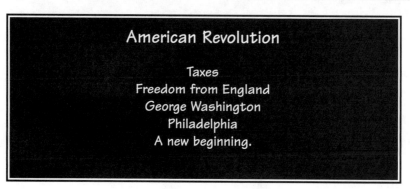

1. **On the first line we'll write the words American Revolution for our title.** Insert your topic.

> **Thinking about Mechanics:** Which words in a title need to be capitalized? (proper nouns—ones that name a particular person, place, or thing) Do not capitalize articles (a, an, it, the) unless they are the first words in title.

2. **Earlier we circled five words that capture our topic. How should we order these words? What would be the most effective way to order these ideas about American Revolution ?** Place words after the title as suggested until five words are listed. If students change their mind about using a previously selected word, ask what to use instead. Praise thoughtful revisions.

> **Thinking about Mechanics:** How do we show that a word starts a new line of the poem? (capitalize the first word in each line of a poem)

3. **Which descriptive word (or phrase) best describes our topic?** Choose one and add it to the poem.

INDIVIDUAL BRAINSTORMING & COMPOSING

Explain that each student will write a five-line poem. Ahead of time decide whether students will write about (1) a topic of their choice, (2) a topic from the brainstormed list, or (3) themselves. Have students fold a sheet of notebook paper in half. Label one side "People/Places/Objects/Events/Ideas" and the other side "Describing Words."

As you circulate around the room to help students get started, spend a little time with each student brainstorming topics. Read back portions of students' poems so that they can hear what they have created so far. Make positive comments about word choice. Demonstrate how to use a thesaurus to get ideas for more effective words.

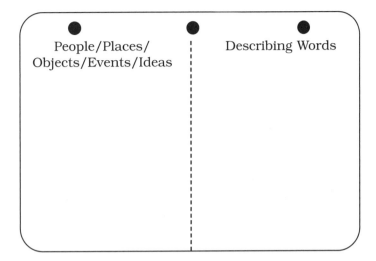

RESPONDING TO STUDENTS' WRITINGS/REVISING

As young writers complete their drafts of their five-line poems, ask them to find a revising partner—someone new with whom they haven't worked. Have the revising partner read his/her five-line poem out loud to the other person to see if it captures the essence of the topic in a very tiny capsule. Write the following on the board, a chart, or the overhead to guide the revising teams:

> - Make two positive comments about how the people/places/objects/events/ideas or the describing words are great choices for the topic. For example:
>
>   Wow, "loud music" and "fast and wild" really capture what Max is about.
>
> - Ask questions to help the writer consider how effective is the impact of one or more words. For example:
>
>   How does the phrase "long driveways" capture who Max is? (One possible response: "Well, I like skateboards and I'm always looking for long driveways." Another possible response: "Well it really is about skateboarding. Maybe I should think of another word.") NOTE: Both responses are fine. Let the writer be the judge.

PUBLISHING

Depending on the poem topic, tell students one of the following: They'll display their autobiographic poems (1) so their new classmates (*audience*) can get to know each other better (*purpose*) or (2) so they can learn how others think about the chosen topic.

Name Tags/Business Cards

Write the autobiographic poems on "Hello, my name is" name tags or enter the information on a word processor and print the poem on business card paper. Have the students wear them throughout the day or share/trade the business cards during free time.

> **Hello,**
> **my name is** *Max*
> *Skateboards,*
> *Long driveways*
> *Loud music*
> *Fast and Wild*

Quilt

Write the science or social studies five-line poems on sticky notes, then place them on chart paper in "quilt" fashion. If desired, preline the chart paper. Use tape to attach the sticky notes more firmly at the bottom of each "quilt piece." Here's a partially completed class poem quilt.

Mr. Castle's Class of 20XX					Mr. Castle's Class of 20XX
			Jessie Soccer Choir Horses Tough		
		Danny Fish Swim Surf Friendly			
Mr. Castle's Class of 20XX					Mr. Castle's Class of 20XX

LESSON 38

Comparison Poem

OUTCOME Each student will write a poem describing a descriptor or a feeling.

MOTIVATORS

1. Stretch a rubber band as you involve students in ridiculous mini-stories or silly boasting sessions using adjectives that compare. ("er" is used to compare two and "est" is used to compare more than two)

> My _____ is _____.
> My _____ is _____ "er" than a _____.
> My _____ is the _____ "est" in the _____.

   Ask for three volunteers to assist you by coming to the front of the classroom and stretching the rubber band. Tell students that they have the privilege of assisting, as long as they have control of their rubber band. (Don't snap or lose it.)

2. Bring to class magazine advertisements that claim a product tastes better, gets your clothes cleaner, or makes the environment fresher.
   Do a quick Science lesson in which an experiment results in test subjects being fast, faster, fastest; thick thicker, thickest; or moldy, moldier, moldiest.

3. Read a comparison poem and ask students what it means. (Four sample poems are provided at the end of this lesson.) Repeat with another comparison poem. Ask students how the poems are similar and different.

Sad

Sadder than a lost doll
Sadder than an empty refrigerator
Sadder than a homeless cat
Sadder than an old building about to be demolished
Sadder than a bank with no money
Sadder than a grandpa in a nursing home
  with no visitors
That's how sad I am.

Tall

Taller than a red ant
Taller than my old beat-up teddy bear
Taller than my four-year-old sister
Taller than my drooling Golden Retriever
That's how tall I am.

431

GROUP BRAINSTORMING

Now we are going to compose a comparison poem about our class (or use another topic).

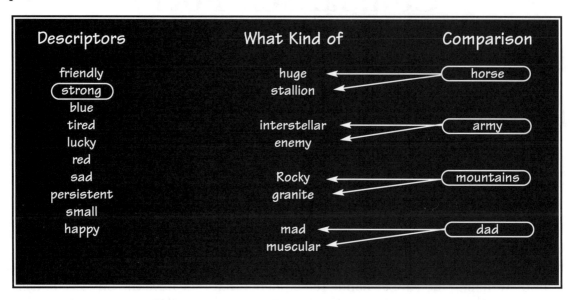

Descriptors	What Kind of	Comparison
friendly	huge	horse
(strong)	stallion	
blue		
tired	interstellar	army
lucky	enemy	
red		
sad	Rocky	mountains
persistent	granite	
small		
happy	mad	dad
	muscular	

Key Questions

1a. What is one word that describes our class? How do you/we look? act? feel?
Write students' responses on the board, chart paper, or overhead under the "Descriptors" column.

1b. Out of all our ideas about our class, which descriptor is really strong and/or accurate? Choose a withdrawn or uninvolved student to select a describing word. Circle it.

NOTE: Brainstorm the "comparison" next. Leave room on the board to record the "What Kind of" ideas (adjectives) so they'll fit in front of the nouns they describe.

2a. To what can we compare ourselves? Who or what are you _____er or more _____ than? Write students' responses under the "Comparison" column.

2b. Out of all these ideas, which four are the most powerful comparisons? Choose a withdrawn or uninvolved student to select the most powerful comparisons. Circle them.

3a. What kind of _____? Insert the selected comparison. **How can we describe _____?** Write students' responses under the "What Kind of" column.

3b. From the "What Kind of" column, which describing word (adjective) shall we choose to describe our comparison word? Choose a withdrawn or uninvolved student to select a describing word. Circle the describing word.

4. Repeat steps 3–6 for each comparison.

GROUP COMPOSING

Before you write a comparison poem, let's compose one together to see how much fun comparison poems are to create and how powerful they can be.

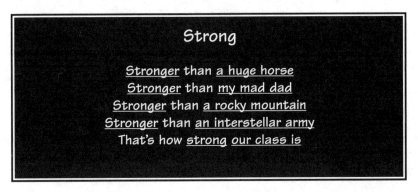

> ### Strong
>
> <u>Stronger</u> than <u>a huge horse</u>
> <u>Stronger</u> than <u>my mad dad</u>
> <u>Stronger</u> than <u>a rocky mountain</u>
> <u>Stronger</u> than <u>an interstellar army</u>
> That's how <u>strong</u> <u>our class is</u>

   1. **Which descriptor did we choose as the focus of our poem? Let's change the word we choose to a comparative form. Should we add (-er) or use the word "more"?**

Thinking about Mechanics: Which sounds better? _____er or more _____?

NOTE: Adjectives (brown, tall) have comparative forms (browner, taller) and superlative forms (brownest, tallest). When an adjective has more than two syllables, the word "more" or "most" is usually used to show comparative and superlative forms. For example:

Cooperative

More cooperative than a hungry lion
More cooperative than a self-assembled bike
More cooperative than a new computer
More cooperative than my stepdad
That's how cooperative
our rent collector is.

---

   2. **Which lines begin with this descriptor?** Ask the whole class for a response. Write the chosen descriptor at the beginning of each line of the comparison poem.

   3. **From our list of comparisons, which shall we choose?** Ask withdrawn or uninvolved students to select four or five. Circle these.

   4. **Which describing word makes the most powerful comparison?** Circle one for each comparison.

   5. **How do we want to order our comparison phrases? Which of these comparisons do we want to place first in our poem? last? in between?** Write *than* or *than a/an* followed by each chosen comparison phrase to the poem.

> **Thinking about Mechanics:** Many people use "than" when they should be using "then." The word "than" is used to compare two topics, as in this lesson. "Then" is a word used to indicate time order, as in "We went to the fair, then we went to the barbecue."

6a. How shall we complete our last line? Since we are describing our class , we'll write the words "That's how strong we are" to complete our comparison poem. Add this ending to the poem.

6b. If you were describing yourself, you'd write "That's how _____ I am" or "That's how I feel."

6c. If you were describing someone else, like your sister, you'd write, "That's how smart my sister is." If you were describing something like an oak tree, you'd write, "That's how tall the oak tree is."

INDIVIDUAL BRAINSTORMING & COMPOSING

Tell students they get to create their own powerful comparison poems using a descriptor or a feeling of their choice. Direct students to fold their notebook paper in thirds and crease the paper. Have students write "Descriptors" at the top of the first column, "What Kind of" at the top of the middle column, and "Comparison" on the third column. Ask students why they will brainstorm the middle column last. (They need to choose a comparison before they can consider what kind of person, place, or thing.)

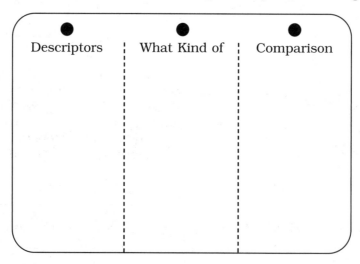

As students begin brainstorming descriptors, encourage them to select something personally relevant or unusual. Once young writers have selected one descriptor, encourage the brainstorming of powerful comparison words. Next encourage students as they choose their best comparisons and brainstorm "what kind of" words (adjectives).

Since word choice is critical to creating a powerful poem, encourage the following spelling strategies during drafting, instead of avoiding the use of interesting words:

- Make your best guess.

- Write the letters you know.

- Sound it out.

- Draw a picture or symbol.

- Leave an empty line to mark the place.

RESPONDING TO STUDENTS' WRITINGS/REVISING

1. As students finish the rough drafts of their comparison poems, have them find a revising partner. Have each young author read his/her poem aloud to his/her partner to see if it creates a powerful image so others can understand. Write the following on the board or overhead and encourage peer teams to evaluate and revise.

> - Make two or three specific comments about the comparisons. For example:
>
>   Your diamond ring comparison is really a powerful way to help me feel how lucky you are. The adjective interstellar shows me how huge and strong the army is.
>
> - Ask questions to assist students in celebrating powerful phrases and rethinking others. For example:
>
>   What is your strongest comparison?
>   What might be a more powerful comparison than _____?
>
> - Make one suggestion to make the comparison poem "come alive" for readers.

After revising teams have finished, signal poem writers to reread their poems, considering ways to replace overused words and make the images in their poems even stronger. Show teams how to use a thesaurus.

2. Before publishing, have revising partners trade poems and look for spelling errors that might hinder the reader in fully understanding the meaning of the poem. Return the comparison poem to the young writer with these suggestions for checking spelling:

- Close your eyes and picture the word in your mind.

- Break the word into smaller parts/syllables.

- Write it different ways until it looks right.

- Find the word somewhere around you such as on a crayon, on a sign, or in a book.

- Use a handheld or computer spell checker.

- Ask someone.

PUBLISHING

Explain that students will display their comparison poems on a soda bottle display (*format*) so each student (*audience*) will remember how he/she felt (*purpose*) and also shared with others (*audience*) so they understand our feelings (*purpose*).

Soda Bottle Display

Materials

Soda holder pattern, pencil, tagboard or butcher paper, scissors, empty/washed 2-liter plastic soda bottle with cap, glue

Directions

1. Trace the soda bottle display pattern onto tagboard or butcher paper.

Strong

Stronger than a huge horse
Stronger than my mad dad
Stronger than a rocky mountain
Stronger than an interstellar army
That's how strong our class is.

2. Cut out the soda bottle display.

Cooperative

More cooperative than a hungry lion
More cooperative than a self-assemble
    bike
More cooperative than a new
    computer
More cooperative than my stepdad
That's how cooperative
    our rent collector is.

3. Bend the two neck joints. If you are using a large bottle, increase the neck area so the rectangular area that will display the poem will hang down, not stick out horizontally from the bottle.

4. Use pointed scissors (or a large nail) to carefully poke a hole in the center of the display so you can cut out the hole that you'll place over your bottle. If the neck of your bottle is larger, snip a few of the lines around the hole.

5. Write or glue your poem in the rectangular display.

6. If your soda bottle is empty, fill it with water; screw on the cap tightly, then carefully place the poem holder on your bottle.

Sad

Sadder than a lost doll
Sadder than an empty refrigerator
Sadder than a homeless cat
Sadder than an old building about to be demolished
Sadder than a bank with no money
Sadder than a grandpa in a nursing home with no visitors
That's how sad I am.

Tall

Taller than a red ant
Taller than my old beat-up teddy bear
Taller than my four-year-old sister
Taller than my drooling Golden Retriever
That's how tall I am.

Strong

Stronger than a huge horse
Stronger than my mad dad
Stronger than a rocky mountain
Stronger than an interstellar army
That's how strong our class is.

Cooperative

More cooperative than a hungry lion
More cooperative than a self-assembled bike
More cooperative than a new computer
More cooperative than my stepdad
That's how cooperative our rent collector is.

LESSON 39

Auto/Bio Poem

OUTCOME   Each student will create a pattern poem that describes someone's life (a brief character sketch).

MOTIVATORS

1. Read the poem "Martin Luther"* without sharing the title and last line that contain his name. Ask students to guess who the poem is about. Inquire how students figured it out.

Martin Luther

Minister
Just, Courageous, Eloquent, Fair
Lover of Freedom, Justice, and Equality
Who believed the world could be a better place
Who wanted Peace, Respect, and Hope
Who used Preaching, Nonviolence, and Love
Who gave Help, Time, and His Life
Who said "let freedom ring"
King

*All efforts to locate the original source of this poem have been unsuccessful. We will gladly credit the source in a future reprinting of the book.

   Read your own Auto/Bio poem without sharing the first and last lines that contain your name. Ask students to guess who wrote the poem. See the examples on the next page for ideas.

2. Display two Auto/Bio poems side by side (on wall charts or the overhead). Line by line ask how these poems are similar and different. The comparison will help students analyze the poem pattern. A reproducible copy of these poems is provided at the end of this lesson.

Dan	**Cherlyn**
Helpful, talented, shy,	Thoughtful, playful, organized,
Lover of motorcycles,	Loved by her mom and three dogs,
Who hates to be in debt,	Who dreams of a smart, sensitive
Who enjoys quality firework displays,	man on a motorcycle,
Who hunts for silver and gold,	Who would like to lie on a
Who surfs the Internet all night,	sunny beach for a millennium,
Who knows chocolate candy	Who plans to snorkel
solves all problems,	in warm Caribbean waters,
Who wants a better job,	Lover of good teaching,
Who would like to live in Canada,	Believer in success for all students,
Resident of North Dakota,	Who fears being too critical,
My best friend	Resident of the universe,
	Sunflower

NOTE: In the poem titled "Dan," the words "My best friend" were used in place of Dan's last name.

GROUP BRAINSTORMING

Today we're going to brainstorm and write poems about ourselves and each other at school. Since students are going to write a Bio poem about our school, special brainstorming categories have been chosen that better fit qualities of a school.

Our School	Cares About	Wants	Feels
fun	football	a computer	overpopulated
competitive	the environment	be prepared for future	hungry
loud	gymnastics	a day off	angry
friendly	our teacher	a road trip	tired
huge	science fest	a school counselor	happy

Fears	Says	Believes	Plans
detention	"Teachers are great!"	in ourselves	make the 1st string
drug dealers	"Say no!"	parents don't understand	save money
Ms. Taske	"Go, Fight, Win!"		get a good job

Key Questions

1. **What is one word that describes our school? What kind of school is our school? What are some words that describe the people in our school?** Write students' responses on the board, overhead, or chart paper under the brainstorming category "Our School."

2. **About what do students at our school care? About what do teachers and staff care? What is an issue that is important to everyone here? Whom do we all admire?** Write students' responses under the brainstorming category "Cares About."

3. **What do students want? What do teachers want? What do other people at our school want? What is something we strive for? What do we wish? What is something students work toward?** Write students' responses under the brainstorming category "Wants."

4. **How does a student at our school feel? How does our principal make us feel? How do you feel on the first day of school? How do you feel on the last day of school? When something disappointing happens, how do you feel?** Write students' responses under the brainstorming category "Feels."

5. **What do students fear at our school? What do teachers fear on our campus? Which class is known as the most difficult? Which teacher is thought to be the most strict? What do you dread about school?** Write students' responses under the brainstorming category "Fears."

6. **What do students say about our school? What do teachers or the principal say? What do people/students/teachers say about our principal/vice principal? What words do our teachers use to make us feel good? What cheers do we say at sporting events?** Write students' responses under the brainstorming category "Says."

7. **What do students believe about our school? What makes us proud of our school? What does our school's "mission statement" say we believe?** Write students' responses under the brainstorming category "Believes."

8. **What do students plan? What plan(s) do teachers/administration have for students? What do parents plan for us?** Write students' responses under the brainstorming category "Plans."

GROUP COMPOSING

Ahead of time write the phrases and blanks on the board, chart paper, or overhead.

Now let's organize our ideas into an Auto/Bio poem.

> ## Panthers
>
> Friendly, competitive, loud,
> Who care about the environment,
> Who want everyone to be prepared for the future,
> Who feel overpopulated,
> Who fear drug dealers,
> Who believe in ourselves,
> Who plan to go to college,
> Located in sunny Oklahoma,
> Stillwater High.

1. **Since we are describing our school, let's put the name of our school mascot on the top line.** Insert this information on the board, overhead, or chart paper.

2. **From the list of describing words we generated, which best describe our school?** Circle three words. **Now from the describing words that we circled, which one shall we put into our poem first?** Choose an uninvolved or withdrawn student to select an idea. **second? third? last?** Add the three words as suggested to the group poem.

3. **Out of all the things we care about, which idea shall we put in our poem?** Choose a student who needs to succeed to select an idea. Add this idea to the poem.

4. **Of all the things we want and strive for at our school, which best represents the way it is at our school?** Choose an uninvolved or withdrawn student to select an idea. Add this idea to the poem.

5. **Out of all the feelings we generated about our school, which shall we share with the people who read our poem?** Choose a student who needs to succeed to select an idea. Add this idea to the poem.

6. **Out of all the things we fear at our school or in the world, which shall we choose to include in our poem?** Choose an uninvolved or withdrawn student to select an idea. Add this idea to the poem.

7. **Of all the things we and other people say about our school, which best represents our school?** Choose a student who needs to succeed to select an idea. Add this idea to the poem.

8. **Out of all our beliefs about our school, which shall we include in our poem?** Choose an uninvolved or withdrawn student to select an idea. Add this idea to the poem.

9. **Of all our plans for ourselves and our school, which shall we include in our poem?** Add this idea to the poem.

10. **Where are we located? What descriptor can we add to our location?** Add this information to the poem.

    NOTE: This information was not brainstormed earlier.

11. **What name should we put on the last line?** (optional) **Let's put the name of our school on the last line. Add this information to the poem.**

    NOTE: This information needs to be brainstormed since it was not brainstormed earlier.

INDIVIDUAL BRAINSTORMING & COMPOSING

There are a number of topic options. Choose one before beginning the lesson.

1. Have everyone brainstorm and write about themselves (Auto/Bio poems).

2. Pair students and have them brainstorm and write about their partner (Bio poems).

3. Brainstorm people your students know about whom they could write a poem (Bio poems). Have students choose one person.

4. Have all students pay tribute to a special person.

    NOTE: Writing about someone students know on a day-to-day basis is much easier than writing about someone who is famous, yet not personally known. A U.S. president or rock star is an example of a person who is famous, yet not (usually) personally known.

Encourage students to create their own ideas for poem lines. The reproducible Ideas for Auto/Bio Poem Lines can be found at the end of this lesson.

Ideas for Auto/Bio Poem Lines

Title	First name or nickname
Related to ___	To whom is person related? loved by?
	Son of/daughter of/mother of/father of/dog or cat of ___?
Descriptors	What kind of person? What words describe this person?
Who feels ___	How do you feel now?
Who thinks ___	What do you think? wonder?
Who fears ___	What do you fear? scared of? afraid of?
Who loves ___	Who do you love? hate?
Who needs/gives ___	What do you need? give?
Who likes ___	What like to do? want? wait for?
Who cares about ___	About whom/what do you care?
Who believes ___	What do you believe?
Who sees ___	What would you like to *see*?
Who says ___	What did/will you say? What were you quoted as saying?
Who travels ___	Where do you like to *travel*?
Who changes ___	What would you like to *change*?
Who dreams ___	What do you dream about?
Who used to ___	What did you used to do?
Who plans ___	What do you plan to do?
Resident of ___	Where do you live?
Final destination ___	What is your final destination?
End	Last Name

NOTE: Except for the first and last lines, there is no prescribed order to the lines of the poem. Ordering lines will be addressed in the revising step.

Once your writers have selected ideas for each poem line, have them turn a sheet of notebook paper sideways. Direct them to fold the paper in half, in half again, crease the folds, and reopen the paper. Direct students to write four of the brainstorming categories they selected across the top of the paper and four just below mid page.

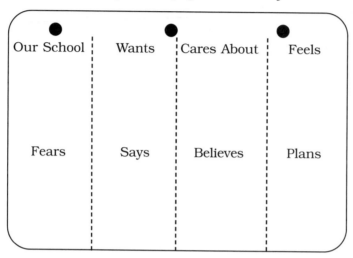

Beginning Writers These students can use a shortened poem format. Here is one possible format:

> _____
> (first name)
> _____ and _____,
> (two describing words)
> Who loves _____ and _____,
> (two people/animals/things/ideas loved)
> Who needs _____ and _____,
> (two needs)
> Resident of _____,
> (where lives)
> _____.
> (last name)

Advanced Writers These students can be encouraged to make each line especially powerful, and/or brainstorm and compose additional lines.

RESPONDING TO STUDENTS' WRITINGS/REVISING

As your young writers complete drafts of their poems, request they find a revising partner—someone new with whom they haven't worked. Have the revising partner read his/her poem out loud to the classmate to see which lines are the most powerful.

Write the following on the board, chart, or overhead to guide the peer-revising teams:

- Star the three most powerful lines. Decide what makes them strong.

- Ask yourselves, "Which lines would be better positioned to earlier or later in the poem?" Use arrows and lines to show where to move the lines for a greater effect.

- Ask yourselves, "Would a different line work better than one of the current lines?" If so, delete the old line and compose a new line.

After this exploration is completed, ask each writer to strengthen his/her poem. Then ask to check capitalization, punctuation, and spelling.

PUBLISHING

Explain that students will display their Auto/Bio poems on wrap-around cans (*format*) and share with classmates and school staff (*audience*) to celebrate a special occasion (*purpose*).

Wrap-around Can

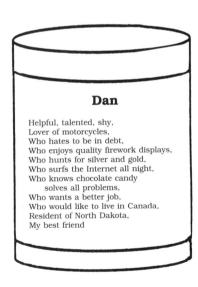

Dan

Helpful, talented, shy,
Lover of motorcycles,
Who hates to be in debt,
Who enjoys quality firework displays,
Who hunts for silver and gold,
Who surfs the Internet all night,
Who knows chocolate candy
    solves all problems,
Who wants a better job,
Who would like to live in Canada,
Resident of North Dakota,
My best friend

Materials

cans (28-oz. fruit cans, 46-fluid oz. fruit juice cans, or 6-lb. 4-oz. vegetable cans display the poem well; smaller cans can be used too), markers, colored butcher paper, scissors, tape, glue

Directions

NOTE: These directions will be easy for students to follow if you first demonstrate.

1. Ask more Advanced Writers to recopy or word-process their revised poems on a clean sheet of paper, then sign and date them. Allow Beginning Writers to clean up their drafts, then sign and date them.

2. Have each student choose a clean can that will be large enough to display his/her Auto/Bio Poem. Some sharing of cans may be necessary to get the right size or pre-cut the paper to fit the can.

3. Lay the butcher paper on a table. Line up the bottom edge of the can with the left bottom edge of the butcher paper.

4. Next, make a mark on the butcher paper to indicate where the top of the can reaches.

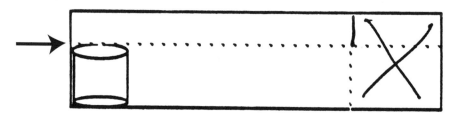

5. Tape the left edge of the butcher paper to the middle of the can, then roll the paper around the can until the paper overlaps.

6. Mark the butcher paper where the paper overlaps, unwind the paper, and remove the tape.

7. Cut out the butcher paper strip that will wrap around the can.

8. Glue the Auto/Bio Poem to the center of the butcher paper strip. Wrap and tape the paper to the can.

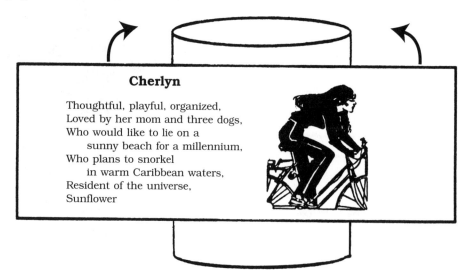

Cherlyn

Thoughtful, playful, organized,
Loved by her mom and three dogs,
Who would like to lie on a
    sunny beach for a millennium,
Who plans to snorkel
    in warm Caribbean waters,
Resident of the universe,
Sunflower

Sample Auto/Bio Poems

Dan

Helpful, talented, shy,
Lover of motorcycles,
Who hates to be in debt,
Who enjoys quality firework
    displays,
Who hunts for silver and gold,
Who surfs the Internet all night,
Who knows chocolate candy
    solves all problems,
Who wants a better job,
Who would like to live in Canada,
Resident of North Dakota,
My best friend

Cherlyn

Thoughtful, playful, organized,
Loved by her mom and three dogs,
Who dreams of a smart, sensitive
    man on a motorcycle,
Who would like to lie on a
    sunny beach for a millennium,
Who plans to snorkel
    in warm Caribbean waters,
Lover of good teaching,
Believer in success for all students,
Who fears being too critical,
Resident of the universe,
Sunflower

Ideas for Auto/Bio Poem Lines

Title   First name or nickname

Related to ___   To whom is person related? loved by?
                              Son of/daughter of/mother of/father of/dog or cat of ___?

Descriptors   What kind of person? What words describe this person?

Who feels ___   How do you feel now?
Who thinks ___   What do you think? wonder?
Who fears ___   What do you fear? scared of? afraid of?
Who loves ___   Who do you love? hate?
Who needs/gives ___   What do you need? give?
Who likes ___   What like to do? want? wait for?

Who cares about ___   About whom/what do you care?
Who believes ___   What do you believe?
Who sees ___   What would you like to *see*?
Who says ___   What did/will you say? What were you quoted as saying?

Who travels ___   Where do you like to *travel*?
Who changes ___   What would you like to *change*?
Who dreams ___   What do you dream about?
Who used to ___   What did you used to do?
Who plans ___   What do you plan to do?

Resident of ___   Where do you live?
Final destination __   What is your final destination?

End   Last Name

Ideas for Auto/Bio Poem Lines

Title   First name or nickname

Related to ___   To whom is person related? loved by?
                              Son of/daughter of/mother of/father of/dog or cat of ___?

Descriptors   What kind of person? What words describe this person?

Who feels ___   How do you feel now?
Who thinks ___   What do you think? wonder?
Who fears ___   What do you fear? scared of? afraid of?
Who loves ___   Who do you love? hate?
Who needs/gives ___   What do you need? give?
Who likes ___   What like to do? want? wait for?

Who cares about ___   About whom/what do you care?
Who believes ___   What do you believe?
Who sees ___   What would you like to *see*?
Who says ___   What did/will you say? What were you quoted as saying?

Who travels ___   Where do you like to *travel*?
Who changes ___   What would you like to *change*?
Who dreams ___   What do you dream about?
Who used to ___   What did you used to do?
Who plans ___   What do you plan to do?

Resident of ___   Where do you live?
Final destination __   What is your final destination?

End   Last Name

LESSON 40

Modern Nursery Rhymes

OUTCOME Each student will rewrite one or more nursery rhymes to make them up-to-date.

MOTIVATORS

1. Recite one or two nursery rhymes you recall from childhood. Ask students which nursery rhymes they remember.

2. Read the names of some nursery rhymes. Ask students to raise their hands when they remember one. For fun jot down the total recalls for each nursery rhyme. Add other nursery rhymes you know to the list.

"Humpty-Dumpty" "Mary Had a Little Lamb"
"Little Bo Peep" "Ba-a Ba-a Black Sheep"
"Jack and Jill" "Three Little Kittens"
"Hey Diddle, Diddle" "This Little Pig"
"Two Blackbirds" "Old King Cole"
"Old Mother Hubbard" "Hickory, Dickory, Dock"
"Little Miss Muffett" "Little Boy Blue"
"Jack Be Nimble" "A Crooked Man"

Ask volunteers to recite various popular nursery rhymes. Suggest your class hum one or two favorite nursery rhymes so that students can experience its rhythm. Students from other cultures and countries may know other nursery rhymes. Encourage them to get the words from older family members.

3. Share some modern nursery rhymes. Ask students which nursery rhyme was rewritten to create each modern version. A reproducible can be found at the end of this lesson.

Chelsie Is Careful
("Jack Be Nimble")
Chelsie is careful,
Chelsie is brave,
Chelsie walks six blocks
To school every day.

Little Bo Derik
("Little Bo Peep")
Little Bo-Derik has lost her bike
    And doesn't know where to find it.
Relax, and it'll come home,
    Dragging its handlebars behind.

This Foxy Mom
("This Little Piggy")
This foxy mom went to Hardees,
Her little brats stayed home.
This foxy mom had a burger,
The brats had none.
This foxy mom went yum, yum, yum,
All the way home.

Old Joe Slow
("Old King Cole")
Old Joe Slow was a friendly old janitor,
and a friendly old janitor was he.
He cleaned all the floors.
He shut the school doors.
He emptied the trash and waved at me.

President and Governor
("Jack and Jill")
President Clinton and Governor Jesse went to Washington
    to pass an environmental bill.
Clinton was voted down and it broke his pride
    and the Governor was selected President just after.

4. Give each student a large sheet of newsprint paper. Ask students to choose a favorite nursery rhyme and illustrate it with pencil, crayons, and/or markers. A list of nursery rhymes can be found at the end of this lesson. Have students draw modern characters in a modern setting. When students have finished, share their drawings. Post them around the room.

GROUP BRAINSTORMING

We're going to rewrite an old nursery rhyme so we can entertain some younger children with modern versions they'll understand.

NOTE: If "Jack and Jill" is too difficult for your students, model the Group Brainstorming and Group Composing on a simpler nursery rhyme, such as "Two Blackbirds." A list of nursery rhymes can be found at the end of this lesson.

Male	Female	Where	Reason
Frank	Emily	to the store	get some red hots
Matt	Juanita	to the street fair	tried the rides
Steve	Michelle	to the used car lot	find transportation to the prom
Harold	Sandy	up the river	locate a speedboat

Unfortunate Result	Other Results
the dogs chased them home	
lost her purse	
broke her glasses	
lost his homework	
failed a class	
broke his tooth	

Key Questions

1. **What teenage boy's or man's name could we use in our nursery rhyme?** Choose a low-achieving student to answer this easy question and get him/her involved right away. List students' ideas for names on the board, chart, or overhead under the "Male" column.

   > **Think about Mechanics:** What do we need to do to each person's name? (capitalize)

2. **What teenage girl's or woman's name could we use?** Choose a low-achieving student to answer this easy question and get him/her involved right away. List students' ideas for names on the board, chart, or overhead under the "Female" column.

3. **Where could these two teenagers/adults go instead of "up the hill"?** List students' ideas for locations under the "Where" column. Praise phrases that tell "where," especially those with rhythm like the original nursery rhyme.

4. **Out of all these ideas for where they could go, which one shall we choose for our nursery rhyme?** Choose a low-achieving student to answer this easy question and get him/her involved right away. Circle the chosen location.

5. **What did they do there? What did they hope to get? Why did they go?** List students' ideas under the "Reasons" column. Praise phrases/clauses that give a reason, especially those that have the rhythm of the original nursery rhyme.

6. **Out of all these reasons why, which one shall we choose for our nursery rhyme?** Choose a low-achieving student to answer this easy question and get him/her involved right away. Circle the chosen reason.

7. **On the way back/home, what unfortunate event occurred or took place?** List students' ideas under the "Unfortunate Result" column. Praise phrases that give an unfortunate result, especially those that have the rhythm of the original nursery rhyme.

8. (optional) **On the way home, what interesting or amazing event took place?** List students' ideas under the "Other Results" column. Praise phrases/clauses that have the rhythm like the original nursery rhyme.

GROUP COMPOSING

Now let's use our ideas to rewrite an old nursery rhyme. We'll create a modern version of "Jack and Jill" for some young children.

> ## Tony and Ed
>
> Ed and Tony went to the used car lot
>   to find transportation for the prom.
> Ed found a rusty Ford truck that emptied his pockets
>   and offended his girl friend.
> And Tony followed empty-handed after him.

1a. **We need the names of two people.** These can be two men, two women, or a man and a woman. **Which two names shall we choose? Which names go with our nursery rhyme?** Circle the two chosen names.

1b. **Which person shall we make the main character? Which name shall we place in our modern nursery rhyme first? second?** Try to avoid sexual bias. Insert the names in the first line of the poem.

Line 1

2. **(Beginning Writers) Let's add the verb "went" to our nursery rhyme. What more interesting or accurate word could we use?** (jogged, drove, flew) Add the chosen idea to the nursery rhyme.

3a. **Out of all our places they could go, which one should we choose?** Before adding this to the nursery rhyme, ask about mechanics.

> **Thinking about Mechanics:** Which place do we need to capitalize? (proper names of places) We would capitalize "Peggy's Computer Store" because it is a specific store, but not "store" because it could be any store.

3b. **Which preposition should we use?** Suggest several or display the chart for students.

> **Thinking about Mechanics:** Which prepositions fit our modern nursery rhyme instead of *up*?

Prepositions

above	by	out
across	down	over
around	in	past
behind	in front of	through
below/beneath	inside/into	toward
beside	near	under/underneath
between	on top of	up

3c. **Now that we have our preposition and where our people are going, let's add this information to our nursery rhyme.**

Line 2

4. **Which activity did we choose for our characters to do?** (or) **Why did they do it?** Add this phrase to the nursery rhyme.

Line 3

5. **What name goes in line 3?** Add the name to line 3.

6. **What unfortunate event shall we choose for this nursery rhyme?** Pause for at least 30 seconds to give students time to think. Praise ideas as students share them. After about 6–8 ideas ask a student who has been listening carefully to select one idea. Add this to the nursery rhyme.

Line 4

7. **What name goes in line 4?** Add the name to line 4.

8. Ask students to raise hands to volunteer their opinions. **Shall the second person repeat the same awful event, or a different one?** Ask an involved, but quiet student to decide.

   NOTE: An interesting or amazing result could be selected for the second person. Add this idea to the nursery rhyme.

9. **Now let's hum our draft to see how similar it is to the rhythm in the "Jack and Jill" nursery rhyme.** Ask students where their nursery rhyme doesn't fit. As a group decide to keep or change the rhythm.

Ed and Tony

Ed and Tony went to the used car lot
   to find transportation for the prom.
Ed found a rusty Ford truck that emptied his pockets
   and Tony followed sad-faced after him.

---

10. (optional) **Which lines rhymed in "Jack and Jill"? Do our lines rhyme? How can we change our nursery rhyme to make it rhyme?**

    NOTE: Rhyming increases difficulty 100-fold, and should be optional or used with Advanced Writers.

INDIVIDUAL BRAINSTORMING & COMPOSING

Rewriting nursery rhymes is a difficult type of writing because it requires careful word choices and tons of revising, revising, and more revising.

   Beginning Writers   These young authors should write their own versions of "Jack and Jill." A Brainstorming Assistant for "Jack and Jill" can be found at the end of this lesson.

   Advanced Writers   These young authors will benefit from creating their own version of "Jack and Jill" first. Later encourage them to select and modernize their own nursery rhymes. To do this, they first need to create their own brainstorming assistants. (The purpose of the brainstorming assistants is to guide students to generate multiple ideas before choosing one idea to use.) To help Advanced Writers create brainstorming assistants, pull them aside after they complete the "Jack and Jill" nursery rhyme.

1. Explain that nursery rhymes, like sentences, are composed of pieces.

   Nouns—Ask yourself, "Who or what is doing something?"
   Pronouns—he, she, it, him, her, them, etc.

   Adjectives—Ask yourself, "What kind of _____?"

Verbs—Ask yourself, "What did _____ do? What will _____ do?"
Adverbs—Ask yourself, "How did he/she/it do it?"
Prepositional Phrases—See the previous list.

Conjunctions—and, but, or, nor, so, yet, for

"Jack and Jill"
Brainstorming Assistant

Male	Female	Where	Reason

Unfortunate Result   Other Results

---

2. Select another nursery rhyme. A list of nursery rhymes can be found at the end of this lesson. The typical difficulty level of the nursery rhymes has been marked with stars: 1 star—easy, 3 or 4 stars—extremely difficult. Guide students to start with a rhyme marked 1 or 2 so they can experience success before moving up.

   Have an Advanced Writer select a main word from the first line of the nursery rhyme that could be replaced by something modern. Underline it and brainstorm up-to-date alternatives. Repeat for other main words.

With this knowledge Advanced Writers will be able to create their own brainstorming assistants for any nursery rhyme. Consider requiring the creation of brainstorming assistants since their purpose is to guide students to consider multiple ideas before choosing one to use.

   Advanced Writers can be encouraged to keep or add rhyme to their modern nursery rhyme(s). Bring to class some rhyming dictionaries from your school or public library. Here's a sixth modernized draft of "Jack and Jill" and also the final rhyming version.

(Sixth Draft)
   Matt and Kate went to the mall
   to buy some software.
   They spent all their allowance
   and thought it was funny
   Until they found it worthless.

> **(Fifteenth and Final Version)**
> Matt and Kate went to the mall
>   to buy a video game.
> Matt spent his money,
>   They thought it funny
> Until they found the game was lame.

RESPONDING TO STUDENTS' WRITINGS/ REVISING

As students finish the rough drafts of their modern nursery rhymes, ask them to find a revising partner with whom they haven't worked. Have each revising partner read his/her modern nursery rhyme out loud to the other person using the rhythm of the original nursery rhyme as much as possible. Direct partners to do the following, then repeat for the other writer.

- Together find and count the "places" in the nursery rhyme that are modern or up-to-date. For example, in the "Matt and Kate" nursery rhyme, the ideas "mall" and "video game" are modern.

- Consider other spots in the nursery rhyme that can be modernized. Make these changes.

- Remove or change words to fashion the new nursery rhyme to better fit the beat or rhythm of the original nursery rhyme. HINT: Hum the original nursery rhyme as you silently read the modern version. Which lines sound good? Which don't? Cross out or add words as needed.

Before publishing, trade compositions and look for capitalization, spelling, and punctuation errors that might keep readers/listeners from understanding and enjoying the nursery rhyme.

PUBLISHING

Share with your students that you are very pleased with the modern versions of the nursery rhymes they wrote. Explain that they will create mitt puppets (*format*) to use with the nursery rhymes to entertain (*purpose*) kindergarten classes and nursery school children (*audience*). The puppet will be used to help maintain the children's interest while they read/say their nursery rhyme.

Mitt Puppets

Materials

one or two sheets of construction paper or butcher paper, glue, scissors, crayons or colored markers, miscellaneous decorations

Directions

Tell students to decide on one or two characters in their nursery rhyme to illustrate.

1. Fold a sheet of construction paper in half.

2. Cut around the top of the mitt. Shape the top for your particular puppet. (If the student has a large hand, use two 8-1/2 × 11-inch pieces of construction paper.) Place one hand on the folded sheet of paper. Put the little finger against the fold, spread fingers a little but tuck in the thumb. Trace around the hand. Leave a one-inch margin around the outline as the mitt puppet is cut out.

3. Place a thin strip of glue around the top and down the open side of the construction paper. Close and press. Then let the glue dry.

   NOTE: To create wide creatures (such as a horse or a whale) use 18 × 36-inch construction paper or butcher paper. When reading the nursery rhyme, the student holds his/her hand horizontally, instead of vertically.

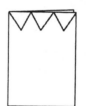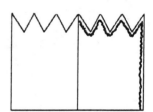

4. Draw and/or glue on decorations that add to your character. You can use yarn, aluminum foil, buttons, cotton balls, and small pieces of construction paper to decorate your mitt puppet.

5. Use the mitt puppets to present the modern nursery rhyme(s) to the young children. Your puppet(s) will help maintain the children's interest while you read/say your nursery rhyme.

"Jack and Jill"
Brainstorming Assistant

Male	Female	Where	Reason

Unfortunate Result

Other Results

A List of Nursery Rhymes

Little Miss Muffett**

Little Miss Muffett
Sat on a tuffet,
Eating her curds and whey;
There came a great spider,
And sat down beside her,
And frightened Miss Muffett away.

_____ Miss/Ms./Mr./Mrs. _____
Sat on a _____,
Eating her _____ and _____,
There came a _____ _____,
And sat down beside _____,
And _____ Miss/Ms./Mr./Mrs. _____ away.

Hickory, Dickory, Dock*

Hickory, Dickory, Dock,
The mouse ran up the clock.
The mouse struck one,
The mouse ran down.
Hickory, dickory, dock.

Hickory, dickory, dock.
The _____ ran up the _____.
The _____ _____,
The _____ _____ _____.
Hickory, dickory, dock.

Ba-a Ba-a Black Sheep**

Ba-a Ba-a Black Sheep, have you any wool?
    Yes, sir, yes, sir, three bags full:
One for my master, one for my dame,
    But none for the little boy who cries in
    the lane.

Ba-a Ba-a _____ _____, have you any _____?
    Yes, sir, yes, _____, _____ _____ full:
One for my _____, one for my _____,
    But none for the _____ _____ who _____
    _____.

Two Blackbirds*

One named Jack.
The other named Jill.
Fly away, Jack!
Fly away, Jill!
Come again, Jack.
Come again, Jill.

One named _____.
The other named _____.
_____, _____!
_____, _____!
_____, _____.
_____, _____.

Old Mother Hubbard**

Old Mother Hubbard
    Went to the cupboard,
To get her poor dog a bone.
    But when she went there
The cupboard was bare
    And so the poor dog had none.

_____ _____ _____
    Went to the _____,
To get _____ a _____.
    But when _____ went there
The _____ was _____
    And so the _____ _____ _____.

Hey Diddle, Diddle**

Hey diddle, diddle, the cat and the fiddle
The cow jumped over the moon.
The little dog laughed to see such a sport,
And the dish ran away with the spoon.

Hey diddle, diddle, the _____ and the _____
The _____ jumped over the _____.
The _____ _____ _____ to see such a sport,
And the _____ ran away with the _____.

This Little Pig**

This little Pig went to Market,
This little Pig stayed at Home,
This little Pig had Roast Beef,
This little Pig had none,
This little Pig cried wee, wee, wee,
All the way home.

This _____ _____ went to _____,
This _____ _____ stayed at _____,
This _____ _____ had _____ _____,
This _____ _____ had none,
This _____ _____ cried _____, _____, _____,
All the way _____.

Three Little Kittens****

Three little kittens lost their mittens,
    and they began to cry,
Oh! mother dear, we very much fear
    That we have lost our mittens.
Lost your mittens! You naughty kittens!
    Then you shall have no pie.
Mee-ow, mee-ow, Mee-ow, mee-ow,
    No, you shall have no pie.
Mee-ow, mee-ow, mee-ow.

_____ _____ _____ lost their _____,
    and they began to _____,
Oh! _____ dear, we very much fear
    That we have lost our _____.
Lost your _____! You _____ _____!
    Then you shall have no _____.
_____, _____, _____, _____,
    No, you shall have no _____.
_____, _____, _____, _____.

Humpty Dumpty***

Humpty Dumpty sat on a wall
Humpty Dumpty had a great fall.
All the King's horses and
All the King's men couldn't
Put Humpty together again.

_____ _____ _____ on _____
_____ _____ _____.
All the _____'s _____ and
All the _____'s _____ couldn't
Put _____ together again.

Mary Had a Little Lamb****

Mary had a little lamb,
Its fleece was white as snow;
And everywhere that Mary went
The lamb was sure to go.

It followed her to school one day,
Which was against the rule;
It made the children laugh and play
To see a lamb at school.

_____ had a _____ _____,
Its _____ was _____ as _____;
And everywhere that _____ went
The _____ was sure to go.

It followed her/him/them to _____ one day,
Which was against the rule;
It made the _____ _____ and _____
To see a _____ at _____.

Little Boy Blue****

Little Boy Blue, come, blow your horn;
The sheep's in the meadow, the cow's in
    the corn.
Where's the boy that looks after the sheep?
He's under the haystack, fast asleep.

_____ _____ _____, come, _____;
The _____'s in the _____, the _____'s in
    the _____.
Where's the _____ that looks after the _____?
He's/She's under the _____, _____.